Rheingauer Monographien

The German Brewing Industry

Dirk Schiereck / Christof Sigl-Grüb / Christian Voigt (Editors)

A collaborative publication from

SMG Publishing AG

Verlag Wissenschaft & Praxis

The German Library – CIP-Affiliation

The German Library lists this publication in the German national bibliography; detailed bibliographic data is available on the Internet at http://dnb.ddb.de.

CH-9000 St. Gallen, Teufener Strasse 25

Tel.: +41 (0)71 226 10 60, Fax: +41 (0)71 226 10 69

homepage: www.smg-ag.com, e-mail: contact@smg-ag.com

SMG™ Publishing AG
ISBN 3-907874-43-9

Verlag Wissenschaft & Praxis
ISBN 3-89673-343-5

Printed in Germany

Preface

Although scientific research on mergers and acquisitions is exuberant, comparably little can be found on M&A activities focusing on specific industries. This book is one of the few M&A books concentrating on one single industry and its special regularities, value drivers and merger motives. But this is only one of the reasons for presenting this collection of articles. This book is first and foremost a documentation of a project course that brought together research and teaching more closely. It gives graduate students at the European Business School the opportunity to gain insights and practical experience in scientific research.

The book is a compilation of articles which emerged from the 'Project Course M&A – the German Brewing Industry' in the summer term 2005, a course offered to 8th semester students at the European Business School. The design of this project course has a special character. Departing from a single industry, students are asked to filter and elaborate on relevant aspects of finance related to M&A activities in this industry. In the course of their examinations they do not only have to bring their results in paper form but also present it and discuss it with their fellows as well.

The industry which was chosen for the 2005 course is the German brewing industry. The reasons why its respective companies are appreciative study objects are manifold:

- Over the last decade, quite a big number of take-overs have changed this industry irreversibly. Big international players emerged from this consolidation process. The number of deals is exuberant.
- Still, the branch as a whole is in a deep flux. Decreasing sales volumes and revenues and changing markets demand a high degree of flexibility and efficiency from producers, providing the ground for further activities in the field of M&A.

- Particularly the German brewing industry is still quite fragmented with a great number of historically grown companies with a strong regional focus.
- With respect to newly opening Eastern markets, Germany plays an important role as a basis from which Eastern markets are entered due to its geographical location.
- The large number of exchange listed firms provide a stable basis for drawing empirical inferences.

Due to the underlying concept, the articles in this book cover a wide range of M&A-related topics. Starting with descriptive issues of brewing companies and deals, continuing with an empirical evaluation of trading and transaction valuation of aquirers and targets, going further to the issue of constructing industry indices and finally widening the focus to Central and Eastern European beer markets, this book provides insights into an industry which can hardly be found in one single source and in this compactness. On top, insights on depicted transactions are provided in the form of case studies.

Oestrich-Winkel,
December 2005

Dirk Schiereck
Christof Sigl-Grüb
Christian Voigt

The participants of the 'Project Course M&A – The German Brewing Industry' visiting the Radeberger brewing plant in Frankfurt.

Overview of Content

Table of Content

A Case Study: The Acquisition of Holsten Brauerei AG by Carlsberg A/S

by
Jochen Gast and Christian Johansson

1 Introduction

In recent years, the German brewing industry has seen tremendous changes. Big international brewery groups have discovered their interest in the German market, which is, even though shrinking, the third largest beer market in the world. To enter this heavily fragmented and regionalized market, foreign corporations have launched a series of acquisitions racing for the best pieces of the German beer-cake. One of the most spectacular take-overs of the recent past was the acquisition of Holsten, the second biggest German brewery group, by Carlsberg, the Danish beer-multi in January 2004. In the following, after having introduced both main actors, we will explain the details of this deal and the strategic rational behind it as well as the risks inherent in the deal. We will furthermore describe the market's reaction to the take-over and, as far as it is already recognizable, evaluate the acquisition's success.

2 The Main Characters

2.1 Facts and Figures

The Carlsberg brewery was founded in 1847 near Copenhagen, Denmark. Since then it has become the fifth biggest brewery group in the world producing in 40 countries and selling beer for more than € 4.5b in 140 countries each year. In addition to beer, the 31.375 Carlsberg employees produce and sell sodas and water, which together sum up to about one fifth of Carlsberg's production volume. Naturally, Carlsberg's core market can be found in Northern Europe, but the group is also active throughout all of Western and Eastern Europe as well as in Asia.[1]

Holsten, on the other side, sells more than 80% of its output within Germany, especially in the northern and eastern federal states. It was founded in 1879 in Altona near Hamburg and, just like Carlsberg, produces and sells beer, soft drinks and water. Before the take-over, the Holsten AG was Germany's second biggest brewery group. Nevertheless, it then only employed 2.840 people and had less than one fifth of Carlsberg's market capitalisation. Therefore, we can state that in this case presented, Carlsberg, a big multinational corporation, acquired the much smaller national player Holsten.[2]

Chart 1: Comparison of Carlsberg and Holsten (figures as of end 2003)

	Carlsberg	Holsten
Turnover (in mio. EUR)	4.657	752
Sales – Beer (in mio. hl)	81,4	9,1
Sales – Soft Drinks (in mio. hl)	21,2	3,8
Earnings (in mio. EUR)	203	6,7
Market Capitalization (in mio. EUR)	2.112	367
Employees	31.375	2.840

Source: Own depiction based on Carlsberg (2005), p. 4; Holsten (2004), p. 1, 3.

2.2 Holsten – Background and History

The year 2003 did not start well for Holsten. The new German regulation about can deposits, which became active on January 1st, nearly wiped out the can market segment completely, an area that used to be a traditional strength of the Holsten group.[3] Because management had missed to prepare properly for this important shift in market conditions, Holsten lost about 8.5% of its revenues within the first

[1] Cf. Carlsberg (2005a), p. 1.
[2] Cf. Holsten (2005b).
[3] Cf. CSFB Research (2003), p. 11f.

half of 2003. A new strategy that would allow regaining the lost market share quickly was not in sight.[4]

In this situation, Christian Eisenbeiss, so far the owner of a 34% stake in Holsten and chairman of the supervisory board acquired a 14.37 % package from Commerzbank, which gave him control over 49.37% of Holsten's shares. Rumors hold that the intention behind this deal was to gain a majority position in Holsten, which now could more easily be sold to strategic investors with an interest in acquiring the German brewery. Even though Eisenbeiss made publicly clear that he was not interested in selling Holsten, speculations thrived leading to a rise in share prices from € 20 in February to around € 35 in June (see Chart 2).[5]

On July 17th Eisenbeiss finally announced that he planned to sell his 49,37% stake. Holsten's management immediately started to search for a strategic investor that would take the majority position in the brewery group. During the following months, several big multinational breweries were discussed as potential buyers, which made the share price rise to around € 50 each.[6]

In September, the full extent of the decline in sales caused by the can deposit problem became public, and still no workable growth strategy seemed to be in place. So far, no strategic investor could be found and because of the newly published bad figures a successful search seemed more and more unrealistic. Share prices started to fall again and finally, on December 10th, Holsten's management announced the end of the search for an investor, thereby causing stock prices to fall below € 25.[7]

Only 40 days later, on January 20th 2004, Carlsberg suddenly announced that it would buy 51% of Holsten's shares including the 49,37% of C. Eisenbeiss. Furthermore, Carlsberg offered the remaining shareholders to buy their stocks for

[4] Cf. Holsten (2003), S. 2.
[5] Cf. Hönighaus (2003).
[6] Cf. Fischer (2003).
[7] Cf. Rössig (2003).

€ 38, the same price that Eisenbeiss had received. The Holsten management was not informed of the bid. Negotiations were held with Eisenbeiss directly.[8]

Chart 2: Share Prices of Holsten, Jan. 1999 to Dec. 2004

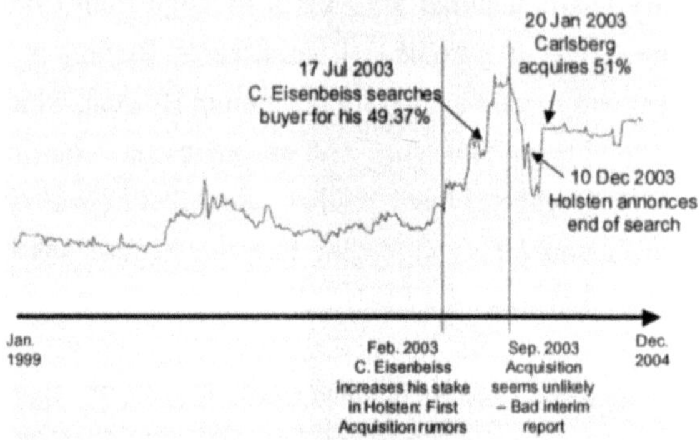

Source: Own depiction based on Yahoo! Finance (2005).

Interestingly, share prices started to rise several days before the announcement of the take-over. This is why Bafin, the German exchange supervisory authority, has started investigations because of the suspicion of insider dealing. It furthermore suspects share price manipulation in form of the (wrong) announcement of Holsten's management in December that the search for an acquirer was given up. This had lowered the share price to around € 25, thereby reducing the take-over price to fit the buyer's expectations. Given the complexity of the transaction announced on January 20th, it is hard to believe that in December all negotiations had failed as it was announced by Holsten. Especially Eisenbeiss is suspected to have beaten down the share price deliberately in order to reach an agreement with Carlsberg. Based on the lower stock price, Carlsberg could offer the remaining shareholders only € 38 per share while only a few month earlier the stock was traded at over € 50. Up to now, no results of the investigations have been published.[9]

---

[8] Cf. Rössig / Clausen (2004).
[9] Cf. Finanzen.net (2004); Netzeitung (2004).

2.3 Carlsberg – Background and Growth Strategy

As Chart 3 illustrates, Carlsberg has dramatically grown in the course of the last three years. Between 2000 and 2003, Carlsberg could more than double its beer sales now aiming for the mark of 100m hectoliters a year. Of course, this development is not the result of an internal growth but of a consequent acquisition strategy focusing on growing markets. Appendix 1 shows a list of preceding take-overs by the Carlsberg group.

Chart 3: Carlsberg's Growth Story

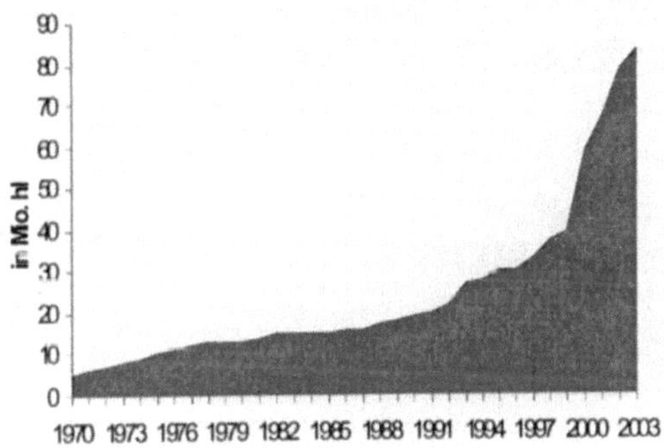

Source: Carlsberg (2004a), p. 24.

In the course of its expansion, Carlsberg follows a clear-cut strategy: Since the Danish brewery already is market leader in Northern Europe, the main focus of their acquisition activities are Western Europe and especially the fast growing markets in Eastern Europe and Asia.

In its newly entered markets, Carlsberg wants to stay concentrated on the production and sale of beer only and, in the first place, aims at promoting the Carlsberg brand, the group's international premium beer. Other brands that may be acquired in the course of such acquisitions merely serve as rounding offs on a regional and local level. The only supra-regional and internationally promoted brand is Carlsberg. It is Carlsberg's strategy to attain a dominant position in every market served.

The Danish brewery group states that it is planning to further participate in the actual consolidation of the beer business, which means that further M&A activities are likely.[10]

3 The Take-Over of Holsten

3.1 Reasons for the Take-Over of Holsten

As the brands of the Holsten brewery group occupy a dominant position in the northern part of Germany (Schleswig Holstein, City of Hamburg, Mecklenburg-Vorpommern, Lower Saxony and Saxony), the acquisition fits to Carlsberg's portfolio from a geo-graphical point of view.

Chart 4: Holsten's Core Markets

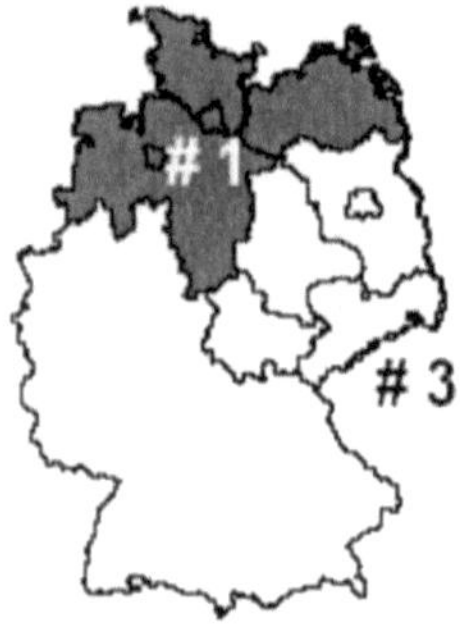

Source: Carlsberg (2004a), p. 8.

Carlsberg is already the market leader in Denmark and Scandinavia and the take-over further enlarges its "Northern European Platform". Because of the high taxes on alcohol in Northern Europe, 25% of Danish beer consumption is served by "private" (sometimes illegal) imports from Germany.[11] This makes Northern Germany highly relevant for a Danish brewery; it can be seen as a natural extension of Carlsberg's own home market.

---

[10] Cf. Carlsberg (2005a), p. 8.
[11] Cf. ABG Sundal Collier (2004), p. 3.

Another major reason for the take-over is Holsten's powerful distribution network within Germany. Carlsberg hopes to strengthen its international brand as well as the local brands by using Holsten's far-reaching network in the retail, hotel and catering industry. On the other side, Holsten, traditionally one of Germany's most exported beers (1,6m hl p.a.) is used to reinforce the export and licensing portfolio of the Carlsberg group. Especially Russia is, due to governmental support of beer aimed at reducing the consumption of Vodka, Europe's fastest growing beer market, and in the UK, Holsten already has a strong market position combined with a good image. As Carlsberg has a presence in both countries as well, the Holsten brand will further benefit from those sales channels while Carlsberg will profit from Holsten's positive image and its contacts.
Aside from the positive effects of combined sales, other synergies are anticipated. Carlsberg quantifies the total synergies attainable with seven million euros in 2004, € 14m in 2005 and, starting from 2006 on, annual synergies of € 17m. 70% of these planned synergies consist of real cost-savings made possible e.g. by merging sales forces and administrations. In the course of realization, Holsten's work force is reduced by 209 employees. The costs of obtaining these synergies are estimated at € 35m Euros.
Another source of synergies not yet mentioned is the better utilization of existing production capacities of the Holsten group. Before the take-over, Carlsberg's beer for the German market was brewed externally while Holsten was not able to fully use its existing capacities. The acquisition now gives Carlsberg control over its German production and helps to secure existing Holsten sites. Furthermore, Holsten's headquarters will be used as the local HQ of Carlsberg Germany.[12]

Besides the reasons provided by the Carlsberg management, other reasons should be mentioned that are generally associated with M&A transaction. These reasons are usually not provided by the management of the bidder; either because their shareholders do not benefit or because they are even unknown to the management itself.

---

[12] Cf. Carlsberg (2004a), pp. 4-12.

Following the categorization provided by Trautwein, the previously stated reasons can be classified as rational choices benefiting the bidder's shareholders, like e.g. efficiency gains, market power gains or gains based on better information.[13] However, other rational motives for acquisition might only benefit the bidder's management, often described as the empire-building theory. This theory argues that managers benefit from increased power, reputation and profits due to acquisitions, which lead to principal agent problems, so that losses for the shareholders are accepted by the management for their own benefits.[14]

Another theory argues that M&A transactions might be the outcome of a process which is not based on rational choice but in which the acquirer has very optimistic expectations. This is often combined with the "winner's curse" in auctions, where the acquirer provided the highest offer of all bidders, which is typically above the fair value of the target.[15]

These reasons might underlie any acquisition and may be true for the Carlsberg-Holsten deal as well, even though the Danish brewery obviously does not provide any information on these motives.

3.2 The New Brand Structure

An analysis of the planned brand structure shows how Carlsberg is realizing its strategy of promoting only one international premium brand: Carlsberg. Before the acquisition, the Holsten group included, next to four regional brands and Duckstein, a national specialty, three beers that were promoted on a national level, namely Holsten, Licher and König Pilsener. Out of these three national brands, only Holsten was kept while Licher and König Pilsener were resold.

Within the newly planned brand hierarchy, the only beers that are promoted nationwide are the international premium brand Carlsberg and Duckstein, which still is a national specialty. Holsten and Tuborg, which already belonged to Carlsberg, are

[13] Cf. Trautwein (1990), pp. 283-295.
[14] Cf. Mueller (1969), p. 644; Amihud / Lev (1981), p. 615; Jensen (1986), p. 323, Trautwein (1990), p. 287.
[15] Cf. Roll (1986), p. 200; Trautwein (1990), p. 289; Barney (1988), p. 78.

now supra-regional brands that focus on their strong core markets in northern Germany. The regional brands stay in place and it is planned to further strengthen them.[16]

Chart 5: The Evolution of the Brand Structure

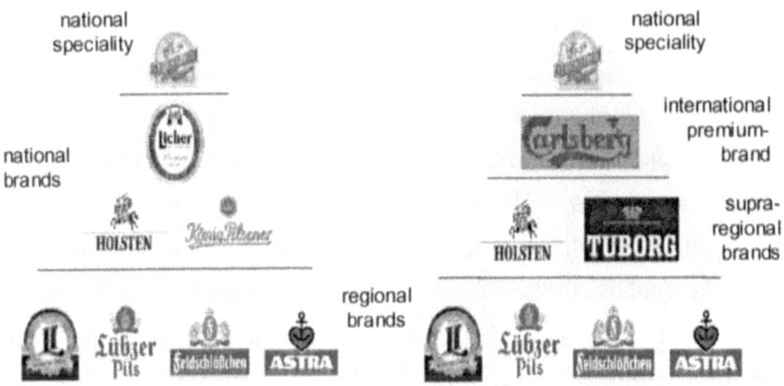

Source: Own depiction based on Carlsberg (2004a), p. 7.

As mentioned above, Carlsberg did not integrate the Holsten group as a whole, but sold several parts of it. Because of Carlsberg's strategy to focus on beer, only Hansa-Brunnen, the non-alcoholic beverages subsidiary of Holsten, was sold. As Hansa-Brunnen's main product mineral water is a commodity, there is heavy pressure on the margins in this business, which is another reason for the sale.

The resale of Licher and König Pilsener must be seen on the one hand as a step towards regional focusing and on the other hand as a means of financing the deal that otherwise might have overextended the buyer's financial means. Carlsberg furthermore wants to use the cash generated by this sale to further develop the remaining brands. In the case of König Pilsener it would have been too expensive to reach a leading position in König Pilsener's relevant market. Even though Licher already had such a position, Hessen, Licher's home market, did not fit into

[16] Cf. Carlsberg (2004a), p. 7.

the regional concept of Carlsberg. As mentioned before, two more national premium brands would not have fit into the strategic concept of Carlsberg.[17]

3.3 The Transaction

3.3.1 Course of Events

The deal can be divided into several transactions. The first one took place on January 20th, 2004. On that day, Carlsberg entered into conditional agreements to acquire 51% of the Holsten Brauerei AG from the Eisenbeiss family and other parties for € 38 per share. At the same time "back-to-back" on-sale agreements to sell two selected breweries, namely König-Brauerei and Licher Privatbrauerei to Bitburger brewery were announced. Furthermore, Carlsberg had a put option on the mineral water business.[18] The deals with the Eisenbeiss family and the sell-off to Bitburger were both conditional on regulatory approvals and on Carlsberg obtaining at least 75% of Holsten in a public offering, which started after the deal with the Eisenbeiss family was announced.

The public offer enabled Carlsberg to buy 97,55% of Holsten until end of March and consequently fulfilled the conditions. Finally, Carlsberg increased its stake to 98,14% until the end of 2004. On January 27th, 2005, Carlsberg decided to conduct a squeeze-out in order to take Holsten privately.[19]

3.3.2 Financial Terms

This section will analyze the future prospects as presented by the acquirer's management. The acquisition price per share was € 38. This implied an equity value of the company of € 523m for the 13.75m shares. The net debt accounted for € 542m, which sums up to an enterprise value of € 1,065m. The disposal of the breweries for € 469m and the mineral water business for € 159m can be deducted from the enterprise value, so that the value of the acquired part of the Holsten Brauerei by Carlsberg equals € 437m. This value includes net debt of € 314m.[20]

---

[17] Cf. Schorbus (2004).
[18] Cf. Carlsberg (2004b).
[19] Cf. Holsten (2005a), p. 7.
[20] Cf. Carlsberg (2004a), pp 10-11.

Chart 6: The Decomposition of the Transaction Value

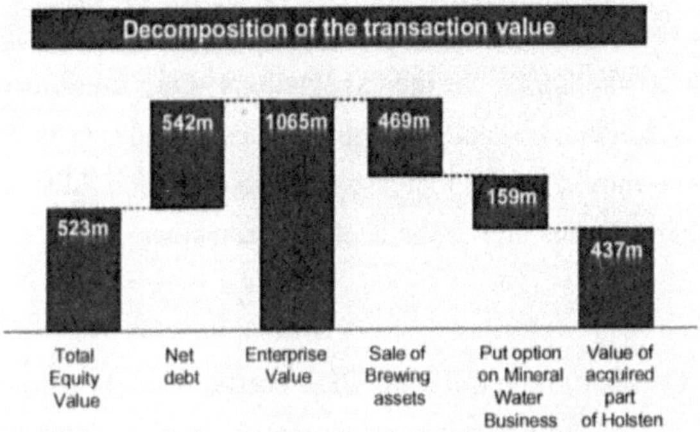

Source: Own depiction based on Carlsberg (2004a), p. 10.

This acquisition price was paid in expectation of the future sales and EBIT / EBITDA values as shown in the table below. In addition to the shown estimates, Carlsberg identified synergies as mentioned above in Section 3.1. However, Carlsberg would have to invest another € 35m in order to achieve the synergies according to their own estimates.[21]

Chart 7: Carlsberg's expectation of Holsten

Assets to be acquired by Carlsberg (Carlsbergs expectations pre-synergy)	2001	2002	2003E	2004F
Sales	532	506	441	521
EBITDA	37	48	48	57
EBIT	-3	8	1	7
EV/Sales		0.9x	1x	0.8x
EV/EBITDA		9.1x	9.1x	7.7x

Source: Adopted from Carlsberg (2004a), p. 11.

Furthermore, the multiples demonstrate another valuation technique and give an idea, whether the price is adequate in comparison to other transaction. Appendix 2 provides an overview of comparable transactions worldwide and shows that the Carlsberg transaction is rather at the lower end.

[21] Cf. Carlsberg (2004a), pp 11-12.

3.4 Risks of the Acquisition

This section will give a brief overview over the most important risks with respect to the acquisition. A major risk is whether or not the expectations about the future development of the Holsten Brauerei can be met. Carlsberg forecast a sales growth of 18% in 2004. The main driver should be the increase in sales of PET bottles in Germany, recovering market shares losses due to the declining can sales caused by the can deposit scheme.

It is questionable whether the German market accepts PET bottles as a substitute for cans. Furthermore, the sale of PET bottles might affect the image of Holsten in a negative way, so that overall increase in sales based on PET bottles of 18% seems too optimistic. On the other hand, Carlsberg wants to establish its own brand in Germany and exploit revenue synergies, even though it has always been difficult to establish foreign brands on the German beer market.

In addition to that, the German beer market is saturated and declining steadily.[22] Moreover, Carlsberg is not acting as a consolidator in the fragmented German market, as two of Holsten major brands were directly resold. So, the market in general can be regarded as a threat for Carlsberg, especially as Carlsberg is known for expansion in fast-growing markets rather than for expansion into markets in downturn or for successes in restructuring.[23]

Another threat is the growing market share of discounters and private labels, which increases the risk of a further drop in prices.[24] These risks appear to be underestimated by Carlsberg and in the paid acquisition price.

[22] Cf. CSFB Research (2003), p. 5-7.
[23] Cf. ING Financial Markets (2004); see also Appendix 1.
[24] Cf. CSFB Research (2003), p. 18.

3.5 Reactions to the Announcement of the Acquisition

3.5.1 Analysts' Opinions

The general tendency of the opinions towards the deal ranges from neutral to negative, which seems to concur with the findings of the previous section that imply that the acquisition price does not reflect all the risks incorporated in the transaction. Appendix 3 provides some analysts' statements which corroborate this hypothesis.

By taking a deeper look at two analysts' reports, the major differences in expectations between analysts and Carlsberg's management can be shown. BNP Paribas (BNP) analysts expect in their own estimates a return on investment (ROI) of 3%, 4.7% and 5.4% in 2004, 2005 and 2006 based on Carlsberg's expected future sales. The differences arise from the fact that BNP incorporates the € 35m investment necessary to exploit the synergies and by eliminates € 5m due to the establishment of the Carlsberg brand in Germany, which is doubted yet. The expectations lead BNP Paribas to the conclusion that the required ROI will not be achieved until 2021, and positive value, in terms of economic value added, will not be created until 2030.[25]

Despite the fact that Deutsche Bank advised of Carlsberg in the acquisition, Deutsche Bank research (DB) provided even worse estimates for the future (see Appendix 4). Similar to BNP, DB incorporated the € 35m investment to achieve synergies into the calculation. Furthermore, DB adjusted the expected sales to € 485m in 2004, growing by € 10m to € 495m in 2005 and € 505m in 2006, which is € 36m below Carlsberg's expectations. Therefore, they estimate a lower EBITDA and EBIT, providing higher multiples and finally a return on investment of 2.4% in 2004, 3.6% in 2005 and 4.2% in 2006, which is even lower than the BNP estimations.[26]

The overall expectation and perception of the transaction should be reflected in the recommendation of the Carlsberg share. Therefore, a brief overview shall be pro-

[25] Cf. BNP Paribas Equities (2004).
[26] Cf. Deutsche Bank (2004).

vided at this point. While Deutsche Bank, BNP Paribas, ING Financial Markets, Handelsbanken Capital Markets, Carnegie and Sendal Collier provided sell, underperform or reduce recommendation at end of January 2004, only Danske Equities had a buy recommendation.[27] Unfortunately, the effect of the acquisition on the group is not that crucial, so that the recommendations cannot be attributed solely to this acquisition. However, it demonstrates that the deal is not seen as a major gain for Carlsberg as most of the analysts believe the share to be overvalued.

3.5.2 Market Reaction

This section provides details on the market reaction. What has to be kept in mind at this point is that the effect of the announcement has to be attributed to the combination of three transactions. Firstly, the acquisition of Holsten, secondly, the disposition of the two breweries to Bitburger and finally the possible sale of the mineral water business, which leads to a substantial change in the risk structure of the remaining Holsten assets.

However, in accordance with the analysts' opinions of the deal, the market reacted with a 4.1% loss to the announcement of the deal (Appendix 5). The reasons for the reaction can be manifold and hence cannot be clearly determined. One aspect is definitely hubris, the overestimation and over optimistic expectation of Carlsberg's management, which led to an unrealistic high acquisition price. This would confirm the analysts' opinions on the deal. Furthermore, investors might have assumed opportunistic behaviour by Carlsberg's management, alleging the management that the aim was to acquire a major brewery, independent from the consequences for the shareholders. Probably, both aspects played a role in the market's reaction. This reaction is rather unusual for take-overs in the brewing industry as research on the announcement effects on the acquirer shows.[28] Other more general studies provide mixed results. Nevertheless, the bidder's abnormal returns are generally below the target's returns.[29]

---

[27] Cf. Deutsche Bank (2004); BNP Paribas Equities (2004); ING Financial Markets (2004); Car-Negie (2004); Handelsbanken Capital Markets (2004); Danske Equities (2004); ABG Sundal Collier (2004).

[28] Cf. Geiger / Roediger (2005).

[29] Cf. Zawadzky / Gerbig (2005).

Looking at the target, Holsten's shareholders gained from the announcement of the deal. The return on the day of the announcement was 9.3%. Although this positive reaction has to be regarded with respect to the dubious price movements in the days prior to the announcement, which was already discussed in Chapter 2.2, the reaction demonstrated that the investors treated the acquisition as a success for Holsten. It created strong abnormal returns, which is in line with the findings of the analysis of the announcement effects of M&A transactions. [30]

4 Ex-Post Analysis

This section will provide an ex-post analysis of the transaction with the information available in May 2005.

The disposal of König Pilsener and Licher took place on June 23rd, 2004 and July 1st, 2004 respectively, which was in line with expectations.[31] The Hansa-Brunnen AG, which changed its name to Hansa-Heemann AG in 2004, was sold for € 79m, implying an enterprise value of € 176m.[32] This exceeded the expectation by € 17m that were based on the put option announced by Carlsberg at the time of the acquisition. The whole deal led to a reorganization of the brands in Germany, which resulted in the positioning shown in Appendix 6, slightly deviating from the original plans.

So far, the acquisition seems to be successful. However, the critical issue at the time of the acquisition was the sales development as well as the general market development. Even though the Holsten group achieved a sales growth and generated €488m sales in the fiscal year 2004,[33] the forecast sales of € 521m were not achieved in 2004, affirming the analyst's expectations (DB research expected € 485m). The total sales quantity for the remaining parts of Holsten increased by 9.8% from 4.7m hl to 5.2m hl domestically, while the sales abroad increased by 10.2% to 1.8m hl. The positive trend was caused by increased sales of different

[30] Cf. Zawadzky / Gerbig (2005).
[31] Cf. Holsten (2005), p. 7.
[32] Cf. Nordic Business Report (2004); Holsten (2005), p. 7.
[33] Cf. Holsten (2005), p. 10.

brands, including sales of Carlsberg in Germany and Holsten's sales abroad promoted by the joint activities with Carlsberg. Thus, the synergies were already used in 2004 and helped generating growth. Nevertheless, the growth target of 18% was clearly missed.[34]

Another issue was the increase of market share through PET bottles and the recovery of losses caused by decreasing can sales. Even though the PET bottle sales for Holsten tripled to 172,000 hl, the losses from can sales of the years prior to the acquisition were neither offset, nor did PET bottles strongly contribute to the overall sales growth. As a result, Carlsberg was not able to reach it operational aims with Holsten in 2004.

Furthermore, the German beer market further declined in 2004, which was mainly caused by the overall economic situation and the consequences of the can deposit system, which were not offset by PET bottles. This trend is still threatening Holsten's future. Especially the growth of discounters as a distributional channel increases the pressure on prices and margins, so that the future prospects remain challenging.

Nevertheless, as shown in Appendix 7, the long term's performance of the Carlsberg share was not affected in a negative way. However, it is unclear whether the influence of Holsten on the Carlsberg group is positive, after the short shock following the announcement of the acquisition, or whether the influence of Holsten on the Carlsberg group is too small to notice, so that even negative effects of the acquisition were overlaid by other news from the group's operations. Due to the ex-post analysis, the latter is more probable, as the success of acquisition and post-acquisition performance of Holsten appears to be poor.

5 Conclusion

The acquisition of Holsten by Carlsberg was a surprise for the market in many respects. On the one hand, the timing was surprising, as Holsten's management had

---

[34] Cf. Holsten (2005a), p. 8-10.

announced that talks with possible acquirers had ended and Holsten would not be sold. On the other hand, Carlsberg's move into the declining German market was rather unexpected for many investors. Carlsberg had always focused on fast-growing markets, so that the strategic rationale of this acquisition was unclear or at least diverging from the preceding strategy.

We showed that there were some seemingly convincing strategic reasons behind this acquisition (e.g. the regional fit). Nevertheless, the basic questions were whether this acquisition was the right choice and whether Carlsberg would be able to improve Holsten's performance again, after Holsten had suffered from the new can legislation and other problems.

Now, almost one and a half year later, first answers to these questions can be derived. Although Holsten continued its restructuring process and increased its performance, the aims Carlsberg used to justify the acquisition price were not met. Especially the expected sales growth of 18% was too optimistic, as both the PET bottle and the Carlsberg brand acceptances are still low in the German market. The only positive news came from the sale of the mineral water business for a higher price than originally expected. Therefore, we come to the conclusion that the acquisition has not proven to be successful so far and it remains doubtable whether it will create value within short or medium term.

Altogether it remains questionable whether or not this transaction was completely rational and fully in line with shareholders' interests. However, we found out that the long-term performance of Carlsberg was not affected in a negative way by the acquisition, which can be explained by the small impact of Holsten on the Carlsberg group.

Appendix

Appendix 1: M&A Activity of Carlsberg 2001-2003

Date	Type	Country	Company	Subject (Partner)	Share-holding
15-Dec-03	A	Poland	Carlsberg Breweries	Carlsberg Breweries increases shareholding in the Polish Carlsberg Okocim S.A.,to	85%
10-Nov-03	A	Bulgaria	Carlsberg Breweries	Carlsberg Breweries increases shareholding in the Bulgarian brewery Shumensko Pivo to	89%
14-Oct-03	A	Poland	Carlsberg Breweries	Carlsberg Breweries increases shareholding in Carlsberg Okocim to	79%
22-Sep-03	A	Serbia	Carlsberg Breweries	Carlsberg Breweries acquires 51% of the shares in Pivara Celarevo	51%
14-Aug-03	A	Vietnam	Carlsberg Breweries	Carlsberg Breweries increases shareholding in Vietnam	75%
1-Aug-03	D	Asia	Carlsberg Breweries	Carlsberg Breweries terminates Asian J/V and takes full control over Carlsberg Asia	100%
16-Jul-03	D	Switzerland	Carlsberg Breweries	Feldschlösschen Getränke AG sells its soft drink bottling plant in Eglisau	
1-Jul-03	D	Germany	Carlsberg Breweries	Carlsberg Breweries sells its German subsidiary Hannen's production facilities	
10-Jun-03	A	China	Carlsberg Asia	Carlsberg Asia acquires Dali Beer (Group) Ltd. Company and Yunnan Dali Beer Joint Stock Company	100%
6-Jun-03	A	Turkey	Carlsberg Breweries	Carlsberg increases shareholding in Türk Tuborg	95.3%
27-May-03	A	Kazakstan	Carlsberg Breweries	BBH acquires Ak-Nar Brewery	100%
26-Mar-03	A	Poland	Carlsberg Breweries	Carlsberg Breweries increases shareholding in Carlsberg Okocim	75%
23-Jan-03	A	China	Carlsberg Asia	Carlsberg Asia has through Carlsberg Brewery Hong Kong Ltd. acquired Kunming Huashi Brewery Company Ltd.	100%
9-Jan-03	D	Denmark	Carlsberg Breweries	Rent a Cooler sold to Eden Springs Ltd.	
6-Jan-03	A	Bulgaria	Carlsberg Breweries	Pirinsko Pivo Brewery, public tender increases shareholding	94.5%
20-Dec-02	A	Poland	Carlsberg Breweries	Carlsberg Breweries acquires 9.9% of shares in Carlsberg Okocim S.A.	71.47%
7-Nov-02	A	Kazakstan	Carlsberg Breweries	BBH acquires 76% of IRBIS brewery and invests Euro 45m to increase capacity	76%
2-Aug-02	A	Bulgaria	Carlsberg Breweries	Pirinsko Pivo Brewery	67%
1-Jul-02	(D)	Lithuania	Carlsberg Breweries	Sells its shareholding in Svyturys Utenos Alus to BBH. BBH holds 76% of shares	
28-Jun-02	A	Bulgaria	Carlsberg Breweries	Shumensko Brewery	59.4%
30-May-02	I	Russia	Carlsberg Breweries	Baltika (BBH) invests USD 50m in a new brewery in Russian Far East	
23-May-02	A	Croatia	Carlsberg Breweries	Panonska Brewery (40%) shareholding increased	80%
8-May-02	I	Ukraine	Carlsberg Breweries	BHH invests USD 50m in a new brewery	
14-Feb-02	D	Nordic	Carlsberg Breweries	Rent a Cooler	
29-Jan-02	A	Laos	Carlsberg Breweries	Carlsberg Asia (CBHK) acquires shareholding in Lao Brewery	25%
28-Jan-02	A	Russia	Carlsberg Breweries	BBH acquires shareholding in Voronezh Brewery	70%
21-Jan-02	A	South Korea	Carlsberg Breweries	Carlsberg Asia increases shareholding in Hite Brewery Co. Ltd.	25.1%
7-Jan-02	A	Italy	Carlsberg Breweries	Carlsberg Italia (75%) shareholding increased	100%
30-Nov-01	(D)	Russia	Carlsberg Breweries	Sells half of its shareholding of 99.9% in Vena Bewery to BBH	49.9%
8-Oct-01	D	Lithuania	Carlsberg Breweries	BBH sells Kalnapilis Brewery (86.6%)	
19-Sep-01	A	Turkey	Carlsberg Breweries	Türk Tuborg (50.01%) public tender	82.46%
9-Aug-01	A/M	Poland	Carlsberg Breweries	Acquisition Bosman, Kasztelan and Piast breweries. Merger with Okocim. New name Carlsberg Okocim	61%
6-Jul-01	A	Turkey	Carlsberg Breweries	Türk Tuborg (2.24%) shareholding increased	50.01%
3-Jul-01	A	Poland	Carlsberg Breweries	Okocim (50.01%) public tender	80.38%
17-May-01	A	Poland	Carlsberg Breweries	Okocim (31.8%) shareholding increased	50.01%
14-Feb-01	M	World wide	Carlsberg A/S	Carlsberg Breweries established	60%
14-Feb-01	D	Nordic	Carlsberg A/S	CCNB restructure	

Mergers (M), Acquisitions (A), Divestments (D), Joint Ventures (J/V) and Investments (I) - since Jan 1, 2001 by Carlsberg A/S and Carlsberg Breweries A/S (Carlsberg Breweries) and BBH = Baltic Beverages Holding, 50% owned by Carlsberg Breweries

Source: Carlsberg (2005b).

Appendix 2: Comparable Transactions

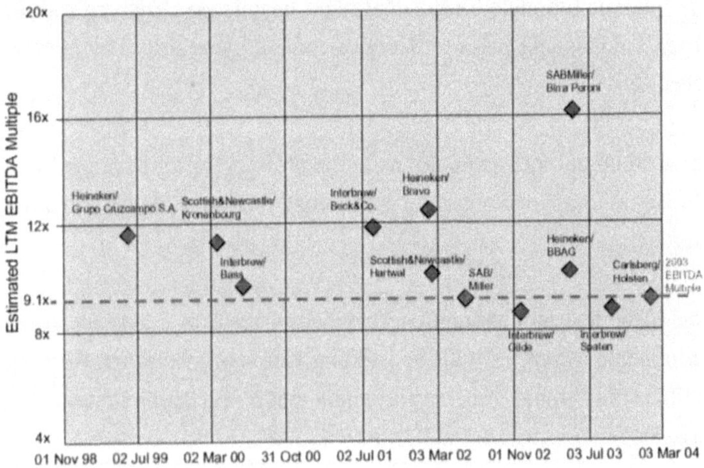

Source: Own depiction based on Inbev (2004), p. 10.

Appendix 3: Analysts' opinions on the acquisition

BNP Paribas Equities: "However, we would not be surprised if Carlsberg investors had to wait a further 20 years before this proposed acquisition creates value! We neither understand the financial nor strategic rationale of the acquisition, and believe that Carlsberg faces sufficient problems (restructuring in its existing markets) already without adding to them by seeking a major acquisition in the highly competitive, regional and declining German beer market"

ING Financial Markets: „The positives of the deal are weak... The geographical argument for expanding the position in north-west Europe is not a strong one. We cannot see the big synergies between Denmark and Northern Germany. And by already selling a part to Bitburger, Carlsberg has also not prepared itself to become the leading consolidator. ...and the negatives are strong. We believe Carlsberg paid a relatively high EV / EBITDA 2004F multiple in view of the weakness of the portfolio, the necessary additional investments in marketing, the uncertainties in the deal and the dilution in cash EPS. It is a pity that the upcoming positive newsflow on Russia will be overshadowed by this new strategic direction. "

Carnegie: "The economic rationale for the deal relies heavily on Carlsberg's ability to reverse Holsten's collapsing sales and deliver on all synergies. The strategic rationale is unclear."

Handelsbanken: "Although other acquisitions in the brewery sector have seen even worse in value creation terms, we regard this as a good reason not to get too exited about the deal now."

Danske Equities: "The deal will strengthen Carlsberg's northern European market position and bring some synergies with its existing German operations. Although the deal seems financially sound, it is hard to argue that it is a major strategic leap forward for Carlsberg."

Sources: BNP Paribas Equities (2004); ING Financial Markets (2004); Carnegie (2004): Handelsbanken Capital Markets (2004); Danske Equities (2004).

Appendix 4: Comparison of Carlsberg and Deutsche Bank's expectations for Holsten

Operations remaining with Carlsberg (Comparison of expectations)	2003E	2004F	2005F	2006F
Cost of the Acquisition (Expectation Carlsberg)		437	437	437
Cost of the Acquisition (Expectation DB)		472	472	472
Sales (Expectation Carlsberg)	441	521	531	542
Sales (Expectations DB)	441	485	495	505
EBITDA (Expectations Carlsberg)	48	64	74	81
EBITDA (Expectations DB)	48	59	65	70
ROI (Expectations Carlsberg)		4,00%	5,90%	7,00%
ROI (Expectations DB)		2,40%	3,60%	4,20%
EV/EBITDA (Expectations Carlsberg)		6,8x	5,9x	5,4x
EV/EBITDA (Expectations DB)		8,1x	7,3x	6,8x

Source: Carlsberg (2004a); Deutsche Bank (2004).

Appendix 5: Announcement effects on Carlsberg and Holsten

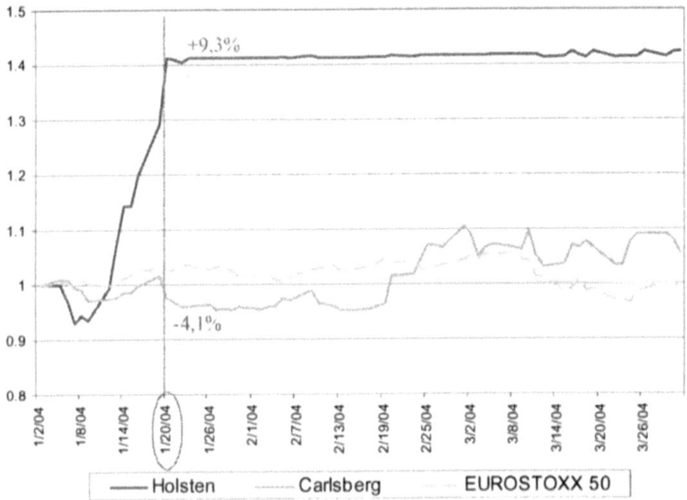

Source: Own depiction based on Yahoo! Finance (2005).

Appendix 6: New Structure of the German Portfolio

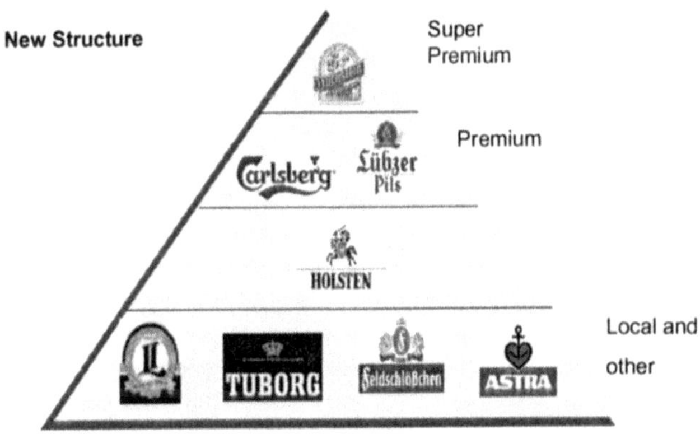

Source: Depiction based on Holsten (2005a), p. 2.

Appendix 7: Carlsberg vs. DAX from 01/01/04 to 22/03/05

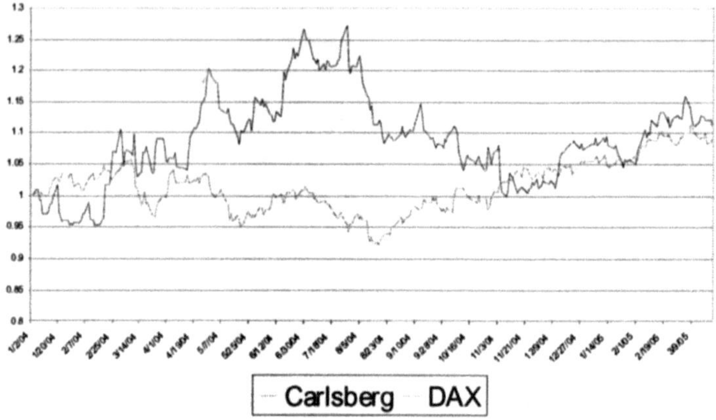

Source: Own depiction based on Yahoo! Finance (2005).

References

ABG Sundal Collier (2004): Research Allert: Carlsberg, January 21st 2004.

Amihud, Yakov / Lev, Baruch (1981): Risk Reduction as a Managerial Motive for Conglomerate Mergers, in: The Bell Journal of Economics, Vol. 12, Iss. 2, pp. 605-617.

Barney, Jay B. (1988): Returns to Bidding Firms in Mergers and Acquisitions: Reconsidering the Relatedness Hypothesis, in: Strategic Management Journal Vol. 9, Iss. 5, pp. 71-79.

BNP Paribas Equities (2004): Carlsberg, Research alert, January 20th 2004.

Carlsberg (2004a): Expanding Carlsberg's Northern European Leadership – Carlsberg Breweries Acquisition of Holsten-Brauerei, Copenhagen 2004.

Carlsberg (2004b): Carlsberg News, Information to Shareholders, February 19th 2004 <http://info.carlsberg.com/NR/rdonlyres/e3rcg6gdozw77kmhniypdjyfecsgnxbqyh4apsjl6iblectxiaeyuhxxsro3yvkersh5khk3ap6o7f/5618_CarlsbergNyt_UK_web.PDF>; date of retrieval: 10.05.2005.

Carlsberg (2005a): Annual Report 2004, Copenhagen 2005.

Carlsberg (2005b): Acquisitions <http://info.carlsberg.com/Info/frameset.htm>; retrieval: 10.05.2005.

Carnegie (2004): Company Update: Carlsberg, January 23rd 2004.

CSFB Research (2003): The German Beer Industry – The Consolidators' Challenge, June 4th 2003.

Danske Equities (2004): Carlsberg, January 21st 2004.

Deutsche Bank (2004): Carlsberg, January 21st 2004.

Finanzen.net (2004): Holsten-Übernahme durch Marktmanipulation verbilligt?, <www.finanzen.net>; date of retrieval: 22.01.2004.

Fischer, Oliver (2003): Großaktionär Christian Eisenbeiss will Anteile abgeben, in: Financial Times Deutschland, dated: July 17th, 2003.

Geiger, Florian / Roediger, Tobias (2005): M&A Announcement Effects of Bidders in the German Brewing Industry, Working Paper, Oestrich-Winkel.

Handelsbanken Capital Markets (2004): Equity Research: Company Update: Carlsberg, January 21st, 2004.

Holsten (2003): Interim Report 1st Half of 2003, Hamburg 2003.

Holsten (2004): Annual Report 2003, Hamburg 2004.

Holsten (2005a): Annual Report 2004, Hamburg 2005.

Holsten (2005b): Press file <http://www.holsten.de/cms/startordner/800_deutsch/1052.html>; date of retrieval: 10.05.2005.

Hönighaus, Reinhard (2003): Großaktionär Eisenbeiss bleibt Holsten vorerst treu, in: Financial Times Deutschland, dated: June 19th, 2003.

Inbev (2004): Investors presentation <http://www.inbev.com/pdf/ITW-ABV_FINAL.pdf>; date of retrieval: 10.05.2005.

ING Financial Markets (2004): Company update: Carlsberg, January 20th, 2004.

Jensen, Michael C. (1986): Agency Costs of Free Cash Flow, Corporate Finance and Takeovers, in: American Economic Review, Vol. 76, pp. 323-329.

Mueller, Dennis C. (1969): A Theory of Conglomerate Mergers, in: Quarterly Journal of Economics, Vol. 83, pp. 643-659.

Netzeitung (2004): Anzeichen für Manipulationen des Holsten-Kurses <http://www.netzeitung.de/wirtschaft/277826.html>; date of retrieval: 22.05.2005.

Nordic Business Report (2004): Carlsberg A/S divests German Mineral Water and Soft Drink Operations, dated: May 14th, 2004.

Rössig, Sabine (2003): US-Großaktionär Eisenbeiss kann gewünschten Preis offenbar nicht erzielen – Aktienkurs bricht ein, in: Financial Times Deutschland, dated: December 12th, 2003.

Rössig, Sabine / Clausen, Sven (2004): Dänischer Konzern zerschlägt Hamburger Brauerei-Gruppe – Bitburger kauft Premiummarken, in: Financial Times Deutschland, dated: January 21st, 2004.

Roll, Richard (1986): The Hubris Hypothesis of Corporate Takeovers, in: The Journal of Business, Vol. 59, Iss. 2, pp. 197-217.

Schorbus, Axel (2004): Zerschlagung durch Carlsberg gebilligt / Kaum Kritik der Holsten-Aktionäre an Rückführung auf den Kern, in: Frankfurter Allgemeine Zeitung, dated: June 24th, 2004.

Trautwein, Friedrich (1990): Merger Motives and Merger Prescriptions, in: Strategic Management Journal, Vol. 11, Iss. 4, pp. 283-295.

Yahoo! Finance (2005): <finance.yahoo.com>; date of retrieval: 01.05.2005.

Zawadzky, Felix / Gerbig, Jörg (2005): Event Study: M&A Announcement Effects on Targets in the German Brewery Market, Working Paper, Oestrich-Winkel.

B M&A-Activities in the German Brewing Industry

I Descriptive Statistics – Merger Waves and Multiples

by
Mirko Jablonsky and Patrick Zenz-Spitzweg

1. Introduction

1.1. Objective of the Study

The German beer market, being the largest in Europe, plays a very important role in the international beer market, not only due to its size, but also due to its long history and its worldwide known and popular products. The market is characterised by a very high level of competition from both large breweries and a high number of smaller breweries with a more regional focus. In addition to that, market influencing effects such as decreasing beer consumption, low profit margins, low pricing levels and high excess capacities, fostered the competitiveness of the market in the last years. Currently the market is in a phase of consolidation, which can be seen by the strong mergers and acquisitions (M&A) activities. As German beer drinkers associate themselves very much with local beer brands, hence are very loyal, it is generally hard to build up market shares with new brands on the German beer market. Accordingly, larger German breweries try to acquire smaller producers in order to enlarge their product and brand portfolio and to be able to enter new regional markets. Furthermore, large international breweries, such as Carlsberg and Interbrew, play an important role in this consolidation process as they also try to enter the German beer market.[1]

The main objective of this paper is to analyse recent M&A activities on the German beer market. Several questions are addressed in this context. Firstly, it is of

[1] Cf. Bowley / Shackleton / Bleakley et al. (2003), pp. 3-5; Bowley / Shackleton / Bleakley et al. (2004), pp. 1-3.

special interest whether there were years with abnormal high M&A activity in the last decade or not. Secondly, the chapter endeavours to analyse the multiples and the prices paid respectively for breweries within these transactions in order to compare these prices to those ones paid in international transactions. In this perspective, the development of prices paid in the last years will also be considered.

1.2. Course of Analysis

In order to analyse the desired objectives, the following approach was chosen for the chapter. After an introduction in part 1, part 2 provides the theoretical background of the topic. Firstly some basic considerations regarding the German beer market are provided in order to get a deeper understanding of the specific circumstances of the beer market in Germany. Secondly, the concept of multiple valuations is addressed, as it is the crucial theoretical background of the following chapter. In part 3, M&A activity on the German beer market is explained in detail. Thereafter follows an analysis of selected transactions on the German beer market. The chapter finishes with a comparison of German and international transactions. Finally, part 4 provides a short conclusion and gives a brief future outlook.

2. Theoretical Background

2.1. Basic Considerations Regarding the German Beer Market

The German beer market is one of the largest in the world. In terms of production, it ranks at third position with a total output of approximately 105.8m hl in 2004, equaling around 10% of the worldwide production, just behind the United States (235m hl in 2001) and China (227.1m hl in 2001). However, the total volume of production has been decreasing in the last years, a trend expected to continue in the future.[2]

Out of the 105.8m hl, 91.9m hl are used for consumption in Germany, the remaining 13.9m hl are exported. Although more than 13% of production is used for exportation, large amounts of overproduction exist. Per capita consumption is estimated to be at 117.7 liters p.a., which is together with Ireland the highest in

[2] For a table of the top 10 beer markets in 2001 see appendix 1.

Europe. Over 2/3 of the consumed beer is "Pils", followed by "Export" (7%) and "Weizen" (6%).[3] Imports only account for 3%. Accordingly, brand loyalty (especially in Bavaria) is extremely high, which makes it hard for international brands to enter the market. This can also be seen by the relatively small number of international brands being successful on the German beer market.[4]

The German beer market itself is highly fragmented. Currently approximately 1,270 breweries exist in Germany, which produce about 5,000 different types of beer. Around 60% of the total beer production is produced by the ten largest breweries. The remaining share is produced by small- and medium-size breweries mainly acting on a local and regional basis. Some of these small and medium breweries, however, are extremely successful. Although they have disadvantages in comparison to large breweries in terms of financial restrictions, marketing possibilities, market penetration, reputation etc., they are able to maintain solid positions on regional markets. This is caused by the strong loyalty of German beer consumers towards products coming from their region. The regional breweries foster this phenomenon by concentrating their marketing activities on certain regional areas and by e.g. sponsoring local events. For large breweries it is therefore difficult to enter these regional markets and to change the consumption habits of regional customers.[5]

As already mentioned in the introduction, the German beer market was characterised in the last years by a high level of M&A activities and an overall trend towards consolidation. This can easily be seen when comparing the market positions in terms of production volume of leading breweries within the last decade.[6] In 1996, Brau und Brunnen was the largest brewery in Germany with a portfolio of strong regional (e.g. Gilden Kölsch) and national brands (e.g. Jever) and a total volume of production of 9.7m. hl. From the year 1996 to 2001, production declined by 2.7m hl to 7.2m hl, resulting in a fifth position on the German market. Being in a financially difficult situation, Brau und Brunnen was acquired by the Radeberger

[3] For a graph illustrating the consumption by beer type see appendix 2.
[4] Cf. Gohlke (2002), pp. 23-25.
[5] Cf. Gohlke (2002), pp. 23-25.
[6] Please see appendix 3 for a table comparing market shares in 1996, 2001 and 2004.

Gruppe (a company belonging to the Oetker-Gruppe) in 2004. By means of this acquisition, Radeberger became the largest brewery in Germany with a total volume of production of 14m hl. However, Radeberger has always been an important player on the German beer market, having ranking at second position in the last ten years.

Currently Interbrew ranks at second position in the German beer market. Interbrew's position, however, has not always been that strong. As already mentioned, it is extremely hard to build up market shares on the German beer market by organic growth. Therefore, Interbrew steadily improved its position by various acquisitions. While Interbrew was not among the top ten brewers in 1996, through the acquisition of "Beck's" (also to strengthen its international portfolio) and "Diebels" (German market leader in the "Alt" segment) in 2001 the company became the third largest player in the German market. Furthermore, in November 2002 Interbrew acquired the large brewery "Gilde" and as a result increased its production volume by another 4.5m hl.

The third largest player on the German market in terms of volume is currently Bitburger, with a total output of over 8m hl, but like in the case of Interbrew, Bitburger was only able to better its market position by means of acquisitions, too. From 1996 till 2001, production volume remained at a constant level of about 4.6m hl, ranking number seven on the German market. One of the most important transactions of Bitburger was the acquisition of "Wernesgrüner" in February 2002.

Adding up the production volume of the respective three largest producers in Germany in the years 1996, 2001 and 2004 underlines the described consolidation activity. The production of the three largest producers accounted for 23.5m hl in 1996, 27.1m hl in 2001 and even 34.1m hl in 2004, which equaled 32.2% of the total production. According to an industry report from CSFB, 30% of the market by volume changed hands between 1999 and 2002. This led to an increase in the market share of the ten biggest brewers from 46% in 1999 to 65% in 2002 in terms of volume and to a level of 79% in terms of industry EBITDA.[7]

[7] Cf. Bowley / Shackleton / Bleakley et al. (2003), pp. 21-23.

2.2. The Concept of Multiple Valuation

The basic objective of all valuation techniques is to come up with a figure, which is a good indication of the value of a company. The valuation of companies is very much discussed in literature as it is a very complex topic and allows for many variations which consequently can lead to differing results.[8] This is also due to the fact that the various valuation methods strive for different goals. The two main possibilities of calculating the value of a company is firstly valuations in terms of capital markets, and secondly valuations in terms of analysing and valuing the assets and liabilities of a company or respectively valuations based on future cash-flows.[9]

The most important valuation techniques are Discounted Cash Flow (DCF) and Comparable Company Trading Multiple Analysis. For the purpose of a DCF-valuation, the future free cash-flows are forecast and discounted to its present value using the company's specific costs of capital as discount factor.[10] Comparable Company Trading Multiple Analysis comprise two kinds of multiples, market multiples and transaction multiples. Market multiples reflect the value of a company as perceived by the market. In practice, the most common market multiples are enterprise value / revenues, enterprise value / EBITDA and enterprise value / EBIT. The enterprise value is defined as market capitalisation[11] of the company plus interest bearing debt minus cash. Calculating multiples for a number of similar companies, a so-called peer group, allows then to compare the values of the different companies or to estimate the value of a not publicly listed company.[12]

Transaction multiples work similar to market multiples. However, the difference is that transaction multiples are not based on share prices (as in the case of market multiples), but on values of transactions. Hence, transaction values represent prices actually paid for companies in the past. Furthermore, transactions multiples differ

[8] For further information regarding the pricing of M&A transactions, cf. Palepu / Healy / Bernard (2000), pp. 15-10.
[9] Cf. Betsch / Groh / Lohmann (1998), pp. 141-142, p. 170; Levy / Sarnat (1994), pp. 688-691.
[10] Cf. Copeland / Koller / Murrin (2000), pp. 132-136.
[11] The market capitalisation is defined as: number of shares outstanding multiplied by share price.
[12] Hockmann / Thießen (2002), pp. 198-203.

from trading multiples, since they often encompass premiums. Accordingly, one therefore searches for comparable transactions from the same industry in order to calculate the multiples. The most common transaction multiples are based, like market multiples, on revenues, EBITDA and EBIT figures. To come up with the transaction multiple, one has to divide the amount paid for the company in a transaction, by the revenues of the company, or the EBITDA or EBIT figure respectively. The figures taken for the calculation are usually the last twelve month (LTM) financials. This leads then to a multiplier, the desired transaction multiple. As transaction multiples are based on transaction volumes and LTM figures, they are historical in nature.[13]

Calculating the multiples of various deals in an industry allows getting an idea of prices paid on average. Hereby, it is of crucial importance to identify transactions which have very comparable businesses. The selected companies should be from the same or from a very similar industry and should produce the same products or offer the same services. In addition, they should have approximately similar margins, size and market positions. Otherwise the comparability of the multiples is not given. This peer group of companies can then be used to calculate mean and median values of multiples paid within different transactions as well as to get an approximation for a price range by evaluating the minimum and maximum values.

However, calculating and analysing transaction multiples is also associated with certain difficulties and shortcomings. One reason, as already mentioned, is the fact that transaction multiples can contain a control premium. This means that an investor paid more than the actual value of the company due to strategic reasons. The reasons can inter alia be based on considerations regarding possible synergy effects or the elimination of competitors. Furthermore, control premiums can vary by industry, by country, by the attitude of the bidder (friendly, hostile, competitive) etc. Therefore, one has to carefully take into account the specific circumstances of a transaction before interpreting the results of the calculated multiples.

[13] Cf. Hockmann / Thießen (2002), pp. 198-203.

3. Merger Statistics

The following part further examines the M&A activity in the German beer industry. Within the past ten years the German market has experienced a tremendous transformation process. The market shares of the large, nationwide operating breweries have increased while the number and importance of the smaller or regional breweries has decreased. At the same time international brewing corporations entered the German market through acquisitions of leading German breweries such as Holsten and Gilde. Furthermore, the polarisation of customer demand towards premium products on the one hand and low-price products on the other has further increased the need for consolidation. Hence, these processes have reshuffled the brewing landscape in Germany.

3.1. M&A Activity in the German Brewing Market

According to Thomson Financial, 244 mergers and acquisitions of breweries and related businesses have been executed between 1989 and the first quarter of 2005. However, after deducting transactions in which the target was not a brewer, but a company from a related business (e.g. a service provider such as a distributor) and deducting several other transactions that were mistakenly part of the set, the number of transactions decreased to a total of 163.

Appendix 4 gives an overview of the distribution of transactions over time. The mean number of transactions in the time considered was 10.2 while the median was 10. The chart suggests intense activities especially in 1991 and 2003. Furthermore, the graph does not promote the notion of a merger wave, since a constant activity can be observed throughout the considered period. However, an analysis of merger activity simply on the basis of the number of transactions does not really reveal the market dynamics.

The picture changes if one considers the transaction volumes. As can be seen in Appendix 5, transaction volumes picked up in 2001 and since then have constantly exceeded a level of USD 500m per year in the following years.

The underlying data sample for the next steps consists of only 26 transactions due to a lack of data for the remaining 137 out of the total sample of 163 transactions. Some of these 26 transactions were split over two years in the data sample due to the fact that the respective acquisitions were divided into two steps, since for example the acquirer could not obtain the desired percentage holding already in the first place or he was required to place a mandatory offer to the retail investors following the purchase of holdings from the major shareholders exceeding the legally defined hurdle rate of 30%. Examples include the acquisition of Gilde and Hofbrauhaus Wolters by Interbrew and Brau und Brunnen by Radeberger. This drove the final number of transactions down to 22.[14]

In 2001, transaction volumes exceeded USD 1.5 billion driven by the take-over of Beck's by Interbrew (now InBev). In 2002, volumes decreased to roughly USD 500m. This could be ascribed to a difficult economical environment with a generally lower M&A activity across all industries. Yet the comparably high values for 2003 (despite a still generally recessive environment) and the low number of transactions, which in the end determined the market volumes for the respective years (see below), suggest a fairly independent development of M&A activity in the brewing industry and indicate that the transaction values for the years are in the end driven by a few large transactions.

The largest transaction in 2002 was the take-over of Gilde by Interbrew. In 2003, activity recovered and reached a volume of approximately USD 1.1 billion. The year saw among others the acquisitions of Spaten Group by a group of investors and the acquisition of Radeberger Group by Dr. Oetker. In 2004, transaction volumes peaked with a total volume of USD 1.7 billion. The take-over of Brau und Brunnen by Dr. Oetker and Holsten by the Danish brewer Carlsberg constitute the biggest transactions in 2004.

However, the statistics also reveals that in 2001 and 2002 a single transaction determined the transaction volume of the respective year (take-over of Beck's in

[14] Note: while the number of transactions has been adjusted, the transaction volume for each part of the transaction has been accounted for in the year in which the respective phase of the transaction took place.

2001 and the take-over of Gilde in 2002). Moreover, in 2003 the acquisitions of Radeberger by Dr. Oetker and of Spaten Group by Interbrew as well as in 2004 those of Holsten by Carlsberg and Brau und Brunnen by Dr. Oetker had a major impact on the volume figures for the respective years. Hence, a few transactions significantly influenced the picture of the total M&A activity.

In contrast to the finding above, the impression of stronger M&A activities in the last years can be underlined if certain transactions are considered, which due to a shortage of relevant data fell out of the original set of transactions. These transactions include the € 100-130m acquisition of 45% of Karlsberg (Germany) by Heineken (June 2002), the approximately € 50m acquisition of 49% of Wernesgrüner by Bitburger (February 2002), the approximately € 97m acquisition of 80% of Diebels by Interbrew (July 2001) and the approximately € 100m acquisition of 49% of Bayerische Brau Holding by Heineken (February 2001).

Summarising, it becomes obvious that the German beer market is in a phase of consolidation reflected in an increased M&A activity.

3.2. Selected Transactions in the German Market

The analysis of the transaction characteristics includes a set of eight transactions. Transaction volumes have been converted to USD at the exchange rate prevailing at the announcement day of the deal. The set of transactions comprise the larger transactions within the considered time frame (2001-2004) with volumes exceeding USD 50m.

Transactions exercised in two steps, are accounted for as one. Furthermore, transaction values have been grossed up to 100%. The above mentioned adjustments were necessary in order to ensure comparability within the set of transactions and with international transactions (see following part). An overview of the considered transactions can be found in appendix 6.

The analysis reveales a range between 0.86 and 2.23 for the transaction value / sales multiple (all figures derive from the last twelve month) with the mean and median being 1.64. Transaction value / EBITDA multiples were in a range between 4.2 and 12.8 times EBITDA with a mean of 8.8 and a median of 9.0. Transaction value / EBIT multiples came in a range of 5.2 and 54.6 times EBIT. The mean for this multiple is 25.3 and the median 22.1. The transaction values as a multiple of hl production volume lies in a range between USD 71 and USD 285 with a mean of USD 134 and a median of USD 110 per hl.

Comparing the transaction multiples, the take-over of Beck's by Interbrew and Holsten Brewing Business by Carlsberg seem to be the outstanding transactions. The very low EBIT and EBITDA multiples in the acquisition of Stuttgarter Hofbräu are due to a comparably high profitability (EBIT margin of 43.9% in 2003) while at the same time growth opportunities for the regional brewer are fairly limited. Since the company derives a significant part of its turnover through real estate assets and other non-beer brewing activities, the transaction will not be considered in the following.

In the light of the highest transaction value / EBITDA and transaction value / hectolitre production multiples, the price paid in the Beck's acquisition appears to be high. However, through the take-over of Beck's the Belgian Interbrew could significantly improve its standing, becoming the second largest brewer by market share in the third largest beer market in the world. Beck's is not just one of the few nationally sold brands, but the only German brand with significant exports. Furthermore, the company's major brands Beck's and Hasseröder were still growing despite a stagnant market development. Accordingly, Interbrew paid a strategic premium when acquiring Beck's.

The second outstanding transaction was the acquisition of the Holsten Brewing business by Carlsberg. While the transaction values as multiples of sales and hl production constitute the lower bound of the respective ranges, the EBIT multiple is the highest within the analysed set of transactions. By the time of the transaction, the brand Holsten (including Landskrone, Feldschlößchen, Astra and Lübzer - without König Pilsener, Licher and the water business) had generated an EBITDA of approximately USD 60m and an EBIT of approximately USD 10m over sales of USD 636m in the twelve months preceding the transaction. Hence, Holsten had a miserable EBIT margin of only 1.6%. On the other side, it was the largest German brewer with an outstanding and strong position in northern Germany and the adjacent Denmark, home of Carlsberg, which made Holsten an attractive target for a variety of potential acquirors, including Radeberger (Dr. Oetker) and Heineken. Analysts of SG (Société Generalé) and Merrill Lynch commented the price as being too high.[15]

The preceding findings suggest that strategic premiums have been paid in the larger transactions. In order to test, whether a linear relationship between size and market share of the target (implies high transaction value for large targets) and price (as a multiple of sales or hl output respectively) exists, several regressions have been conducted. A regression analysis with the transaction value as the independent variable and the transaction value / EBITDA or transaction value / hl output multiple respectively as the dependent variable yielded for both regressions a positive slope coefficient. The slope coefficient is a measure of the response of the dependent variable (price) to variations of the independent variable (transaction value). It is calculated as the covariance of the two variables divided by the variance of the independent variable. For the transaction value / EBITDA multiple the value was 0.0054 and the regression was significant on a 1% level (p-value < 0.01). R^2, the coefficient of determination, which measures how much of the variation of the dependent variable is caused by changes in the independent variable, is 0.808 (80.8%). Eight observations have been included in the analysis.[16]

For the transactions value / hl output multiple the slope coefficient was 0.1760. The regression is again significant on a 1% level. R^2 for this investigation is 0.9216 (92.2%). Only five observations could be included in the analysis due to a lack of data for the remaining three.[17]

These results show that the larger the transaction value, the higher is the price (as multiple) paid for the target. If one assumes that the larger the transaction values the bigger and the more important (higher market share) the target is, it can again

---

[15] Cf. Merrill Lynch (2004); SG (2004).
[16] Cf. Appendix 9.
[17] Cf. Appendix 10.

be concluded that strategic premiums have been paid. It could also indicate that larger breweries operate more profitably and are therefore valued higher. As already discussed in 2.1, Brau und Brunnen, the second largest transaction in the sample, was in a difficult financial situation at the time of the take-over and by no means a very profitable business. Accordingly, the aforementioned correlation of transaction price and profitability does not exist. However, the small number of observations does not permit any substantial conclusions.

3.3. German vs. International Transactions

In order to evaluate the M&A dynamics in the German beer industry, a comparison of the German transactions to international transactions (in which the target is not a German company) appears reasonable. The national set of transactions is the same as used in the preceding section. The international set of transactions comprises 27 transactions, which took place roughly within the same timeframe, between March 2000 and August 2004.[18]

As with the national transactions, transaction values are grossed up to 100%. The set of transactions is truly global with both acquirers and targets coming from all parts of the world. The regions US, South America and Europe are especially well presented due to the fact that they dispose of well-developed beer markets, which imply a large number of brewers originating from or being active in these markets.[19]

Transaction values for the international transactions fall into a range between USD 213m and USD 19.9 billion. The average transaction value was USD 2.5 billion and the median USD 1.7 billion. This compares to a range of only USD 73m to USD 1.6 billion for the smallest and largest transaction respectively in the German market. Hence, international transactions were on average more than four times larger than the national transactions. Even the largest German transaction, the take-over of Beck's by Interbrew, can be considered to be small by international standards, since the transaction value was well below international average. However,

[18] Cf. Appendix 7.
[19] An overview over the following statistics can be found in Appendix 8.

it has to be mentioned that half of the international transactions (n = 13) had a lower transaction value. The median for both sets of transactions is below the mean, which indicates that a few large transactions, especially the USD 19.9 billion merger of AmBev and Interbrew, had a strong impact on the results.

For the international transactions the range of transaction value / sales multiple lay between 0.47 and 4.62 with a mean of 2.24 and a median of 2.1. The respective EBITDA range is 5.0 to 19.9 transaction value / EBITDA, with a mean of 10.4 and a median of 9.9. The EBIT multiples come in a range between 5.2 and 41.8 with a mean of 19.1 and a median of 16.1. The transaction values as multiples of hl output are in a range of 52 and 587 USD per hl with a mean of USD 196 and a median of USD 160.

The ranges, into which the respective multiples fall, are not considered here due to the significant difference in the number of transactions between the two sets of transactions. The result shows that on average higher sales, EBITDA and hl output multiples have been paid in international transactions than in national transactions while the EBIT multiple is higher for the national transactions. The lower sales, EBITDA and hl output multiples reflect the market characteristics as explained in 2.1. That means that the highly fragmented and shrinking German market with its huge structural problems such as a high overcapacity does not encourage acquirers to pay prices comparable to those paid in international transactions. Furthermore, the comparably low profitability of German brewers certainly has an impact on transaction prices. This leads to low valuations in terms of EBITDA and sales, which have been found to be the more precise valuation measures. Deriving the respective EBIT multiple from a transaction value based on EBITDA valuation leads consequently to a high EBIT multiple. Accordingly, EBIT multiples are on average higher for the German transactions as in the international transactions. Although this could also be due to a very conservative tax oriented accounting, low EBIT margins in Germany are in the first place due to high production costs. Since at the same time beer prices are comparably low in Germany, this translates in low net income for most of the breweries.

A further explanation of the low prices paid for German breweries may be found in the size of the transactions. In the preceding part it has been shown that a positive correlation between the transaction value and prices paid exist. As German transactions are relatively small in the international context, this may be an explanation for the low prices for German Breweries. To investigate this hypothesis, a regression of the transaction value (independent variable) and the EBITDA or hl output variable respectively (dependent variable) has been conducted for the set of international transactions as well.

The slope coefficient for the transaction value / EBITDA regression is a mere 0.0001, while the test has proofed not significant (p-value of 0.469). R^2 is 0.0229 (2.3%). 25 observations have been included in the analysis.[20]

The result for the transaction value / hl output regression does not change this picture. The slope coefficient is positive (0.0015), however, the result is not significant (p-value 0.840) either, and R2 is 0.0021 (0.2%) only. 21 observations have been included in this regression analysis.[21]

Hence, as the results have proofed not to be significant, the H_0 hypothesis, which claims that no causal relationship between the transaction volume and the price paid exists, cannot be ruled out. In other words, it is not clear whether there is a relationship between the transaction value and the price. Therefore, we cannot use the relatively small size of the German transactions to explain the lower prices paid for German breweries.

When comparing the list of acquirers, it becomes obvious that international transactions are undertaken by large Anglo-American brewing corporations as well as international brewers from northern Europe. InBev (or its predecessors AmBev and Interbrew) is the most active company in terms of M&A activity, both in Germany and internationally, with nine deals over a five year period. Carlsberg and Scottish & Newcastle are also major drivers in the consolidation of the global brewing

[20] Cf. Appendix 11.
[21] Cf. Appendix 12.

business. German brewers have not been involved in any international transactions on the buy side, due to their relatively small sizes and lack of financial strength.

4. Conclusion and Future Outlook

As discussed in the paper, one can easily see by the data analysed within the study that the beer market in general, and the German beer market in particular, has experienced a tremendous transformation process. One of the main reasons is that international and national breweries can almost only successfully enter markets in Germany by means of M&A.

Although transaction activities within the analysed years has constantly been at a high level, no specific merger waves can be seen in terms of number of transactions. Nevertheless, in terms of transaction volumes, an increased activity can be observed since 2001. However, it must taken into account that the data is partly very much influenced by exceptionally large transactions, such as the take-over of Beck's by Interbrew.

The analysis of the transaction multiples shows a wide range of sales, EBITDA and EBIT multiples. Some of the multiples paid within transactions seem difficult to justify and would require a detailed analysis of the strategic rationale and the specific circumstances of the deals. However, the result of the regression analysis shows that as the transaction value increases, the price paid for a target increases, too.

The comparison of German transactions international transactions has produced some interesting findings. On average, the international transactions analysed within the data sample were four times larger than on the German market. Furthermore, one can observe that higher sales, EBITDA and hl multiples were paid in international transactions while the EBIT multiple paid was on average higher German transactions. Obviously, the structural problems of the German market do not encourage international investors to pay prices as high for German breweries as paid for international ones. The higher EBIT multiple in Germany can be explained by high production costs, low beer prices and a conservative tax accounting methods.

The current trend on the German and on the international beer market is likely to continue, so that large companies will dominate the national and international markets even more in the near future. Large breweries will carry on expanding their businesses and entering the German beer market while mergers and acquisitions seem to be the most reasonable way for further consolidation, taking the specific characteristics of the German beer market into account. The role of German breweries in terms of international M&A activity seems doubtful.

There is further need for additional research especially in the analysis of the rational for the multiples paid in the different transactions. This could help to understand differences on multiples paid in Germany and the ones paid in international transactions. Furthermore, it will be of special interest to observe the long-term development of multiples in the future.

Appendix

Appendix 1: Top 10 Global Beer Markets

Rank	Market	2001A Volume(1)	Market Concentration(3)	01-07E Growth
#1	USA	235.0	79%	(0.3%)
#2	China	227.1	23	5.1
#3	**Germany**	**101.1**	**26**	**(0.5)**
#4	Brazil	83.9	93	3.3
#5	Russia	63.0	52	10.1
#6	UK	58.3	61	(0.8)
#7	Mexico	52.0	100	3.0
#8	Japan	48.8	94	(4.9)
#9	Spain	31.1	78	3.3
#10	Poland	24.9	78	3.3
Total Top 10 Markets		**925.3**		
As % of global volume		*68%*		

Germany as % of Global Volume	**7.4%**

Appendix 2: Consumption by Beer Type

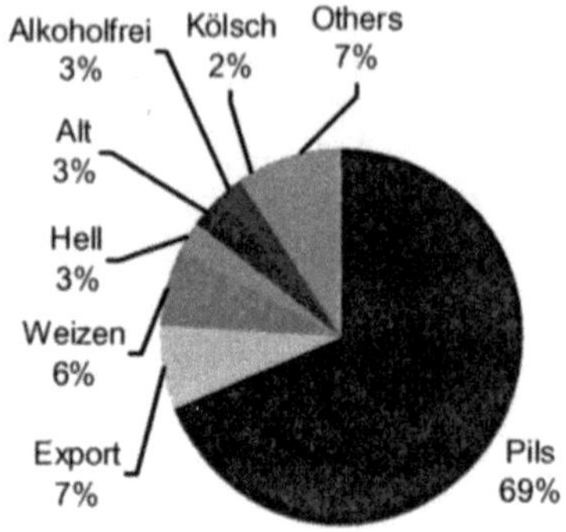

Appendix 3: Comparison of Market Shares

	2004		2001		1996	
Brewers	Volume (m Hl)	Ranking	Volume (m Hl)	Ranking	Volume (m Hl)	Ranking
[illegible]	14.0	#1	9.4	#2	7.9	#2
Interbrew	12.1	#2	8.2	#3	n.a	n.a
[illegible]	8.0	#3	4.7	#7	4.6	#7
Brauholding International	5.7	#4	n.a	n.a	n.a	n.a
[illegible]	5.6	#5	3.0	#10	n.a	#9
Krombacher	5.3	#6	4.6	#8	4.2	#8
HOLSTEN	5.0	#7	9.5	#1	5.7	#4
[illegible]	3.6	#8	6.7	#6	5.9	#3
Karlsberg	3.3	#9	n.a	n.a	n.a	n.a
[illegible]	2.3	#10	n.a	n.a	n.a	n.a

Appendix 4: Number of Transactions in the German Beer Market

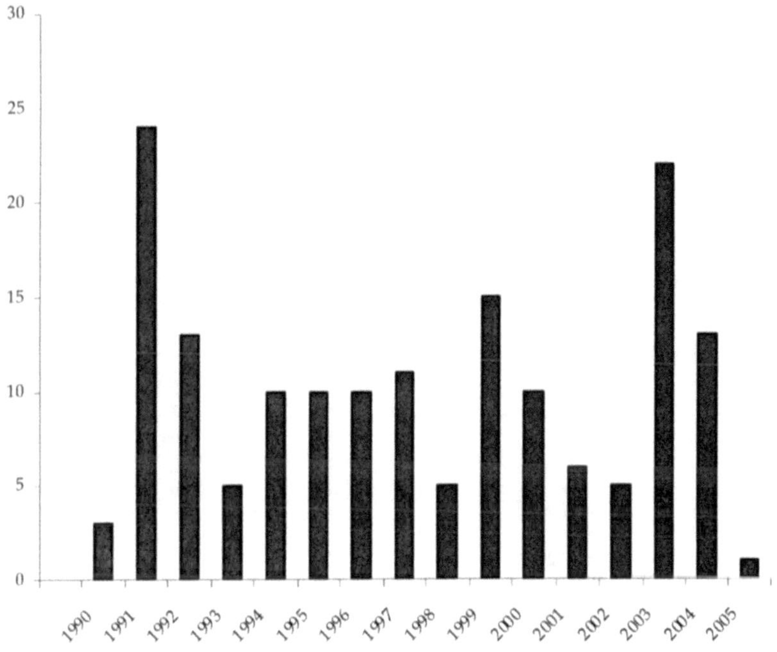

Source: Thomson Financial; own calculations.

Appendix 5: Number of Transactions in the German Beer Market

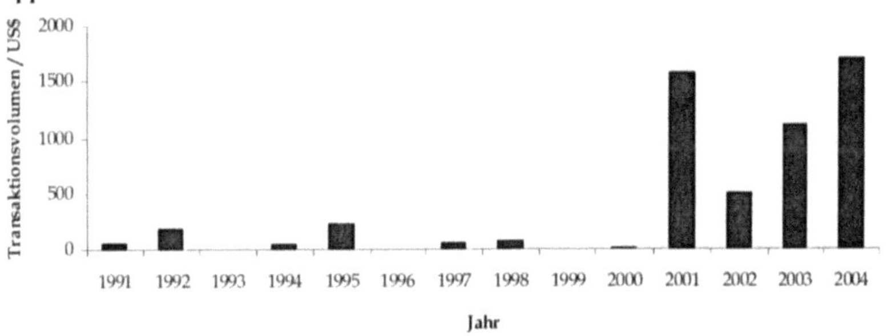

Source: Thomson Financial; own calculations.

Appendix 6: Analysis of Selected Transactions (National)

Date Announced	Target	Acquiror	Transaction Value	Transaction Value as a Multiple of LTM: Sales	EBITDA	EBIT	Production ($/ Hl)
Feb 04	Brau und Brunnen	Dr.Oetker	798	1,20	12,1	n.m.	111
Jan 04	König and Licher	Bitburger	589	2,23	9,0	22,1	n.a.
Jan 04	Holsten Brewing Business	Carlsberg	549	0,86	9,1	54,6	71
Dez 03	Stuttgarter Hofbräu	Radeberger	73	1,53	4,2	5,2	n.a.
Sep 03	Dinkelacker-Schwabenbräu	Brauerei Beck's	86	2,12	6,1	25,0	n.a.
Sep 03	Spaten	Interbrew	537	1,34	8,9	n.a.	110
Nov 02	Brauerei Gilde	Interbrew	478	1,75	8,6	n.a.	106
Aug 01	Brauerei Beck's	Interbrew	1.585	2,11	12,8	19,9	285

Source: Company announcements; own calculations.

Appendix 7: Selected Transactions Analysis (International)

Date Announced	Target	Acquiror	Transaction Value	Transaction Value as a Multiple of LTM: Sales	EBITDA	EBIT	Production ($/ Hl)
Aug 04	Sun Interbrew	InBev	2.397	2,97x	15,8x	28,9x	123
Jun 04	Harbin	Anheuser Busch	830	4,62	19,9	34,2	n.a.
Mrz 04	Ambev	Interbrew	19.908	4,47	12,9	15,6	284
Feb 04	Carlsberg Breweries	Carlsberg A/S	8.849	1,50	8,6	16,1	109
Jan 04	Oriental Brewery	Interbrew	1.963	n.a.	10,7	n.a.	273
Dez 03	Chongquing Brewery	Scottish & Newcastle	325	2,95	7,5	41,8	74
Mai 03	Birra Peroni	SABMiller	647	1,14	12,6	n.a.	147
Mai 03	Centralcer	S&N	746	n.a.	9,6	n.a.	226
Mai 03	BBAG	Heineken	2.131	2,10	10,2	23,9	168
Apr 03	Bulmer	S&N	442	0,47	7,3	13,7	n.a.
Sep 02	Florida Bebidas+COCECA	Heineken	916	n.a.	n.a.	n.a.	482
Jul 02	UCP Backus y Johnston	Bavaria	2.016	4,23	14,8	22,8	395
Mai 02	Miller Brewing	SAB	4.993	1,18	8,3	10,4	100
Mai 02	Quinsa	Ambev	1.689	3,36	10,8	26,9	137
Feb 02	Hartwall	S&N	1.979	2,82	9,9	13,6	123
Feb 02	Bravo	Heineken	400	n.a.	12,5	n.a.	160
Jan 02	Hite Brewery	Carlsberg Asia	810	1,45	n.a.	5,2	85
Dez 01	Carling Assets	Coors	1.700	2,13	8,5	15,5	170
Dez 01	San Miguel (SMC)	Kirin Breweries	4.055	1,74	12,1	19,7	n.a.
Nov 01	Cerveceria Honduren.a.	SAB	553	2,21	8,8	11,1	587
Jan 01	Cia Cervecerias Unidas SA	Anheuser Busch Inc	1.820	3,18	13,1	25,6	186
Nov 00	Bavaria	Molson	213	1,00	5,5	n.a.	65
Jun 00	Bass Brewing Assets	Interbrew	3.478	1,25	9,7	14,4	n.a.
Mai 00	Orkla Brewing Assets	Carlsberg	1.234	1,74	9,8	23,1	52
Mai 00	Whitbread Brewing Assets	Interbrew	662	0,64	5,0	9,7	n.a.
Apr 00	Unicer	VSGPS	506	1,95	5,9	11,5	n.a.
Mrz 00	Kronenbourg	S & N	2.656	2,47	11,2	17,9	167

Source: Company announcements; own calculations.

Appendix 8: Comparison National vs. International Transactions

National Transactions	Transaction Value	Transaction Value as a Multiple of LTM: Sales	EBITDA	EBIT	Production ($/ Hl)
Mean	587	1,64x	8,8x	25,3x	137
Median	543	1,64	9,0	22,1	110
Max	1.585	2,23	12,8	54,6	285
Min	73	0,86	4,2	5,2	71

International Transactions	Transaction Value	Transaction Value as a Multiple of LTM: Sales	EBITDA	EBIT	Production ($/ Hl)
Mean	2.516	2,24x	10,4x	19,1x	196
Median	1.689	2,10	9,9	16,1	160
Max	19.908	4,62	19,9	41,8	587
Min	213	0,47	5,0	5,2	52

Source: Company announcements; own calculations.

Appendix 9: Transaction Value / EBITDA multiple Regression Analysis (National Transactions)

Regression Statistics	
Multiple R	0,899167484
R Square	0,808502164
Adjusted R Square	0,776585858
Standard Error	1,334580605
Observations	8

ANOVA	*Degree of Freedom (df)*	*SS*	*MS*	*F*	*Significance F*
Regression	1	45,11886683	45,11886683	25,3319467	0,002373046
Residual	6	10,68663235	1,781105391		
Total	7	55,80549918			

	Coefficients	*Standard Error*	*t Stat*	*P-value*	*Lower 95%*	*Upper 95%*	*Lower 95,0%*	*Upper 95,0%*
Intercept	5,704138316	0,782936557	7,285569013	0,000340619	3,788361581	7,619915051	3,788361581	7,619915051
X Variable 1	0,005356521	0,001064262	5,033085207	0,002373046	0,002752366	0,007960676	0,002752366	0,007960676

Appendix 10: Transaction Value / hl Output Multiple Regression Analysis (National Transactions)

Regression Statistics	
Multiple R	0,959986121
R Square	0,921573353
Adjusted R Squ	0,895431138
Standard Error	27,35954786
Observations	5

ANOVA	Degree of Freedom (df)	SS	MS	F	Significance F
Regression	1	26387,93153	26387,93153	35,2523048	0,009550495
Residual	3	2245,634577	748,5448591		
Total	4	28633,5661			

	Coefficients	Standard Error	t Stat	P-value	Lower 95%	Upper 95%	Lower 95,0%	Upper 95,0%
Intercept	-2,339460849	26,41292735	-0,08857257	0,935003088	-86,3971839	81,7182622	-86,3971839	81,7182622
X Variable 1	0,176008323	0,02964418	5,937365139	0,009550495	0,081667311	0,270349335	0,081667311	0,270349335

Appendix 11: Transaction Value / EBITDA Multiple Regression Analysis (International Transactions)

Regression Statistics	
Multiple R	0,151526219
R Square	0,022960195
Adjusted R Square	-0,019519796
Standard Error	3,393610912
Observations	25

ANOVA	Degree of Freedom (df)	SS	MS	F	Significance F
Regression	1	6,224654467	6,224654467	0,540494344	0,46965873
Residual	23	264,8816855	11,51659502		
Total	24	271,10634			

	Coefficients	Standard Error	t Stat	P-value	Lower 95%	Upper 95%	Lower 95,0%	Upper 95,0%
Intercept	10,10178198	0,815271749	12,39069303	1,163E-11	8,415263878	11,78830007	8,415263878	11,78830007
X Variable 1	0,000125409	0,000170582	0,735183204	0,46965873	-0,000227467	0,000478285	-0,000227467	0,000478285

Appendix 12: Transaction Value / hl Output Multiple Regression Analysis (International Transaction)

Regression Statistics	
Multiple R	0,046777522
R Square	0,002188137
Adjusted R Square	-0,050328277
Standard Error	143,3790018
Observations	21

ANOVA	Degree of Freedom (df)	SS	MS	F	Significance F
Regression	1	856,5455655	856,5455655	0,041665766	0,840428726
Residual	19	390593,2253	20557,53817		
Total	20	391449,7708			

	Coefficients	Standard Error	t Stat	P-value	Lower 95%	Upper 95%	Lower 95,0%	Upper 95,0%
Intercept	191,7618757	37,25748051	5,146936216	5,73198E-05	113,781073	269,7426785	113,781073	269,7426785
X Variable 1	0,001496384	0,007330831	0,204121938	0,840428726	-0,013847223	0,01683999	-0,013847223	0,01683999

References

Betsch, Oskar / Groh, Alexander / Lohmann, Lutz: Corporate Finance, Frankfurt 1998.

Bowley, Andy / Shackleton, Ian / Bleakley, Michael / Matthews, Jennifer (2004): The German Beer Industry, CSFB Research Report (16/02/2004), pp. 1-7.

Bowley, Andy / Shackleton, Ian / Bleakley, Michael / Matthews, Jennifer (2003): The German Beer Industry, CSFB Research Report (04/06/2003), pp. 1-78.

Copeland, Tom / Koller, Tim / Murrin, Jack: Valuation – Measuring and Managing the Value of Companies, 3rd edition, New York 2000.

Gohlke, Christian: Der deutsche Biermarkt, in: M&A Intern, No. 8, October 2002, pp. 23-28.

Hockmann, Heinz J. / Thießen, Friedrich: Investment Banking, Frankfurt am Main 2002.

Levy, Haim / Sarnat, Marshall: Capital Investment and Financial Decisions, Fifth Edition, Essex 1994.

Merrill Lynch (2004): Update on Carlsberg (21/01/2004).

Palepu, Krishna G. / Healy, Paul M. / Bernard, Victor L.: Business Analysis and Valuation, 2nd edition, Boston / Harvard 2000.

SG (2004): Carlsberg takeover of Holsten (21/01/2004

II Trading Multiples in the German Brewing Industry

by
Diana Diekmann and Heiko Weber

1 Introduction

1.1 Objective of the Study

The German beer market is an extremely atomistic and fragmented market with a total of 1,274 breweries, of most which are small and privately owned companies. Furthermore, the German beer industry is one of the largest industries in the world with a total annual production volume of almost 106m hl. Despite the continuously decreasing beer per-capita consumption, averaging at 117.7 l in 2003, the Germans are still one of the most important beer consumers in the world after the Czech Republicans and the Irish. At the same time, however, the average retail beer price in Germany is one of the lowest in Europe, mainly due to the weak retail environment and low beer exercise rates.

In light of the highly fragmented market structure, fierce market competition and many breweries being stuck in the middle-price segment a consolidation momentum has started to pick up in the German market. Many international players have started scrutinising the German beer market in order to identify attractive brands possibly to help them build large market positions in the long-run. A higher level of market concentration, resulting in economies of scale and pricing power benefits, is also perceived as a method of increasing the level of profitability for many breweries. Therefore, a consolidation process may allow the industry to achieve a better pricing policy and to reduce over-capacities in the production. Since major global breweries as well as other investors are starting to meticulously investigate the German brewing industry for investment opportunities, it is vital for them to get an overview of the traded values of breweries. The enterprise and equity values of the listed brewery companies are of particular interest to those investors.[1]

The main objective of this paper is two-fold. The primary objective is to value German brewery companies by means of trading multiples, providing an overview on how breweries should be traded in efficient markets. The secondary objective is then to group the evaluated companies according to market size and geographical scope, possibly arriving at some conclusions on how much a potential investor should pay to acquire certain brewery types. Considering the information constraints on privately owned companies, the study only analyses the trading multiples of German breweries listed on the German stock exchange.

1.2 Course of Analysis

The contribution of this study is its extensive theoretical overview and empirical examination of trading multiples for German brewery companies in order to provide an overview of typical multiple ranges for certain brewery clusters in Germany which potential investors could use to assess privately owned breweries.
Firstly, the paper sets the issue in its wider context by providing basic concepts and theories of multiples, in particular of trading multiples. A side from defining the equity and enterprise trading multiples extensively, their main advantages and disadvantages will be summarised briefly.

Having set the theoretical foundation, the study will focus on the empirical examination of the different types of trading multiples with respect to all listed German brewery companies and some selected international companies. It will be analysed whether the breweries' multiples differ with regard to their market sizes, product ranges and geographical locations. This will allow analysts to apply the most adequate multiples for different brewery companies in the future, thus achieving a better estimation of the correct value of the particular firm being examined. In order to accomplish this goal it is necessary to previously identify the appropriate data sample for the analysis, to filter out unnecessary information and data and to

[1] Cf. CSFB Equity Research (2003), pp. 3-21.

calculate the various equity and enterprise multiples for each firm for a predefined time series.

Finally, the empirical results will be summarized, providing the basis to conclude whether trading multiples can and should be used in the German brewing industry. In particular, the question of which particular types of multiples should be applied will be stressed at the end. Based on these findings, averaged market multiples could be applied to privately owned companies in the same sector to determine their intrinsic values, but due to lack of information this is not feasible in the context of this paper.

2 Conceptual Foundation of Valuation Methodologies

2.1 Definition of Trading Multiples

In general, there are three main valuation methodologies used in finance to evaluate companies: Discounted Cash Flow (DCF), Transaction Multiple and Trading Multiple Analysis.[2] While the DCF analysis focuses on the present value of anticipated free cash flows in order to determine the value of a firm, multiple analysis examines the value based on multiples paid for comparable companies in sale transactions ("transaction multiples") or on market trading multiples of comparable companies ("trading multiples").[3] The following study will merely concentrate on trading multiples for examining the German brewing industry.

As a public market valuation technique, trading multiples indicate how the secondary market values a company with respect to particular financial measures (e.g. earnings, sales, etc.). Companies with common characteristics (i.e. industry, size, expected earnings growth, product mix, geographical spread, etc.) should be valued similarly in an efficient market. Furthermore, the trading multiple analysis is an ex-post analysis because the analyst has to scrutinise historical and prospective multi-

[2] Cf. Engel (2003), pp. 243-245.
[3] Cf. Damodaran (1996), pp. 9-15.

ples in order to derive at a value for the business being investigated. Unlike transaction multiples, trading multiples do not include a control premium.[4]
The market value of the business being valued depends on a benchmark company and the market assumptions on prospective earnings, cash flow, etc. of the examined company.[5] This relationship is also presented in the following formula:

Formula 1: Market Value

$$Market\ Value = market\ assumptions \times comparable\ trading\ multiples$$

To hold true, the formula has to fulfil two assumptions: Firstly, stock market efficiency is assumed which means that the market correctly determines the value of the freely traded assets. Secondly, certain key ratios are adequate proxies for detailed and reliable valuation work.

Trading multiples can be broadly distinguished into two categories, equity and enterprise multiples. Whilst equity multiples are ratios solely concentrating on the company's equity stake, enterprise multiples are ratios affecting the enterprise value. The enterprise value can be calculated by adding a company's market capitalisation (used in equity based multiples) and its net debt (total debt - including long and short-term debt reported in the balance sheet - minus cash and investments). Therefore, the enterprise value is the value of the productive assets of a firm. Equity multiples are mostly used by retail investors because they are understandable, straight-forward and easy to calculate. Enterprise multiples are used by financial analysts as these types of multiples avoid some of the worst accounting distortions.[6]

The application of the publicly traded comparable companies' analysis features several advantages relative to other valuation methodologies. It is a very flexible and easily applicable valuation technique for most industries and companies. Furthermore, it is an analysis closely linked to financial markets by using stock prices; many analysts use the method for evaluating companies in an initial public offering

[4] Cf. Thommen / Schellenberg (2002), pp. 381-382.
[5] Cf. Ferris / Petitt (2002), p. 72.
[6] Cf. Benninga / Sarig (1997), pp. 305-312.

(IPO). On the other hand, however, there are some disadvantages. Comparable companies are difficult to identify because every company is unique in some respect. In particular for companies with a small market capitalisation, the use of comparables can be misleading as the relative illiquid shares might be falsely priced in the market. Growth prospects for the business being valued are only implicitly considered.[7] Despite these disadvantages, however, trading multiples are a commonly applied valuation methodology.

2.2 Equity Multiples

2.2.1 Cash Flow Multiple

Cash flow multiples are widely used by investors in Europe, in particular for cyclical companies. Then primarily focuses on the cash flow generated by the business being valued. As the advantage of this multiple is that it is not dependent on any accounting methodologies as it corrects for different depreciation policies and that it has several close parallels to the DCF analysis. On the other hand, however, there might be distortions when using this multiple because the cash flows of only one period are analysed and the definition of cash flows among companies might be inconsistent. Furthermore, the multiple can be flawed when the different capital structures and tax rates are neglected in the use of cash flow multiples. This multiple also requires a lot of gathering of information before it can be applied.[8]

The following formula indicates how to calculate the cash flow multiple:

Formula 2: Cash Flow Multiple

$$Cash\ Flow\ Multiple = \frac{Equity\ Value}{Cash\ Flow}$$

[7] Cf. Damodaran (1996), pp. 14f.
[8] Cf. Benninga / Sarig (1997), pp. 325f.

2.2.2 Price/Earnings Ratio

The Price/Earnings (P/E) Multiple is a very popular valuation multiple because it is an indicator easy to understand and to calculate.[9] Consensus prospective earnings per share (EPS) figures are widely available for most companies. Another reason for the frequent application of this multiple is that it includes the earnings which are distributed to the shareholders. In theory, a high P/E ratio should mean high earnings growth.[10] Similarly to cash flow multiples, however, P/E multiples can be distorted due to the negligence of the firm's unique capital structure and differing tax rates. Non-core business activities influence the company's earnings, thus making it difficult to apply this multiple to 'comparable' companies which don't have these identical business activities. The earnings can also be falsified due to different accounting methodologies with regard to inventory, depreciation and amortization of goodwill. Unlike the cash flow multiple, P/E multiples are not applicable to cyclical industries because the multiples would then be very volatile.[11]

The P/E ratio can be determined by applying the following formula:

Formula 3: Price/Earnings Multiple

$$P/E\ Multiple = \frac{Price\ per\ share}{Diluted\ EPS} = \frac{Market\ Capitalization + Options}{Normalised\ net\ income\ after\ preference\ dividends}$$

2.3 Enterprise Multiples

2.3.1 Sales Multiple

The sales multiple is an enterprise multiple which eliminates the impact of the debt/equity mix of comparables and can also be used for companies making financial losses (as opposed to equity multiples). It is especially applicable to enterprise valuation when all comparables have similar profit margins and, hence, profitability. If no information about a company's earnings is available, this multiple can nevertheless be applied. In practice, this multiple is commonly used as a bench-

[9] Cf. Damodaran (1996), pp. 291-315.
[10] Cf. Ferris / Petitt (2002), pp. 104-106.
[11] Cf. Ross et al. (2002), pp. 121-123.

mark for transactions in certain industries. Despite its advantages, the sales multiple is based on the assumption that the comparable companies have an identical profitability and growth in different periods. Considering that it focuses on the revenues of only one particular period, the sales multiple can also be very volatile over time.[12]

The sales multiple can be calculated by using the following ratio:

Formula 4: Sales Multiple

$$Sales\ Multiple = \frac{Enterprise\ Value}{Sales}$$

2.3.2 EBIT Multiple

The EBIT multiple, which is another type of enterprise multiple, is used when primarily focusing on the earnings of an examined business. Similar to the EBITDA multiple, the EBIT ratio does not depend on the capital structure, leverage and tax rate of comparable companies. The disadvantage, however, is that this multiple does not eliminate any effects of different depreciation and accounting policies between the business being valued and comparables. This is the main reason why most financial analysts prefer using the EBITDA instead of the EBIT multiple when valuing firms.[13]

The EBIT multiple is calculated as follows:

Formula 5: EBIT Multiple

$$EBIT\ Multiple = \frac{Enterprise\ Value}{EBIT}$$

[12] Cf. Damodaran (1996), pp. 338-353.
[13] Cf. Benninga / Sarig (1997), pp. 322-325.

2.3.3 EBITDA Multiple

The EBITDA multiple is a well-understood enterprise metric which financial analysts often use for cyclical industries. One of the key advantages is that this multiple is independent of the differing capital structures, leverages and tax rates of comparable companies. Furthermore, the EBITDA multiple eliminates some of the accounting differences between firms, for instance differences in depreciation and amortization policies. On the other hand, differences in the levels of capital expenditure and capital intensity might distort the EBITDA multiple. Furthermore, the multiple assumes that companies have the same growth rate over time. When the EBITDA of the business being valued is negative in the examined time period, the multiple cannot be applied.[14]

The EBITDA multiple is the ratio of the firm value divided by the EBITDA:

Formula 6: EBITDA Multiple

$$EBITDA\ Multiple = \frac{Enterprise\ Value}{EBITDA}$$

3 Analysis of Trading Multiples in the Brewing Industry

3.1 Description of the Data Sample and Multiple Calculation

The data used for the analysis of the trading multiples in the brewing industry stems from the financial database Datastream[15] and comprises financial information for a time series from 1993 to 2004 for 51 breweries.[16] As one of the central aspects in the analysis of the multiples of the German brewing industry lies in an international comparison, it is important to separate data for listed German breweries from data of international und multinational breweries. The data analysis encompasses 19 German breweries and 32 foreign enterprises.

[14] Cf. Ferris / Petitt (2002), S. 70-74.
[15] Cf. Datastream (2005).
[16] The time series varies in depending on the availability of data, the date of initial public offering, the starting date of the accounting year and possible later mergers and acquisitions.

As previously mentioned in the introduction, the German brewery market has a highly atomized structure and consists of more than 1,200 breweries. This structure is also reflected in the financial data for the listed German breweries since the market size of breweries strongly diverges from the size of international breweries. As can be taken from the following table, which depicts average values for the entire data sample, the market capitalisation, the sales and the earnings of international breweries are substantially higher than those of local firms.

Table 1: Average Data for German and Foreign Breweries (2003, in T€)

	Average			
	MarketCap	Sales	EBITDA	EBIT
Germany	115.657	132.189	21.387	8.743
Overseas	4.082.432	4.112.279	817.782	512.212

This can firstly be drawn back to the atomized structure of the German market. Secondly, the existence of large multinational corporations with many brands, being also active in other sectors besides the brewery market, pulls up the average values for foreign firms and distorts the results. Whereas the activities of German breweries clearly concentrate on the production of beer and very few other non-alcoholic beverages, many of the large international firms have moved into sectors such as the production of liquors and other strong alcoholic beverages. Furthermore, it can be seen that international firms have been more active in various growth strategies through mergers and acquisitions, entrances into new markets and the expansion of product lines than German breweries. All these reasons explain the lower average values for German breweries in comparison to other publicly traded international breweries.

Even though all international breweries were taken into account when calculating average values, only larger and regionally selected breweries were taken into consideration for further and deeper investigation of multiple evolution and structure. This is reasonable since the focus of the paper predominantly lies on German breweries rather than on international breweries, and the international ones are only drawn on for reasons of comparison. To ensure a representative sample of international breweries and to increase the comparability of the financial data and the calculated multiples, most of these selected international enterprises (65%) originated in Europe. As the also somewhat atomised market structure in the United Kingdom can be compared to that of Germany, the analysis strongly focuses on British companies in the context of the international data sample (about 50% are British companies). Furthermore, breweries in other European countries such as Hungary (Brau Union) and the Netherlands (Heineken) were contemplated. The remaining 35% consist of breweries from the United States of America (e.g. Anheuser Bush), South America (Quilmes and Ambev) and other multinationals (e.g. SABMiller).

The German data sample comprises all publicly listed German breweries. As the main characteristic of the German beer market is its regional orientation, the 19 breweries were separated into five geographic clusters. The regional market of most of the publicly listed German breweries lies in Bavaria (42%). Next to these, 21% find their origin in Baden-Wuerttemberg, 10% in North Rhine-Westphalia, 10% in Lower Saxony and 17% in the rest of Germany. Generally it can be generally said that no correlation between the regional origin and the size of the company can be observed. The market capitalisation goes from € 2.7m in the case of Park & Bellheimer to over € 375.7m for Stuttgarter Hofbräu. Appendix 1 shows the key financial figures for the listed breweries in Germany sorted by the above described geographic clusters.

The calculation of the multiples was made with the above described data sample. Due to the lack of quarterly or half-yearly reports, it was not possible to adjust the end-of-financial year data of various breweries that report in other months than December in order to have financial data for the exact same timeframe for every enterprise. As the analysis is focused on the contemplation of the time series and a great variety of multiples, it is assumed that calendarization is not necessary and no serious distortions will arise due to this. Further preparatory steps such as the analysis of the product portfolio of each firm were taken in order to categorize the companies and to identify possible benchmarks. Having calculated the various multiples, the results were contemplated, taking into consideration the following factors: the development of the multiples in the specific time frame, the mean and the median in the time frame, maximum and minimum values, the standard deviation and ultimately the multiple for the lastly considered date (2003). By using these values the selection of the most appropriate multiple for the German brewing industry was enabled. Exhibits 2 to 6 in the appendix show the statistical overview of the various multiples.

In the closer analysis of the multiples, factors such as enterprise size, product portfolio, geographic origin and margins were regarded for possible clustering. As the highest coherences and correlation were discovered with respect to the regional focus of the breweries, this was the central criterion for clustering. Nevertheless, the other above mentioned aspects were not neglected and are highlighted in cases of notable insights.

3.2 Calculation and Analysis of Trading Multiples

3.2.1 Equity Multiples

3.2.1.1 Cash Flow Multiple

As described before, the equity value based multiple of cash flow sets cash flows generated by the company in relation to the company's price. The equity value used for the calculation of the multiple in this study is the market capitalisation and the cash flow drawn on is the net cash flow at the end of the financial year.
The cash flow multiples calculated for the German breweries are highly volatile and no clear trends can be recognised in the course of time. This can mainly be drawn back to changes in the denominator of the calculation, that is, the net cash flow of the breweries. Firstly, it can be observed that neither stability nor clear trends in the net cash flows can be identified in the time spread. This can also be said about the market capitalisation. Secondly, it can be assumed that due to the relatively small size of all breweries, the susceptibility of the multiples to smaller changes in the cash flows is extremely high.

A geographic differentiation does not give further insights into the development of these multiples and their values. A closer examination of the five regional clusters neither gives information about the evolution of the multiples nor about their values and the ranges in which these values move in. This allows for the conclusion that different regional preference structures and consumption habits are not reflected in the relation of the market value towards the net cash flow. A very interesting insight can be recognised when comparing the multiples of breweries with a wider product range that includes non-alcoholic beverages (such as sodas and water) to those of breweries with a portfolio restricted to beers. Hereafter breweries with a narrower product line record higher volatilities than breweries with wide portfolios. A possible explanation for this realization is that the risk of the product line and the effects of adverse movements on the cash flow that can arise if one specific brand is not performing well are reduced through a diversification into other consumer segments. This of course leads to a higher constancy in cash flows and thus, when assuming relatively constant market capitalisations, to less volatile multiples. Another possible way to increase the explanatory power and constancy of the cash flow multiple would be to analyse the results sorted firstly by market capitalisation and secondly by the height of the cash flow. However, neither approach has results that are significant and can be interpreted.

The multiples calculated for the rest of the world do not differ very much from the German results. Due to the inconsistency and volatility of the cash flows the cash flow multiples for the benchmark firms abroad are also highly volatile. The highest volatility is recognised in British firms. This can be explained by the greater size of multinational enterprises like Heineken and Anheuser-Bush and their highly diversified product portfolios in comparison to British firms. It can also be recognised that multinational firms demonstrate slightly growing multiples in the course of time. No insights can be gained when clustering the enterprises by size or by the height of the cash flows.

3.2.1.2 Price/Earnings Ratio

The second equity multiple analysed in this paper is the price/earnings multiple. In this study the multiple is calculated by dividing the market capitalisation with the firms' earnings.

The findings of the observation of the price/earnings multiples in the course of time are very similar to those already described for the cash flow multiple. There is no clear trend to be recognised in the development of the multiples for German breweries. These highly fluctuating ratios can be partly attributed to the fact that due to the smaller size of the firms they react faster to small changes in value of the earnings. Furthermore, the lack of stability in the market capitalisation and the earnings lead to highly volatile and unsteady multiples.

Unlike the cash flow multiple, clear differences can be recognised in relation to the regional clustering of the enterprises. In Bavaria, for example, rather volatile values are recorded, but a clear trend is seen towards values of around 40. Interestingly, most of the firms experienced a growth in the multiple around the turn of the century due to falling earnings coupled with slightly growing market capitalisations, but most of these outliers balanced out in the first years of the 21st century. The same peek as in Bavaria is can be observed to a lesser extent for the breweries in BadenWuerttemberg. Furthermore, the multiples move on lower levels than in Bavaria and balance out around values of about 20. In North Rhine-Westphalia a peek at the turn of the century cannot be observed, but despite highly volatile values a trend can be recognised toward negative values. This can be explained by the negative earnings reported by the breweries in North Rhine-Westphalia in the last years. Further trends are neither recognised for the other geographical clusters nor for the differentiation over the portfolio diversification. Beyond, similar to the cash flow multiple, no change and trend in the multiples can be drawn back to the market capitalisation or the height of the earnings of the respective firms.

In contrast to the multiples calculated for German breweries, the price/earnings ratios for international breweries are relatively stable over the course of time. The values recorded in Europe are stable on different levels between 2 and 15 and hence substantially lower than those in Germany. These stable values can be attributed to a growth in both the market capitalisation and the earnings. Furthermore, the generally higher level of earnings in international firms has the consequence that small fluctuations do not have great influence on the multiples. This can also be said about the multiples of other non-European breweries, which also present relatively stable values (except the Argentinean brewery Quilmes) on different levels between 10 and 20. These international values are consistent with the average value of the price/earnings ratio of the entire industry (beverages - brewers) that lies at 17.7[17]

3.2.2 Enterprise Multiples

3.2.2.1 Sales Multiple

The sales enterprise value based multiple is calculated by setting a company's sales in relation to its enterprise value.

The variety of sales multiples calculated for the German and international brewing industry seem to be the first results that exhibit certain constancy over time and where comparable values can be identified for the different breweries and regions. German breweries have sales multiples between 0 and 2. This stability is reflected in the close conformity of the mean and the median (which shows that no extreme values and outliers are found) and the very low standard deviation. These values are relatively stable for each enterprise and only move in a margin of about 0.7. About 50% of the breweries – for this issue no regional trend could be identified – experienced a slight increase of the multiples in the late nineties followed by a decrease towards the original values in the past years.

A clear regional differentiation regarding the level of the sales multiple improves further comparability and applicability. The Bavarian breweries can, for example, be clustered into two groups: while one group reflects multiples between 0 and 1, the other group shows multiples between 1 and 2. The margin of fluctuation is relatively small (this is seen in the very low standard deviation) and stable for each enterprise. In Baden-Wuerttemberg, a decreasing tendency of the sales multiples on different levels for many enterprises can be drawn back to descending enterprise values in this region. But nevertheless, stable movements in a narrow range on levels between 0 and 2 can be recognised for breweries in this state as well. Also North Rhine-Westphalia exhibits very stable multiples between 0 and 1. In contrast, no clear trends can be recognised for Lower Saxony, as on the one hand Einbecker shows decreasing but stable values from 2 to 1 and, on the other hand, Hof-

---

[17] Cf. Yahoo! Finance (2005).

bräuhaus Wolters exhibits growing multiples to values up to 5. Interestingly, both breweries show sinking sales figures and enterprise values. In the rest of Germany, rather stable or slowly decreasing multiples can be explained by a slight increase in the sales figure for all of the firms. Hence the sales multiple shows stability for enterprises with rising enterprise values and decreases with stable enterprise values. A categorization by size is not advisable as the correlation between size (measured on the basis of the enterprise value) and the sales multiple is very low (ρ=0,037).

In contrast to Germany, sales multiples for foreign breweries exhibit somewhat less stable and mostly rising multiples. A growth in the multiples in Europe from values of around 1 to values around 2 could be discovered for most of the enterprises. In particular at the turn of the century most of the multiples experienced a growth phase that was later balanced out again. These rising multiples can mainly be drawn back to rising enterprise values and relatively stable sales figures. Therefore, in the past years other European breweries have shown higher multiples than those in Germany. In the rest of the world, no clear rising or falling trend can be recognised, but it can be seen that the multiples move on higher levels than in Germany and Europe.

3.2.2.2 EBIT Multiple

The EBIT multiple is very simple to calculate and sets the company's EBIT in relation to its enterprise value. The EBIT multiples calculated for the German brewing industry are more volatile than the EBITDA multiples. Furthermore, no clear levels, in which these values move, can be recognised. These findings are backed by very high standard deviations and grave differences between the values of the mean and the median. These fluctuations in the EBIT multiple can of course be attributed to different levels of amortization and depreciation in the period of time considered and different investment patterns of the various enterprises.

The highest fluctuations in Germany are registered in Bavaria and no state-wide trend in the EBIT multiple can be identified. A falling trend on different levels can, on the other hand, be recognised in Baden-Wuerttemberg and North Rhine-

Westphalia, where the high volatilities can be attributed to high jumps and outliers in certain years in between. No significant correlation between neither the size of the firm nor the product portfolio and the EBIT multiples can be seen.

In contrast to these highly fluctuating multiples in Germany, multiples in Europe and the rest of the world are very stable. In Europe, especially the UK, the values are stable on levels between 10 and 20 whereas the multiple in the rest of the world moves between 10 and 15. This stability can be explained by the size of the firms and a lower susceptibility of depreciations on the height of the earnings and the multiple.

3.2.2.3 EBITDA Multiple

The next enterprise value based multiple to be looked at is the EBITDA multiple. As described before, this multiple sets the company's EBITDA in relation to the enterprise value.

The EBITDA multiples calculated for the German brewing industry are relatively stable over the time spread but move on different levels for every enterprise. These levels range from 0 to about 20, but are usually between 4 and 7. Furthermore, no clear trend towards a specific level can be recognised for the industry. The causality for the stable multiples is not very clear, as sinking enterprise values in Germany are coupled with slightly volatile EBITDAs. Nevertheless, relatively low standard deviations are evidence of their stability.

Just as described for the sales multiple, the Bavarian breweries can be clustered into the same two groups regarding the level of the EBITDA multiple. While the movements for both groups are stable, the multiples of the first group move around values of 10 and around values of 3 of the second group. These groupings can neither be drawn back to the height of the enterprise value nor the EBITDA figure. As all enterprises have very different financial figures and the groupings cannot be drawn back to different heights of these, it is important to point out that these groups are the result of setting two values (in this case EBITDA and enterprise value) in relation to one another. In Baden-Wuerttemberg, the multiples show a clear declining tendency. This can be attributed to falling EBITDA figures coupled with a relatively stronger descent in the enterprise value. A much higher volatility can be recognised for multiples in the first years of the 21st century of breweries in North Rhine-Westphalia. Before this highly fluctuating phase, most multiples moved around the value of 4 and afterwards balanced out at different levels. This situation is also backed by the highest standard deviations in North Rhine-Westphalia in comparison to other German states. The rest of Germany exhibits stable EBITDA multiples between 4 and 6. Interestingly, the multiples of breweries with a wide product portfolio are generally steadier than those of breweries that only specialise in the production of beer. This can of course be drawn back to a minor susceptibility to bad results of non-performing brands.

The multiples calculated for European breweries are somewhat higher (they move between 7 and 11) than those common multiples for German breweries. The stable movements can be explained by a constant rise in both the enterprise values and the EBITDAs. The breweries analysed in the rest of the world register higher fluctuations and higher values than in Europe. Particularly in the recent years, many international breweries have experienced a growth in enterprise values.

4 Conclusion and Final Remarks

The objective of this study was to empirically analyse the German brewing industry with the help of trading multiples in order to conclude whether there are adequate and representative multiples from comparable companies to determine specific private entity values within the sector for consolidation purposes.

The analysis of the different trading multiples has revealed that in particular enterprise instead of equity multiples are preferable within the German brewery sector. The application of cash flow multiples to evaluate breweries is not advisable. This derives from the fact that the net cash flows have been highly volatile over time and that there have been no long-term cash flow trends. Furthermore, it is notable that especially breweries with a narrow product range are characterised by fluctuating cash flow multiples due to their strong dependencies on certain products. German breweries share the same multiple characteristics than global breweries. Consequently, the cash flow multiple may not be considered a plausible multiple for evaluating the industry.

Having analysed the other equity multiple, the price/earnings ratio, one can conclude that this earning-based multiple has also fluctuated over time. Similarly, the high volatility is triggered by the lacking stability in equity and earnings. Unlike with the cash flow multiples, however, there are explicit differences in the multiples across geographic regions. The regional differences with regard to P/E ratios can also be seen when comparing German with international breweries. International companies have achieved stable multiples over time due to simultaneously increasing earnings and market capitalisation. On the other hand, German multiples have been very volatile. Similarly to cash flow multiples, the P/E ratio is not applicable to the German brewery sector due to its inconsistent performance.

When applying enterprise multiples to the German market, the results are quite different. Though the use of EBIT multiples is not recommendable because they neglect the big impact of different depreciation and amortization policies among firms on their earnings and consequently on the multiples, the use of both the EBITDA and sales multiple is advisable for the brewery market. The empirical results have revealed that the sales multiple reflects certain stability over time, since the enterprise values have generally grown in line with sales. Furthermore, an explicit geographical differentiation among breweries enhances the comparability of the sale multiple. The use of sales multiple may therefore lead to a rather fair and exact valuation of a brewery's entity value.

The evaluation of EBITDA multiples within the brewery sector has shown that the multiples are relatively stable, though at different levels. There is no clear trend to be seen between certain brewery types and the level of the EBITDA multiple in Germany. Nevertheless, the EBITDA multiple is the most reliable and adequate multiple in the brewing industry because it is relatively closely linked to the actual cash flows and earnings central to company valuation.

Having highlighted the adequacy of EBITDA and sales multiple for assessing the German brewing industry, it is vital to stress on the importance of finding proper comparable companies in the multiple valuation. As seen in the empirical analysis, the market size and position of a brewery as well as the product range generally have an influence on the calculated multiple. Particularly its geographical scope in which a brewery operates has a very high influence on the multiple. Hence, it is important to carefully scrutinize the market for representative companies. Due to the high fragmentation of the market however, this may be quite difficult in Germany. Another adverse market structure is that the market of listed brewery companies is very illiquid because many firms have a small free float and a small market capitalisation. Due to the market structure, analysts may face severe problems when evaluating the German brewing industry. As the number of listed breweries is relatively small in comparison to the number of private ones, one has to select the most similar comparable company and then make adjustments to the inherent risks and growth prospects of the firm being examined. This has to be done very carefully in order not to misgauge the correct value of the brewery company. Only if this process is done correctly, trading multiples may gain momentum and may become vital as valuation methodologies in the consolidation procedure within the brewing industry.

Again, it has to be stressed that the German brewery differs from many other industry sectors with respect to the limited data availability (only 19 brewery companies are listed in Germany), the partly available but misleading market information (no listed German brewery company has a market capitalisation of more than €540 Mio and not a free float of more than 24%), and the atomistic market structure with many inherent uniqueness. It may therefore be difficult to correctly apply trading multiples in German brewing industry to assess market values. Therefore, it is advisable to use multiples as a benchmark and value range for company valuation but couple the analysis with other valuation methods such as DCF.

Appendix

Appendix 1: Key Financial Data for German listed Breweries (in T€, 2003)

	MV	Earnings	EV	Sales	EBITDA	EBIT
Bavaria						
AKTIEN BRAU.KAUFBEURI	10.4	209	7.921	18.742	2.42	378
ALLGAEUER BRAUHAUS	31.407	745	31.493	21.261	2.415	808
BAY.BIERBRAUEREI	7.5	169	6.699	5.91	629	285
BUERG.BRAUH.INGOLSTA	20.88	277	29.862	17.316	5.256	1.04
INNSTADT-BRAUEREI	8.641	n/a	14.904	1.48	1.04	414
SEDLMAYR	713.4	17.804	796.919	309.252	62.212	37.079
WUERZBURGER HOFBRAI	33	764	42.289	32.908	5.308	2.056
KULMBACHER BRAUEREI	64.68	5.518	104.767	200.01	30.059	8.517
Baden-Württemberg						
BRAUEREI MONINGER	3.04	646	1.221	13.702	1.482	670
DINKELACKER BRAUEREI	180	7.635	128.101	117.744	19.027	11.052
RAVENSBURGER BAU	18.1	n/a	-6.617	33.573	2.249	1.775
STUTT.HOFBRAEU	375.75	38.905	367.066	81.499	56.708	50.728
North Rhine-Westphalia						
PARK & BELLHEIMER	2.7	-55	15.561	35.057	5.157	1.363
DOM-BRAUEREI	15.093	-10.035	25.444	22.081	-5.38	-8.589
Lower Saxony						
EINBECKER BRAUH.	42.12	2.281	49.027	39.596	7.764	2.817
HOFBRAUHAUS WOLTERS	7.9	529	7.896	1.553	1.423	543
Rest of Germany						
HOLSTEN-BRAUEREI	366.987	6.668	641.016	752.091	111.384	37.726
BRAU UND BRUNNEN	291.785	7.473	368.627	647.81	90.298	15.954
MNZ AKTIEN BRAUEREI	4.1	n/a	3.976	159.999	6.903	1.498

Appendix 2: Statistical overview – Cash Flow multiples

	Cash Flow					
	Mean	Median	Min.	Max.	*Std. Dev.*	2003*
Bavaria						
Aktien Brau Kaufbreuen	n/a	n/a	n/a	n/a	n/a	n/a
Allgäuer Brauhaus	n/a	n/a	n/a	n/a	n/a	n/a
Bayerische Bierbrauerei	n/a	n/a	n/a	n/a	n/a	n/a
Bürgerliche Brauhaus Ingolsta	-7.157,39	-797,91	-30.000,00	178,46	12.895,96	178,46
Innstadt Brauerei	n/a	n/a	n/a	n/a	n/a	n/a
Sedlmayr	88,38	65,45	-26,93	226,62	128,32	226,62
Würzburger Hofbräu	346,64	18,79	-42,33	1.391,30	*697,73*	56,70
Kulmbacher	-373,77	30,14	-2.940,00	183,06	*1.136,72*	72,84
Baden-Württemberg						
Brauerei Moninger	0,81	1,74	-1,32	2,02	1,86	2,02
Dinkelacker Brauerei	183,01	33,45	15,68	766,82	*327,20*	23,03
Ravensburger Brau	n/a	n/a	n/a	n/a	n/a	n/a
Stuttgarter Hofbräu	51,01	49,44	-132,80	216,62	*141,47*	49,44
North-Rhine Westfalia						
Dom Brauerei	-22,05	-1,86	-199,64	19,83	*67,43*	19,83
Park & Bellheimer	27,17897	2,792141	-1,2552301	80	45,78909	2,792141
Lower Saxony						
Einbecker	n/a	n/a	n/a	n/a	*n/a*	n/a
Hofbrauhaus Wolters	n/a	n/a	n/a	n/a	n/a	n/a
Rest of Germany						
Holsten	2.084,09	24,41	-2.644,23	18.040,00	*6.249,00*	24,41
Brau & Brunnen	321,00	4,28	-133,46	2.917,85	*975,51*	2.917,85
Mainzer Aktienbrauerei	1,7573939	1,7573939	1,757393913	1,7573939	n/a	1,7573939
Great Britain						
Belhaven	1.841,44	2.010,25	-137,65	4.861,43	*1.836,53*	-137,65
Eldridge	31,74	-9,50	-273,41	670,05	340,51	-240,39
Fullers	2,97	-2,76	-30,22	54,18	26,43	-24,46
Greene King	-27,03	90,67	-1.403,07	1.071,61	706,45	90,67
Jennings	97,09	40,26	-20,01	286,56	120,63	-7,03
Wolverhampton & Dudley	223,45	118,69	-191,82	1.482,12	473,44	-191,82
Scottish Newcastle	237,37	25,57	-299,83	2.545,45	*877,73*	102,43
Europa						
Brau Union	-6,226302	1,9987456	-56,2412949	11,171101	24,914051	5,9366131
Heinecken	33,21	31,23	-55,07	127,42	*61,35*	21,56
USA						
Anheuser	4.629,82	454,37	-453,61	19.509,79	*7.401,65*	19.509,79
Worldwide						
SAB Miller	32,16	31,59	-69,60	144,41	*72,92*	23,75
AmBew	100,1417	42,93113	-22,443632	337,1482	161,5906	60,09558
Quilmes	121,453	15,87832	-180,08173	1058,855	389,0977	1058,855
Inbev	2,896609	-3,208801	-41,363169	59,36721	50,69003	32,04761

*Multiples for the year 2003 – Exceptions: Innstadt Brauerei (1998), Ravensburger Brau (1999), Park & Bellheimer (2001), Mainzer Aktien Brauerei (2001).

Appendix 3: Statistical Overview – Price/Earnings Multiples

	P/E					
	Mean	Median	Min.	Max.	*Std. Dev.*	2003*
Bavaria						
Aktien Brau Kaufbreuen	64,60	58,37	41,53	111,08	22,46	49,76
Allgäuer Brauhaus	n/a	n/a	n/a	n/a	n/a	n/a
Bayerische Bierbrauerei	n/a	n/a	n/a	n/a	n/a	n/a
Bürgerliche Brauhaus Ingolsta	909,62	188,07	75,38	6.131,20	2.110,74	75,38
Innstadt Brauerei	n/a	n/a	n/a	n/a	n/a	n/a
Sedlmayr	58,58	50,89	40,07	84,80	23,34	40,07
Würzburger Hofbräu	42,73	42,73	42,26	43,19	*0,66*	43,19
Kulmbacher	27,31	12,56	-36,56	166,78	*59,51*	11,72
Baden-Württemberg						
Brauerei Moninger	190,49	0,43	-223,12	1.813,33	666,00	4,71
Dinkelacker Brauerei	59,40	34,81	20,58	147,49	*46,54*	23,58
Ravensburger Brau	3,81	3,81	3,81	3,81		0,00
Stuttgarter Hofbräu	22,84	17,18	9,66	58,69	*15,45*	9,66
North-Rhine Westfalia						
Dom Brauerei	76,59	1,40	-43,88	736,74	*234,28*	-1,50
Park & Bellheimer	-7,42	-2,19	-262,70	97	96	-49,09
Lower Saxony						
Einbecker	64,52	63,84	18,47	93,05	25,15	18,47
Hofbrauhaus Wolters	9,28	5,78	4,43	19,37	5,64	14,93
Rest of Germany						
Holsten	24,50	24,47	-19,02	55,04	20,11	55,04
Brau & Brunnen	9,29	-1,61	-49,42	106,73	40,37	39,05
Mainzer Aktienbrauerei	6,04	6,10	5,58	6,32	0,25	0,00
Great Britain						
Belhaven	9,21	9,43	5,56	12,65	2,19	9,69
Eldridge	10,36	12,36	-4,39	16,24	7,39	-4,39
Fullers	9,17	8,30	4,30	15,64	3,86	4,79
Greene King	13,58	13,20	9,03	27,49	5,12	11,14
Jennings	8,73	10,96	-3,26	12,73	6,05	8,70
Wolverhampton & Dudley	-11,66	11,91	-130,41	35,57	56,60	13,45
Scottish Newcastle	-1,11	16,75	-160,96	39,93	57,40	-160,96
Europa						
Brau Union	2,32	1,32	1,02	6,95	2,02	3,20
Heinecken	22,94	22,01	13,70	35,19	6,83	13,70
USA						
Anheuser	23,16	25,65	12,77	30,50	5,69	24,80
Worldwide						
SAB Miller	15,74	16,18	11,61	20,35	3,34	17,77
AmBew	11,75	8,72	5,12	27,66	9,09	7,06
Quilmes	20,94	10,31	-1,30	106,96	35,11	106,96
Inbev	9,23	16,90	-16,09	19,19	16,92	16,37

*Multiples for the year 2003 – Exceptions: Innstadt Brauerei (1998), Ravensburger Brau (1999), Park & Bellheimer (2001), Mainzer Aktien Brauerei (2001).

Appendix 4: Statistical Overview – Sales Multiples

	Sales					
	Mean	Median	Min.	Max.	Std. Dev.	2003*
Bavaria						
Aktien Brau Kaufbreuen	0,71	0,73	0,42	1,14	0,23	0,42
Allgäuer Brauhaus	0,95	0,70	0,67	1,48	0,46	1,48
Bayerische Bierbrauerei	1,59	1,63	0,98	2,03	0,40	1,13
Bürgerliche Brauhaus Ingolsta	1,81	1,73	1,30	2,43	0,41	1,72
Innstadt Brauerei	9,16	9,46	7,94	10,07	1,10	10,07
Sedlmayr	2,02	2,09	1,40	2,58	0,59	2,58
Würzburger Hofbräu	1,81	1,73	1,19	2,59	0,52	1,29
Kulmbacher	0,60	0,63	0,49	0,75	0,08	0,52
Baden-Württemberg						
Brauerei Moninger	0,40	0,39	0,05	0,98	0,32	0,09
Dinkelacker Brauerei	1,48	1,37	1,09	2,13	0,37	1,09
Ravensburger Brau	0,33	0,33	-0,20	0,86	0,75	-0,20
Stuttgarter Hofbräu	3,03	3,05	1,51	4,61	1,15	4,50
North-Rhine Westfalia						
Dom Brauerei	0,83	0,80	0,45	1,40	0,31	1,15
Park & Bellheimer	0,59	0,57	0,43	1,01	0,16	0,44
Lower Saxony						
Einbecker	1,61	1,64	1,08	1,95	0,30	1,24
Hofbrauhaus Wolters	3,92	4,03	0,27	18,98	5,41	5,08
Rest of Germany						
Holsten	0,57	0,52	0,44	0,85	0,14	0,85
Brau & Brunnen	0,65	0,62	0,30	1,28	0,30	0,57
Mainzer Aktienbrauerei	0,98	0,89	0,02	2,11	0,66	0,02
Great Britain						
Belhaven	1,32	1,24	1,05	1,81	0,26	1,57
Eldridge	1,43	1,55	0,95	1,72	0,31	1,19
Fullers	0,74	0,66	0,50	1,15	0,23	0,50
Greene King	1,94	2,03	1,62	2,31	0,23	1,81
Jennings	1,82	1,82	1,43	2,60	0,36	2,07
Wolverhampton & Dudley	1,82	1,81	1,36	2,35	0,29	2,01
Scottish Newcastle	1,96	2,01	1,30	2,59	0,42	1,30
Europa						
Brau Union	0,15	0,14	0,09	0,27	0,06	0,22
Heinecken	1,91	1,63	1,12	2,93	0,64	1,51
USA						
Anheuser	2,86	3,21	1,34	3,79	0,85	3,54
Worldwide						
SAB Miller	1,84	1,95	1,24	2,37	0,45	1,24
AmBew	1,60	1,31	1,09	2,91	0,75	1,31
Quilmes	1,98	1,18	0,45	8,52	2,68	8,52
Inbev	2,25	2,01	1,64	3,33	0,76	1,64

*Multiples for the year 2003 – Exceptions: Innstadt Brauerei (1998), Ravensburger Brau (1999), Park & Bellheimer (2001), Mainzer Aktien Brauerei (2001).

Appendix 5: Statistical Overview – EBITDA Multiples

	EBITDA					
	Mean	Median	Min.	Max.	Std. Dev.	2003*
Bavaria						
Aktien Brau Kaufbreuen	4,03	3,74	3,03	5,92	0,95	3,27
Allgäuer Brauhaus	-13,45	6,05	-59,43	13,04	39,98	13,04
Bayerische Bierbrauerei	64,39	19,48	9,80	307,79	101,37	10,65
Bürgerliche Brauhaus Ingolsta	9,74	9,73	5,68	12,35	1,83	5,68
Innstadt Brauerei	23,66	14,33	11,14	45,50	18,98	14,33
Sedlmayr	11,80	12,81	9,64	12,97	1,88	12,81
Würzburger Hofbräu	10,18	9,23	7,19	14,49	2,64	7,97
Kulmbacher	4,69	3,98	3,08	7,78	1,69	3,49
Baden-Württemberg						
Brauerei Moninger	1,86	3,64	-15,21	7,14	6,65	0,82
Dinkelacker Brauerei	8,37	8,30	3,32	13,24	2,85	6,73
Ravensburger Brau	0,55	0,55	-2,94	4,04	4,93	-2,94
Stuttgarter Hofbräu	9,40	8,85	5,07	17,55	4,04	6,47
North-Rhine-Westfalia						
Dom Brauerei	5,70	3,77	-4,73	24,42	8,03	-4,73
Park & Bellheimer	5,79	4,64	3,02	12,86	2,93	3,02
Lower Saxony						
Einbecker	9,92	9,96	6,31	13,46	2,10	6,31
Hofbrauhaus Wolters	4,66	4,23	1,73	16,77	4,26	5,55
Rest of Germany						
Holsten	5,08	5,45	3,72	6,79	1,10	5,76
Brau & Brunnen	4,81	4,44	1,45	8,19	2,12	4,08
Mainzer Aktienbrauerei	1,90	1,58	0,58	3,22	0,97	0,58
Great Britain						
Belhaven	7,15	7,05	5,52	8,92	1,02	8,07
Eldridge	-3,51	8,09	-64,46	10,56	29,89	-64,46
Fullers	4,29	3,83	2,32	7,68	1,70	2,49
Greene King	8,57	8,50	6,52	13,37	1,82	7,49
Jennings	8,02	9,05	-15,26	21,16	9,64	7,87
Wolverhampton & Dudley	8,32	7,89	5,56	12,91	2,07	7,48
Scottish Newcastle	20,46	9,85	8,55	111,15	31,93	9,35
Europa						
Brau Union	1,07	0,67	0,54	2,68	0,74	1,50
Heinecken	9,63	8,42	6,03	14,59	2,99	7,10
USA						
Anheuser	11,03	12,30	6,35	14,08	2,48	12,26
Worldwide						
SAB Miller	6,75	6,54	5,72	8,02	1,00	5,82
AmBew	5,96	5,38	3,33	8,79	2,63	3,33
Quilmes	7,10	5,14	2,51	23,62	6,77	23,62
Inbev	-28,09	8,07	-137,58	9,05	72,99	7,45

*Multiples for the year 2003 – Exceptions: Innstadt Brauerei (1998), Ravensburger Brau (1999), Park & Bellheimer (2001), Mainzer Aktien Brauerei (2001).

Appendix 6: Statistical Overview – EBIT Multiples

	EBIT					
	Mean	Median	Min.	Max.	*Std. Dev.*	2003*
Bavaria						
Aktien Brau Kaufbreuen	11,58	21,80	-136,77	48,62	53,14	20,96
Allgäuer Brauhaus	19,30	25,77	-6,86	38,98	23,59	38,98
Bayerische Bierbrauerei	4,48	24,28	-82,19	75,63	52,16	23,51
Bürgerliche Brauhaus Ingolsta	45,65	46,54	28,71	62,05	11,11	28,71
Innstadt Brauerei	7,07	21,72	-36,54	36,03	38,44	36,03
Sedlmayr	23,12	21,98	21,49	25,87	2,40	21,49
Würzburger Hofbräu	11,86	23,90	-101,70	47,08	46,75	20,57
Kulmbacher	14,90	16,46	-24,02	49,06	21,84	12,30
Baden-Württemberg						
Brauerei Moninger	-0,38	7,23	-262,52	80,33	97,91	1,82
Dinkelacker Brauerei	31,62	16,71	11,59	78,24	25,47	11,59
Ravensburger Brau	0,40	0,40	-3,73	4,52	5,83	-3,73
Stuttgarter Hofbräu	13,34	10,89	7,24	26,94	6,65	7,24
North-Rhine Westfalia						
Dom Brauerei	14,33	10,06	-15,87	88,51	29,70	-2,96
Park & Bellheimer	19,24	19,75	-30,34	67,84	29,16	11,42
Lower Saxony						
Einbecker	40,41	36,41	17,40	61,21	14,63	17,40
Hofbrauhaus Wolters	11,32	9,03	4,32	33,64	8,89	14,54
Rest of Germany						
Holsten	16,06	14,08	11,42	36,18	7,31	16,99
Brau & Brunnen	7,89	-1,70	-15,64	70,57	26,44	23,11
Mainzer Aktienbrauerei	3,28	3,62	2,06	3,86	0,62	2,65
Great Britain						
Belhaven	8,32	8,25	6,38	10,19	1,14	9,30
Eldridge	7,39	10,34	-12,72	13,46	9,95	-12,72
Fullers	6,14	5,50	3,20	10,62	2,34	3,60
Greene King	10,75	10,18	8,31	16,92	2,31	9,88
Jennings	12,36	11,66	-10,34	36,74	11,93	9,84
Wolverhampton & Dudley	12,10	10,41	7,16	21,75	4,53	10,41
Scottish Newcastle	10,51	13,52	-36,83	26,99	17,46	26,99
Europa						
Brau Union	1,86	1,09	0,90	5,42	1,54	2,37
Heinecken	13,90	12,70	9,17	21,24	4,09	10,27
USA						
Anheuser	14,51	15,96	8,44	18,61	3,25	15,62
Worldwide						
SAB Miller	9,68	9,55	8,09	11,08	1,20	10,04
AmBew	8,45	6,56	4,59	15,04	4,58	4,74
Quilmes	10,98	6,96	-1,24	47,54	15,14	47,54
Inbev	3,87	13,58	-27,27	15,57	20,79	12,94

*Multiples for the year 2003 – Exceptions: Innstadt Brauerei (1998), Ravensburger Brau (1999), Park & Bellheimer (2001), Mainzer Aktien Brauerei (2001).

References

Benninga, Simon/Sarig, Oded (1997): Corporate Finance – a Valuation Approach, New York.

CSFB Equity Research (2003): The German beer industry – The consolidators challenge, London.

Damodaran, Aswath (1996): Investment Valuation – Tools and techniques for determining the value of any asset, New York.

Datastream (2005): Company accounts and financial ratios, Downloaded on: 18/03/2005.

Engel, Ronald (2003): Seed-Finanzierung wachstumsorientierter Unternehmensgründungen, in: Achleitner /Kaserer (Hrsg.): Entrepreneurial and Financial Studies, Band 1.

Ferris, Kenneth/Petitt, Barbara (2002): Valuation – Avoiding the Winner's Curse, Upper Saddle River.

Ross, Stephen/Westerfield, Randolph/Jaffe, Jeffrey (2002): Corporate Finance, 6th edition, New York.

Thommen, Jean-Paul/Schellenberg, Aldo (2002): Rechnungswesen – Finanzierung – Investition – Unternehmensbewertung, 5. überarbeitete Auflage, Zürich.

Yahoo! Finance (2005): Industry centre – Beverages – Brewers, http://biz.yahoo.com/ic/346.html, accessed on 06/06/2005.

III Transaction Multiple Valuation in the German Brewing Industry

by

Sarah Ali Khalil Ibrahim and Katharina von Bassewitz

1 Introduction

1.1 Objective of the Study

In the course of the last years, the European brewing industry has been largely dominated by Mergers and Acquisitions (M&A).[1] The following paper focuses on one distinct European brewing market: Germany. In 2000 Germany was in fact the largest European beer market exhibiting the second highest per capita beer consumption among European countries. In addition to its large market size, the German brewery market exhibits other characteristics, namely very high fragmentation, diverse export opportunities inherent to the market, strong regional loyalties and large overcapacities stemming from ever-decreasing beer consumption,[2] which differentiate this market from others. In Germany consolidation has recently also gained momentum and is likely to remain the dominant theme for some years.[3]

Acknowledgement of the relevance of M&A transactions undertaken in the brewing industry on the one hand and the possibility to evaluate the latter with the aid of multiple valuations on the other hand, sets the ground for this paper. The objective of this paper therefore is to assess the valuation levels of Germany-related transac-

[1] Cf. Deutsche Bank (2003), p. 3.
[2] Cf. Deutsche Bank (2000), p. 154; Credit Suisse First Boston (2003), p. 3.
[3] Cf. Credit Suisse First Boston (2003), p. 3.

tions[4] and to explore the underlying rationales for divergences from international multiple levels.

1.2 Course of Analysis

Following the brief introductory discussion on the German brewing industry in Chapter 1, this paper first elaborates multiple valuation by exploring the differences between trading and transaction multiples and the corresponding advantages as well as disadvantages in Section 2.1. Then, the three most commonly applied multiples for transaction valuation – namely sales, EBIT and EBITDA - are discussed with regard to their benefits and shortfalls in 2.2. Subsequently, Section 2.3 outlines general drivers of variations in multiples.

Chapter three, the main part of the paper, constitutes an analysis of German and International transaction multiple levels for the period July 1999 until August 2004. The chapter commences with an in depth description of the data set underlying the analysis. Thereafter, the sales, EBIT and EBITDA multiple levels yielded in German M&A transactions are explored and compared to international levels in Section 3.2. This evaluation is followed by an analysis of the main value drivers underlying the brewing industry, which intends to derive possible explanations of the comparably low Germany-related transaction multiple levels (3.3).

Finally, Chapter 4 recapitulates the major findings of the analysis undertaken and comments on necessary improvements regarding further research efforts. Ultimately, the paper concludes by providing for a critical outlook on the future development of the consolidation-dominated German brewing industry.

---

[4] Transactions in which a Germany company is either target or acquirer are in the following referred to as Germany-related transactions. Analogously, those transactions without any German involvement are called non-Germany-related transactions.

2 Multiple Valuation Foundation

2.1 Conceptual Basics of Multiple Valuation

Among the wide universe of common valuation methods, the earnings- and cash flow-based methodologies depicted are the most widely applied valuation techniques. Besides the "Ertragswertverfahren", real options and the common discounted cash flow (DCF) analysis, multiples constitute a distinct subcategory. Multiples can fundamentally be divided into trading as well as transaction multiples.[5]

Chart 1: Earnings- and Cash Flow-Based Valuation Methods

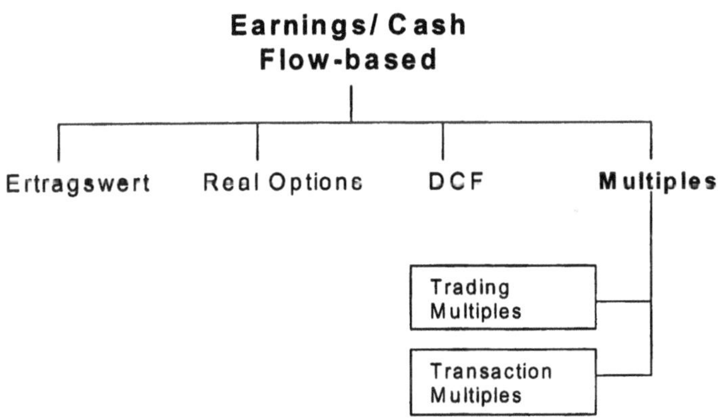

Source: Adopted from Deutsche Bank (2004), p. 18.

In a trading multiple valuation the company to be valued is compared to publicly traded companies which exhibit high conformity to the company regarding industry, business and financial characteristics.[6] Because this methodology draws upon share prices it is recognised as a pure capital market assessment and the resulting values are regarded as reliable indicators of the value of a company for minority investments because the multiples do not include control premiums.[7]

[5] Cf. Deutsche Bank (2004), p. 18.
[6] Cf. Ferris / Pécherot Petitt (2002), p. 72.
[7] Cf. Morgan Stanley (2005), p. 34.

The main advantage of trading multiples is that they are widely used due to their conceptual simplicity and the attached ease of communicability.[8] In addition, trading multiples are based on publicly available information which alleviates their computation. Another benefit is that the company to be valued is placed in an industry context, which provides for benchmarking possibilities.[9]

The main shortfall, on the other hand, is that this type of valuation is static. Also, it is often hard to find a large sample of companies that are truly comparable in the relevant aspects and adjustments for differences in the latter are very complex. If the peer group lacks conformity, multiples lose significance and distortions can be substantial.[10] In addition, trading multiple valuations implicitly assumes market efficiency, i.e. trading levels should mirror all information available, industry trends, underlying growth patterns and business risks. Analogously, it can be argued that multiples are inadequate valuation tools if the market is inefficient in some form.[11] And even if the market is regarded to be efficient, it becomes very difficult to find plausible explanations for wide multiple ranges for apparently similar companies.[12]

The fields of applications include the establishment of relevant benchmarks for private as well as publicly traded companies, the analysis of the break-up value of a conglomerate by establishing benchmarks for business divisions and the derivation of benchmarks regarding operating performance. Additionally, trading multiples allow for the determination of undervalued companies, key industry players and the identification of possible acquisition targets.[13]

In a transaction multiple valuation, in contrast, the value of the company to be valued is based on historic transaction prices, i.e. prices paid in a comparable transaction. Hence, transaction multiples summarise how the M&A market has

---

[8] Cf. Ferris / Pécherot Petitt (2002), p. 74.
[9] Cf. Morgan Stanley (2005), p. 34.
[10] Cf. Ferris / Pécherot Petitt (2002), p. 74.
[11] Cf. Damodaran (1999), p. 14f.
[12] Cf. Morgan Stanley (2005), p. 34.
[13] Cf. Morgan Stanley (2005), p. 34.

historically valued comparable transactions in order to derive relevant benchmarks.[14]

Analogously to trading multiples, the benefits of transaction multiples include their wide-spread use related to their conceptual simplicity and the attached ease of communicability. Transaction multiples are also based on public information. Nonetheless, data obtainment might be more difficult as many M&A transactions are private. Another advantage is the direct reflection of supply and demand. Further, transaction multiples are useful indicators of trends such as consolidation and magnitude of foreign purchasers.[15] In general, the value of transaction multiples include premium or discounts respectively, which are attributable to the context-specific nature of M&A transactions. In addition, deal multiples are highly dependent on the number of strategic buyers, potential synergies and the inherent risks of the specific business. Further, transaction multiples include control premiums as well as premiums paid for strategic value and synergies and, as a consequence, indicate the level of premiums paid in different industries.[16]

The shortfalls, on the other hand, are mainly linked to the difficulty of finding directly comparable deals. Even in the presence of comparable transactions, those historic deals may be of limited relevance due to structural changes taken place in an industry or due to the inherent dynamics of M&A markets. As a consequence, the quality of transaction multiples is largely determined by the comparability and relevance of historic transactions. Another problem attached to transaction multiple valuation is the availability of data due to limited disclosures and the historic nature of data obtainable. And finally, deal-specific factors can cause wide multiples ranges because not all aspects of transactions are captured by multiples and premiums. Ultimately, the market conditions at the transaction date, e.g. business cycle stage or scarcity of assets, can have substantial impacts on valuation levels.[17]

---

[14] Cf. Deutsche Bank (2004), p. 35.
[15] Cf. Morgan Stanley (2005), p. 63.
[16] Cf. Deutsche Bank (2004), p. 35.
[17] Cf. Morgan Stanley (2005), p. 53.

The fields of application include the valuation of a company in a change of control situation, the analysis of acquisition affinity in certain industries, the levels of prices paid and the determination of demand for certain assets mirrored by frequencies of transactions and premiums paid.[18]

2.2 Overview of the Most Commonly Applied Multiples

From a computation point of view, multiples can be divided into equity and enterprise value multiples as depicted in Chart 2, whereby the difference between the two types is the reference parameter of the enumerator.[19]

Chart 2: Equity Value vs. Enterprise Value Multiples.

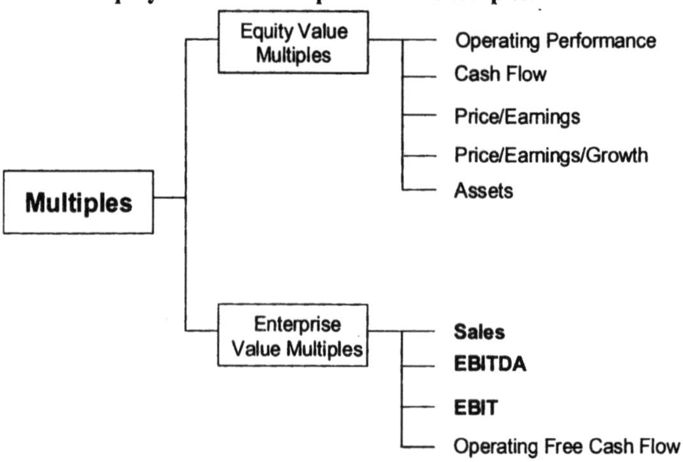

Source: Deutsche Bank (2004), p. 36.

M&A valuations predominantly apply enterprise value multiples. As a consequence, this paper focuses on the latter. Due to the high data requirements in form of cash flow statements, the operating free cash flow multiple is excluded from further discussion. Subsequently, the sales, EBIT and EBITDA multiples will be explored with regard to their computation, advantages and disadvantages.

[18] Cf. Morgan Stanley (2005), p. 63.
[19] Cf. Benninga / Sarig (1997), p. 330.

2.2.1 Sales Multiples

The sales multiple sets a company's sales in relation to its enterprise value (EV):[20]

Formula 1: Sales Multiple

$$Sales\ Multiple = \frac{Enterprise\ \ Value}{Sales}$$

This multiple is mainly used for companies without earnings data[21] and can be regarded as a fairly good measure if margins are similar among companies operating in the same industry. The main shortfall of the sales multiple is that it does not indicate profitability in any way. Therefore, one has to account for differences in sales growth and cost structures. As a consequence, it is questionable if sales are a meaningful measure for valuation purposes.[22]

2.2.2 EBIT Multiple

The EBIT multiple sets a company's earnings before interest and tax (EBIT) in relation to its EV:

Formula 2: EBIT Mulitple

$$EBIT\ Multiple = \frac{Enterprise\ \ Value}{EBIT}$$

EBIT multiples are widely applied in practice. However, it is intuitive that they are only computable if EBIT figures are positive. The main advantage of EBIT multiples is their focus on operating results. Further, EBIT figures are not distorted by differences in financial leverage and country-specific taxation and usually exhibit

[20] The enterprise value is calculated as the sum of equity value and net debt. Equity value refers to the market value of a company's equity, i.e. its market capitalisation, and represents the value of flows available to all equity holders after debt and preferred claims have been serviced. Net debt, on the other hand, comprises all interest-bearing debt positions, pension provisions, minority interests, redeemable preferred stocks, finance leases net of excess cash, cash equivalents and marketable securities.

[21] Cf. Ferris / Pécherot Petitt (2002), p. 10.

[22] Cf. Benninga / Sarig (1997), p. 326f.

high correlations with enterprise values.[23] The main shortfall of the EBIT multiple is that differences in depreciation methods of the company to be valued and the comparables can possibly have substantial impacts upon the resulting multiples. Additionally, the underlying M&A strategy may dilute operative perspective.[24]

2.2.3 EBITDA Multiple

The EBITDA multiple sets a company's earnings before interest, tax, depreciation and amortisation (EBITDA) in relation to its EV:

Formula 3: EBITDA Multiple

$$EBITDA\,Multiple = \frac{Enterprise\ \ Value}{EBITDA}$$

Again, EBITDA multiples are only applicable to companies with positive EBITDA figures. Like EBIT multiples, EBITDA multiples have a strong operational focus and are not distorted by differences in financial leverage and country-specific taxation. In addition, given that EBITDA figures exclude depreciation and amortisation components, they are valuable for comparisons of companies that reside in different phases of investments.[25] EBITDA multiples are particularly well-suited for cross border transactions and companies with intense recent acquisition activity. The main shortfall of EBITDA multiples is the implicit assumption of identical growth and capital intensity of both the target and the reference company. In addition, the exclusion of depreciation and amortisation components can lead to distortions in the cases of leasing and outsourcing. EBIT might be better indicator, for instance, when comparing companies with very large leasing and outsourcing contracts to other with none or small ones.[26]

---

[23] Cf. Benninga / Sarig (1997), p. 325; Ferris / Pécherot Petitt (2002), p. 10.
[24] Cf. Deutsche Bank (2004), p. 43.
[25] Cf. Benninga / Sarig (1997), p. 325; Ferris / Pécherot Petitt (2002), p. 10.
[26] Cf. Deutsche Bank (2004), p. 42.

2.3 Drivers of Variation in Multiples

Having explored the most commonly applied transaction multiples, it is now to be elaborated what drives variation in multiple levels. As displayed by the following exhibit, the three value drivers to be further analysed in section three are growth, profitability and company size.

Chart 3: Drivers Underlying Variations in Multiples

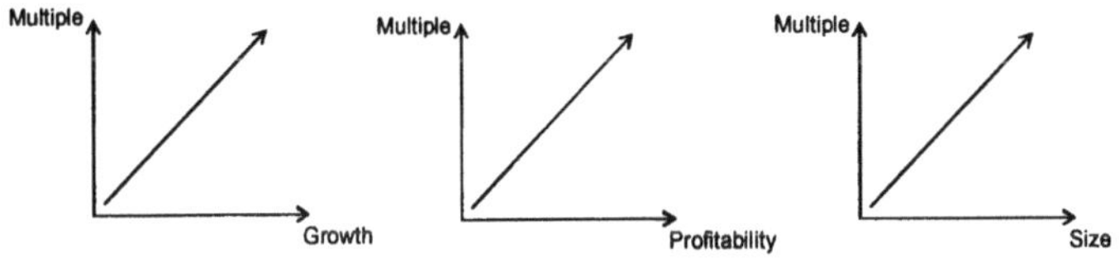

Source: Morgan Stanley (2005), p. 53.

As depicted, multiple levels generally increase with rising growth, profitability and company size, i.e. prices paid for companies with better prospects regarding those three elements should be higher. EBIT and EBITDA multiples show high sensitivity for growth, whereas sales multiples are largely determined by underlying profitability. While it is assumed that size has a positive effect on the multiple level, the effect of growth and profitability can additionally be explained theoretically. Future growth leads to higher future cash flows under the assumption that growth is not value destroying. A higher level of profitability implies that fewer investments are necessary in order to achieve the same increase in cash flows.[27]

A further possible value driver is the intensity of investments. However, the effect of the intensity of investments on the multiple has to be regarded with caution. On the one hand, it might be argued that a high intensity of investments leads to a high asset turnover. Thus, multiples should tend to be of a rather low level. Furthermore, a high intensity of investments could imply a lack of profitability as capacities are not optimally used. On the other hand, fixed assets, particularly real estate, possibly include a high level of hidden reserves.

[27] Cf. Morgan Stanley (2005), p. 53.

The value drivers already mentioned are applicable for both, trading and transaction multiples. Besides those, there are certain drivers that exclusively relate to the latter. Most prominent is the premium paid on the transaction as it might add value to the fair value on a stand-alone basis.[28] The advisor could be a value driver, since his or her competence and industry experience may affect the transaction price.

Subsequently, the outlined value drivers and their applicability to the German brewing industry will be analysed in Section 3.3.

3 Analysis of Transaction Multiples in the German Brewing Industry

3.1 Description of the Data Set

The number of M&A transactions undertaken in the international brewing industry between July 1999 and August 2004 amounted to 871. Those transactions comprised 76 deals where German brewery companies represented the target and 68 where German brewery companies acted as bidders.

It is reasonable to state that M&A activities in the German brewing industry feature a national focus. German companies were mainly targeted by other German brewery companies. In 15 out of the 76 deals with German targets the bidder was either unknown or foreign.[29] The Belgian company Interbrew was particularly active with eight acquisitions of German breweries. German acquirers also targeted mainly German companies. Only seven out of the 68 transactions by German acquirers were targeted at foreign companies, whereby Poland was the most attractive market to German acquirers.[30]

Despite the magnitude of transaction taken place in the international brewery market, the availability of public information about the deals is rather limited. It was

[28] Cf. Morgan Stanley (2005), p. 63.

[29] Out of those 15 bidders three are unknown, one is from Austria, two from the Netherlands, eight from Belgium and one from Denmark.

[30] The targets of German bidders included five companies in Poland, one in South Korea and one in the UK.

only possible to gather reliable information for 34 out of 871 deals on an international level. This data set serves as the basis for the analysis undertaken in Chapter 3. For the German market, the number of transactions that can be analysed shrank to seven due to limited data availability. Those transactions are strongly influenced by international key players of the industry. Interbrew was involved in four of these acquisitions whereas Carlsberg acquired one German company. It is also to be mentioned that only three out of the seven targets were publicly listed companies.

It is not unusual that information about transactions is very limited as companies are often not willing to publish information on acquisition price or other acquisition-related details. However, the small number of public information can also be partly explained by the structure of the German brewery market. In the light of the very high fragmentation of the market, German breweries tend to be relatively small in size and mainly privately held. Hence, scarcity of information is to some extend the natural consequence of the prevailing market structure.

3.2 Initial Evaluation of the Assessed Transaction Multiples

The following subsections elaborate on the finding of the transaction multiple analysis undertaken. While the different multiples, namely sales, EBIT and EBITDA are presented, it is to be mentioned that those are at the most indicative.[31] Due to the small data sample, the findings obtained are not very reliable, which impedes the derivation of any universally valid explanations.

3.2.1 Description of Sales Multiple Levels

Out of the 34 analysed transactions, sales multiples could be obtained for 22 transactions. These 22 transactions can be divided into 16 non-Germany-related and six Germany-related transactions. Generally, it can be stated that the non-Germany-related sales multiples are higher than the Germany-related sales multiples. As illustrated by exhibit 4, the range of the non-Germany-related multiples is between 1.1x and 12.4x, whereas the range of the German sales multiples lies between 0.6x

[31] For an overview of all transaction multiple levels assessed please refer to Appendix 1.

and 3.2x. The difference in ranges is also reflected by the differences in the median and the mean. While the median for the non-Germany-related transactions is 8.1x and the mean 6.7x, those values are 1.2x and 1.5x respectively for the Germany-related transactions.[32]

Chart 4: Sales Multiples for the Germany-Related Transactions

ANNOUNCE DATE	BIDDER/ TARGET	SALES MULTIPLE
Feb 04	Radeberger/ Brau und Brunnen	0.6x
Jan 04	Bitburger/ Holsten	NA
Jan 04	Carlsberg/ Holsten	1.0x
Sep 03	Interbrew/ Spaten	1.3x
Nov 02	Interbrew/ Gilde Brauerei AG	1.8x
Aug 01	Interbrew SA/ Brauerei Beck & Co	3.2x
Jul 01	Interbrew SA/ Diebels GmbH & Co KG	1.2x

Source: Credit Suisse Forst Boston (2005).

Concerning the sales multiples' development over time, it is to note that there is no clear trend for the non-Germany-related transactions. The Germany-related multiples, however, show a declining trend.[33]

Assessing the Germany-related sales multiples in more detail, it should be highlighted at this point that the highest multiple was paid by Interbrew SA for Brauerei Beck & Co The lowest multiple was paid Radeberger for Brau und Brunnen.

3.2.2 Description of EBIT Multiple Levels

Out of the 34 analysed transactions, EBIT multiples could be obtained for 18. However, only one EBIT multiple is available for Germany-related transactions. While the EBIT multiple for the Brauerei Beck & Co is 25.3x, and therefore lies in the range of the non-Germany-related transactions, which is between 11.6x and 28.4x, it is not feasible to compare the two groups any further due to the lack of data.

[32] Please refer to Appendix 10.
[33] Please refer to Appendices 2 and 3.

3.2.3 Description of EBITDA Multiple Levels

Out of the 34 analysed transactions, EBITDA multiples could be obtained for 30 transactions. These 30 transactions can be divided into 23 non-Germany-related and seven Germany-related transactions. Analogously to the sales multiples, the EBITDA multiples tend to be higher for the non-Germany-related transactions than for the Germany-related transactions. However, the ranges differ to a lesser extend for EBITDA multiples than they do for the sales multiples. For the non-Germany-related multiples, the range lies between 7.6x and 14.1x, whereas the range of Germany-related multiples lies between 6.5x and 13.0x, as highlighted by exhibit 5. The median and mean for non-Germany-related transactions are 10.2x and 10.5x respectively. For the Germany-related multiples, in contrast, the median and mean both amount to 8.9x.[34]

Chart 5: EBITDA Multiples for the Germany-Related Transactions

ANNOUNCE DATE	BIDDER/ TARGET	EBITDA MULTIPLE
Feb-04	Radeberger/ Brau und Brunnen	7.3x
Jan-04	Bitburger/ Holsten	9.0x
Jan-04	Carlsberg/ Holsten	9.1x
Sep-03	Interbrew/ Spaten	8.9x
Nov-02	Interbrew/ Gilde Brauerei AG	8.6x
Aug-01	Interbrew SA/ Brauerei Beck & Co	13.0x
Jul-01	Interbrew SA/ Diebels GmbH & Co KG	6.5x

Source: Credit Suisse First Boston (2005).

Concerning the EBITDA multiples' development over time, there is a rather high volatility between the different non-Germany-related transactions. The Germany-related EBITDA multiples, on the other hand, are more stable over time.[35]

Assessing the Germany-related sales multiples in more detail, it is to note that the highest multiple was paid by Interbrew SA for Brauerei Beck & Co. Interbrew SA paid the lowest multiple in the context of the Diebels GmbH & Co KG acquisition.

[34] Please refer to Appendix 10.
[35] Please refer to Appendices 4 and 5.

3.3 Evaluation of Multiple Levels with Value Drivers

Subsequent sections elaborate six selected value drivers, which appear particularly interesting in the context of the German Brewing Industry, namely growth, profitability, size, intensity of investments, transaction advisor and premium. They intend to provide for possible explanations for the level of multiples paid for German targets presented in Section 3.2. Nonetheless, as mentioned before no universally valid conclusion can be drawn due to the small data sample.

3.3.1 Growth

Particularly in Germany saturation, the demographic development, government interference via drink-driving regulations and lifestyle changes are causing decreases in German beer consumption.[36] Thus, the limited growth prospects for the German beer market might be one reason for the lower level of Germany-related multiples in comparison to non-Germany-related multiples.

In order to explore the effect of growth on the related multiple level, it makes sense to compare the past growth of the targets as a proxy for future growth with the respective multiple level. In this analysis it is only possible to compare the multiples of the three publicly listed targets, since only for those growth development data is accessible. Out of these three transactions, the Radeberger / Brau und Brunnen transaction has the lowest sales multiple, 0.6x, as well as the lowest EBITDA multiple, 7.3x. For the Carlsberg / Holsten transaction the second lowest sales multiple with 1.0x was paid. However, it was worth the highest EBITDA multiple with 9.1x. The Interbrew SA / Gilde Brauerei AG deal consequently shows the highest sales multiple with 1.8x and the second highest EBITDA multiple with 8.6x.

First of all, none of the three targets has had stable growth over the last years. Thus, past growth does not seem to be a good proxy for the future. Particularly Brau und Brunnen and Holsten are difficult to assess. While Brau und Brunnen shows a sales growth of 12% for the period September 2002 to September 2003,

[36] Cf. Credit Suisse First Boston (2003), pp. 6f.

the prior period was characterised by a decline in sales of 16%. Holsten, in contrast, shows a decline in sales of 10% for the period September 2002 to September 2003 and a decline of 24% for the period September 2000 to September 2001 after two following years of high growth. The sales growth of Gilde Brauerei AG for the period 2001 to 2002 was 3%, followed by a 5% growth for the period 2002 to 2003.[37]

3.3.2 Profitability

The German brewery market is highly fragmented. As shown in the exhibit below, market profitability is linked to the level of market concentration. In comparison to the Western European average, German brewers show a low level of profitability. While the first earn about € 20 per hl of EBITDA, the latter only realize about € 9 per hl of EBITDA.[38] The difference in profitability is reflected in the level of multiples.

Chart 6: Market Profitability is Linked to Market Concentration

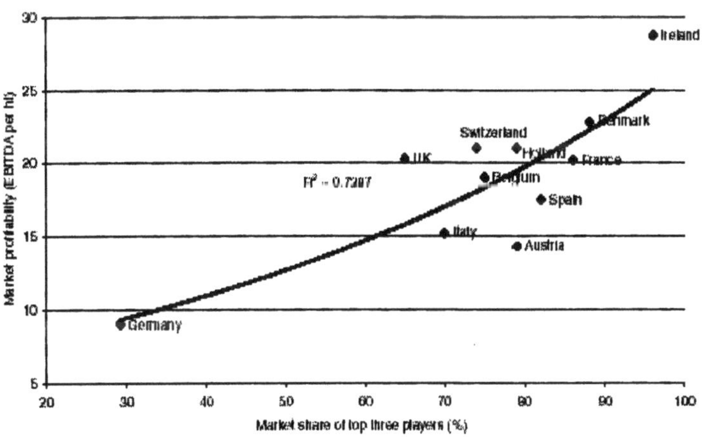

Source: Credit Suisse First Boston (2003), p. 22.

In the analysis of whether the difference in multiple levels of the observed German transactions can be partly explained by the different profitability levels, EBITDA

[37] Datastream (2005); please refer to Appendix 11.
[38] Cf. Credit Suisse First Boston (2003), p. 3.

margins as well as return on capital employed are compared. As for the analysis on growth effects, it is only possible to explore those transactions where a publicly listed company was targeted.

The profitability of Brau und Brunnen, Holsten und Gilde Brauerei AG is, like growth, not stable. There is neither stability in EBITDA margins nor in return on capital employed. It is also not possible to state that in general one company is more profitable than another. Consequently, the effect of profitability on the multiple level from a domestic perspective cannot be proven.[39]

3.3.3 Size

Having analysed the 34 transactions, no clear link between size and multiple level could be detected. Regarding only the Germany-related transactions, there is also no clear relation between size and multiple level. For example, while Brau und Brunnen exhibits the highest sales figures, it shows the lowest sales multiple.[40]

3.3.4 Intensity of Investments

Given the fact that the intensity of investments could only be calculated for three transactions, it is difficult to conclude whether it drives value or destroys it. However, focusing either on the transaction between Carlsberg / Holsten and the transaction between Radeberger / Brau und Brunnen or the transaction between Carlsberg / Holsten and the transaction between Interbrew / Gilde Brauerei AG, it is to be assumed that a high intensity of investments might drive the multiple level. The supposition is further affirmed, taking into account the fact that brewery companies usually possess a high level of real estate.

[39] Please refer to Appendix 12.
[40] Please refer to Appendices 6, 7, 8 and 9.

Chart 7: Relationship between EBITDA Multiple and Intensity of Investments

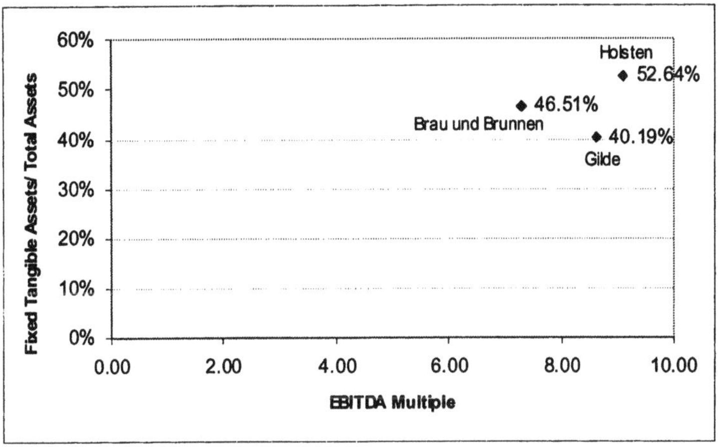

Source: Own exhibit based on data obtained from Datastream (2005) and Credit Suisse First Boston (2005).

3.3.5 Transaction Advisor

The analysis whether the advisor has an impact on the multiple level could not be accomplished due to the small number of transactions. Considering that the individual advisor only counselled at very few of those transactions, no reliable analysis was possible.

3.3.6 Premium

As briefly described in Section 2.3, the premium often contributes a significant part to the transaction multiple level. As in our sample, most of the acquirers targeted at private companies, it was not possible to calculate a premium. For the others, the lack of coherent data impeded the computation of the premiums. Nonetheless, some theoretical issues shall be addressed at this point. It seems reasonable to assume that with regard to the brewing industry high premiums are largely attributable to strategic rationales. The underlying data sample of this paper did not include any financial investors and a strong dominance of strategic investors in the brewing industry in general is assumable. To what extend a strategic advantage can be obtained from extending e.g. regional coverage, the brand portfolio or the customer base is obviously context- and acquirer-specific. In general, however, higher strategic synergies of different kinds could possibly justify high premiums paid. This seems a particularly appealing explanation for prices paid by international investors because they gain entrance to a very lucrative European beer market concerning per capita consumption and export possibilities. Also, in an era of increasing consolidation pressures, scarcity of targets or binding obligations that are tied to other M&A transactions could be other sources of high premiums observed when comparing trading with transaction multiples.

4 Concluding Remarks and Outlook

The primary objective of this paper was to analyse the transaction multiples in the German brewing industry. Detailed information about transactions in general is rarely published. Taking into account the average transaction size on the German market and the fact that this market is dominated by private players, the information availability is even lower. Consequently, although the market consolidated substantially with about 76 Germany-related and 871 non-Gemany-related transactions between July 1999 and August 2004, the data sample usable for analysis is relatively small with 7 and 17 transactions respectively. As highlighted before, the consequence of this scarcity of information is that it is very difficult to define clear findings regarding the drivers of multiple levels.

The analysis undertaken yielded the following results: Germany-related transaction multiples are generally lower than non-Germany-related transaction multiples. The sales multiple level in German lies between 0.6x and 3.2x and the EBITDA multiple for Germany-related transaction is between 6.5x and 13x.[41] The difference Germany-related as compared to non-Germany-related multiple levels can be partly explained by the limited growth prospects of the German market and the lower profitability of German brewery companies. While the findings have to be regarded with caution, other types of analysis did not lead to meaningful results. Firstly, the data sample was way too small to find statistical evidences and secondly, the lack of stability in growth and profitability of the German brewery com-

[41] For an overview of all transaction multiple levels assessed please refer to Appendix 1.

panies makes a reliable judgement of its impact on transaction multiples nearly impossible. Thus, regarding solely the Germany-related transactions, it was not possible to find an explanation of the different multiple levels.

For a solid analysis more data input would be needed. In the absence of public data on the relevant transactions, data obtainment could be pursued by a very time-consuming and rather difficult approach. Essentially, for each transaction, all data provided by the press, would have to be thoroughly assessed. Thus, any information, might it be the rough size of the transaction, the locations or the acquirer and the target, their products, or the strategic rationale for the acquisition and acquisition appetite of certain companies has to be gathered. This way, a more thorough analysis might be facilitated and multiple levels might be better explained by strategic drivers.

Due to the large acquisitions in 2004, the potential targets are scarce on the German brewery market. It is to expect that one of three big private companies – Bitburger, Krombacher and Warsteiner – will be the next target.[42] Furthermore, it might be possible that the multiple level will rise as a consequence of the strategic importance underlying to acquire one of the last three large German breweries that are privately held.

[42] Cf. Credit Suisse First Boston (2004), p. 3.

Appendix

Appendix 1: Transaction Multiple Ranges for Germany-Related Transactions

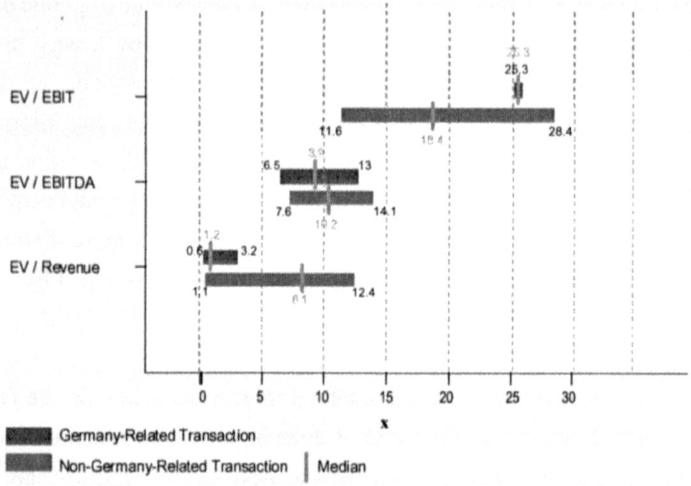

Source: Own figure based on data from Credit Suisse First Boston (2005).

Appendix 2: Non-Germany-Related Sales Multiple Levels over Time

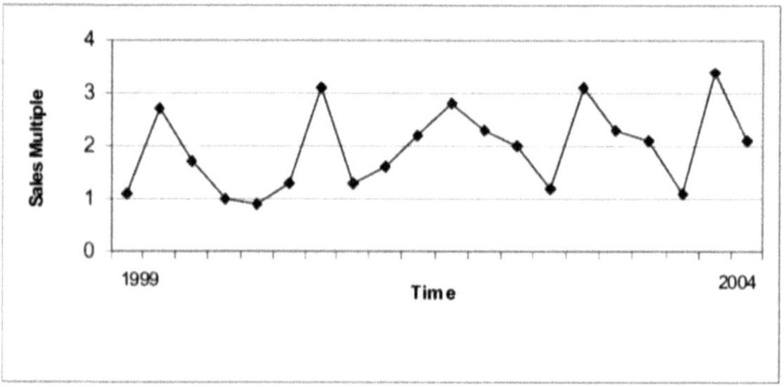

Source: Own figure based on data obtained from Datastream (2005) and Credit Suisse First Boston (2005).

Appendix 3: Germany-Related Sales Multiple Levels over Time

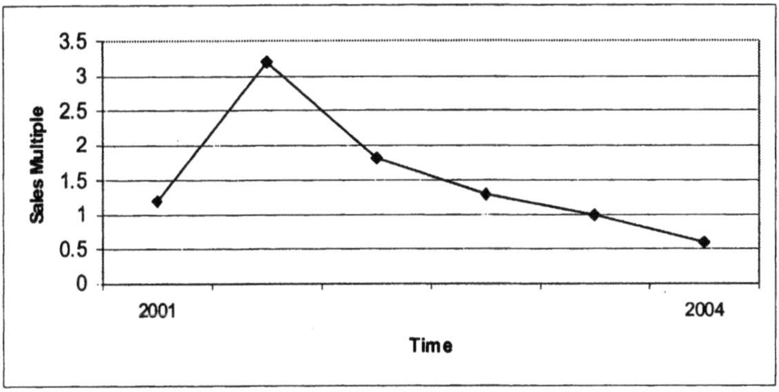

Source: Own figure based on data obtained from Datastream (2005) and Credit Suisse First Boston (2005).

Appendix 4: Non-Germany-Related EBITDA Multiple Levels over Time

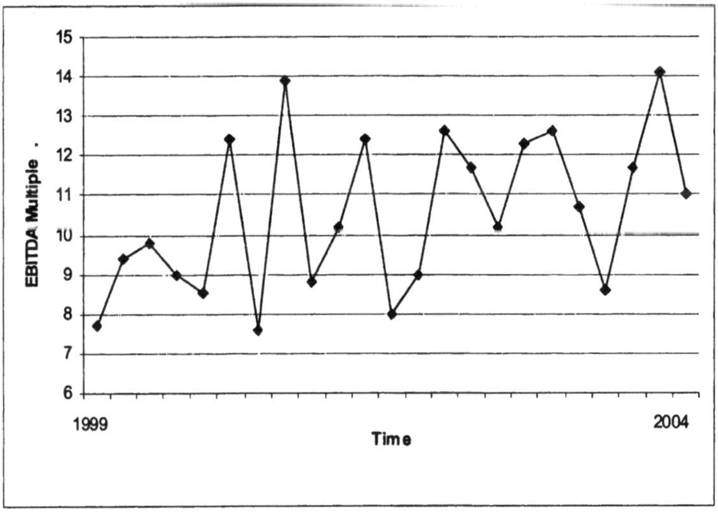

Source: Own figure based on data obtained from Datastream (2005) and Credit Suisse First Boston (2005).

Appendix 5: Germany-Related EBITDA Multiple Levels over Time

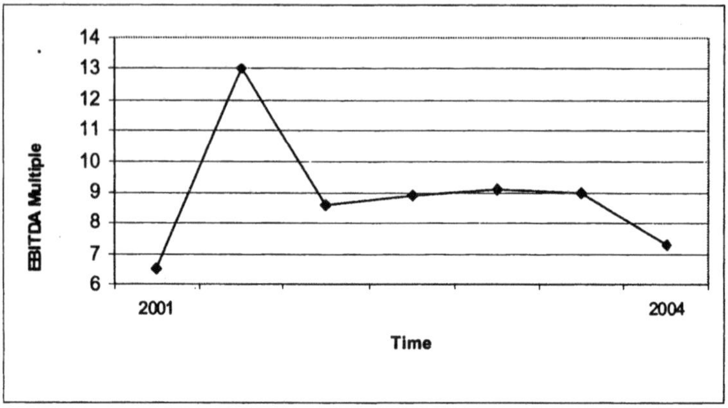

Source: Own figure based on data obtained from Datastream (2005) and Credit Suisse First Boston (2005).

Appendix 6: Non-Germany-Related Sales Figures in Relation to Sales Multiple Levels

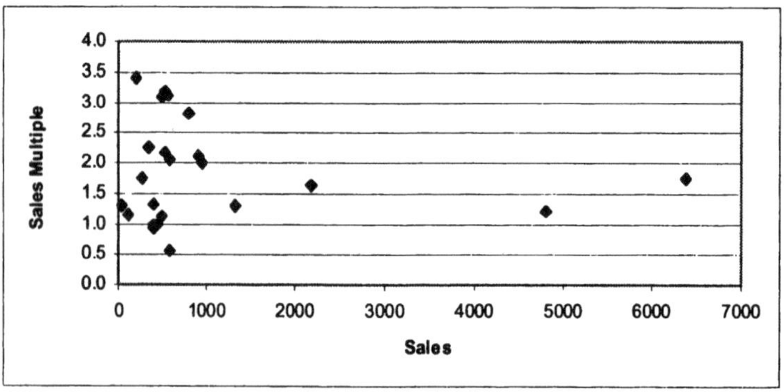

Source: Own figure based on data obtained from Datastream (2005) and Credit Suisse First Boston (2005).

Appendix 7: Germany-Related Sales Figures in Relation to Sales Multiple Levels

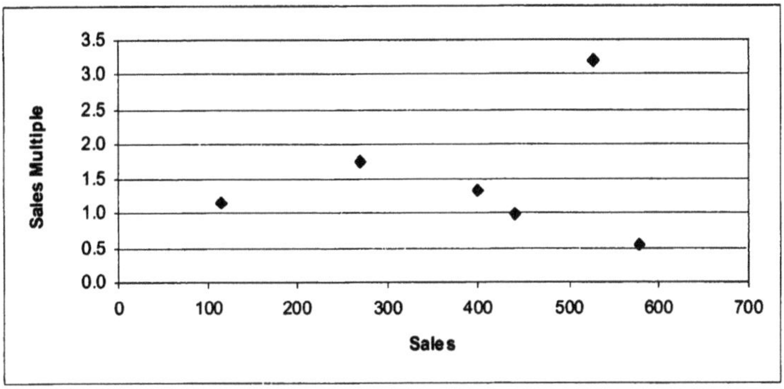

Source: Own figure based on data obtained from Datastream (2005) and Credit Suisse First Boston (2005).

Appendix 8: Non-Germany-Related Sales Figures in Relation to Sales Multiple Levels

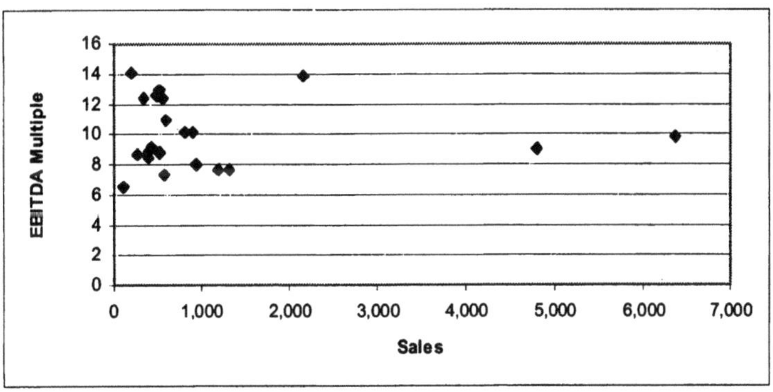

Source: Own figure based on data obtained from Datastream (2005) and Credit Suisse First Boston (2005).

Appendix 9: Germany-Related Sales Figures in Relation to EBITDA Multiple Levels.

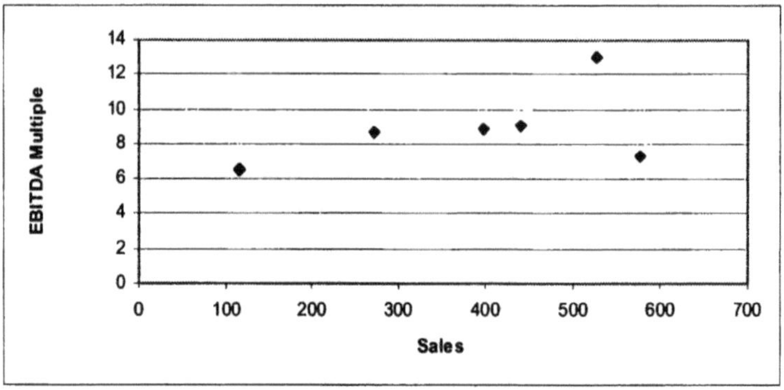

Source: Own figure based on data obtained from Datastream (2005) and Credit Suisse First Boston (2005).

Appendix 10: Overview Basic Statistics Related to Multiples Analysed

	ADJ. PURCHASE PRICE AS A MULTIPLE OF			EQUITY PURCHASE PRICE AS A MULTIPLE OF		
ANNOUNCE DATE	SALES MULTIPLE	OPER. CASH FLOW (EBITDA)	OPER. INCOME (EBIT)	NET INCOME	BOOK VALUE	VAL TRA CUR
Total number of transactions	26	30	18	11	13	
MAX	3.4x	14.1x	28.4x	54.7x	7.7x	
MEDIAN	1.8x	9.6x	19.7x	36.8x	2.8x	
MEAN	1.9x	10.2x	19.0x	34.4x	3.3x	
MIN	0.6x	6.5x	11.6x	14.4x	0.4x	
Number of Non-Germany related transactions	16	23	17	12	13	
MAX	12.4x	14.1x	28.4x	54.7x	7.7x	
MEDIAN	8.1x	10.2x	18.4x	33.5x	2.6x	
MEAN	6.7x	10.5x	18.2x	33.7x	3.0x	
MIN	1.1x	7.6x	11.6x	14.4x	0.4x	
Number of Germany related transactions	6	7	1	0	1	
MAX	3.2x	13.0x	25.3x	0.0x	7.1x	
MEDIAN	1.2x	8.9x	25.3x	0.0x	7.1x	
MEAN	1.5x	8.9x	25.3x	0.0x	7.1x	
MIN	0.6x	6.5x	25.3x	0.0x	7.1x	
Number where German company is acquiror	1	2	0	0	0	
MAX	0.6x	9.0x	0.0x	0.0x	0.0x	
MEDIAN	0.6x	8.1x	0.0x	0.0x	0.0x	
MEAN	0.6x	8.1x	0.0x	0.0x	0.0x	
MIN	0.6x	7.3x	0.0x	0.0x	0.0x	
Number where German company is target	6	7	1	-1	1	
MAX	3.2x	13.0x	25.3x	0.0x	7.1x	
MEDIAN	1.2x	8.9x	25.3x	0.0x	7.1x	
MEAN	1.5x	8.9x	25.3x	0.0x	7.1x	
MIN	0.6x	6.5x	25.3x	0.0x	7.1x	

Source: Credit Suisse First Boston (2005).

Appendix 11: The Development of Sales Growth of the Three Publicly Listed German Targets

		9/30/1998	9/30/1999	9/30/2000	9/30/2001	9/30/2002	9/30/2003
BRAU UND BRUNNEN							
	Sales	719,751	758,252	706,270	687,730	577,714	647,810
	Sales Growth	-11%	5%	-7%	-3%	-16%	12%
Holsten							
	Sales	752,589	893,805	1,081,416	820,661	833,958	752,091
	Sales Growth	0%	19%	21%	-24%	2%	-10%
Gilde Brauerei AG							
	Sales	107,676	126,288	109,841	128,310	131,950	138,141
	Sales Growth	-3%	17%	-13%	17%	3%	5%

Source: Own table based on data obtained from Datastream (2005).

Appendix 12: The Development of EBITDA Growth of the Three Publicly Listed German Targets

		9/30/1998	9/30/1999	9/30/2000	9/30/2001	9/30/2002	9/30/2003
BRAU UND BRUNNEN							
	EBITDA Margin	1%	-4%	-6%	-2%	16%	2%
	ROCE - published	5%	-21%	-33%	-36%	1547%	35%
Holsten							
	EBITDA Margin	10%	9%	10%	10%	13%	15%
	ROCE - published	9%	9%	9%	4%	9%	8%
Gilde Brauerei AG							
	EBITDA Margin	21%	12%	13%	5%	17%	20%
	ROCE - published	24%	11%	10%	2%	20%	26%

Source: Own table based on data obtained from Datastream (2005).

References

Benninga, Simon Z. / Sarig, Oded H. (1997): Corporate Finance – a valuation approach, New York.

Credit Suisse First Boston (2005): Latest Public Beer Compaq.

Credit Suisse First Boston (2004): The German beer industry – The consolidation continues, 16th of February 2003.

Credit Suisse First Boston (2003): The German beer industry – The consolidator's challenge, 4th of June 2003.

Damodaran, Aswath (1996): Investment valuation – tools and techniques for determining tha value of any asset, university edition, New York.

Datastream (2005): Data German Brewery retrieved 18th March 2005.

Deutsche Bank (2004): Venture Valuation, Course Material – Lecture held at the European Business School, Winter Term 2004.

Deutsche Bank (2003): Global Equity Research European Brewing – Dangerous liason, 5th of June 2003.

Deutsche Bank (2000): Global Equity Research – Global Brewing, 6th of November 2000.

Kenneth, R. Ferris / Pécherot Petitt, Barbara S. (2002): Valuation – avoiding the winner's curse, Upper Saddle River.

Morgan Stanley (2005): Gesamtbewertung, Course Material – Lecture held at the European Business School, Summer Term 2005.

C Case Study: The Acquisition of Würzburger Hofbräu AG by Kulmbacher Brauerei AG

by
Sebastian Schels and Tim Knipps

1 Introduction

The German beer market is characterised by unique features – it is highly dynamic and is currently going through substantial changes. This is based mainly on its historically high fragmentation, which is a cause for the high number of small and regional breweries. In fact, no single beer brand in Germany has ever had a market share of more than 10%. Another indicator for the high fragmentation is the fact that 38% of all German breweries have a smaller market share than 2%.[1]

This greatly fragmented beer market has been shrinking since the beginning of the 1990s when the total beer sales started to decline. This trend is currently even reinforced by an in-creasing popularity of wine, a higher health consciousness among the German population, an aging population and unfavourable economic and political circumstances which lead to decreasing customer confidence and growing uncertainty. Moreover, the increasing market shares of discounters and private labels, a consequence of a vanishing brand loyalty and a greater than ever price consciousness, also create pressure for German breweries. [2]

The logic consequence of these developments is a shake-out of the highly fragmented German beer industry through numerous mergers and acquisitions. It thus stands to reason that it is of high importance and interest to dedicate attention to recent take-over deals and analyze them from a financial point of view.

---

[1] Cf. Deutscher Brauer Bund (2005).
[2] Cf. Kulmbacher Brauerei AG (2004), pp. 3-6.

This paper thus analyzes the acquisition of Würzburger Hofbräu AG by Kulmbacher Brauerei AG within this dynamic market. This transaction is of interest for a variety of reasons. On the one hand, it will be shown that the strategy behind the take-over differs from the strategic rationale of most other comparable transactions.

Also, the shareholder structure of the target is of high interest for the transaction, as an investor that has held the majority of shares for more than 100 years is emotionally linked to Würzburger Hofbräu AG and therefore tried to assure that his interests are taken into account in the acquisition. As it will be shown, this had a decisive impact on the overall outcome. Moreover, the transaction process is worthy of note because the acquirer had to struggle collecting a squeeze-out majority and did not succeed in doing so before the very last day of the period of the mandatory offer, May 27th, 2005.

2 The Acquirer: Kulmbacher Brauerei AG

2.1 Company Background

The Kulmbacher Brauerei Aktiengesellschaft was founded in 1846 as Reichelbräu. In the year 1895 the company was changed into an 'Aktiengesellschaft'. 91 years later, in 1986, Schörghuber Unternehmensgruppe acquired a 49.9% stake in the company. By the year 1996, Reichelbräu – now unifying Sandlerbräu, Mönchshof and EKU, was finally renamed to Kulmbacher Brauerei AG. Today, the brewery has its core market in the north of Bavaria, Saxony and Thuringia and belongs to the top 20 breweries in Germany.[3]

2.2 Product Portfolio

Within the product portfolio, one can clearly recognise the regional focus of Kulmbacher Brauerei AG. Under the roof of Kulmbacher, the company runs seven different beer brands, namely Kulmbacher, Mönchshof, EKU, Kapuziner, Sternquell, Braustolz and Scherdel. In the section 'non-alcoholic beverages', the com-

[3] Cf. Kulbacher Brauerei AG (2005c).

pany offers mineral water called Bad Brambacher.[4] Recent developments of the most important brands are presented briefly in the following chapter.

Kulmbacher beer is a supra-regional premium brand with a leading position in North Bavaria. However, it experienced a decline in total sales (hl) in 2004 due to negative influences by bad weather conditions and national economic developments, as well as the German 'Einwegpfand', a law for deposits on one-way drink containers.[5]

The Mönchshof brand once more grew stronger last year – new target groups were addressed by a high variety of beers under the Mönchshof brand, market leader in Bavaria for the segment of flip-top bottles.[6]

EKU beer experienced a very weak development in the time before 2003, being the main cause for losses of Kulmbacher Brauerei AG by the end of the nineties. In the year 2004 the brand reached an increase in sales (hl) for the first time in several years. According to the annual report of Kulmbacher, this is an effect of a consequent regional marketing approach for EKU beer.[7]

2.3 Corporate Strategy

According to its annual report, Kulmbacher Brauerei AG's strategy is to take into consideration people's need for a feeling of belonging and a general tendency of identification with one's home. Kulmbacher is thus focusing on a culturally and historically developed variety of beer brands deeply incorporated into the lives of those people living in the company's relevant markets.[8]

Therefore, Kulmbacher brewery pursues its goals through a regionally focused marketing approach that does without nation-wide advertising campaigns, but focuses on sympathetic actions like support of regional sports teams, society and

---

[4] Cf. Kulmbacher Brauerei AG (2005d).
[5] Cf. Kulmbacher Brauerei AG (2004), pp. 3-14.
[6] Cf. Kulmbacher Brauerei AG (2004), p. 14.
[7] Cf. Kulmbacher Brauerei AG (2004), p. 14.
[8] Cf. Kulmbacher Brauerei AG (2004), p. 9.

maintenance of tradition[9]. These strategic issues are in line with the transaction rationale as Würzburger Hofbräu disposes of a variety of locally established brands that could complement the offer of Kulmbacher and could be integrated in the company's regional marketing strategy.[10]

2.4 Shareholder and Holding Structure

In order to understand the rationale behind a take-over transaction, it is important to know the shareholder and holding structure of the acquirer. In this case, the biggest share of the acquirer Kulmbacher Brauerei AG (62.6%) is owned by Brau Holding International AG, a joint venture of Schörghuber Unternehmensgruppe and Heineken. The acquisition of Würzburger Hofbräu through Kulmbacher thus gets an international perspective as Heineken is interested in increasing its stake in the German market. However, such strategic issues behind the purchase are mentioned in Chapter 4.[11]

IREKS, a bakery goods producer in Kulmbach, holds a share of 26.0% of the company. The rest amounts to 11.4%, a total of 383,040 shares, and is publicly traded at the stock exchanges in Frankfurt/M. and Munich.[12] Chart 1 gives an overview of the current shareholder and holding structure of Kulmbacher Brauerei AG.[13]

[9] Cf. Kulmbacher Brauerei AG (2004), p. 9.
[10] Cf. Würzburger Hofbräu AG (2005a).
[11] Cf. Kulmbacher Brauerei AG (2005e).
[12] Cf. Kulmbacher Brauerei AG (2005a).
[13] Cf. http://www.ireks.de/.

Chart 1: Holding Structure of Kulmbacher Brauerei AG

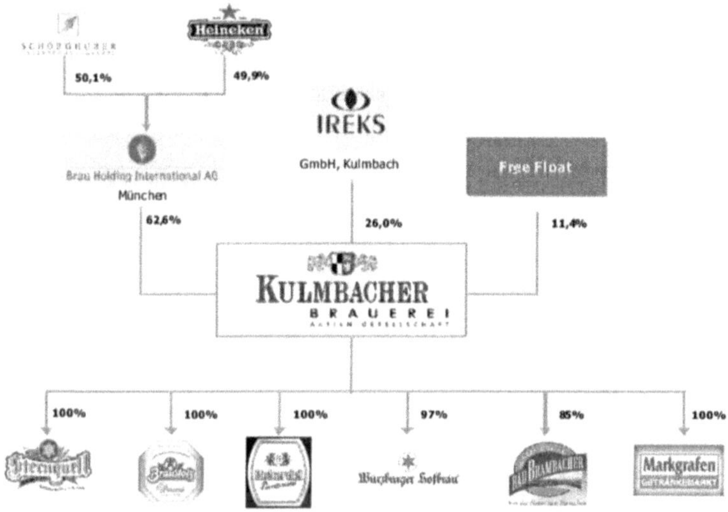

Source: Kulmbacher Brauerei AG (2005d); Kulmbacher Brauerei AG (2005c).

2.5 Financial Data

As shown in Chart 2, Kulmbacher Brauerei AG is currently following a stable and sound financial development.

Chart 2: Financial Development of Kulmbacher Brauerei AG

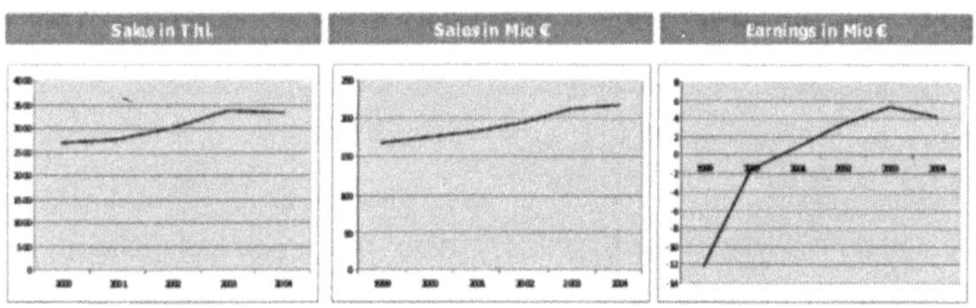

Source: Kulmbacher Brauerei AG (2004), pp. 24-36; http://www.comdirect.de/; http://www.lz-net.de.

However, all three graphs indicate a slight slowing down of a recently strong upward trend. The whole industry has had to suffer from a relatively cold summer in 2004 after record breaking temperatures in 2003. Furthermore, political and economic developments contributed to put the sector under pressure. In contrast to this negative market environment, Kulmbacher Brauerei AG showed relative strength: beer sales increased by 0.8% and could withstand the negative influences. This is shown by the first graph: it indicates the development of the overall sales which amount to 3.3m hl in 2004. This figure splits up into 2.2m hl of beer sales and the remainder being sales of non-alcoholic beverages.[14]

In contrast to the sales figures, earnings decreased sharply in the year 2004. The reason for this development is that Kulmbacher had to pay taxes on income for the first time since several years – even though the company had deferred deficits. The tax payment of EUR 1.4m brought down earnings from € 5.5m to € 4.3m in 2004.[15]

3 The Target: Würzburger Hofbräu AG

3.1 Company Background

Würzburger Hofbräu AG was founded in 1643 during the Thirty Years' War when Swedish soldiers had drunken up all of their wine supply, forcing the Würzburg inhabitants to look for a substitute. The beer they consequently brewed finally became so popular that in the 19th century it was drunk all over Germany. In the year 1887 Würzburger Hofbräu beer was one of the first German beers to be exported to the USA. Today, the company offers a traditional beer in a regional premium sector. With its annual output of 360,000 litres of beer, Würzburger Hofbräu AG can be classified as a rather small brewery.[16]

3.2 Product Portfolio

Like the Kulmbacher brewery, Würzburger Hofbräu AG's product portfolio is mainly targeted at a regional market. In addition to Würzburger Hofbräu, the company also offers Werner Bräu, Lohrer Bier and Wächtersbacher as regional beer brands. These breweries are situated in the north of Bavaria and in Hessia, east of

[14] Cf. Kulmbacher Brauerei AG (2004), pp. 3-14.
[15] Cf. Kulmbacher Brauerei AG (2004), pp. 16-17.
[16] Cf. Würzburger Hofbräu AG (2005e); Würzburger Hofbräu AG (2004), p. 5.

the breweries of Kulmbacher. As will be shown later, the location of the breweries played a decisive role in the transaction.[17]

3.3 Corporate Strategy

When examining the corporate strategy of the target, it is important to look at the distribution channels. Würzburger Hofbräu AG's distribution channels are typical for a small and regional brewery: 47% of its sales are generated through catering industry, 46% through retailers and 3% through export, leaving a remainder of 4% distributed through other channels.[18] This leads to a high dependency on the development of beer demand in pubs and restaurants as well as the distribution situation in the German retail sector. However, these two fields are not developing in favour of Würzburger Hofbräu as sales through catering industry are stagnating and recent developments in the German retail sector especially put small breweries under pressure. A strong growth of discounters and private labels, as well as the introduction of the German 'Einwegpfand' are factors especially affecting smaller regional breweries.[19]

The brewery has thus been searching for a suitable big and strong partner in its industry that could purchase the company and support it in its operations and financial situation. Another goal has been to find suitable take-over targets which, after their integration, could strengthen the current market position and increase earnings. It wants further to focus on the premium beer market in order to become less dependent on the middle price segment, since it is broadly anticipated that this segment will vanish over the next years.[20]

3.4 Shareholder and Holding Structure

The shareholder structure of Würzburger Hofbräu AG plays a central role in analysing the transaction. Before the initiation of the deal, 9.3% of Würzburger Hofbräu's shares were publicly traded on stock exchanges in Frankfurt/M. and Mu-

---

[17] Cf. Würzburger Hofbräu AG (2005f).
[18] Cf. Würzburger Hofbräu AG (2004), p. 5.
[19] Cf. Würzburger Hofbräu AG (2005d).
[20] Cf. Würzburger Hofbräu AG (2005d); Würzburger Hofbräu AG (2004), p. 7; Belz (2005).

nich. However, the biggest part, being 90.7%, was held by a family called Finck who has held these shares for more than 100 years. August von Finck, who had held the shares of Würzburger Hofbräu AG until they were purchased by Kulmbacher, is the tenth richest German with total private means of $ 6.3bn. The family is the beneficiary of the founder of Allianz AG Holding. Today they still own 5 % of the German insurance company.[21]

The von Finck family was a long-time investor in Würzburger Hofbräu AG and such shareholders usually have their specific interests. For one thing, it can be assumed that the family was connected emotionally to Würzburger Hofbräu. They are likely to have an interest in the long-term survival of the company, and thus probably favoured to sell their shares to the brewery that would offer a stable environment to Würzburger Hofbräu AG.[22] Chart 3 displays the shareholder structure and subsidiaries of Würzburger Hofbräu AG.

Chart 3: Shareholder and Holding Structure of Würzburger Hofbräu AG

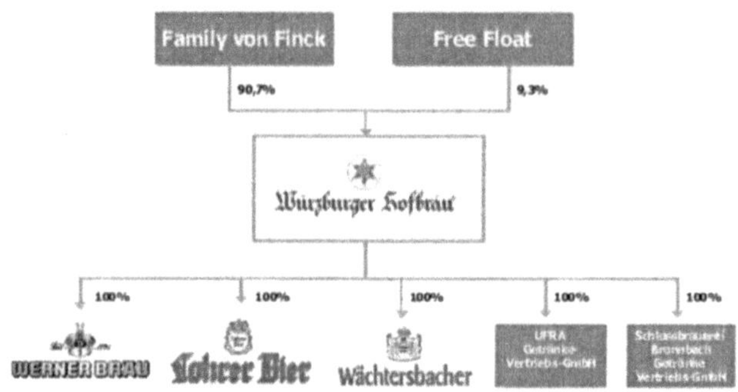

Source: Würzburger Hofbräu AG (2004), p. 32.

3.5 Financial Data

Chart 4 gives an overview of the most important financial data of Würzburger Hofbräu AG. Sales in hl and in € both declined by 5% in 2004. This is above all due to a relatively weak summer in 2004 compared to the previous year. The whole

[21] Cf. http://www.marx-forum.de/geschichte/deutschland/milliard_AF.html.
[22] Kulmbacher Brauerei AG (2005e), pp. 1-5; www.lz-net.de; Interview from 05/20/2005 with Dr. Metzel, Kulmbacher Brauerei AG, Public Relations Dept.

beverage market had to suffer from this negative environment; there was also an influence on Würzburger. In fact sales measured in € declined slightly less than sales in hl due to an increase in prices of Würzburger Hofbräu's beer.[23].

Chart 4: Financial Development of Würzburger Hofbräu AG.

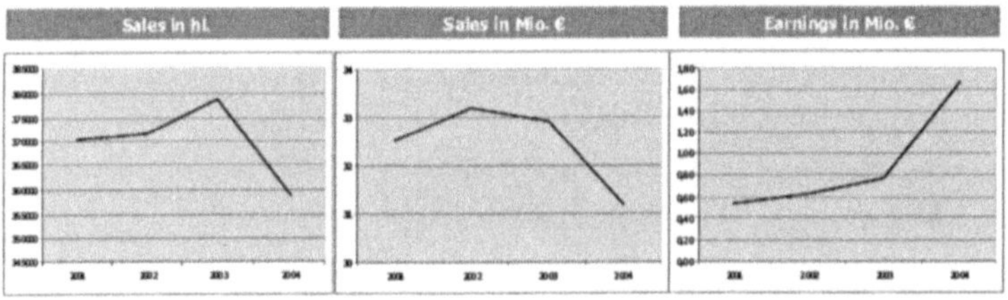

Source: Würzburger Hofbräu AG (2004), p. 10; Würzburger Hofbräu AG (2003), p. 10; Würzburger Hofbräu AG (2002), p. 10.

In contrast to the sales figures, earnings increased sharply by nearly 120%. One reason to be identified by the examination of the company's annual report is a realization of cost reductions, especially in the field of human resources. Operation costs could be lowered by € 1.6m and personnel costs by € 0.2m. To conclude the comparison of the two companies, Chart 5 gives an overview of the most important financial data of both breweries.[24]

[23] Cf. Würzburger Hofbräu AG (2004), pp. 4-10; Würzburger Hofbräu AG (2003), p. 10; Würzburger Hofbräu AG (2002), p. 10.
[24] Cf. Würzburger Hofbräu AG (2004), pp. 5-6.

Chart 5: Comparison of Basic Financial Data (2004)

	Kulmbacher Brauerei	Würzburger Hofbräu
Sales in Mio. €	217	31
Sales in Mio. hl.	2,15	0,36
Sales of non alcoholics in Mio. hl.	1,27	-
Earnings in Mio. €	4,3	1,5
Market Capitalization in Mio. €	79,97	41,00
Employees	987	165

Source: Würzburger Hofbräu AG (2004), pp. 4-10;
Kulmbacher Brauerei AG (2004), p. 1-29.

4 Strategic Rationale

There are different explanations for the successful completion of the acquisition. On the one hand, Würzburger Hofbräu was set under pressure to look for a strong partner. On the other hand, Kulmbacher Brauerei had strategic motivations for the purchase and finally, the von Finck family was able to bring in its interests.

4.1 Würzburger Hofbräu Under External Pressure

Würzburger Hofbräu had an interest to be acquired by Kulmbacher Brauerei for several reasons. However, those motivations stem above all from external influences. On the one hand, as already described above, the overall beer market has been declining due to decreasing beer consumption. Small breweries like Würzburger Hofbräu are highly affected by this development, and thus feel a pressure to enter a strong partnership. On the other hand, the high fragmentation of the German beer market paves the way for mergers and acquisitions in this industry. Especially smaller companies are under pressure to look for a strong partner that pursues a strategy which is conductive to the company's long-term survival. In the optimal case, this partner leaves the purchased company an independent entity. For Kulmbacher, both those arguments hold true. Next to the fact that Kulmbacher is a potent regional brewery, it was clearly communicated from the beginning that in the case of a purchase, Würzburger Hofbräu would remain independent.[25] Moreover, the transaction made sense for Würzburger Hofbräu because this way they can profit from the successful regional marketing strategy of Kulmbacher already described earlier in Chapter 2.3.

Other factors that created an external pressure for Würzburger to look for a strong partner include a high growth rate of discounters and private labels. This let to decreasing margins. Especially smaller players are restricted in their ability to react to these new circumstances. Moreover, the German "Einwegpfand" introduced in 2003 and an increase in beer taxes are mostly only bearable through product diversification, new packaging formats, new tastes like mild beers and so-called "mixeries". This poses a major disadvantage especially for smaller breweries. In a letter to the company's shareholders and employees, the CEO of Würzburger Hofbräu thus comes to a very pessimistic assessment of the company's environment and argues that it is therefore vital for the long-term success to find a strong partner in the beer industry. Hence, one can say that Würzburger Hofbräu was pushed towards a strong partnership – be it through being purchased or through establishing a close cooperation.[26]

4.2 Kulmbacher Brauerei AG's Strategic Decision

For Kulmbacher Brauerei, the decision to foster the transaction was a more strategic one. The company was not so much pushed towards purchasing Würzburger Hofbräu – they had other reasons, the most important being the strengthening and expansion of their geographic market position. According to the public relations department of Kulmbacher, it was the main goal to strengthen the strategic line of breweries which goes from Chemnitz in the east to Kulmbach in the west.[27] The acquisition of Würzburger Hofbräu extended this line in the west and manifested the current market position while opening up the alternative to foster expansion towards Hessia and North Rhine-Westphalia. Chart 6 shows these geographic strategic aspects.

---

[25] Interview from 05/20/2005 with Dr. Metzel, Kulmbacher Brauerei AG, Public Relations Dept.
[26] Cf. Würzburger Hofbräu AG (2005d).
[27] Interview from 05/20/2005 with Dr. Metzel, Kulmbacher Brauerei AG, Public Relations Dept.

Chart 6: Geographic Expansion Strategy of Kulmbacher Brauerei AG

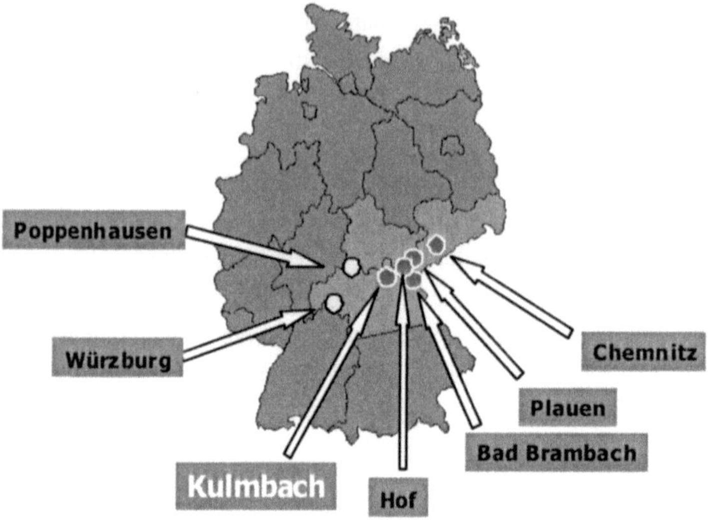

The dots with a circle indicate Kulmbacher's current breweries, the other ones Würzburger's two production sites. However, while this constellation might suggest that Kulmbacher would be able to realise substantial cost reductions through the exploitation of synergies, the public relations department emphasized that this is not the case. The overriding reason for the purchase was the company's strategy to lock its core market and open up alternatives for future expansion towards the west.[28]

This is also in line with the company's expansion strategy which focuses on regional markets and their successive and healthy enlargement by acquiring breweries that are treated cooperatively and that are left independently. The company also follows this approach for its other small regional breweries and intends to also follow this path in the future. A pitfall of this strategy is certainly that major synergies in the field of purchasing, distribution and personnel cannot be realized. Kulmbacher even assured to not lay off any employees from Würzburger Hofbräu. Thus, it cannot be argued that Kulmbacher purchased Würzburger Hofbräu in order

[28] Interview from 05/20/2005 with Dr. Metzel, Kulmbacher Brauerei AG, Public Relations Dept.

to lower cost through realization of synergies. The acquisition can therefore be called strategic, implying that Kulmbacher pursued its geographic positioning strategy but not a strategic purchase in the usual sense as this would imply a comparably high purchase price – a strategic purchase price. And as it will be shown later, the purchase price is comparably low when analyzing transaction multiples (see Chapter 6).[29]

However, while not playing a major role in this transaction, synergies have occured and will be realized in the field of logistics, purchase, personnel (without any layoffs) and IT. This should lead to cost advantages in the short-term, but their relative importance can almost be neglected according to the public relations department of Kulmbacher Brauerei AG.[30]

4.3 Shareholders' Interests

As already shown before, Schörghuber Unternehmensgruppe and Heineken hold a 62.6% stake in Kulmbacher Brauerei through their joint venture Brau Holding International. It can thus be assumed that these two parties represent certain interests in the transaction. Furthermore, the von Finck family held a 90.7% share in Würzburger Hofbräu and finally sold their stake to Kulmbacher on 24th March 2005.

According to Kulmbacher, Heineken and Schörghuber did not take any major influence on the transaction – Kulmbacher is acts absolutely independently and is manages its operations without any pressure or influence from Brau Holding International. However, for Heineken the transaction was nonetheless a positive contribution to their overall strategy as they have not yet succeeded in entering the German market on a broad scale. An enlargement of their share in the regional market was thus sensational and part of their overall internationalisation strategy.[31]

[29] Interview from 05/20/2005 with Dr. Metzel, Kulmbacher Brauerei AG, Public Relations Dept.
[30] Interview from 05/20/2005 with Dr. Metzel, Kulmbacher Brauerei AG, Public Relations Dept.
[31] Interview from 05/20/2005 with Dr. Metzel, Kulmbacher Brauerei AG, Public Relations Dept.

On the other hand, the von Finck family played a major role in the transaction and finally favored to sell their 90.7% share to Kulmbacher brewery for various reasons. As already mentioned before, their history of more than 100 years of investment in Würzburger Hofbräu AG surely contributed to a rather emotional attitude towards the transaction. What surely contributes to this attitude is that the brewing industry with its long history and tradition is more emotional than many other sectors. The von Finck family favored a new investor which could secure a survival of Würzburger Hofbräu in a very dynamic market in the long-run. The long-term investor rather preferred a new owner which guarantees the independence of Würzburger and which does not lay off too many of the current employees.[32]

All these factors hold true for Kulmbacher. For the von Finck family it was easily recognisable that Kulmbacher Brauerei follows a strategy of leaving its subsidiaries as independent entities, as the company managed to do with its other breweries. It can thus be said that Heineken was surely open towards the purchase of Würzburger by Kulmbacher and that the von Finck family did most likely foster and support it, in order to realise their long-term interests in the company.[33]

5 The M&A Deal

5.1 The Transaction

The Kulmbacher Brauerei AG entered a Stock Purchasing Agreement (SPA) with the major shareholder of Würzburger Hofbräu AG, the von Finck family, on January 20th, 2005 with respect to March 24th, 2005. Kulmbacher bought 80,700 shares which correspond to 80.7% of equity and voting rights of Würzburger Hofbräu.

On the basis of the same SPA of January 20th, 2005 with effect on March 24th, 2005, the NG (Nordbayerische Getränkebeteiligungs-GmbH & Co. KG) bought 10.000 shares (10% of equity and voting rights) of Würzburger Hofbräu AG. These voting rights belong to Kulmbacher according to the German Take-over Act[34] be-

[32] Interview from 05/20/2005 with Dr. Metzel, Kulmbacher Brauerei AG, Public Relations Dept.
[33] Interview from 05/20/2005 with Dr. Metzel, Kulmbacher Brauerei AG, Public Relations Dept.
[34] § 30 Abs. 1 Satz 1 Nr. 1 WpÜG.

cause Kulmbacher Brauerei AG owns 100% of the capital of Nordbayerische Getränkebeteiligungs-GmbH & Co. KG.

In total, Kulmbacher owned 90.700 shares of Würzburger after the completion of the initial SPA which equalled to 90.7% of the target's equity and voting rights with effect from March 24th, 2005. The price agreed upon in the SPA was € 375.00 per share. This has been the only transaction of the acquirer in order to take over the control of the target. In compliance with the German Take-over Act[35], Kulmbacher Brauerei AG did not acquire any shares of Würzburger Hofbräu AG within a period of three months before publishing the decision to launch an offer or within the period of the publication of the bidding documents.[36]

On March 3rd, 2005, the Bundeskartellamt (Federal Cartel Office) accepted that Kulmbacher Brauerei AG would gain control over Würzburger Hofbräu AG.[37]

On March 29th, 2005, Kulmbacher announced a mandatory offer for the left over 9,300 shares. The shares of Würzburger Hofbräu AG are listed at the Munich Stock Exchange as well as at the over-the-counter market at the Frankfurt Stock Exchange. Within the last three months before publishing the mandatory offer, the Munich stock exchange only stated stock prices for Würzburger Hofbräu for less than a third of all trading days. A couple of these subsequently stated stock prices differed more than 5 % from each other. On March 28th, 2005, the BaFin, the Federal Financial Supervisory Authority, published an estimated average share price for the three months period for Würzburger of € 393.75 per share. But BaFin called the share price invalid because it did not comply with German law[38] in the sense of a mandatory weighted average domestic share price due to the stock price movements bigger than 5 % in between two subsequent statements. Therefore, the share price published by BaFin was not a legal minimum price for the mandatory offer.

[35] § 30 Abs. 1 Satz 1 Nr. 1 WpÜG.
[36] Cf. Kulmbacher Brauerei AG (2005a), pp. 13–14.
[37] Cf. Bundeskartellamt (2005).
[38] § 31 Abs. 1 WpÜG in connection with § 5 Abs. 1, 2 WpÜG-AngVO.

In conclusion, a fair price for the mandatory offer had to be determined by a company valuation according to § 5 Abs. 4 WpÜG-AngVO.[39]

On April 23rd, 2005, the Kulmbacher Brauerei AG announced according to § 35 Abs. 2 WpÜG to conduct a public mandatory offer in order to buy all shares of the Würzburger Hofbräu AG. The payment in return is reasonable in the sense of the WpÜG and has been approved by the board of directors to be fair and appropriate.[40]

Chart 7: Schedule of Events

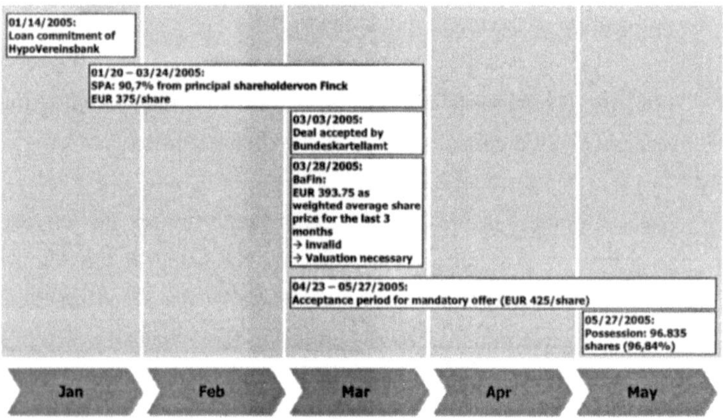

From April 23rd to May 27th, 2005 the minority shareholder could accept the mandatory offer at € 425 per share. Kulmbacher received a loan commitment by HypoVereinsbank for € 4.1m on January 14th as well as on January 19th, 2005. This included the maximum liabilities for 9,300 outstanding shares (about € 4m plus additional costs).

At the beginning, the remaining shareholders of Würzburger reluctantly accepted the deal. Within a month, Kulmbacher could only incrementally increase their share of the target's equity (see Chart 8). The share volume traded for the manda-

[39] Cf. BaFin (2005).
[40] Cf. Würzburger Brauerei AG (2005b), p. 1.

tory offer was low and Kulmbacher could only increase its share from 90.7% to 91.4%. Before the deadline, the mandatory offer was accepted and Kulmbacher could increase its share from 91.40% to 96.84% of Würzburger Hofbräu's equity and voting rights.[41]

5.2 Capital Market Reaction

Looking at the share price reaction of Kulmbacher Brauerei AG it becomes obvious that the market appreciated the deal and the strategy behind it. The share rose from the day Kulmbacher announced the acquisition of the control of Würzburger Hofbräu AG. Within the period of the SPA the share price of Kulmbacher gained about 26%, which is mainly due to the M&A activities concerning Würzburger. Initially trading at € 24.55 on January 20th, 2005, Kulmbacher's share price increased to € 30.90 at the end of the SPA and a positive correlation between the deal and the share price development seems plausible. The mandatory offer did not seem to meet the expectations of the market as the share price went down. During the period to accept the mandatory offer, the share price of Kulmbacher fluctuated between € 28.00 and € 30.00. On several occasions Kulmbach announced its increasing share of Würzburger, but Kulmbacher's share price always hit a resistance at € 30.00. This might have been related to the price of the mandatory offer that had been based on a company valuation of Würzburger.

[41] Cf. Kulmbacher Brauerei AG (2005b): Press Release May 31st, 2005.

Chart 8: Share Price of Kulmbacher Brauerei AG within the Period of the Transaction

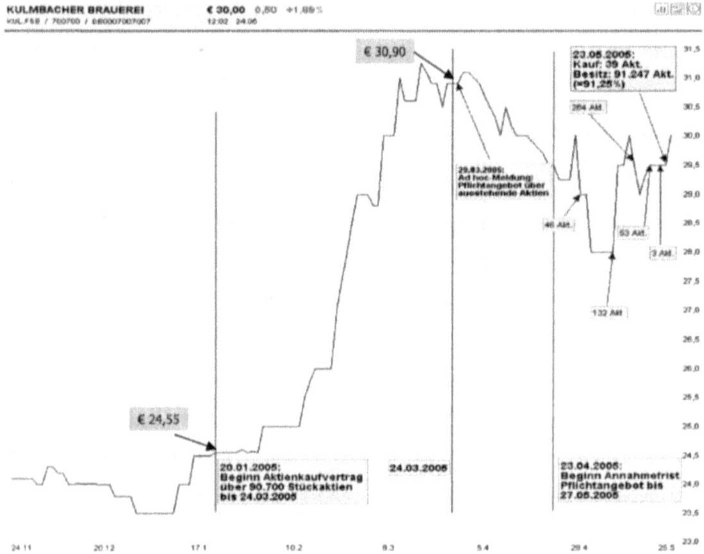

6 Financial Rationale

6.1 Valuation of the Target

Since the weighted average domestic share price published by BaFin was invalid due to stock price movements higher than 5 % in between two subsequent trading days, Kulmbacher ordered CMS GmbH Wirtschaftsprüfungsgesellschaft in Stuttgart to conduct a valuation of Würzburger Hofbräu AG.[42] For their valuation report, CMS chose the income approach ("Ertragswertverfahen"). The income approach calculates the company value by discounting future financial net profits derived from future success ("Ertragüberschussrechnung"). The valuation report used a method dividing future earnings in two phases. For the first phase until the 2013, future earnings were discounted with an adequate target rate and the present values added up. In Phase II a constant annual amount of net earnings ("perpetuity") was assumed and then discounted. In conclusion, CMS calculated a company value for

[42] In compliance with § 5 Abs. 4 WpÜG-AngVO.

Würzburger Hofbräu AG including all subsidiaries of € 37.2m Having issued 100,000 shares, the proportional company value of Würzburger equaled € 372 per share.[43]

In conclusion, the price of the mandatory offer is clearly above the price of the initial SPA with the principal shareholder von Finck family. The price is also higher than the price calculated by CMS according to their company valuation of Würzburger Hofbräu. Kulmbacher chose € 425 per share (14 % above the stated company value) for their mandatory offer in hope of a high acceptance quote by the minority shareholders.[44]

6.2 Analysis of Comparable Transactions

In comparison to other transactions in the beer industry, a transaction volume of € 38m is still relatively low.[45] This becomes obvious when looking at transaction multiples (LTM). The sales multiple of 1.15 is at the lower end of the range for the German Brewing industry as well as the transaction multiple for hectoliters. The EBITDA multiple is noticeably low for the Würzburger transaction.

Chart 9: Multiples of comparable transactions

					Multiples (LTM)		
Date	Target	Buyer	Stake	Transaction volume in Mio €	Sales	EBITDA	(€/ Hl)
Mai 05	Würzburger Hofbräu AG	Kulmbacher Brauerei	96,84%(1)	38(2)	1,15	6,2	106
Feb 04	Brau und Brunnen	RB Brauholding	61,7%	222	1,20	12,1	111
Jan 04	Holsten	Carlsberg	100,0%	1.338	1,39	8,6	122
Jan 04	König and Licher	Bitburger	100,0%	589	2,23	9,0	n.a.
Jan 04	Holsten Brewing Business	Carlsberg	100,0%	549	0,86	9,1	71

(1) May 27th, 2005: 96.8357 shares after the deadline of the mandatory offer

(2) € 34.012.500 for 90.7% of Würzburger Hofbräu's shares (EUR 375/share) + maximum liabilities for all remaining shares (EUR 425/share).

The main reason for the relatively low multiple can be partly explained by the strategic rationale of the deal (see Chapter 4). This deal was a strategic one, but not

[43] Cf. Kulmbacher Brauerei AG (2005a), pp. 19–23.

[44] Interview from 05/20/2005 with Dr. Metzel, Kulmbacher Brauerei AG, Public Relations Dept.

[45] € 34,012,500 for 90.7% of Würzburger Hofbräu's shares (€ 375/share) + maximum liabilities for all remaining shares (€ 425/share).

in the sense of cost synergies. Cost synergies were not the main reasons for the deal but rather strategic synergies: Kulmbacher wanted to strengthen their regional strategy, now protecting the Chemnitz-Würzburg axis even more. What is more, Würzburger saw better opportunities of operating independently within the Kulmbach network due to recent market trends and the principle shareholder von Finck aimed to fulfill his responsibility concerning the continuing existence of the brewery, as well considering the employees of Würzburger. On top of that, there had only been two bidders for the take-over deal, Kulmbacher Brauerei AG and Radeberger Brauholding.[46] The two companies had calculated a similar enterprise value for Würzburger Hofbräu AG. In the end, Kulmbacher convinced the major shareholder.

As already mentioned briefly, a key reason why the transaction price was relatively low was the seller's interests. The von Finck family held 90.7 % over 100 years and was interested in the continuing existence of the brewery and the brand. The von Finck family did want to sell the control of the Würzburger Hofbräu AG. They had been looking for a strategic investor for a couple of years. It was also a precondition for them that not a single employee would be laid off. In total, Würzburger Hofbräu AG will remain independent in terms of their company policy, decisions and actions. Or to summarize and to put it with the words of Reinhard Meier, CEO Würzburger Hofbräu AG: "Everything stays the same except for one change: the shares of Mr. August von Finck will be transferred to the new principal shareholder, the Kulmbacher Brauerei AG."[47]

7 Conclusion

The Kulmbacher Brauerei AG now owns 96,835 shares of Würzburger Hofbräu AG which corresponds to 96.84 % of the equity and voting rights of Würzburger.[48] The Kulmbacher Brauerei AG will take control of the board of Würzburger Hofbräu. Nevertheless, Würzburger Hofbräu will widely remain independent within the Kulmbacher network.

---

[46] Cf. Kallmeyer (2005).
[47] Cf. Würzburger Hofbräu AG (2005a).
[48] Cf. Kulmbacher Brauerei AG (2005b).

The case is a good example of a take-over transaction in the German beer industry. It was mainly driven by a strategy of the acquirer to lock the current core market and to open up possibilities to expand into the west of Germany. Unlike in most other such transactions, synergies did not play an overriding role for the acquirer. Therefore, Würzburger will neither be broken up nor will be any employees laid off. In conclusion, the regional strategy will be further pushed by Kulmbacher including the new subsidiary. The expansion strategy will now take place from a reinforced Chemnitz-Würzburg axis.

Furthermore, it was found out that the target company had a pressure to find a strong partner in a vastly changing and consolidating market. After a year long search, the von Finck family and Würzburger Hofbräu AG finally found a strong and potent partner, able and willing to secure the long-term success of the brewery in a very dynamic market environment. For the future it is anticipated that the consolidation in the German beer market will continue, and international players like Heineken will continue to try and find their way into this very lucrative market.

References

BaFin (2005): www.bafin.de.

Belz, Franz-Martin (2005): Past, Present and Future of the German Brewing Industry; Presentation at the Institute for Brewing and Distilling, Centenary Video Link Conference, January 12th, 2005, Technische Universität München.

Bundeskartellamt (2005): <http:www.bundeskartellamt.de>.

Deutscher Brauer Bund (2005): http://www.brauer-bund.de/index1.html.

Kallmeyer, Ulrich (2005): Speech at the discussion forum with the European Business School Radeberger Brauholding, May 30th, 2005, Frankfurt.

Kulmbacher Brauerei AG (2004): Geschäftsbericht 2004, Kulmbacher Brauerei Aktien-Gesellschaft, Kulmbach.

Kulmbacher Brauerei AG (2005a): Angebotsunterlage – Öffentliches Kaufangebot (Pflichtangebot) der Kulmbacher Brauerei AG an die Aktionäre der Würzburger Hofbräu AG, Kulmbach.

Kulmbacher Brauerei AG (2005b): Press Release May 31st, 2005, Kulmbach.

Kulmbacher Brauerei AG (2005c): <http://www.kulmbacher.de/de/klbag/001/002/001_002_ ueberuns_geschichte.php>.

Kulmbacher Brauerei AG (2005d): < http://www.kulmbacher.de/de/klbag/001/004/001_004_ ueberuns_gruppe.php>.

Kulmbacher Brauerei AG (2005e): http://www.kulmbacher.de/de/klbag/003/003/003_003_ ueberuns_gruppenstruktur.php.

Kulmbacher Brauerei AG (2005e): <http://www.kulmbacher.de/de/cms/newsDownload/ 101/Presse-Information_KBAG.pdf>.

Würzburger Hofbräu AG (2002): Geschäftsbericht über das Geschäftsjahr 2003/2004, Würzburg.

Würzburger Hofbräu AG (2003): Geschäftsbericht über das Geschäftsjahr 2003/2004, Würzburg.

Würzburger Hofbräu AG (2004): Geschäftsbericht über das Geschäftsjahr 2003/2004, Würzburg.

Würzburger Hofbräu AG (2005a): Press release of January 21st, 2005, <http:www.wuerzburger-hofbraeu.de/wueho/aktuell/news/art56,313.html>.

Würzburger Hofbräu AG (2005b): Gemeinsame Stellungnahme nach §§ 39, 27 Abs. 1 WpÜG des Vorstands und des Aufsichtsrats der Würzburger Hofbräu AG zum Pflichtangebot der Kulbacher Brauerei AG, Kulmbach an die Aktionäre der Würzburger Hofbräu AG, Würzburg zum Erwerb ihrer Aktien an der Würzburger Hofbräu AG. <http://www.kulmbacher.de/ de/klbag/files/Gemeinsame_Stellungnahme_Vorstand_und_Aufsichtsrat.pdf >.

Würzburger Hofbräu AG (2005c): <http://www.wuerzburger-hofbraeu.de/start/ ?fCMS=71e138da0d264421cda73013b5b49f48>.

Würzburger Hofbräu AG (2005d): <http://www.wuerzburger-hofbraeu.de/wueho/aktuell/ news/art56,313.html>.

Würzburger Hofbräu AG (2005e): <http://www.wuerzburger-hofbraeu.de/wueho/brauerei/ chronik/index.html>.

Würzburger Hofbräu AG (2005f): <http://www.wuerzburger-hofbraeu.de/start/>.

D Short and Long Term Performance of M&A Activities in the German Brewing Industry

I M&A Announcement Effects on Bidders in the German Brewing Industry

by

Florian Geiger and Tobias Roediger

1 Introduction

1.1 Objective of the Study

Historically, most breweries in Germany have been small, family-owned businesses serving mainly regional areas. Still in 2003, 1,268 of the 1,801 independent breweries in EU member countries were situated in Germany (> 85%), compared with 16 in France and 61 in Great Britain.[1] In recent years the German beer industry has changed drastically. Germany, as the third-largest market by volume in the world, is an important and attractive beer market.[2] However, during the last decade the beer consumption in Germany has decreased steadily. Mainly through the population age profile and lifestyle changes (e.g. shift from beer to wine) it is expected that until 2015 the German beer market will decrease down to further 30% in volume.[3] As a result breweries in Germany are consolidating in order to improve their market position as well as allow for collectively addressing pricing and the rational closure of excess capacity. In this context, merger and acquisition (M&A) activities allow for consolidation-induced profitability improvements through taking advantage of reduced administration costs, economies of scale, increased pricing power, distribution benefits and cross-selling of brands.[4] Between 1999 and 2002 around 30% of ownership of the market (by volume) changed hands via M&A in Germany, leading to an increased share of the top 10 players from 46% to

[1] Cf. Deutscher Brauer Bund (2003).
[2] Cf. CSFB (2003), p. 3.
[3] Cf. Ernst&Young (2003).
[4] Cf. CSFB (2003), p. 22; Hall (1979), p. 32.

65%.[5] However, empirical studies show that announced synergy levels of mergers could not have been realised in many instances.[6] In this context, this study examines the M&A announcement effects on bidders in Germany by examining the market valuation of M&A activities in the German brewing market. Although sufficient literature exists about general announcement effects of acquirers in many industries, the German brewing industry has not been analysed before. With regard to the strong consolidation activity in the German brewing market it seems important to examine this ongoing trend. Using event study methodology, capital market reactions to transaction announcements are empirically tested.

1.2 Course of Analysis

In the context of this research an event study is carried out in order to derive an understanding of the M&A announcement effects on bidders in Germany. In order to build a basis for further analysis a theoretical background is given in the first place. A literature review is provided in order to give valuable insights about general announcement effects of M&A (Section 2). Section 3 characterises the empirical part of the analysis and presents the event study analysis, covering M&A announcements between 1989 and 2004. In a first step the theoretical findings are analysed and hypotheses to be tested in the event study are derived (Section 3.1). After an introduction of the procedure and methodology of the analysis (Section 3.2), the data base selection criterion (Section 3.3) are explained. In Section 3.4 the results of the event study are presented. In this context, a sub-sample analysis (3.4.2) and a multivariate regression (3.4.3) are used to examine in depth the impacts of different parameters on the announcement effects of acquiring firms. In Section 3.5 the hypotheses derived in the theoretical part of this paper are compared to the empirical findings in order to derive general, applicable patterns for the impact of M&A announcements on the shareholder value of acquiring companies in the German brewing industry. The paper finishes with a conclusion and gives an outlook about the implications for further research in Section 4.

---

[5] Cf. CSFB (2003), p. 21.
[6] Cf. Tremblay / Tremblay (1988), p. 33 for US comparison.

2 Review of Literature

The existing literature on announcement effects of bidding companies is quite voluminous. The following literature therefore does not constitute a numeration of every existing paper, but a summary of the most important ones. This should be considered sufficient to derive a general understanding about the view literature holds on the effects of M&A announcement on the share price of bidding companies.

The literature on M&A agrees on the fact that shareholders of target companies benefit the most from M&A transactions and receive far higher premiums than acquirer shareholders. Indeed, the literature review on bidder effects shows that there is an ambiguous view of the impact of M&A announcements. Some studies find positive reactions to announcements while others find negative ones. On the one hand, Jarell / Poulsen examine shareholder wealth effects for acquiring companies and observe significant positive abnormal returns for a data sample of 450 tender offers between 1963-1986.[7] The same results are obtained by Kohers / Kohers for acquirers of high-tech targets, regardless of whether the acquisition is financed with stock or with cash.[8] Fuller / Netter / Stegemoller also observe positive abnormal returns. However, they find that target characteristics, especially their old ownership (public, private) influence the announcement effects on bidding companies.[9] For Germany there are only few representative studies. A study from Gerke / Garz / Oerke in 1995 analyses take-over premiums of German companies from 1987-1992. They find that the target experiences significant average abnormal returns of 2.2% over a [-1;1][10] event window while bidding companies do not reap significant abnormal returns. However, if the target is an east German company, the bidding company generates significant positive abnormal returns.[11] One of the very few studies that focus on the M&A activities within the brewing sector is conducted by Franks / Broyles / Hecht. Focusing on the brewing industry in the UK they find positive stock price reactions around the announcement date.

[7] Cf. Jarell / Poulsen (1989), pp. 12-13.
[8] Cf. Kohers / Kohers (2000), p. 40.
[9] Cf. Fuller / Netter / Stegemoller (2002), pp. 1763-1993.
[10] In the course of this study a time window will be expressed in the form $[t_0;t_1]$.
[11] Cf. Gerke / Garz / Oerke (1995), pp. 811-819.

Furthermore, their study shows that the market seems to anticipate mergers at least three months prior to the announcement date.[12]

On the other hand, some event studies observe negative abnormal returns after M&A announcements. A negative interpretation by the stock market is found by Andrade / Mitchell / Stafford with negative returns of -0.7% for a event window of [-1;1] and a data sample of 3,688 mergers from 1973-1998.[13] Furthermore, especially many long-term event studies find negative stock performances of acquiring companies. Agraval / Jaffe / Mandelker, for instance, analyse over 1,000 US transactions between 1955 and 1987. They focus on the abnormal returns of acquirers spanning a time frame of 5 years beginning with the announcement date. They find a negative performance of -10% for the acquiring firms.[14] However, this study focuses primarily on the short-term impact and the announcement effect itself. Therefore, long-term event studies are not in the focus of this paper.

3 Empirical Analysis

3.1 Derivation of Hypotheses

A comparison of research in the field of abnormal acquirer leads to ambiguous findings. A clear effect for the share price of the acquiring firm seems not deductible. It seems that industry specific characteristics and general market conditions influence the stock price reactions to M&A announcements. The most comparable study was undertaken by Franks / Broyles / Hecht who find positive abnormal returns for the UK brewing industry.[15] Furthermore, a general hypothesis on acquirer abnormal returns is given by Mandelker with the perfectly competitive acquisition market hypothesis.[16] Following this theory, the competition among acquiring firms will cause the value of expected benefits from merging to be paid to the shareholders of the firm being acquired. As a consequence, no abnormal returns

[12] Cf. Franks / Broyles / Hecht (2001), pp. 1522-1525.
[13] Cf. Andrade / Mitchell / Stafford (2001), p. 110.
[14] Cf. Agraval / Jaffe / Mandelker (1992), pp. 1605-1622.
[15] Cf. Franks / Broyles / Hecht (2001), pp. 1522-1525.
[16] Cf. Mandelker (1974), pp. 303-335.

or (as empirical evidence on the UK brewing industry showed) only small positive abnormal returns can be expected.[17]

Hypothesis I: As a reaction to M&A announcements, bidders experience no or only slight positive share price effects in the German brewing industry.

After deriving a general understanding of the capital market reaction to M&A announcements on bidders in the German brewing industry the analysis goes more into detail. In order to understand the market valuation the following hypotheses are formulated. This displays what parameters of the transactions are rewarded by capital markets positively and which are not.

In the introduction of this paper it was shown that the primary reasons for M&A in the brewing industry seem to be reduced administration costs, economies of scale, increased pricing power, distribution benefits and crossselling of brands. Those advantages appear to be correlated to the size of the target and of the acquirer. In this context, both the size of the acquiring firm and the value of the target company can be a factor that influences abnormal returns. It seems especially interesting to analyse how the relative size of the acquirer to the target influences abnormal returns of the acquirer. This allows deriving an understanding of whether capital markets reward a "merger of equals" more than smaller acquisitions. However, it does not seem clear in which direction and to what extend this parameter influences the abnormal returns of the bidding company. On the one hand, the risk of integration rises when both companies are similar in size. On the other hand, positive effects like higher scale advantages, better growth opportunities and a better market position could be realised more easily. As a result, these two effects are expected to cancel each other out.

Hypothesis II: There is no relationship between the relative market value of the bidder to the target and abnormal returns.

---

[17] For an overview of the hypotheses and their criterion, see appendix 1 on page 20.

After analysing size effects of the acquirers and the target companies it is important to examine the business situation. In order to analyse the performance of the companies involved, this paper uses the market-to-book value of the respective companies. The market-to-book value is the market evaluation of the company's assets and its efficiency to use those assets. This serves as a basis for profitability, growth, dividends and other factors that influence the value of a company.[18]

Looking at the performance of the acquiring firm, this paper postulates that a higher performance (higher market-to-book value) should implicate higher abnormal returns. This should be the case since the acquiring company could apply its efficient use of assets to the target company. Through know-how and technology transfer potential synergy effects can be expected to be higher. Furthermore, a higher valuation shows more trust of capital markets in the business model and management of the bidding company. This should lead to higher abnormal returns.

Hypothesis III: The better the performance of the acquiring firm, the higher the abnormal returns should be.

In a normal M&A transaction one of the main value drivers is the profitability and performance of the target company. Similarly, capital markets should weigh an acquisition of a well performing target higher than the acquisition of a badly performing target. For the analysis the market-to-book value and also the EBITDA/Sales margin is used to describe the performance of the target company.

Hypothesis IV: A better performance of the target firm should yield higher abnormal returns.

Cross-border acquisitions allow companies to enter new markets by directly acquiring market shares. As a result the strategic implication of a cross-border acquisition can be higher. Market reactions to cross-border M&A are often very different from those of domestic M&A.[19] As a consequence higher wealth creation ef-

[18] Cf. Block (1995), p. 63

[19] Cf. Kaplan / Weisbach (1992), pp. 107-138.

fects for acquiring firms are detected.[20] Based on these results, hypothesis V states that cross-border M&A should yield higher returns than domestic M&A.[21] In order to test this hypothesis, a dummy variable is used. This variable is set to be 1 if the M&A transaction is a cross-border transaction and 0 if it is a domestic German transaction.

Hypothesis V: Cross-border M&A should yield higher abnormal returns than domestic M&A.

3.2 Event Study Approach

The effects of events on share prices are analysed in event studies. Such a study is based on real market data and requires markets to be semi-strongly efficient, meaning that all available public information is taken into account by the market.[22] Further, new information is priced into the share price immediately.[23]

3.2.1 Methodology

Abnormal returns describe the difference between the expected return and the actual return observed in the market.[24] In event studies, two different periods are distinguished: The estimation or regression period, in which the expected return is calculated and the event period or event window, in which abnormal returns are calculated and interpreted. The estimation period in this study is chosen to be the 200 days in the period [-220;-21], while the primary event window is set to be the period [-1; 0]. Apart from [-1;0], other event windows are observed as well in order to compare different reactions of capital markets with regard to abnormal returns. As a matter of fact, the bigger the event window chosen, the more information is incorporated. However, apart from more relevant information, there is also more that distorts the results. In this study, the primary event window [-1;0] is chosen, as the most significant abnormal returns can be observed in this period.

---

[20] Cf. Markides / Ittner (1994), pp. 343-367; Harris / Ravenscraft (1991), pp. 825-844.
[21] For further information on cross-border M&A see for example Shimizu et al. (2004), pp. 307-353.
[22] Cf. Ross / Westerfield / Jaffe (2002), p. 246.
[23] Cf. MacKinlay (1997), p. 13.
[24] Cf. MacKinlay (1997), p. 18.

In contrast to the actual share price, the expected return of a stock cannot be directly observed in the market. There are basically three different models that help to calculate the expected return: The mean adjusted return method, the market adjusted return method and the market model. The mean adjusted return method takes the mean return of the share price during the estimation period as the expected return. The market adjusted return method, on the other hand, takes the market return during the estimation period as the expected return. The market model bases the calculation of the expected return on the CAPM and is expressed by the following formula[25]

Formula 1

$$R_{it} = \alpha_i + \beta_i \cdot R_{mt} + \varepsilon_{it} \qquad E(\varepsilon_{it}) = 0$$

where R_{it} is the return of stock i in period t, α_i the constant return component of stock i, β_i the dependence of stock i on the market portfolio return, R_{mt} the return of the market portfolio in period t, ε_{it} the residual of stock i in period t and $E(\varepsilon_{it})$ the expected residual ε_{it}.[26] Although all three models yield similar results, in this study the market model is the method of choice, since it has several advantages over the other two models. Firstly, it is better suited when looking at daily returns.[27] Secondly, the market model takes into account the individual betas of the stocks and is therefore more accurate when calculating the expected returns. The abnormal return is then derived by rearranging formula 1 to

Formula 2

$$AR_{it} = R_{it} - [\alpha_i + \beta_i \cdot R_{mt}]$$

where AR_{it} is the abnormal return of stock i in period t. The market portfolio in this study is the German M-DAX, as this return most likely reflects the market setting of German breweries. Further, not individual abnormal returns, but cumulative average abnormal returns (CAARs) are looked at in this study. The abnormal re-

---

[25] Cf. Weston / Mitchell / Mulherin (2004), p. 152.
[26] Cf. MacKinlay (1997), p. 18.
[27] Cf. Dyckman / Philbrick / Stephan (1984), pp. 28f.

turns of the individual stocks derived by formula 1 have to be added up in a first step, so that

Formula 3

$$CAR_i = \sum_{t=1}^{T} AR_{it}$$,

where CAR_i is the cumulative abnormal return of stock i in the event window and T the number of days in the event window.[28] In order to cumulate the abnormal returns, the discrete share and market portfolio returns have to be transformed into continuous returns by taking the logarithms.[29] This leads to more accurate results when using linear regression models such as the market model.[30] In a second step, the average of the CARs of the different stocks (transformed back into discrete returns) is used to calculate the CAAR. This step is described by

Formula 4

$$CAAR = \frac{1}{N}\sum_{i=1}^{N} CAR_i$$,

where N is the number of events analysed.[31]

After having calculated the CAAR, the hypotheses are tested in two different ways. Firstly, subsamples are formed. Hypotheses described by a dummy variable are divided into two groups. Then the CAARs of these two groups are compared to each other in order to examine if there is a difference in the CAARs. Hypotheses described by variables that do not have the nature of a dummy are also tested by forming two groups. One group consists of testing variables below the median of this variable, whereas the other group consists of testing variables above the median. In order to verify the subsample analysis, each variable is regressed against the CARs in [-1;0] in addition. Secondly, a multivariate regression analysis is con-

[28] Cf. Dodd / Warner (1983), p. 413.
[29] Cf. Patell (1976), p. 253.
[30] Cf. Fama et al. (1969), p. 4.
[31] Cf. Dodd / Warner (1983), p. 413.

ducted in order to explain the actual influence of each testing variable on the CARs of the stocks in the event window [-1;0].

3.2.2 Tests for Statistical Significance

In order to test the significance of the results, a standard two-tailed t-test is used in most of the cases.[32] When testing the significance of the CAAR in a specific event window, the modified t-test of Dodd / Warner is used in addition.[33] The p-value of the tests, which describes the probability of the true value of the tested parameter to be actually zero, is classified into the levels 1%, 5% and 10%.[34] This study defines the 1% level as being highly significant, the 5% level as being significant and the 10% level as being little significant. When analysing the subsamples, the Wilcoxon rank test is used in addition to the two-tailed t-test. In contrast to the parametric t-test, the Wilcoxon test does not require the sample to be normally distributed, and thus can also be applied to samples that are quite small.[35]

3.3 Data Selection

3.3.1 Data Base Selection Criteria

The M&A transactions used in this study include all European M&A transactions involving a brewery between January 1st, 1980 and March 16th, 2005 where the target of the M&A transaction is a German company. The acquirer, on the other hand, can be a foreign company. Taking these criteria into account, 243 transactions can be found. From this original data sample, 50 transactions have to be eliminated because the bidders are engaged in other industries than beverages. For further 127 transactions, the bidders are not listed or no market information is available on Datastream, the database from which the financial information for the companies involved is collected from. The remaining sample is analysed in this study consists of 66 brewery transactions. The relevant event date is the an-

---

[32] $t-value = \frac{CAAR \cdot \sqrt{N}}{\sigma(CAAR)}$, with σ(CAAR) being the standard deviation of the cumulative abnormal returns of the event window.

[33] Cf. Dodd / Warner (1983), pp. 436f.

[34] Cf. Bayless (1994), p. 124.

[35] Cf. Wilcoxon (1945), pp. 80f.

nouncement date of the deal. In the cases, in which the announcement date lies on a non-trading date the following trading date is taken as the event date.

3.3.2 Characteristics of the Data Sample

The events analysed in this study take place between 1989 and 2005.[36] Chart 1 documents the distribution of the sample over this period, showing there was much hype between 1991 and 1994 and in 2003.

Chart 1: Overview over the distribution of the transactions over time

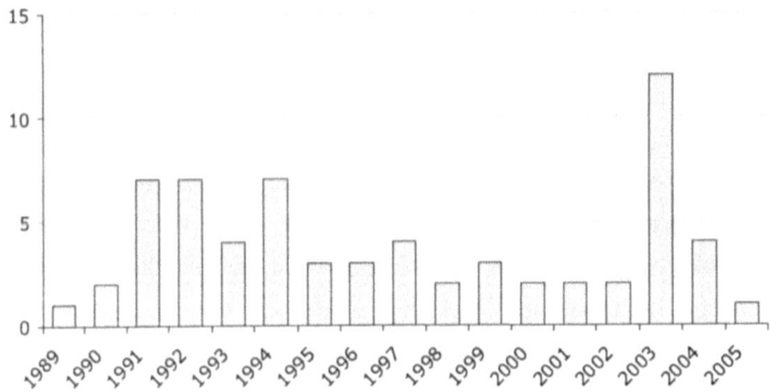

Of these 66 transactions 50 are purely national transactions. Within the remaining 16 transactions, 4 involve Belgian bidders, 3 Danish bidders, 3 Japanese bidders and 3 Dutch bidders. These transactions are referred to as cross-border transactions. The acquirers in our sample are considerably bigger than the targets that they acquire. While the bidders have an average market value of € 1.88bn, the targets only have an average market value of € 299m. Further, the average market-to-book value of the bidders is at 3.59 compared to 2.56 much higher than those of the targets. However, specific deal information such as transaction prices is unfortunately not available for the majority of events, so that this study has to cope with the information available from Datastream. It is worthwhile mentioning that most of the shares of the bidders cannot be considered to be very liquid. Of the 66 M&A

[36] For a list of all events with important variables see appendix 3.

transactions, 17 are not traded between 10% and 20% of the time in the estimation period, 25 are not traded between 20% and 50% and 20 are not traded in over 50% of the time. In fact, only shares of companies of 4 transactions are traded more than 90% of the time. Brown / Warner recognise this fact as being a problem for studies using daily share prices. However, they state that although the beta of illiquid shares is calculated to be too low in these cases, this is compensated by a higher alpha. They conclude that this effect can be neglected and that other models, which take this effect into account, do not yield better results.[37]

3.4 Discussion of Results

3.4.1 Cumulative Average Abnormal Returns

In the majority of event windows looked at, the CAARs are positive. However, only 2 CAARs, which are positive, show appropriate significance levels of 5% and 1% with the modified t-test of Dodd / Warner. The normal two-tailed t-test, on the other hand, does not show enough significance for any of the 4 event windows documented in Table 1. The different event windows show that the smaller the event window chosen, the higher the CAAR is. In addition, the significance level rises as the event window becomes smaller. The higher significance levels observed with the Dodd-Warner t-test may be a result of the lower volatility of share prices during the estimation period. In contrast to Dodd / Warner, the normal two-tailed t-test is based on the volatility of the CARs of the different events and not on the volatility of share prices during the estimation period. As the shares of the bidding companies in this study are not very liquid, the low volatility may thus be a major driver of the higher significance levels of the Dodd-Warner t-test.

Table 1: Statistics of the Cumulative Abnormal Returns

Event Window	Mean	Median	Standard Deviation	Two-tailed t-Test t-value	Two-tailed t-Test p-value	t-Test after Dodd/Warner t-value	t-Test after Dodd/Warner p-value
[-10;10]	0.05%	-0.15%	5.05%	0.081	0.468	0.197	0.422
[-5;5]	-0.03%	-0.13%	4.75%	-0.058	0.477	0.797	0.213
[-1;1]	0.42%	0.03%	2.88%	1.188	0.117	1.931	0.027
[-1;0]	0.62%	-0.03%	4.12%	1.230	0.109	3.091	0.001

[37] Cf. Dyckman / Philbrick / Stephan (1984), p. 29; Brown / Warner (1985), p. 16-18.

This study chooses the even window [-1;0] as the primary event window for all further analyses, as this window shows the highest significance level and also the biggest CAAR of all the event windows examined.[38] Furthermore, the event window [-1;0] seems a logical choice, since it describes the very day of the announcement while taking into account that the announcement might have been published one day after the actual announcement. Thus, movements one day before the published announcements might have taken place. Chart 2 displays the movements of the cumulative average abnormal returns.

Chart 2: Cumulative Average Abnormal Returns in the Window [-20;20]

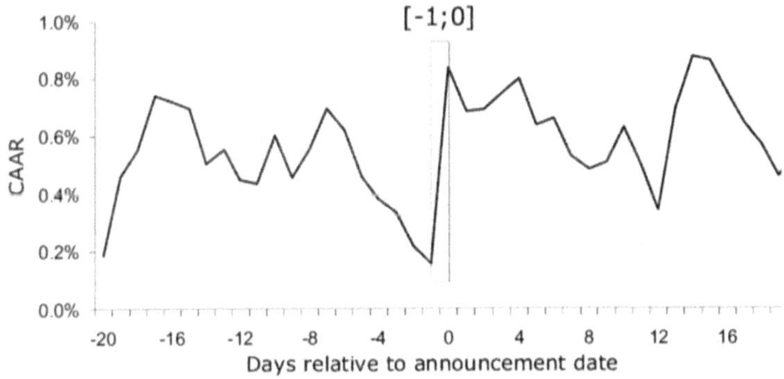

With 0.78%, Danish bidders experience the highest CAAR, followed by Japanese bidders (0.51%), UK bidders (0.22%) and Belgian bidders (0.20%). German and Dutch bidders have negative CAARs (-0.05% and -0.25% respectively).[39] However, the different reactions in the different countries can only be considered as tendencies because the samples are too small to yield stable results. Thus, it is also not appropriate to calculate significances.

---

[38] For a distribution of the CARs in the event window [-1;0] see Appendix 2.

[39] For an overview of the statistics about the countries analysed see Appendix 4.

3.4.2 Comparison of Subsamples

The higher the relation of the market value of the acquirer to the market value of the target company, the smaller is the positive abnormal return of the shares in the event period [-1;0]. However, hypothesis II can be confirmed as the result lacks significance with both the Wilcoxon test and the two-tailed t-test. Thus, as Table 2 shows, no stable relationship can be observed.

Table 2: Subsample Comparison Based on the Criterion "Market Value Acquirer/Market Value Target"

	CARs in [-1;0]				Wilcoxon-Test		t-Test	
	No.	Mean	Median	Standard Deviation	Z-value	p-value	t-value	p-value
Sample > Median	9	0.12%	0.20%	0.38%	-1.64	0.10	0.51	0.62
Sample < Median	9	0.43%	-0.04%	1.81%				

The market-to-book value of the acquirer can also not be significantly linked to the abnormal returns experienced at the announcement of a M&A transaction. However, acquirers with a smaller than median market-to-book value in our sample have a higher CAAR (1.77%) than those acquirers with a higher than median market-to-book value (0.00%). The latter companies do not seem to be affected at all by the market-to-book value. Thus, the results do not support hypothesis III, as documented in Table 3. 21 companies are unaccounted for in this subsample comparison as no market-to-book data is available.

Table 3: Subsample Comparison Based on the Criterion "Market-to-Book Value Acquirer"

	CARs in [-1;0]				Wilcoxon-Test		t-Test	
	No.	Mean	Median	Standard Deviation	Z-value	p-value	t-value	p-value
Sample > Median	24	0.00%	-0.03%	2.99%	-0.32	0.75	1.21	0.23
Sample < Median	21	1.77%	0.01%	6.39%				

The results of the comparison of subsamples concerning the performance of target companies are based on 12 and 18 events as required data is not available in some cases. Thus, the results concerning the characteristics of the target companies are less convincing than the results concerning the characteristics of the acquirers. The reason for this is that the target companies are on average much smaller than the acquirers and are most often not listed nor covered by information providers such as Datastream. The available data shows that a lower market-to-book value and a lower EBITDA/Sales number of the target company is related to a higher abnormal return of the share of the acquirer. However, all the results with regard to the target company characteristics lack significance as displayed in Table 4. All in all, the results do not support hypothesis IV.

Table 4: Subsample Comparisons Based on the Criterion "Market-to-Book Value Target" and "EBITDA/Sales Target"

	CARs in [-1;0]				Wilcoxon-Test		t-Test	
	No.	Mean	Median	Standard Deviation	Z-value	p-value	t-value	p-value
Market to Book Value Target > Median	9	0.12%	0.20%	0.40%	-1.24	0.21	0.51	0.62
Market to Book Value Target < Median	9	0.43%	-0.04%	1.80%				
EBITDA/Sales > Median	6	-0.04%	0.08%	0.42%	-0.33	0.74	1.02	0.33
EBITDA/Sales < Median	6	0.86%	0.12%	2.12%				

Finally, the analysis of the influence of the nationality of the bidding company shows that domestic acquisitions yield a higher positive abnormal return than cross-border acquisitions. Table 5 documents, however, that these results are also not significant. Like hypothesis III and IV, the results of the subsample analysis do not support hypothesis V.

Table 5: Subsample Comparison Based on the Criterion "Nationality of Acquirer"

	CARs in [-1;0]				Wilcoxon-Test		t-Test	
	No.	Mean	Median	Standard Deviation	Z-value	p-value	t-value	p-value
Foreign brewery as acquirer	16	0.13%	0.20%	0.52%	-1.24	0.21	0.55	0.59
German brewery as acquirer	50	0.78%	-0.04%	4.73%				

As the period of acquisition might also be of importance, an additional subsample analysis is conducted. One subsample includes all transactions of and before 1996 and the other subsample includes all transactions after 1996. The results show that the events after 1996 have a much higher CAAR than the events in and before1996. Table 6 documents that these results are significant on a 10% level when looking at the two-tailed t-test.

Table 6: Subsample Comparison Based on the Criterion "Period of Acquisition"

	CARs in [-1;0]				Wilcoxon-Test		t-Test	
	No.	Mean	Median	Standard Deviation	Z-value	p-value	t-value	p-value
Events after 1996	32	1.62%	0.03%	5.46%	-1.04	0.30	-1.89	0.07
Events 1996 and before	34	-0.31%	-0.04%	1.91%				

In order to complement the results of the subsample comparison, Table 7 shows the individual regressions of the variables of each criterion against the CARs in the event window [-1;0]. Except for hypothesis IV, the regression analysis confirms the results of the subsample analysis.

Table 7: Regression of Individual Variables Against the CARs of the Window [-1;0]

	(1)	(2)	(3)	(4)	(5)
Intercept	0.6421	2.0061	0.6140	0.7932	-0.3102
	(0.62)	*(1.75)*	*(0.38)*	*(1.33)*	*(-0.44)*
Market Value Acquirer/ Market Value Target	-0.0002				
	(-0.06)				
Market-to-Book Value of Acquirer		-0.3838			
		(-1.38)			
Market-to-Book Value of Target Company			0.0041		
			(0.01)		
Crossborder Acquisition Dummy				-0.6744	
				(-0.56)	
Period of Acquisition Dummy					1.9281
					*(1.94)**
Adjusted R^2	-0.06	0.02	-0.06	-0.01	0.04
F Value	0.00	1.91	0.00	0.32	3.76
Durbin-Watson Value	2.04	2.05	2.04	1.88	1.94

t-values are in parentheses
Significance levels: *10% **5% ***1%

3.4.3 Multivariate Regression

The multivariate regression is conducted in order to further analyse the influence of the hypothesis criterion on the abnormal returns in direction and strength. The dependent variable are the CARs in the event window [-1;0] while the independent variables are the hypothesis variables and some control variables. The results of the regressions are displayed in Table 8. The "variance inflation factor (VIF)" is below 2 for almost all factors except for the "market value of the target company" and the "variance of returns" variables. The VIF for these two variables is around 5. The VIF describes the impact of collinearity of independent variables on the increase of the variance and indicates in this case that there might be a minor problem with collinearity with the two variables just mentioned.[40] Further, the Durbin-Watson-test displays values that range from 2.68 to 2.91, depending on the model looked at. This might be an indication for muticollinearity and autocorrelation in these

[40] Cf. Craney / Surles (2002), p. 392.

models, although the value for model 6 is at the boundary of being fine.[41] Apart from the variables analysed in the subsamples, several control variables are included in the multivariate regression. These variables are the market value of the target company and the acquirer, the buy-and-hold abnormal return in the estimation period of the acquirer and the variance of returns in the estimation period of the acquirer. The influences of the independent variables on the dependent variable have the same direction as in the subsample analysis for hypothesis III and V. However, the variables for hypothesis II and IV have the opposite directions than in the subsample analysis. This reflects the influence of the low significance levels observed in the subsample analysis and the multivariate regression. However, model 6, which best meets statistical requirements, rejects hypothesis III at a significance level of 5%. The higher the market-to-book value of the acquirer, the lower is the abnormal return in period [-1;0]. The control variables also indicate that the market value of the target company is significantly and negatively related to the dependent variable, whereas the variance of returns in the estimation period of the acquirer is positively related to the dependent variable.

Table 8: Multivariate Regression with the CARs of the Window [-1;0] as Dependent Variable

	(1)	(2)	(3)	(4)	(5)	(6)	(7)
Intercept	5.2523 *(0.85)*	5.2865 *(1.05)*	5.5675 *(1.49)*	5.5413 *(1.66)*	5.6784 *(1.85)*	4.6766 *(1.73)*	6.3055 *(2.31)***
Market Value Acquirer/ Market Value Target	0.0004 *(0.06)*						
Market Value of Acquirer (in € mm)	-0.0001 *(-0.10)*	-0.0001 *(-0.11)*					
Buy-and-Hold Abnormal Return in Estimation Period of Acquirer	0.0061 *(0.11)*	0.0056 *(0.12)*	0.0055 *(0.14)*				
Period of Acquisition Dummy	0.6536 *(0.14)*	0.7299 *(0.20)*	0.7244 *(0.23)*	0.9501 *(0.39)*			
Crossborder Acquisition Dummy	-1.4103 *(-0.19)*	-1.4498 *(-0.24)*	-1.9754 *(-0.65)*	-2.0558 *(-0.77)*	-1.8770 *(-0.77)*		
Market-to-Book Value of Target Company	1.0000 *(0.69)*	0.9692 *(0.88)*	0.9152 *(1.08)*	0.8632 *(1.27)*	0.9535 *(1.61)*	0.9097 *(1.60)*	
Market-to-Book Value of Acquirer	-1.7199 *(-1.33)*	-1.7113 *(-1.63)*	-1.7537 *(-2.08)*	-1.7118 *(-2.42)**	-1.7312 *(-2.65)***	-1.5808 *(-2.61)***	-1.4208 *(-2.18)**
Market Value of Target Company (in € mm)	-0.0189 *(-1.73)*	-0.0189 *(-2.12)*	-0.0187 *(-2.48)**	-0.0184 *(-2.83)***	-0.0187 *(-3.14)***	-0.0183 *(-3.18)***	-0.0137 *(-2.52)***
Variance of Returns in Estimation Period of Acquirer	131.4623 *(1.55)*	130.7009 *(1.91)*	129.0859 *(2.22)**	126.3454 *(2.58)***	132.5565 *(3.09)***	132.0501 *(3.18)***	97.1724 *(2.52)***
Adjusted R^2	-0.83	-0.22	0.08	0.26	0.37	0.40	0.29
F Value	0.45	0.75	1.14	1.65	2.27	2.86	2.48
Durbin-Watson Value	2.87	2.88	2.89	2.91	2.82	2.68	2.80

t-values are in parentheses
Significance levels: *10% **5% ***1%

[41] Cf. Durbin / Watson (1951), pp. 161f.; McClave / Benson / Sincich (2001), p. 798.

3.5 Implications

The acquiring companies experience a positive announcement effect of 0.62% in the event window [-1;0]. Thus, the market seems to honour a consolidation in the brewing industry in general. These findings are in line with the study of Franks / Broyles / Hecht who find a positive effect for the UK brewing industry.[42] Consolidation induced profitability improvements seem realizable through economies of scale, increased pricing power, distribution benefits, cross-selling of brands and reduced administration costs, for example.[43] However, there does not seem to be any relationship between the market value of the acquirer to the market value of the bidder and the announcement effects of M&A transactions on the stock market. Thus, each single transaction is evaluated independently, and general rules are not derivable in this context. Consolidations in the brewing industry appear to be so highly appreciated that the relative sizes of the transaction participants do not matter and are regarded as unimportant. With regard to the performance of the acquirer, a negative relationship to abnormal returns has been identified. This relationship is even significant in the multivariate regression analysis. The reason could be found in the fact that potential synergy effects are outweighed by the market's critical view on the future performance. The market seems to expect a dilution of the performance in this stagnating market. Most striking is the observation within the subsample analysis that the performance of the target company is negatively related to abnormal returns, even if not significantly. However, the multivariate regression shows a positive correlation with this variable to abnormal returns. Thus, the influence seems to be ambiguous. An explanation for the observation of a negative relationship might be that through the change in management hidden potentials in the low performing target firm are realizable and that performance will increase in the near future. Thus, current low performing target companies are connected with a higher abnormal return of the share prices of acquirers.

Another finding indicates that domestic M&A transactions are higher rewarded by capital markets than cross-border M&A deals. Contrary to other empirical findings,

[42] Cf. Franks / Broyles / Hecht (2001), pp. 1522-1525.
[43] Cf. CSFB (2003), p. 22.

there does not appear to be a wealth creation effect for foreign acquiring firms.[44] Rather, domestic transactions are favored by the market. Two effects might explain this observation. Firstly, domestic breweries are more familiar with the German market characteristics, while foreign investors could fail to be successful in this very fragmented market. Secondly, foreign breweries might follow other strategies than German breweries when acquiring a brewery in Germany. In this regard, domestic consolidation strategies are rewarded more highly by the market than market entry strategies or internationalization strategies of foreign acquirers. However, results are not significant enough to draw final conclusions. The significant higher abnormal returns in transactions after 1996, both in the subsample analysis and in the multivariate analysis, show that the importance of consolidation in the German brewing industry has grown over time. The multivariate regression further illustrates a significant relationship between the market value of the target company (negative correlation) and the variance of returns in the estimation period of the acquirer (positive correlation) with the announcement effect. These control variables thus explain part of the market reaction. Therefore, in contrast to the relative size of the target company, the absolute size of the target appears to influence the announcement effect. With regard to the variance, effects are higher, as volatile shares in general react harsher than less volatility shares.

4 Summary and Conclusion

The objective of this paper has been the analysis of announcement effects on the stock price of acquirers to M&A transactions in the German brewing industry.

The results show that acquirers are positively rewarded for buying German breweries (0.62%). While the market-to-book value of the bidding company (significantly) and cross-border acquisitions (insignificantly) are negatively related to abnormal returns, results for the market-to-book-value of the target company (insignificantly) and the relative size of the acquisitions (insignificantly) yield ambiguous results. Further, announcements for acquisitions after 1996 have higher positive abnormal returns than announcements for acquisitions in 1996 and before.

[44] Cf. Markides / Ittner (1994), pp. 343–367; Harris / Ravenscraft (1991), pp. 825–844.

The results seem to underline the importance of consolidations within the German brewing industry.

However, limiting facts of this study include the lack of detailed information about the transactions (e.g. transaction prices). Furthermore, many transactions had to be eliminated due to missing data. Nonetheless, this study should give a thorough view on general market reactions to M&A announcements in the German brewing industry. Future studies on this topic should include more variables, including detailed transaction information to yield more significant results.

Appendix

Appendix 1: Overview of hypotheses and their criteria

Hypothesis		Criteria	Expected Influence
H1	CAAR	CAAR	+/-
H2	Relative Size of Acquisition	Market Value of Acquirer / Market Value of Target	+/-
H3	Performance Acquirer	Market-to-Book Value Acquirer	+
H4	Performance Target	Market-to-Book Value Target and EBITDA/Sales Target	+
H5	Crossboarder Acquisition	Dummy Variable with 1 for Crossborder and 0 for Domestic Transaction	+

Appendix 2: Distribution of CARs in the event window [-1;0]

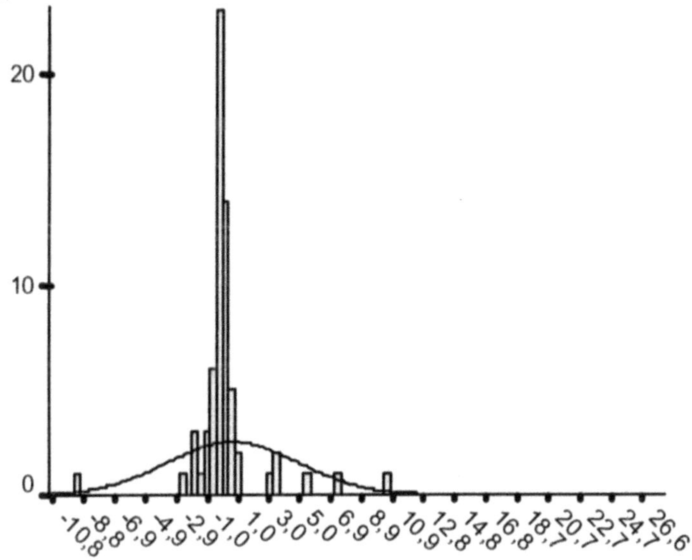

Appendix 3: List of all events with important variables

Acquirer	Announcement Date	Nation	CAR [-1;0]	Market Value Acquirer (in € mm)	Market Value Acquirer/Market Value Target	Market-to-Book Value Acquirer	Market-to-Book Value Target	EBITDA/ Sales Target	Crossborder Transaction	Market Value Target (in € mm)	Buy/Hold Abnormal Return Acquirer	Variance of Returns Acquirer
ALLGAEUER BRAUHAUS	2-Oct-2003	Germany	-0.12%	21.84		5.83			no		11.49%	0.40%
BAVARIA & ST.PAULI	29-May-1995	Germany	-0.17%	127.48					no		19.43%	0.02%
BAVARIA & ST.PAULI	24-Apr-1992	Germany	-0.72%	137.17					no		10.02%	0.01%
BERENTZEN-GRUPPE	3-Feb-2004	Germany	0.10%	24.19		0.56			no		-13.12%	0.09%
BRAU UND BRUNNEN	21-Aug-2003	Germany	0.61%	399.52		9.09			no		79.25%	0.05%
BRAU UND BRUNNEN	8-Jul-2003	Germany	-1.39%	377.52		8.59			no		124.57%	0.05%
BRAU UND BRUNNEN	27-Jan-2003	Germany	-0.25%	220.41		5.02			no		77.19%	0.04%
BRAU UND BRUNNEN	17-Jan-2003	Germany	-0.25%	220.86		5.03			no		76.45%	0.04%
BRAU UND BRUNNEN	29-Nov-2002	Germany	-0.47%	232.53		5.09			no		132.87%	0.04%
BRAU UND BRUNNEN	2-Jun-1995	Germany	0.10%	624.29		3.13			no		-25.03%	0.03%
BRAU UND BRUNNEN	28-Nov-1994	Germany	0.29%	559.75		4.34			no		-10.87%	0.03%
BRAU UND BRUNNEN	7-Mar-1994	Germany	0.38%	688.67	1.97	5.34	3.61	0.30	no	350.20	0.62%	0.02%
BRAU UND BRUNNEN	5-Jan-1994	Germany	-0.18%	727.27		5.64			no		1.83%	0.02%
BRAU UND BRUNNEN	26-Nov-1993	Germany	0.09%	693.30		5.16			no		0.61%	0.03%
BRAU UND BRUNNEN	5-Apr-1993	Germany	0.08%	540.44	11.26	4.02	0.00		no	48.00	-5.71%	0.05%
BRAU UND BRUNNEN	30-Mar-1992	Germany	-0.03%	668.60		4.98			no		-6.51%	0.04%
BRAU UND BRUNNEN	11-Jun-1991	Germany	-0.04%	753.52		5.37			no		-3.21%	0.05%
CARLSBERG	19-Apr-1999	Denmark	0.21%	1,191.05		1.88			yes		-22.62%	0.04%
CARLSBERG	21-Oct-2004	Denmark	0.46%	1,569.40	2.95	1.45	2.76		yes	532.40	-7.59%	0.02%
CARLSBERG	20-Jan-2004	Denmark	-0.83%	1,083.15	1.99	0.95	2.69		yes	518.37	-27.16%	0.03%
DINKELACKER BRAUEREI	2-Mar-1992	Germany	-9.20%	276.10		8.12			no		0.71%	0.01%
DINKELACKER BRAUEREI	17-Apr-1996	Germany	0.13%	213.98		6.21			no		-9.21%	0.04%
DOM-BRAUEREI	30-Jul-1998	Germany	-0.18%	24.38	1.00	1.99	1.99	0.19	no	24.38	-8.41%	0.02%
DORTMUND ACT-BRAUER	3-Jul-1996	Germany	-1.83%	44.54		2.54			no		-29.73%	0.01%
EINBECKER BRAUH.	23-Jun-2000	Germany	7.35%	39.98		3.13			no		-15.19%	0.10%
EINBECKER BRAUH.	26-Sep-1997	Germany	10.51%	58.90		3.58			no		-5.09%	0.01%
GBR.MAERZ	24-Nov-1992	Germany	0.04%	774.61				0.00	no		24.26%	0.01%
GBR.MAERZ	16-Jul-1992	Germany	-0.36%	883.51					no		32.52%	0.01%
GBR.MAERZ	6-Jul-1992	Germany	-0.04%	892.72				0.00	no		33.00%	0.01%
GBR.MAERZ	24-Oct-1991	Germany	-0.04%	685.64					no		4.26%	0.03%
GILDE BRAUEREI	30-Sep-1991	Germany	-1.82%	67.49		1.45			no		9.37%	0.01%
GROLSCH (KON.)	31-Jan-1991	Netherlands	-0.18%	219.19	1.49	2.4	0.00		yes	147.05	28.66%	0.01%
GROLSCH (KON.)	14-Dec-1990	Netherlands	-0.18%	217.14		1.74			yes		29.49%	0.01%

Appendix 3: continued

Acquirer	Announcement Date	Nation	CAR [-1;0]	Market Value Acquirer (in € mm)	Market Value Acquirer/Market Value Target	Market-to-Book Value Acquirer	Market-to-Book Value Target	EBITDA/ Sales Target	Crossborder Transaction	Market Value Target (in € mm)	Buy/Hold Abnormal Return Acquirer	Variance of Returns Acquirer
HEINEKEN	14-Feb-2001	Netherlands	-0.40%	19,943.94		7.23			yes		20.21%	0.04%
HEINEKEN	22-Apr-1997	United Kingdom	0.60%	7,328.86		3.16			yes		-49.98%	0.02%
HOLSTEN-BRAUEREI	31-Jan-2003	Germany	-0.04%	312.12		1.62			no		59.43%	0.06%
HOLSTEN-BRAUEREI	31-Jan-2001	Germany	-0.57%	325.87		2.85			no		71.21%	0.10%
HOLSTEN-BRAUEREI	18-Jan-2000	Germany	28.26%	275.00		2.09			no		14.84%	0.11%
HOLSTEN-BRAUEREI	19-Nov-1999	Germany	-0.40%	191.51	0.12	2.09	2.02	0.00	no	1,651.57	-4.62%	0.08%
HOLSTEN-BRAUEREI	20-Aug-1999	Germany	-0.03%	203.50		2.22			no		-8.08%	0.07%
HOLSTEN-BRAUEREI	11-Nov-1998	Germany	-0.98%	194.60		2.21			no		-10.49%	0.06%
HOLSTEN-BRAUEREI	8-Dec-1993	Germany	-0.14%	233.52		2.99			no		5.53%	0.03%
HOLSTEN-BRAUEREI	23-Jul-1991	Germany	-1.88%	209.22		3.69			no		-8.44%	0.02%
HOLSTEN-BRAUEREI	23-Apr-1991	Germany	0.75%	218.67		3.85			no		2.87%	0.04%
INTERBREW	18-Sep-2003	Belgium	0.20%	10,276.96	57.44		3.39	0.16	yes	178.92	-9.70%	0.00%
INTERBREW	1-Apr-2003	Belgium	0.20%	10,276.96	38.96		5.42	0.14	yes	263.77	4.99%	0.02%
INTERBREW	12-Feb-2003	Belgium	0.20%	10,276.96	1,300.88		1.30	0.92	yes	7.90	5.18%	0.02%
INTERBREW	26-Nov-2002	Belgium	0.20%	10,276.96	29.13		5.00	0.20	yes	352.80	3.41%	0.02%
ISENBECK	13-Jul-1994	Germany	3.31%	13.99					no		-49.02%	0.02%
KIRIN BREWERY	14-Aug-1997	Japan	0.97%	8,300.68		1.37			yes		-9.70%	0.04%
KIRIN BREWERY	20-Nov-1996	Japan	-0.59%	8,711.17		1.71			yes		-0.02%	0.02%
KIRIN BREWERY	29-Dec-1989	Japan	1.16%	11,639.93		3.92			yes		-7.49%	0.01%
KULMBACHER BRAUEREI	20-Jan-2005	Germany	-0.04%	82.49	2.01	2.12	2.74		no	41.00	15.17%	0.01%
KULMBACHER BRAUEREI	25-Sep-2003	Germany	3.30%	67.87		1.74			no		24.91%	0.02%
KULMBACHER BRAUEREI	5-Apr-1991	Germany	-2.38%	54.92		2.47			no		60.94%	0.01%
KULMBACHER BRAUEREI	31-Jul-1990	Germany	2.89%	38.57		2.53			no		-34.24%	0.01%
MNZ AKT.-BIERBRAUEREI	18-Jan-1994	Germany	-0.04%	40.52	2.07	5.29	0.00		no	19.57	-26.86%	0.01%
MNZ AKT.-BIERBRAUEREI	9-Jul-1992	Germany	-0.01%	42.01	2.11	5.49	0.00		no	19.89	4.73%	0.01%
PARK & BELLHEIMER	12-Dec-1995	Germany	0.01%	17.79		2.45			no		3.90%	0.03%
RADEBERGER GRUPPE	7-May-2004	Germany	0.50%	1,061.87	2.79	5.35	2.70		no	381.00	7.69%	0.02%
RADEBERGER GRUPPE	10-Dec-2003	Germany	-0.80%	1,011.30	2.82	5.11	2.54	0.70	no	358.50	80.69%	0.03%
RADEBERGER GRUPPE	30-Jan-2003	Germany	-0.33%	449.82		2.27			no		115.56%	0.05%
SEDLMAYR	11-Sep-1997	Germany	5.17%	146.33	0.65		2.20	-0.54	no	224.51	29.21%	0.03%
SEDLMAYR	4-Nov-1993	Germany	-0.04%	30.83	0.12		7.67	0.21	no	260.76	-49.03%	0.01%
WHITBREAD	1-Sep-1994	United Kingdom	0.01%	3,427.02		1.23			yes		12.15%	0.02%
WHITBREAD	29-Jul-1994	United Kingdom	0.04%	3,156.75		1.12			yes		0.66%	0.02%
Number of Events			66	66	18	53	18	12	66	18	66	66
Minimum			-9.20%	13.99	0.12	0.56	0.00	-0.54		7.90	-49.98%	0.00%
Maximum			28.26%	19,943.94	1,300.88	9.09	7.67	0.92		1,651.57	132.87%	0.40%
Mean			0.62%	1,879.51	81.10	3.60	2.56	0.19		298.92	11.86%	0.04%
Median			-0.03%	294.11	2.09	3.13	2.62	0.18		242.64	3.14%	0.02%
Standard Deviation			4.12%	3,838.10	304.84	2.04	2.04	0.36		378.80	38.29%	0.05%

Appendix 4: Overview of the statistics about the countries analysed

	Frequency	Percentage	Cumulative Percentage	CAAR [-1;0]	Median CARs [-1;0]	Mean: MV Acquirer/ MV Target	Mean: Market to Book Value Acquirer	Mean: Market to Book Value Target	Mean: EBITDA/Sales Target	Mean: Market Value Acquirer (in € mm)	Mean: Market Value Target (in € mm)
Germany	50	75.76%	75.76%	-0.05%	0.21%	2.47	1.43	2.73		1,264.53	525.39
Belgium	4	6.06%	81.82%	0.20%	0.20%	356.60		3.78	0.35	10,276.96	200.85
Denmark	3	4.55%	86.36%	0.78%	-0.04%	2.45	3.97	2.32	0.11	324.03	307.22
Japan	3	4.55%	90.91%	0.51%	0.97%		2.33			9,550.59	
Netherlands	3	4.55%	95.45%	-0.25%	-0.18%	1.49	3.79	0.00		6,793.42	147.05
United Kingdom	3	4.55%	100.00%	0.22%	0.04%		1.83			4,637.54	
Total	66	100.00%									

References

Ad Hoc News (Ed.) (1998): Henninger neuer Vorstand, <http://www.aktiencheck.de/>, Publication Date: 15/07/1998, Accessed: 06/06/2005.

Agrawal, Anup / Jaffe, Jeffrey F. (2000): The Post-Merger Performance Puzzle, in: Cooper, Cary / Gregory, Alan (Eds.): JAI Series: Advances in Mergers and Acquisitions, Vol. 1, pp. 1-59.

Agrawal, Anup / Jaffe, Jeffrey F. / Mandelker, Gershon N. (1992): The Post-Merger Performance of Acquiring Firms: A Re-examination of an Anomaly, in: The Journal of Finance, Vol. 47, No. 4, pp. 1605-1621.

Andre, Paul / Kooli, Maher / L'her, Jean-Francois (2004): The Long-Run Performance of Mergers and Acquisitions: Evidence from the Canadian Stock Market, in: Financial Management, Vol. 33, No. 4, pp. 27-43.

Asquith, Paul (1982): Merger Bids, Uncertainty, and Stockholder Returns, in: Journal of Financial Economics, Vol. 1, pp. 51-83.

Barber, Brad M. / Lyon, John D. (1997): Detecting Long-Run Abnormal Stock Returns: The Empirical Power and Specification of Test Statistics, in: Journal of Financial Economics, Vol. 43, No. 3, pp. 341-372.

Bhagat, Sanjai / Romano, Roberta (2001): Event Studies and the Law: PART 1: Technique and Corporate Litigation, in: Yale Law School-Center for Studies in Law, Economics and Public Policy, Vol. 4, No.1, pp. 1-33.

Boehmer, Ekkehart / Musumeci, Jim / Poulsen, Anette B. (1991): Event-Study Methodology Under Conditions of Event-Induced Variance, in: Journal of Financial Economics, Vol. 30, No. 2, pp. 253-272.

Bollerslev, Tim (1986): Generalized Autoregressive Conditional Heteroscedasticity, in: Journal of Econometrics, Vol. 31, No. 3, pp. 307-317.

Bollerslev, Tim (1987): A Conditionally Heteroscedastic Time Series Model for Speculative Prices and Rates of Return, in: Review of Economics & Statistics, Vol. 69, No. 3, pp. 542-547.

Brockett, Patrick L. / Chen, Hwei-Mei / Garven, James R. (1999): A New Stochastically Flexible Event Methodology with Application to Proposition 103, in: Insurance: Mathematics & Economics, Vol. 25, No. 2, pp. 197-217.

Brooks, Chris (2002): Introductory Econometrics for Finance, Cambridge.

Brown, Stephen J. / Warner, Jerold B. (1980): Measuring Security Price Performance, in: Journal of Financial Economics, Vol. 8, No. 3, pp. 205-258.

Brown, Stephen J. / Warner, Jerold B. (1985): Using Daily Stock Returns: The Case of Event Studies, in: Journal of Financial Economics, Vol. 14, No. 1, pp. 3-31.

Corrado, Charles J. / Zivney, Terry L. (1992): The Specification and Power of the Sign Test in Event Study Hypothesis Tests using daily Stock Data Returns, in: Journal of Financial and quantitative Analysis, Vol. 27, No. 3, pp. 465-478.

Credit Suisse First Boston (Ed.) (2003): The German Beer Industry – The Consolidors' Challenge, in: Credit Suisse First Boston Equity Research, Research Paper, Vol. 04/06/2003, without location.

Credit Suisse First Boston (Ed.) (2004): The German Beer Industry – The Consolidation continues, in: Credit Suisse First Boston Equity Research, Research Paper, Vol. 16/02/2004, without location.

Engle, Robert F. (1982): Autoagressive Conditional Heteroscedasticity with Estimates of the Variance of United Kingdom Inflation, in: Econometrica, Vol. 50, No. 4, pp. 987-1008.

Engle, Robert F. (2001): Garch 101: The Use of ARCH/GARCH Models in Applied Econometrics, in: Journal of Economic Perspectives, Vol. 15, No. 4, pp. 157-168.

Faff, Robert (2004): A Simple Test of the Fama and French Model Using Daily Data: Australian Evidence, in: Applied Financial Economics, Vol. 14, No. 2, pp. 83-92.

Fama, Eugene F. (1998): Market Efficiency, Long-Term Returns, and Behavioral Finance, in: Journal of Financial Economics, Vol. 49, No. 3, pp. 283-306.

Fama, Eugene F. / French, Kenneth R. (1993): Common Risk Factors in the Return on Stocks and Bonds, in: Journal of Financial Economics, Vol. 33, No. 1, pp. 3-56.

Fama, Eugene F. / French, Kenneth R. (1996a): Multifactor Explanations of Asset Pricing Anomalies, in: The Journal of Finance, Vol. 53, No. 1, pp. 55-85.

Fama, Eugene F. / French, Kenneth R. (1996b): The CAPM is wanted, dead or alive, in: The Journal of Finance, Vol. LI, No. 5, pp. 1947-1958.

Fama, Eugene F. / French, Kenneth R. (1998): Value versus Growth: The International Evidence, in: The Journal of Finance, Vol. 53, No. 6, pp. 1975-1999.

Ferris, Stephen P. / Park, Kwangwoo (2002): How Differnet is the Long-Run Performance of Mergers in the Telecommunications Industry?, in: Hirschey, Mark / John, Kose / Makhija, Anil (Eds.): Advances in Financial Economics, Vol. 7, No. 1, pp. 1-21.

Franks, Julian R. / Harris, Robert S. / Mayer, Colin (1988): MeSans of Payment in Takeovers: Resukts for the United Kingdom and the United States, in: Auerbach, Alan J. (Ed.): Corporate Takeovers: Causes and Consequences, Chicago.

Geiger, Florian / Roediger, Tobias (2005): Announcement Effects M&A of Bidder in Germany, Unpublished Working Paper, Oestrich-Winkel.

Gerbig, Joerg / Zawadsky, Felix (2005): M&A Announcement Effects on Targets in the German Brewery Market, Unpublished Working Paper, Oestrich-Winkel.

HWPH Historisches Wertpapierhaus AG (Ed.) (2003), Auktionskatalog zur 3. Präsenzauktion am 20.09.2003 in Würzburg, <http://www.historisches-wertpapierhaus.de/ auktionen/pa3/pa3_2.html>, Publication Date: 20/09/2003, Accessed: 06/06/2005.

Ising, Jan / Schiereck, Dirk / Simpson Marc W. / Thomas, Thomas W. (2004): Long-Term Market Reactions to Large Price Declines and Increases – The Case of Germany; Witten/Herdecke University working paper, 2nd revised Version (June 2004), Witten, pp. 1-45.

Jegadeesh, Narasimhan / Karceski, Jason (2004): Long-Run Performance Evaluation: Correlation and Heteroskedasticity-Consider Tests, Working Paper Emory University, pp. 1-40.

Kothari, S. P. / Warner, Jerold B. (1997): Measuring Long-Horizon Security Price Performance, in: Journal of Financial Economics, Vol. 43, No. 3 pp. 301-339.

Kothari, S. P. / Warner, Jerold B. (2004): Econometrics of Event Studies, in: ECKBO, ESPEN (Ed.): Handbook of Corporate Finance: Empirical Corporate Finance, Elsevier.

Lyon, John D. / Barber, Brad M. / Tsai, Chih-Ling (1999): Improved Methods for Tests of Long-Run Abnormal Stock Returns, in: The Journal of Finance, Vol. 54, No. 1, pp. 165-201.

Mcclave, James T. / Benson, P. George / Sincich, Terry (2001): Statistics for Business and Economics, 8th Edition, Upper Saddle River.

Mikkelson, Wayne H. / Partch, Megan (1986): Valuation Effects of Security Offerings and the Issuance Process, in: Journal of Financial Economics, Vol. 15, pp. 31-60.

Mikkelson, Wayne H. / Partch, Megan (1988): Withdrawn Security Offerings, in: Journal of Financial and Quantitative Analysis, Vol. 23, No. 2, pp. 119-136.

Mitchell, Mark L. / Stafford Erik (1999): Managerial Decisions and Long-Term Stock Price Performance, in: University of Chicago Press: Journal of Business, Vol. 73, No. 3, pp. 1-56.

Nahar, Toby (2005): The Rebound Effect: Long-term Reactions to Large Stock Price Declines and Increases of the AsianTitans50, (unpublished Working Paper), Oestrich-Winkel, pp. 1-46.

Rajand, Mahendra / Forsyth, Michael (2002): Hostile Bidders, Long-Term Performance, and Restructuring Methods: Evidence from the UK, in: American Business Review, Vol. 1, pp. 71-81.

Sammleraktien-Online.De (Ed.) (2005): Moninger Brauerei AG – Brauerei Moninger, Karlsruhe, < http://www.sammleraktien-online.de/html/2/artId/__1112/gid/__deu90deumf90 /article.html >, Publication Date: N/A, Accessed: 06/06/2005.

Serra, Paula A. (2002): Event Study Tests – A brief Survey, in: Working Papers da FEP No. 117, pp. 1-15.

Wilcoxon, Frank (1945): Individual Comparisons by Ranking Methods, in: Biometrics Bulletin, Vol. 1, No. 6, pp. 80-83.

II M&A Announcement Effects on Targets in the German Brewing Industry

by

Jörg Gerbig and Felix Zawadzky

1 Introduction

1.1 Objective of the Study

The German brewery market has experienced a sharp increase in consolidation activity in recent years. Many independent breweries were acquired by larger corporations, mostly from the same industry. Smaller regional breweries tended to be targeted by other German malt brewers, leading to the fact that 80.4% of completed M&A transactions in Germany were conducted by German acquirers. However, the largest transactions were of cross-border type indicating aggressive international consolidation tendencies amongst the significant players on the global market. The biggest transactions included the € 1.712bn acquisition of the traditional German brewing corporation Beck's by the Belgium Interbrew. Interbrew is today called InBev. InBev was formed in 2004 when Interbrew and Companhia de Bebidas das Américas (AmBev) combined to create what is now the world's premier brewer.[1] A further large transaction occurred when the Danish brewer Carlsberg acquired Holsten for € 1.1bn. The trend for rapid consolidation in the brewery segment can be explained by looking at the market's inherent drivers of profitability. In the brewing industry there are five forces that push profitability, and ceteris paribus eventually shareholder value: The first driver can be seen in the reduction in headcount and administrational costs. The second drivers are the pricing-power benefits that can be achieved from an increased market-share. A similar argumen-

[1] Note: The transaction value was at $ 19.7bn and still represents the biggest deal ever conducted in the brewing industry.

tation lies in driver three – economies of scale benefits and capacity rationalisation. Driver four focuses on distributional benefits that can result from an increase in size as brewers can start distributing themselves from a certain point onwards, cutting out wholesalers, and hence increasing profit margins. The last driver of profitability can be derived from volume- and mix-gains from brand cross-selling. This trend can widely be observed by the emergence of mixed beer drinks aimed at younger target-groups.[2]

Mergers and acquisitions, the process of combining two companies in order to achieve a certain strategy and business objective, are transactions of great significance. The success of an M&A transaction has enormous consequences on the shareholder and stakeholder of the participating companies. As only little research has been conducted on M&A transactions in the brewery market, this paper evaluates the effect of announcement effects on targeted firms' shareholder wealth in transaction in the German brewery market.

1.2 Course of Analysis

In the following chapter, the study first gives a brief overview of existing relevant literature and its findings and then proceeds to Chapter 3 by introducing the hypotheses. In Chapter 4, the study offers the reader a description of the data sample of M&A transactions in the German brewery market. Then, the analysis' methodology is presented by determining the event windows, describing the examination of abnormal returns and statistical significances and explaining the analysis of influencing factors. In Chapter 6 the results are evaluated. Based on this evaluation, a conclusion is drawn in Chapter 7.

2 Review of Literature

Although worldwide M&A activity has experienced increasing development over the last 20 years, relatively little related research has been conducted so far. This holds particularly true for empirical research on the subject. However, some exist-

[2] For a graphical illustration of consolidation-induced profitability, see Appendix 1.

ing literature provides relevant findings to our study. Amongst suitable sources there are studies that investigate the role of announcement effects in creating (or destroying) shareholder value in M&A transactions. Furthermore, there is literature investigating the value of mergers and acquisitions per se. The brewery market, however, has not yet been subject to extensive studies. Hence, we have focused on those studies that carry the highest degree of relevance to the aim of our analysis. Bergström and Högfeldt examine the relationship between acquiring and acquired firms' stock returns and the announcement effect. They report total wealth gains for targets at 17% and for acquirors at 0%.[3] Doukas and Holmen investigated 93 tender offers in between 1980 and 1995, concentrating on an 11-day event window. They only concentrate on bidders' abnormal returns and also find them to be at low levels of 1%. They, too, consider tender offers as types of transactions.[4] Van Hulle and Vermaelenand de Wouters consider an event window of six weeks. Their results show a significant abnormal return of 38% for targeted firms and negative abnormal returns of 1% for acquirers.[5] Another one of their studies published in the same year concentrates on a three-months event window and shows positive abnormal returns of 6% for targets and, again, minus 1% for acquiring firms.[6] Eckbo and Langohr examine 52 public tender offers between 1966 and 1982. The study includes 52 targets and 90 acquiring firms. The event window considers the preceding and following eight weeks of the announcement weeks. Again, targeted firms herein experience higher abnormal returns than acquirors with 14% and -3% respectively.[7] Comment and Schwert deliver a sound explanation for the reason why targets often experience higher abnormal returns than bidding firms. Their reasoning is linked to the prevalence of hostile take-over attempts by acquirors, leading to higher necessary premiums in order to convince the targeted firms' shareholders. This, in effect, transfers into higher abnormal returns at the capital markets.[8] While this assumption does hold true in practice, it must be stated that it is not the sole valid explanation for the phenomenon as higher abnormal returns are

---

[3] Cf. Bergström / Högfeldt (1997).
[4] Cf. Doukas / Holmen (2000).
[5] Cf. Van Hulle / Vermaelen / De Wouters (1991 a).
[6] Cf. Van Hulle / Vermaelen / De Wouters (1991 b).
[7] Cf. Eckbo / Langohr (1989).
[8] Cf. Comment / Schwert (1995).

also experienced in M&A transactions where the deal attitude is of friendly or neutral nature.

All of the above described studies used the market model as their respective benchmark return model. The following studies, however, used the Capital Asset Pricing Model (CAPM). Goergen and Renneboog consider the time-frame between the years 1993 and 2000. Their investigation included 66 targets and 75 bidders in a 120-days event window. Their results imply abnormal returns of 15% for targets and 1% for bidding firms.[9] Mulherin and Boone investigated M&A transactions between the years 1990 and 1999 and further enforced the previously described trend. The focus lay on a three-day event window and observed positive abnormal returns of 18% for targets.[10] Finally, Agraval et al. investigated a five-year event window after the announcement date and concluded with negative abnormal returns in the long-run of 10%.

Extant empirical literature documents that the shareholders of target companies in take-over bids experience substantial wealth gains whereas those of the bidder companies experience at best small positive gains and at worst wealth losses (Jarrell / Brickley / Netter[11] and Datta / Iskandar-Datta / Raman[12]). This result is often observed along various sources of the relevant literature. Whilst targets must receive some expectation of gain in order to win the approval of their target shareholders for any merger, those acquirer firm managers, who are unconstrained by pressure from value maximising shareholders, may embark on acquisitions that offer no ex ante gain to stockholders. In a European context, Cybo-Ottone and Murgia[13] show that diversifying mergers are value reducing, whereas focusing mergers are value enhancing. In the winner's curse or hubris hypothesis, over-optimistic acquirers overbid for targets. For example, Roll[14] shows that acquirers who overestimate the value of the target are more likely to successfully complete a merger, resulting in a decline in the acquirer's value to stockholders.

---

[9] Cf. Goergen / Renneboog (2003).
[10] Cf. Mulherin / Boone (2000).
[11] Cf. Jarell / Brickley / Netter (1988), pp. 49-68.
[12] Cf. Datta / Inskandar-Datta / Raman (2003), pp. 351-375.
[13] Cf. Cybo-Otone / Murgia (2000), pp. 831-859.
[14] Cf. Roll (1986), pp. 197-216.

Furthermore, we can summarise that it does not seem to affect empirical results in these cases whether the market model or the CAPM is being used for the respective investigation. For our distinctive investigation into the brewery market we expect our findings to be in line with the trend of previous studies, observing higher positive returns for targets and maybe even negative ones for bidding firms.

3 Introduction of Hypothesis

In order to conduct the empirical analysis, the abnormal returns caused by the M&A transactions are of great interest. The effects of deal- and company-specific characteristics on the share price are examined in the study. Therefore, seven hypotheses are introduced which are based on the current literature on M&A and share price returns.[15]

Hypothesis 1: Announcements of M&A transactions in the brewing industry cause positive abnormal returns with the target company.

To gain control over the target company, the payment of a premium is usually required. The premium, demanded by the target shareholders in order to approve the transaction, is referred to as control premium, since the bidding firm is interested in gaining control over the target's assets. The bidder's rationale is based on the expectation of efficiency which he seeks to obtain. Hence, the target company contains a hidden value for the acquirer in the form of synergies which he seeks to realise. As a result, the bidding firm is able to pay a premium to the target shareholders as the investment still provides it with a positive net present value. Hypothesis 1 is tested by examining the event window on cumulative average abnormal returns.[16]

Hypothesis 2: Cross-border transactions will, according to FDI-theory, cause targets to experience higher CARs than domestic transactions.

[15] See Appendix 2.
[16] Cf. Mulherin / Boone (2000); Bradley / Desai / Kim (1988).

The Foreign Direct Investment Theory (FDI) suggests factors contributing to higher abnormal returns in cross-border transactions than national M&A transactions. The factors mentioned include exchange rate risk, international risk diversification, current condition of the domestic economy, access to technology and differences in tax systems and accounting standards. As a result, cross-border mergers can provide advantages to acquiring companies that are otherwise not available in their home market. Hence, these factors encourage companies to engage in cross-border take-overs and result in higher take-over premiums.[17]

Hypothesis 3: Transactions where acquiring firms belong to the same industry will result in higher CARs for targets, due to higher synergies.

A M&A transaction of two companies from the same sectors will result in higher synergy potential due to a comparable business model. The synergies can be differentiated in cost, capex and revenue synergies. The combined new entity is able to realise cost synergies mainly through economies of scale. Capital expenditure will decrease due to the combination production facilities. The bidder is furthermore able to export his expertise into the target company and encourage knowledge sharing which results in revenue synergies in the long run.[18]

Hypothesis 4: The announcement effects on targets in brewery mergers vary over time.

The merger market is characterized by merger waves. The volume of M&A transactions is very volatile, so there are times of buyer markets and times of seller markets. This implies that in a buyer market the premium the buyer has to pay for the target is larger than the premium he has to pay in a seller's market. Concentrating on brewery mergers it is interesting to see if the premiums paid for targets are decreasing or increasing over time.

---

[17] Cf. Danbolt (1995); Danbolt (2004); Datta / Pinches / Narayanan (1992); Servais / Zenner (1991); Vasconcellos / Madura / Kish (1990); Vasconcellos / Kish (1998).

[18] Cf. Elgers / Clark (1980); Gordon / Yagil (1981); Wansley / Wane / Young (1983).

Hypothesis 5: Smaller companies tend to generate higher CARs in an M&A transaction than larger companies.

Small and large companies' stock prices have different characteristics. Due to imperfection in markets smaller stocks are less liquid than bigger stocks. In the case of a M&A announcement, the share price of an illiquid stock is supposed to react more significantly than a liquid stock.[19]

Hypothesis 6: Hostile transactions will result in higher CARs for targets than friendly ones as higher premiums will have to be offered.

Hostility is perceived if the offer of an acquisition is publicly rejected by the target company. Unwelcome bids threaten stakeholders of the target companies which lead to extensive defensive reactions by the target company's management. Those defensive reactions make the bidder offer higher premiums in order to satisfy the target company's stakeholders. The premiums result in higher abnormal stock price returns of the target company.[20]

4 Sample

4.1 Data Collection and Data Revision

Our data sample consists of 51 M&A-transactions of European companies in the period from 1990 to 2005. The data was taken from Thomson Financial Securities DataTM (TFSD) Mergers & Acquisitions database. The transactions all match four criteria:

They were (i) announced between January 1st, 1999 and January 31st, 2005. The bidders are (ii) European companies, which all derive from former EU-15 countries – namely Austria, Belgium, Denmark, Germany, the Netherlands and Sweden. Both counterparties (iii) are publicly traded for at least 200 days before and 10 days after the announcement date. We did not consider companies that had been

[19] Cf. Moeller / Schlingemann / Stulz (2004).
[20] Cf. Schwert (2000); Comment / Schwert (1995).

involved in an IPO shortly before the beginning of the estimation or event window because their returns will be biased during that period. The (iv) bidder acquired over 50% of the target's shares outstanding and thus, gained full corporate control.

The source for equities information and benchmark indices was Datastream, which is also provided by Thomson Financial Services. The share prices used assume reinvestment of cash dividends paid to shareholders. The average market value of the acquirers is € 437.4m.

4.2 Descriptive Statistics

As Chart 1 shows, 10 of the 51 transactions are of cross border-type and 41 were conducted on a national basis.

Chart 1: Aquiror's Nationality

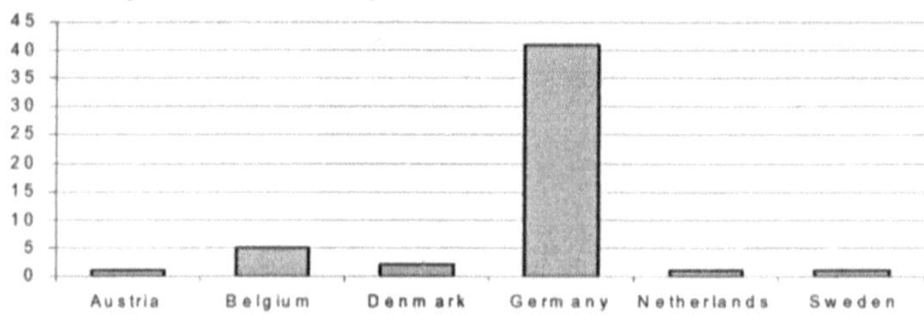

This represents the significant consolidation process that could be observed in the German brewery market, especially on a regional basis. 68.6% of the transactions have been rated as being completed, with the remaining not specifying on a certain status. In terms of deal attitude it could be observed that with 88.2% the absolute majority of the considered transactions were friendly. No hostile take-over was indicated and the deal attitude of the other transactions was either not available or considered to be neutral. The year 2003, as shown in Chart 2, was the year with the highest deal frequency (11), followed by 1997 (5) and years 1993, 1995, 2000 and 2004 with four deals occurring respectively.

Chart 2: Deal Frequency 1990-2005

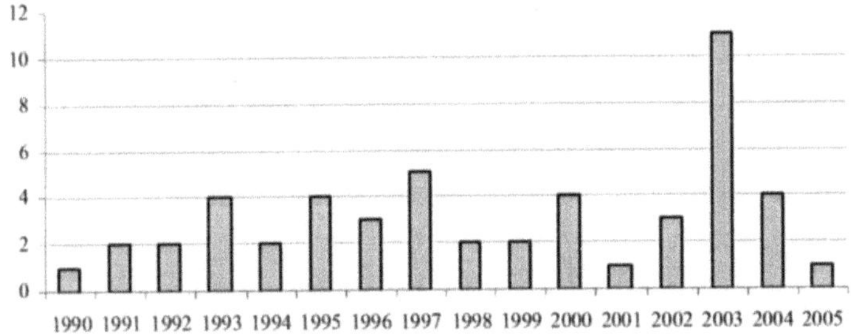

While statements can be made on the deal frequency, no information was available on the respective years' deal volume of M&A activity in the brewery market. Chart 3 indicates that of the 51 transactions included, 32 were carried out between parties of the same industry – breweries. The remaining 19 accounting for cross-industry transactions of which not one specific industry can be identified as the driving force for transactions in the brewery market.

Chart 3: Advisors' Industries (SIC)

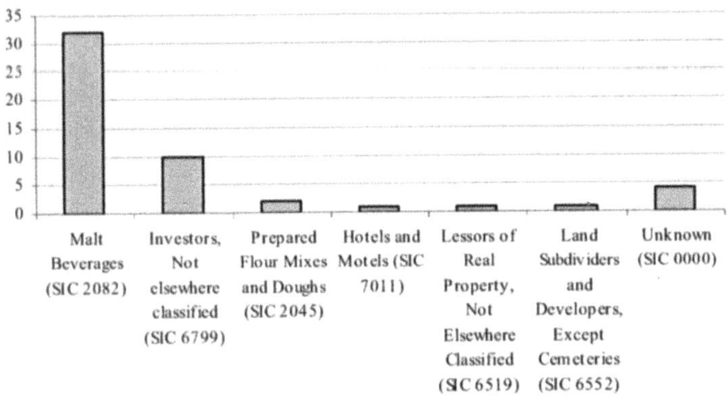

The most bullish singular group in terms of M&A activity however was stated as "Investors – Not elsewhere classified" accounting for almost 20% of total number of transactions.

5 Methodology

The study is based on an event study. An event study is one of the most frequently used analytic methods in finance.[21] The goal of this method is to examine cumulative abnormal returns around an event window. The abnormal return represents the difference between the observed returns and a specific model.[22] In this study we use the market model of Sharpe (1963)[23] also used in Brown / Warner (1980 / 1985) and Dodd / Warner (1983).[24]

5.1 Determination of Event Windows

Having identified the events and the announcement dates, the event windows are fixed. Within this event interval, the announcement effects of the M&A transaction are observed. Hereby it is common to not only take the actual announcement day but extend the event window to several days.[25] The pre-event days include a possible anticipation of the event. The post-event days consider the share price effects of the announcement.[26] For the event study an event window of [-10;+10] is chosen. This event period is in line with the existing literature.[27] Within the event period subintervals of [-5;+5], [-2;+2], [-1;+1], [0;0], [0;+1], [0;+2], [0;+5], [0;+10] are built to interpret the abnormal returns which are found.

5.2 Examination and Aggregation of Abnormal Returns

The abnormal returns describe the difference between the actual ex-post returns and the abnormal returns of the shares over the event period. The determination of the normal and the estimated returns is calculated over the estimation period on the basis of the market model of Sharpe (1963).[28]

---

[21] Cf. Fama / Fisher / Jensen / Roll (1969), pp. 1-21; Brown / Warner (1980), pp. 205-258; Brown / Warner (1985),pp. 3-31; Dodd / Warner (1983), pp. 401-438.
[22] Cf. Peterson (2002), pp. 36.
[23] Cf. Sharpe (1963).
[24] Cf. Brown / Warner (1980), pp. 207-209; Brown / Warner (1985), pp. 3-8; Dodd / Warner (1983), pp. 412.
[25] Cf. MacKinley (1997), pp. 14.
[26] Cf. MacKinley (1997), pp. 15; Cao / Mentz / Schiereck (2004), pp. 15.
[27] Cf. Peterson (2002); MacKinley (1997).
[28] Cf. Sharpe (1963), Cf. MacKinley (1997), p. 18, other studies use the „constant mean return model" instead of the market model, Cf. MacKinley (1997), p. 15; Binder (1998), pp.117-119.

Therefore, the following estimation formula for the calculation of abnormal returns AR of the company i at the day t is used:

Formula 1

$$R_{i,t} = \alpha + \beta R_{m,t} + \varepsilon_{t,\tau}$$

The return of the share at the day t is described by $R_{i,t}$, while $R_{m,t}$ explains the market return at day t. The returns are calculated as log normal returns in order to guarantee a symmetrical distribution. This is advantageous because symmetrical distributions have fewer estimation problems.[29] For the estimation period it is important that there is no overlap with the event period. Consequently, an estimation period of 200 days until 11 days before the announcement [-211;-11] is settled. In literature, the estimation period varies from 100-300 days.[30]

The abnormal returns of the observed shares are calculated over the estimation period with the coefficients α and β:

Formula 2

$$AR_{i,t} = R - (\alpha + \beta R_{m,t} + \varepsilon_{t,\tau})$$

The market model parameters in the study are estimated by the MDAX. This index bases on a representative sample of 100 mid-size German companies from various industries. A broad index is desirable to receive good estimates for the market return. The market model is also the most frequently used model in event studies and is especially useful to examine the daily abnormal returns.[31]

---

[29] Cf. Fama / Fisher / Jensen / Roll (1969), p. 4; a contrary position is argued by Dissanaike / Le Fur (2003).

[30] Cf. Peterson (2002), pp. 37-38; MacKinley (1997), p. 15; for further literature cf. Sallinger (1992), who discusses a post-announcement estimation period instead of a pre-announcement estimation period.

[31] Cf. MacKinley (1997), p. 18; May (1991), p. 322; Brown / Warner (1985), pp. 25-26; Dyckman / Philbrick / Stephan (1984), p. 21.

After having examined the daily abnormal returns, they are aggregated over the event period [d1;d2]. The aggregation of the cumulative abnormal returns (CAAR) is done for all 51 events.

Formula 3

$$CAAR_{i,t} = \frac{1}{51} \sum_{t=d_1}^{d_2} \sum_{i=1}^{55} AR_{i,t}$$

With the help of the cumulative abnormal returns, the announcement effects over the whole event period are examined.[32] The variation in market value is calculated by multiplying the market capitalisation at t-11 and the cumulative abnormal returns of the event windows.[33]

5.3 Examination of Statistical Significance

The statistical significance of the abnormal returns is calculated to examine whether the returns differ significantly from zero. Therefore, two different kinds of tests are accomplished: a parametric and a non-parametric test. Parametric tests are based on the assumption of a specific distribution. The t-test assumes normal distribution of the abnormal returns, for example. For a smaller sample a normal distribution can not be assumed.[34] Therefore non-parametric tests are used for a smaller sample size. They are advantageous because they do not underlie any specific assumptions related to the distribution.[35] For the event study the parametric t-test and the Dodd / Warner-test as well as the non-parametric Wilcoxon-test are used.[36]

---

[32] Cf. MacKinley (1997), pp. 21-27; Brown / Warner (1980), pp. 227-232; Fama / Fisher / Jensen / Roll (1969), pp. 7-9.

[33] Cf. Bradley / Desai / Kim (1988).

[34] Cf. McClave / Benson / Sincich (2002), p. 298.

[35] Cf. Bamberg / Baur (2001), pp. 180, 188.

[36] Cf. Dodd / Warner (1983), pp. 436-437; McClave / Benson / Sincich (2002), pp. 894-899.

5.4 Analysis of Influencing Factors

The analysis of the influencing factors is done in a multivariate regression framework. Even though it can also be accomplished by sub-samples, only a multivariate analysis allows for a combined view of the results.[37] It takes the form:

Formula 4

$$y = \beta_o + \beta_1 x_1 + \beta_2 x_2 + \ldots + \beta_k x_k + \varepsilon$$

The dependent variable of the abnormal returns is explained as a function of the k independent variables x_1, x_2 ... x_k The value β_i determines the contribution of the independent variable to the result of the abnormal returns. Based on the hypothesis the independent variables are defined as follows:[38]

x_1 = NATIONALITY
x_2 = INDUSTRY
x_3 = TIME
x_4 = SIZE
x_5 = ATTITUDE

x_1 describes if the transaction is a national or a cross-border transaction. A dummy is introduced: 0 for national and 1 for cross-border deals. The industry variable x_2 is also given as a dummy variable. It defines whether the companies participating in the transaction are from the same or a different industry. Therefore, the SIC codes of the bidder and target company are compared. Companies with the same SIC code have the dummy variable 0 whereas cross-industry deals are defined as 1. Variable x_3 defines the announcement of the merger and variable x_4 characterises the size of the company being overtaken by giving the market values at the day t-11 of the announcement day. The fifth variable x_5 is defined by the attitude of the deal. Friendly deals are assigned a 0, whereas all other deals are referred to as dummy 1.[39]

---

[37] Cf. Cao / Mentz / Schiereck (2004), p. 17.
[38] Cf. McClave / Benson / Sincich (2002), p. 534.
[39] Cf. McClave / Benson / Sincich (2002), pp. 594-605.

Formula 1 is estimated using OLS. The application of this model is based on several assumptions. The expected value of the prediction errors of the sample is zero. This assumption always holds true for model predictions which contain a constant factor α.[40] Furthermore, the independent variables are not allowed to be dependent linearly. This multicollinearity is improper because the variables are related to different aspects. Nevertheless, multicollinearity is tested by the "Variance Inflation Factor". The name VIF results from the fact that it increases with increasing multicollinearity. Consequently, the exactness of the predicting values is being deteriorated. Another assumption of the multivariate regression is homoscedascity. In order to check for heteroscedascity, a visual examination is accomplished. A diagram with the estimated standardised residuals $\hat{y}$ of the independent variables on the horizontal axis and the standardised residuals of the observation values on the vertical axis. In the case of heteroscedascity a relation between the residuals of the observation values and $\hat{y}$ must be observable. The examination of the error values can also be accomplished by checking for the standardised residuals. Finally, the error values should be statistically independent, meaning that they should not show any correlation. The Durbin-Watson test tests for a possible autocorrelation.[41]

6 Results

6.1 Share Price Reactions

Table 1 shows the result of the share price reaction of the whole sample for years from 1988 to 2004.

[40] Cf. Brooks (2002), p. 146.

[41] Cf. Brooks (2002), pp. 148-164; Backhaus / Erichson / Plinke / Weiber (2003), pp. 77-112.

Table 1: Abnormal Returns of the Sample for the Years 1988-2004

Time Interval for N=51	CAAR	Standard Deviation	Median	P-Value (t-test)	Z-Value (Dodd/Warner)	P-Value (Wilcoxon)	Share Negative	Statistical Significance	ø Value (Mio US$)
[-10;+10]	8,71%	0,2064	4,49%	0,0040	14,3087	0,0156	41,18%	xxxx/****/+++	23,38
[-5;+5]	6,84%	0,1457	2,54%	0,0015	16,9323	0,0051	35,29%	xxxx/****/++++	16,29
[-2;+2]	3,41%	0,0918	2,32%	0,0107	11,5993	0,0036	31,37%	xxx/****/++++	12,83
[-1;+1]	3,14%	0,0845	0,70%	0,0107	14,8630	0,0046	37,25%	xxx/****/++++	11,19
[0]	1,08%	0,0423	0,04%	0,0753	8,5602	0,0971	41,18%	xx/****/++	4,14
[0;+1]	2,76%	0,0712	1,22%	0,0078	16,6838	0,0010	33,33%	xxxx/****/++++	9,26
[0;+2]	2,80%	0,0708	1,01%	0,0067	13,6473	0,0018	35,29%	xxxx/****/++++	9,99
[0;+5]	6,18%	0,1432	1,82%	0,0033	23,7475	0,0051	41,18%	xxxx/****/++++	11,60
[0;+10]	5,68%	0,1388	1,86%	0,0052	13,5892	0,0080	35,29%	xxxx/****/++++	13,95

xxx,xx,x = significant at the 1%, 5%, 10% level according to the t-test.
***,**,* = significant at the 1%, 5%, 10% level according to Dodd / Warner.
+++,++,+ = significant at the 1%, 5%, 10% level according to Wilcoxon Signed-Rank-Test.

In all of the nine event windows the sample shows positive cumulative average abnormal returns (CAAR). The CAAR vary from the minimum of 1.08% for the [0] event window to a maximum value of 8.71% in the case of the [-10;+10] event window. Taking into consideration the median of the cumulative average abnormal returns, all of the event windows generate positive abnormal returns. This also implies that the percentage of negative shares in the sample lies below 50% for every event window. The percentage of negative samples within the event window varies from 31.37% for the [-2;+2] event window and 41.18% for the [0;+5], [0] and [-10;+10] event window. All of the different time periods further show a high value for the statistical significance. The p-value of the t-test and of the Wilcoxon test covered a range of 0.0015 to 0.0753 respectively 0.0010 and 0.0971. This implies that all of the values are significantly abnormal of zero at a level of at least 10%. Also, the z-values of the Dodd / Warner test are very high and show statistically significant and abnormal returns at the 1% level.

Table 1 also shows that the average change in market capitalisation is also increasing for the target companies of brewery mergers. The change in value is calculated by the product of the mean of the market capitalisation of the target companies at t-

11and the cumulative average abnormal returns of the referring event window.[42] All of the nine event windows have positive values for the change in market capitalisation. The effects vary from US$ 4.14m for the [0] event window to US$ 23.38m for [-10;+10] event window. Comparing these values to the average transaction value of US$ 219m, the relative change in market capitalisation to transaction value varies from 1.9% to 10.7%. These percentage increases are slightly higher than the cumulate average abnormal returns, which imply that the larger transactions have higher changes in market values. This size effect is analysed in greater detail later in the multivariate regression. As a conclusion hypothesis 1 that announcements of M&A transactions in the brewing industry cause positive abnormal returns with the target company cannot be neglected.

6.2 Influencing Factors on Share Price Reactions

After having analysed the general announcement effect of mergers in the brewing industry on the share price of target companies, the study determines further factors influencing the share price reaction in a multivariate regression. The analysis focuses on the independent variables stated in the Hypothesis 2 to 6. The expected outcomes have already been explained in the chapter of the introduction of the hypothesis. In the analysis the explaining variables are defined as independent variables. In detail, it is cross-border transactions (NATIONALITY), the industry sector relation defined by the SIC code (INDUSTRY), the time aspect (TIME), the market value of the target companies (MARKET VALUE) and the deal attitude (ATTITUDE).

Table 2 summarises the results of the effects of these explaining factors on the share price of targets at the announcement.

[42] Cf. Bradley / Desai / Kim (1988).

Table 2: Multivariate Regression of the Sample and Test of Hypotheses 2 to 6

Hypothesis	Independent Variable	Expected Impact	Regression Coefficient	P-Value	Statistic Significance	VIF
	Constant c		0,120	0,967		
2	NATIONALITY	+	0,189	0,007	***	1,1595
3	INDUSTRY	-	0,003	0,958		1,1478
4	TIME	+/-	0,000	0,984		1,1679
5	MARKET VALUE	-	0,000	0,732		1,0811
6	ATTITUDE	+	-0,192	0,031	**	1,0540
R	0,4524		Standardfehler	0,194		
R^2	0,2047		P(F-Wert)	0,059	*	
Adj. R^2	0,1163		Durbin-Watson	2,042		

***,**,* = significant at the 1%, 5%, 10% level.

The multivariate regression shows two statistically significant results. There is a positive correlation between the nationality and the announcement effect of the share price at a 1% level and a negative correlation between the deal attitude and the share price development at the 5% level. This implies that cross-border transactions generate higher cumulated average abnormal returns than national brewery mergers. The independent variable ATTITUDE is also statistically significant at the 5% level. Contrary to the expectation, ATTITUDE is negatively correlated with the share price development. Friendly transactions generate higher cumulative abnormal returns than non-friendly transactions. However, this result has to be considered with care. With only six non-friendly transactions this result does not seem to be representative. All of the other independent variables do not show any significant p-value.

The examination of the multivariate regression shows that the chosen combination of independent variables has high explanatory power for the calculated cumulative average abnormal returns. The R^2, which indicates how well the model fits the data, reaches a value of 20.47% and the adjusted R^2 of 11.63%. This implies that the model accounts for 11.63% of the variability with the variables specified and the rest goes back to non specified variables. 11.63% represents a decent value for R^2. The F-statistic, which determines if the model is able to explain the population, has a p-value of 0.059, and thus is significant at the 10% level. The standard error of the estimates is 19.4% which is a fairly good value. It represents the average error of the regression function in estimating the independent variables. The analysis of the autocorrelation by Durbin-Watson gives out a value of 2.042. The critical bounds for five independent variables and a sample size of 51 are 1.34 and 1.77 at a 5% probability error level. This implies that autocorrelation cannot be neglected, but can neither be confirmed. Also the VIF Values do not give hints that any assumption is violated.[43]

In a further analysis presented in the appendix the model is improved by excluding the independent variables TIME and INDUSTRY.[44] In this analysis the value of the adjusted R^2 increases to 14.6% and F-stat p-value decreases to 0.012. This implies that the new model accounts for more of the variability of the cumulative average abnormal returns and has a higher explanatory power for the population. All in all, the model is a good proxy to explain the cumulative average abnormal returns. It is an indicator for the influence of the independent variables on the share price.[45]

7 Conclusion

The consolidation process in the brewing industry advances continually. Hence, the importance of M&A related empirical studies in the brewery context proves to be increasing and has recently gained more attention. The findings of this study about the announcement effects on targets in the German brewing industry appear to be in line with the existing relevant literature.

For the null-hypothesis the study finds significant positive abnormal returns of 8.71% for the 21 day event window. It is hence accepted by our findings, notably in the 1% significance level. Moreover, the nationality-hypothesis is accepted as cross-border deals generate significantly higher returns for target shareholders. This even holds true when excluding the € 1.1bn acquisition of Holsten by Carlsberg.

---

[43] Cf. Backhaus et al. (2003), pp. 77-112.
[44] See Appendix 3.
[45] Cf. Backhaus et al. (2003), pp. 63-73.

With regards to the industry hypothesis no evidence can be established of higher CARs in transactions where acquiring firms belong to the brewery sector. Hence, the hypothesis is rejected. The time hypothesis is also rejected by the study as the findings do not show evidence of announcement effects varying over time. In the brewery sector the size of transaction value does not matter. This leads to the rejections of the size-effect hypothesis. The last hypothesis concerning the deal attitude inherent in past transactions can not be validated by the study as unfriendly acquisitions did not result in higher CARs than neutral or friendly ones. The deal attitude hypothesis is also rejected. However, it must be stated that the sample does not contain sufficient unfriendly transactions to deliver results of high precision.[46]

With regards to recommendations for M&A activity of economic agents interacting in the brewing industry, it can be stated that the consolidation process does imply positive returns for target shareholders and could hence be pursued without substantial fear of loss of shareholder value. However, as other studies concentrating on announcement effects of bidding firms show, moderate positive returns can also be generated by actively pursuing an acquisition-strategy; hence, targeting other firms in the market. As a result, the consolidation process proves to be beneficial with regards to the development of shareholder value in the sector.

[46] See Appendix 4.

Appendix

Appendix 1: Five Forces of Consolidation-Induced Profitability

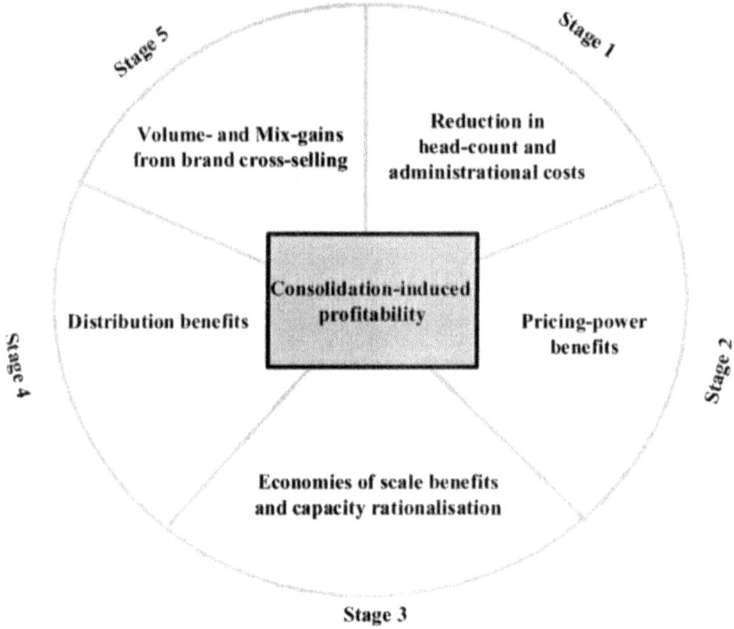

Based on: Sudi Sudarsanam (2003), p. 3.

Appendix 2: Hypotheses

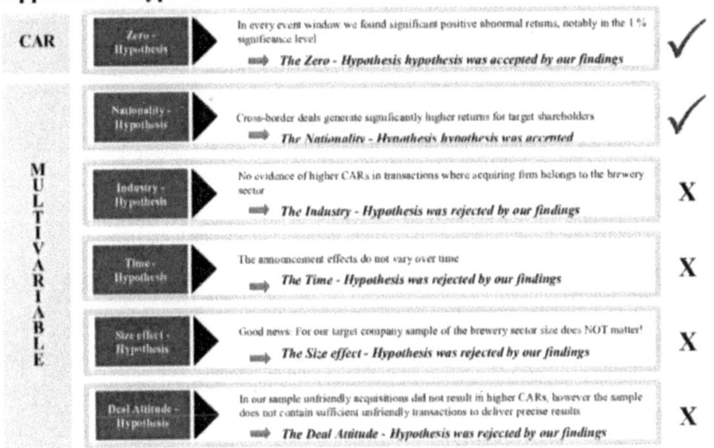

Appendix 3: Improved Model of Multivariate Regression of Sample and Test of Hypothesis [-10;+10]

Hypothesis	Independent Variable	Expected Impact	Regression Coefficient	P-Value	Statistic Sigificance	VIF
	Constant c		0,065	0,053		
2	NATIONALITY	+	0,188	0,004	***	1,0449
5	MARKET VALUE	-	0,000	0,719		1,0020
6	ATTITUDE	+	-0,192	0,027	**	1,0448
R	0,4523		Standardfehler	0,190		
R^2	0,2046		P(F-Wert)	0,012	**	
Adj. R^2	0,1538		Durbin-Watson	2,040		

Appendix 4: Evaluation of Hypotheses

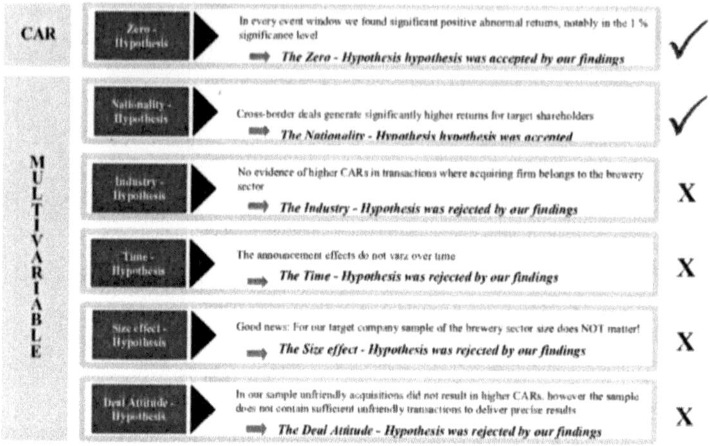

8 References

Backhaus, K. / Erichson, B. / Plinke, W. / Weiber, R. (2003): Multivariate Analysemethoden: Eine anwendungsorientierte Einführung, 10. Aufl., Berlin et al.

Bamberg, G. / Baur, F. (2002): Statistik, 11. Aufl., München / Wien.

Bergström, C. / Högfeldt, P. (1997): The equal bid principle: An analysis of the thirteenth council takeover directive of the European, in: Journal of Business Finance and Accounting, Vol. 24, Issue 3 / 4, pp. 375-396.

Binder, J. J. (1998): Event Study Methodology Since 1969, in: Review of Quantitative Finance and Accounting, Vol. 11, No. 2, pp. 111-137.

Bradley, M. / Desai, A. / Kim, H. (1988): Synergistic Gains from Corporate Acquisitions and Their Division between the Stockholders of Target and Acquiring Firms, in: Journal of Financial Economics, Vol. 21, No. 1, pp. 3-40.

Brooks, C. (2002): Introductory Economics for Finance, Cambridge.

Brown, S. / Warner, J. B. (1980): Measuring Security Price Performance, in: Journal of Financial Economics, Vol. 8, No. 3, pp. 205-258.

Brown, S. / Warner, J. B. (1985): Using Daily Stock Returns: The Case of Event Studies, in: Journal of Financial Economics, Vol. 14, No. 3, pp. 3-31.

Cao, H. Y. / Mentz, M. / Schiereck, D. (2004): Aktienmarktreaktionen auf Rückrufaktionen von Automobilherstellern, Arbeitspapier, European Business School Oestrich-Winkel.

Comment, R. / Schwert, William, G. (1995): Poison or Placebo? Evidence on the Deterrence and Wealth Effects of Modern Antitakeover Measures, in: Journal of Financial Economics, Vol. 39, pp. 3-43.

Cybo-Otone, A. / Murgia, M. (2000): Mergers and shareholder wealth in European banking, in: Journal of Banking and Finance, Vol. 24, Issue 6, pp. 831-860.

Danbolt, Jo (1995): An analysis of gains and losses to shareholders of foreign bidding companies engaged in cross-border acquisitions into the United Kingdom, 1986–1991, in: The European Journal of Finance, Vol. 1, No. 2, pp. 279–309.

Danbolt, Jo (2004): Target Company Cross-border Effects in Acquisitions into the UK, in: European Financial Management, Vol. 10, No. 1, pp. 83–108.

Datta, Deepak, K. / Pinches, Gorge, E. / Narayanan V. K. (1992): Factors influencing wealth creation from mergers and acquisitions: A meta-analysis, in: Strategic Management Journal, Vol. 13, No. 1, pp. 67-84.

Dissanaike, G. / Le Fur, A. (2003): On the Use of Log CAR Measure in Event Studies, in: Journal of Business Finance and Accounting, Vol. 30, No. 7-8, pp. 1165-1170.

Dodd, P. / Warner, J. B. (1983): On Corporate Governance, A Study of Proxy Contests, in: Journal of Financial Economics, Vol. 11, No. 1-4, pp. 401-438.

Doukas, J. A. / Holmen, M. / Travlos, N. G. (2002): Diversification, Ownership and Control of Swedish Corporations, in: European Financial Management, Vol. 8, Issue 3, pp. 281-314.

Dyckman, T. / Philbrick, D. / Stephan, J. (1984): A Comparison of Event Study Methodologies Using Daily Stock Returns: A Simulation Approach, in Journal of Accounting Research, Vol. 22 Supplement, pp. 1-33.

Eckbo, B. E. / Langohr, H. (1989): Information Disclosure, Method of Payment and Takeover Premiums: Public and Private Tender Offers in France, Vol. 24, Issue 2, pp. 363-403.

Elgers, P. / Clark, J. (1980): Merger Types and Shareholder Returns: Additional Evidence, in: Financial Management, Vol. 9, Issue 2, pp. 66-72.

Fama, E. F. / Fisher, L. / Jensen, M. C. / Roll, R. (1969): The Adjustment of Stock Prices to New Information, in: International Economic Review, Vol. 10, No. 1, pp. 1-21.

Goergen, M. / Renneboog, L. (2004): Shareholder Wealth Effects of European Domestic and Cross-border Takeover Bids, in: European Financial Management, Vol. 10, No. 1, pp. 9–45.

Gordon, M. / Yagil, J. (1981): Financial Gains from Conglomerate Mergers, in: Research in Finance, Vol. 3, Issue 2.

Jarrel, G. A. / Brickley, J. A. / Netter, J. M. (1988): The Market for Corporate Control: The Empirical Evidence Since 1980, in: Journal of Economic Perspectives, Vol. 2, No. 1, pp. 49–68.

MacKinley, C. A. (1997): Event Studies in Economics and Finance, in: Journal of Economic Literature, Vol. 35, No. 3, pp. 13-39.

May, A. (1991): Zum Stand der Empirischen Forschung über Informationsverarbeitung am Aktienmarkt: Ein Überblick, in: Zeitschrift für betriebswirtschaftliche Forschung, Vol. 43, No. 4, pp. 313-335.

McClave, J. T. / Benson, G. P. / Sincich, T. (2002): Statistics for Business and Economics, 8th edition, Upper Saddle River.

Moeller, Sara B. / Schlingemann, Frederik P. / Stulz, Rene M. (2004): Firm Size and the Gains from Acquisitions, Vol. 73, Issue 2, pp. 201-228.

Mulherin, H. J. / Boone, A. L. (2000): Comparing acquisitions and divestitures, in: Journal of Corporate Finance, Vol. 6, No. 2, pp.117–139.

Peterson, P. P. (2002): Event Studies: A Review of Issues and Methodology, in: Journal of Business and Economics, Vol. 28, No. 3, S. 36-66.

Roll, R. (1986): The Hubris Hypothesis of Corporate Takeovers, in: Journal of Business, Vol. 59, Issue 2, pp. 197-216.

Sallinger, M. (1992): Value Event Studies, in: The Review of Economics and Statistics, Vol. 74, No. 4, pp. 671-677.

Schwert, William G. (2000): Hostility in Takeovers: In the Eyes of the Beholder?, in: Journal of Finance, Vol. LV, No. 6, pp. 2599-2640.

Servaes, Henri / Zenner, Marc (1990): Taxes and the Returns to Foreign Acquisitions in the United States, in: Financial Management, 1991, Vol. 23, No. 4, pp. 42–56.

Sharpe, W. F. (1963): A Simplified Model for Portfolio Analysis, in: Management Science, Vol. 9, No. 2, pp. 277-293.

Van Hulle, C. / Vermaelen, T. / De Wouters, P. (1991): Regulation, taxes and the market for corporate control in Belgium, Vol. 15, Issue 6, pp. 1143-1170.

Vasconcellos, Geraldo. M. / Kish, Richard J. (1998): Cross-border mergers and acquisitions: the European–US experience, in: Journal of Multinational Financial Management, Vol. 8, pp. 431–450.

Vasconcellos, Geraldo M. / Madura, Jeff / Kish, Richard J. (1990): An Empirical Investigation of Factors Affecting Cross-Border Acquisitions: The United States vs. United Kingdom Experience, in: Global Finance Journal, Vol. 1, Iss. 3, pp. 173–189.

Wansley, James, W. / Lane, William R. / Yang, Ho C. (1983): Abnormal Returns to Acquired Firms by Type of Acquisition and Method of Payment, in: Financial Management, pp. 16-22.

III Long-Term Performance in the German Brewing Industry - Acquirer versus Non-Acquirer

by
Jens Anderson and Jörg Homann

1 Introduction

1.1 Objective of the Study

The German brewing industry is fragmented and currently finds itself in a declining state. As a result, there are overcapacities in the market which have to be shut down. Mergers and acquisitions are one way to solve this problem. Over the past years there have been lots of merger activities in the market, not only domestic breweries, but also global players tried to get a foothold in the German market which is still one of most important worldwide.[1] The question is, whether acquisitions paid off for shareholders of acquirers and non-acquires to the same degree in the long-run?

Gerbig / Zawadzky (2005) already addressed the issue whether target shareholders benefit from take-overs. Their findings suggest that there were positive abnormal returns in the short-term event window surrounding the announcement date.[2]
Similar results presented Geiger / Roedinger (2005) in their work on short-term abnormal performance of acquirers. They conclude that bidders experience slightly positive abnormal returns one day before and at the announcement day itself.[3]

Still unresolved is this question concerning long-term post-merger performance. This paper will hence take on this issue and address the question whether an acqui-

[1] Cf. Credit Suisse First Boston (2004), p. 1 Credit Suisse First Boston (2003), p. 3.
[2] Cf. Gerbig / Zawadzky (2005), pp. 17-18.
[3] Cf. Geiger / Roediger, p. 17.

sition in the German brewing industry will have any long-term impact on returns. Furthermore, the subject is expanded by the question how non-acquirers performed compared to acquirers. Lyon / Barber / Tsai (1999) concluded that analysing long-term abnormal returns is "treacherous".[4] Therefore, it is crucial to find an appropriate model first before starting with the analysis. The first challenge of this paper is to find the appropriate method and then to implement it. Next, it will then dedicate to the objective formulated above.

1.2 Course of Analysis

After the introductory part in Chapter 1 the second chapter reviews the recent literature on the subject of conducting long-term performance analyses. This is done for two reasons. Firstly, to screen suitable methods as references for this study. Secondly, the results of this discussion are taken to formulate the hypotheses to be tested in this seminar paper. After having reviewed the literature, Chapter 3 deals with the sample and data underlying this study. Here, the process of dividing the sample into acquirers and non-acquirers is explained. In the following, Chapter 4 firstly describes the methodology being applicable in general. Secondly, one methodology is chosen, and the course of action including methods and test statistics is explained. Chapter 5 presents the results of the long-term and the short-term studies, analysing the long-term results in a greater depth. In Chapter 6 the conclusion of the main findings of this study will be drawn and consequences pointed out. Finally, general criticism is stated in order to interpret the findings in a better way.

2 Review of Literature and Formulation of Hypotheses

2.1 Review of Literature

So far many events have been examined, reaching from IPO performance over dividend related event, stock splits to merger and acquisitions.[5]

---

[4] Cf. Lyon / Barber / Tsai (1999), p. 1.
[5] Cf. Fama (1998), p. 290.

Agrawal et al. (2000) provide an overview of 22 post-merger performance studies. They admit that their findings might be pure chance, but still they have found long-run underperformance, whether significant or not, at least at one point of each of the articles.[6] Agrawal et al. (2000) also point out the various methodologies employed in order to detect abnormal returns.[7] They discuss four explanations for long-run abnormal returns. Firstly, speed of adjustment[8], i.e. either short-term or long-term; secondly, method of payment hypothesis which states that the method of payment influences post-merger performance[9]; thirdly, performance extrapolation which holds that markets as well as managers extrapolate past performance of a bidding firm in order to assess the acquisition's value; lastly, EPS market myopia assumes that managers tend to pay exaggerated premiums when EPS are expected to rise, which in turn would lead to negative long-run abnormal performance.[10] However, they found ambiguous evidence for basically every hypothesis.[11]

Bearing in mind that long-term event studies results have to be handled with care, a number of M&A studies are summarized in Table 1. To begin with an early study, Asquith (1982) conducts a long-term event study on 196 acquirers and calculates abnormal returns for 240 post-event days using CARs. He finds out that during the pre-press period there are (significant) positive abnormal returns for (successful) bidding firms which then "faded out" over the press date, interim period execution date and finally are significantly negative during the post outcome period for both, successful as well as unsuccessful bidders. In addition, as he observes positive CARs for targets at the announcement date, too. Asquith (1982) concludes that target firms bear potential synergies as they possess unique resources. When resources are appropriated by acquirers, there are chances for a more effective or efficient exploitation which leads to premiums for targets. However, his rationale for negative or only small excess returns for acquirers is that there is a bad post-

[6] Cf. Agrawal et al. (2000), p. 3, pp 50-52.
[7] Cf. Agrawal et al. (2000), pp. 5-39.
[8] Cf. Agrawal et al. (1992), pp. 40-41.
[9] Cf. Franks et al. (1991), p. 253; Agrawal et al. (2000), p. 46.
[10] Cf. Agrawal et al. (2000), pp. 47-49.
[11] Cf. Agrawal et al. (2000), p. 49.

merger integration, that resources are unique to target firms and that the bidder market is competitive.[12]

In contrast to that, Agrwal et al. (1992), who employ two CAPM related models in a study comprising 937 firms, conclude from their findings of negative post-merger performance that this issue generally remains unresolved and argue that either inefficient markets or a slow adjustment to the merger event are responsible for long-run negative abnormal returns. [13]

Mitchell / Stafford (1999) focus on testing various methods. However, they also find underperformance on average among 2,767 firms. As a result, they show that a methodology should be used which accounts for the dependence of event firms abnormal returns. Moreover, they conclude that most of the findings of other scholars are irrelevant as theses studies assume independence in the sample.[14]

Ferris / Park (2001) are the first scholars who concentrated only on one industry, namely that of the highly regulated telecommunication. Hence, their sample only amounts to 9 firms in the smallest and 70 in their largest sample. They find that the acquiring firms underperformed relative to their size, and industry matched control firms. When analysing sub-samples, they are able to conclude that larger firms in contrast to small and medium-sized firms performed well. They account this to synergy effects exploited through the merger.[15]

The second last study reviewed in his chapter is that of Forsyth / Rajand (2002). They investigate 31 firms in the UK. Their findings suggest that hostile bidders experience positive abnormal post-acquisition performance whereas friendly bidders suffer from poor performance. They account this to greater management efforts to ensure a better post-acquisition performance (disciplinary hypothesis).[16]

---

[12] Cf. Asquith (1982), pp. 80-83.
[13] Cf. Agrawal et al. (1992), pp. 1608-1610, pp. 1618-1620.
[14] Cf. Mitchell / Stafford (1999), pp. 31-34, pp. 41-56.
[15] Cf. Ferris / Park (2002), p. 1, p. 31.
[16] Cf. Ferris / Park (2002), pp. 47-79.

Finally, the findings of André / Kooli / L'Her (2004) will be summarised. They find in their long-term post event study including 267 M&A transactions in Canada from 1980 to 2000 both, positive and negative abnormal returns, respectively, depending on whether their calendar-time portfolio is value weighted or equally weighted respectively.[17]

Table 1: Overview of post-event long-term performance studies

Scholar (Year)	Event	Sample Size	Method	Post-Event Period Returns
Asquith (1982)	Mergers a) successful b) unsuccessful	a) 196 b) 86	CARs, annual portfolios of NYSE into 10 control portfolios	240 days negative returns for successful and unsuccessful bidders
Agrawal et. al. (1992)	Mergers 1955-87 (only acquirers)	937	CARs, CAPM related models	60 months negative returns for acquirers
Mitchell / Stafford (1999)	M&A 1961-93	2.767	CARs (Size & BE/ME portfolios, FFTM), BHAR (Size & BE/ME portfolios)	36 month significant and insignificant negative long-term performance
Ferris / Park (2001)	M&A in the Telecommunication Industry 1990-1993	min. 9 max. 70	CARs and BHARs, control firms	3-5 years under-performance for small and mid-sized mergers, positive long-term performance for large mergers and conglomerates
Forsyth / Rajand (2002)	Friendly and hostile bidders in the UK	31	CARs, Market Model	3 years positive CARs for hostile bidders, losses for friendly bidders
André/Kooli/L'Her (2004)	Canadian acquisitions 1980-2000	267	Calendar-time portfolios, FFTM	3 years of poor performance with equally weighted and positive performance with value weighted portfolios

[17] Cf. André / Kooli / L'Her (2004), pp. 27-33, p. 41.

In general, it is justified to state that the more specialised the study is on a particular market, the smaller of course the sample size and the more frequent do positive or negative abnormal returns occur (see Table 1). However, one must still be aware of the fact that the method chosen to conduct a study influences the results.

2.2 Formulation of Hypotheses

When it comes to the null hypothesis, there are manifold arguments supporting any hypothesis. On the one hand one might expect positive CARs as the brewing industry bears synergies for example economies of large scale buying. A technical reason would be that the expected small sample due to the sectoral focus proved to show positive abnormal returns. On the other hand, the industry suffers from large overcapacities. In combination with the facts that the industry is rather atomised, that it is hence not likely that overcapacities will be reduced soon and acquirers are significantly larger than targets, the position is taken that it is reasonable to expect zero long-run abnormal performance. Therefore, the standard null hypothesis (H_0)[18] is formulated: "Acquirers are expected to show zero abnormal performance in the long-run, i.e. over 12, 24 and 36 months respectively".

In terms of non-acquirers, it is intuitively reasonable to expect that there is no abnormal performance in the absence of events: Thus, for non-acquirers H_0 is also: "Non-Acquirers are expected show zero abnormal performance in the long-run, i.e. over 12, 24 and 36 months respectively".

3 Sample and Data Description

Analysing the German brewing market, 244 M&A transactions with at least one listed company were ascertained in the period between December 1989 and January 2005 of which data was accessible. Within these transactions 98 different firms were identified being acquirers of 174 various targets. Due to the restrictions that only companies which are both breweries and German should be part of the investigation, the sample size was reduced to 51 acquirers during the estimated time-

[18] See for example Boehmer et al. (1991), p. 254; Brown / Warner (1980), p. 206; Brown / Warner (1984), p. 4; Agrawal et al. (2000), p. 2, pp. 5-7; Bhagat / Romano (2001), p. 8.

frame. A second restriction results from the application of a long-term investigation. In literature, long-term analyses usually require an event window without any additional event of at least 36 months.[19] Moreover, daily returns for approximately one year before the investigated M&A announcement must be available for the most common methods. The last appreciable restriction is only constraint for the acquirers: All acquiring companies within the sample must exist during the investigation period which means that they must not be targets.

The denoted constraints result in the fact that the acquirer sample size diminishes to five companies, and the end of the investigation the period has to be restricted to December 2001. Their return distribution shows no skewness and seems to be rather normally distributed.[20] Noticeable is the very high number of returns, having a value of zero which reflects the low liquidity and hence a low degree of efficiency of the market which influences the analysis done in this seminar paper in a negative way.

The following event distribution for the acquiring firms can be stated (see Table 2):

Table 2: Event Distribution of Acquirers

	Distribution of Events - Acquirers												
	Jan.	Feb.	Mar.	Apr.	May	Jun.	Jul.	Aug.	Sep.	Oct.	Nov.	Dec	Total
1991									30				1
1992													
1993											4	8	2
1994	18												1
1995													
1996													
1997													
1998							31						1
Total	1						1		1		1	1	5

After having attained the sample of acquirers, in a second step the non-acquiring companies had to be identified. Several requirements for these are similar to those of the acquirers. For setting up the sample, the non-acquirers must be both brewer-

---

[19] Cf. André / Kooli / L'Her (2004), pp. 27-33, p. 41; Kothari / Warner (1997), p. 309; Mitchell / Stafford (1999), pp. 31-34, pp. 41-56; Ferris / Park (2002), pp. 1-5; see also Table 1.

[20] See Appendix 1.

ies and German. Furthermore, they must not have any event – neither in the role of the acquirer nor of the target – during the investigation period.

These constraints reduced the sample size to nine non-acquirers for an investigation period starting in December 1989 and ending in December 1999. When it comes to the return distribution of the non-acquirers, the same result can be stated as previously given for the acquiring firms.[21] Due to the fact that the non-acquiring corporations are in general much smaller than the acquiring ones, there are even more zero returns and therefore less market liquidity. Appendix 3 shows the results of the sample generation.

4 Methodology

4.1 Long-term Performance Study Methods

Being aware of the fact that analysing long-run abnormal returns is "treacherous"[22], it is of utmost importance to make a deliberate choice on the appropriate method. Many of the recent papers composed by renowned scholars do not investigate specific events but rather focus on discussions about the appropriate methodology.[23]

Generally, there are two ways of calculating abnormal returns: The first one is to use CARs and the second one is to use BHARs. Both methods have advantages and disadvantages, which have been vividly discussed in literature.[24] The following chapter will dedicate some arguments to this issue.

First of all, CARs are calculated using continuously compounded returns. This is considered their biggest advantage, since the assumption of normal distribution rather holds with logarithmic returns than with arithmetically computed BHARs.[25] Another advantage of CARs is of a more practical nature: They are easier to handle

---

[21] See Appendix 2.
[22] Cf. Lyon et al. (1999), p. 165.
[23] Cf., for example, Fama (1998), pp. 283-306; Kothari / Warner (2004), pp. 21-41; Kothari / Warner (1997), pp. 301-339; Faff (2004), pp. 82-93; Lyon et al. (1997), pp. 165-201.
[24] Cf. Fama (1998), pp. 291-292; pp. 296-297.
[25] Cf. Brown / Warner (1980), p. 222.

in terms of calculating total and average returns. In contrast, Barber / Lyon (1997) advocate BHARs as they find out in a regression that CARs are biased estimators of CARs, and moreover, they found that continuously compounded returns are negatively biased estimated of long-term abnormal returns.[26] However, there are more pros and cons when it comes to the estimation method of expected returns.

Once having decided about the abnormal return calculation method, one has several options to choose a benchmark method in order to estimate expected returns (see Table 3):

Reference Portfolios can be size decile portfolios, book-to-market decile portfolios or an equally weighted market index. Size decile portfolios are constructed by ranking firms according to some characteristics, for example market value of equity or book-to-market values of equity, etc. and are then used as a control portfolio for abnormal performance measurement. The decile portfolios are rebalanced on an annual basis. The easier alternative is to use an (equally weighted) market index because this approach is less susceptible to mistakes.[27]

In the control firm approach, sample firms are matched to one control firm with regard to specific firm characteristics. These characteristics could be size, book-to-market ratio or a combination of both.[28]

Finally, Barber / Lyon (1997) employ the Fama-French Three Factor Model (FFTM). This model is a multifactor regression which is based on the CAPM.[29] The approach is also referred to as Jensen-alpha Approach.[30] Modifications have been developed as well, for example by Carhart.[31] The returns are obtained by

---

[26] Cf. Barber / Lyon (1997), p. 346, p. 350.

[27] Cf. Barber / Lyon (1997), pp. 353-354; Lyon et al. (1999), pp. 167-168; Jagadeesh / Karceski (2004), p. 4.

[28] Cf. Barber / Lyon (1997), pp. 354-355; Lyon et al. (1999), pp. 172-173; Brown / Warner (1980), p. 223.

[29] Cf. Kothari / Warner (2004), pp. 29-30; Fama / French (1996a), pp. 55-56; Fama / French (1996a), 1982-1987; Fama / French (1993), pp. 3-55.

[30] Cf. Kothari / Warner (2004), p. 28.

[31] Cf. Kothari / Warner (2004), p. 29.

constructing so called monthly calendar-time portfolios. Firms are held in the portfolio for some period after the event date. This is why the number of firms varies from month to month.[32] Besides, the methods presented above have been modified or extended in many ways.

Elaborating on these methods with a focus on test statistics, there are advantages as well as disadvantages associated with each one. Fama (1998) even states that all models are subject to the bad-model problem. This is not severe in short-terms, but the problem increases as the period examined grows.[33] Some of the pros and cons shall be discussed here in short.

There are many authors who tested various methodologies. For instance, Barber / Lyon (1997) experimented with various methods. Concerning reference portfolios, they criticise that they are susceptible to the rebalancing bias and the skewness bias. The former arises due to the monthly portfolio rebalancing, the latter because multi-period abnormals are positively skewed.[34]

The control firms approach avoids the rebalancing bias and the skewness bias when a bootstrapped skewness-adjusted t-statistic is used.[35] However, there are also difficulties regarding control firms. Size matching can yield very different abnormal returns, as book-to-market matched control firms and test statistics can both be misinterpreted. Fama (1998) states: "[...] BE/ME surely do not capture all relevant cross-firm variation in average returns due to expected returns or sample specific patterns."[36] Thus, control firms are also not the magic bullet.

[32] Cf. Lyon et al. (1999), p. 194 ; Brown / Warner (1980), pp. 255-256.
[33] Cf. Fama (1998), p. 291; Lyon et al. (1999), p. 165.
[34] Cf. Barber / Lyon (1997), pp. 342-343.
[35] For details on calculations see Lyon et al. (1999), p. 173.
[36] Cf. Fama (1998), p. 293.

Chart 1: Benchmark Methods and CARs versus BHARs

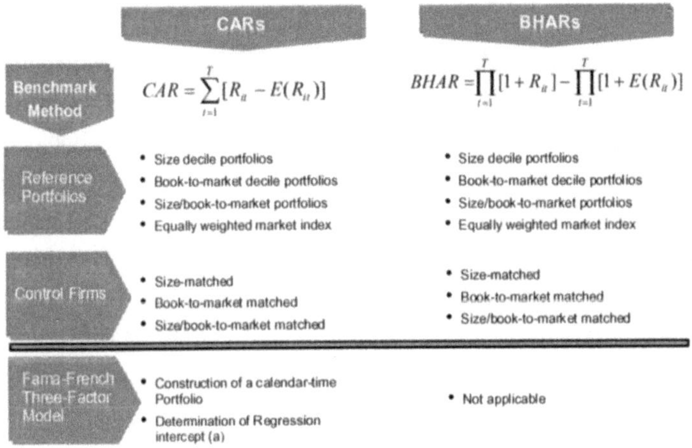

$$R_{it} - R_{ft} = \alpha_i + \beta_i(R_{mt} - R_{ft}) + s_i SMB_t + h_i HML_t + e_{it}$$

Source: Based on Barber / Lyon (1997), p. 360.

With regard to the FFTM and its extensions, it is not considered a good model, either. Firstly, this is so because it is based on the CAPM which is also not deemed to be a good approximation for expected returns;[37] secondly because the FFTM multifactor regression does not provide a comprehensive explanation of average returns.[38] As a closing remark on this discussion, it is Kothari / Warner (1997) who state that the market model can circumvent the failure of using a completely mis-specified model.[39]

Notwithstanding this criticism, there are some advantages of the calendar-time portfolio method used in connection with the FFTM. The calendar-time approach controls well for cross-sectional dependence, since sample firms' returns are aggregated into one portfolio. On the other hand, it does not resemble investor behaviour as BHARs do. Furthermore, calendar-time returns are less skewed. Yet, in

---

[37] Cf. Fama / French (1996b), p. 1957; Bhagat / Romano (2001), p. 30.
[38] Cf. Fama (1998), p. 293.
[39] Cf. Kothari / Warner (1997), pp. 304.

non-random samples, calendar-time portfolios often yield misspecified test statistics.[40]

BHARs, in turn, are skewed and show large cross-correlation due to overlapping event returns in the long-run.[41] The skewness is partly a by-product of cross-correlation within samples.[42] The cross-correlation increases with sample homogeneity (when industries are clustered) and time-horizons.[43] Lyon et al. (1999) take the bootstrapped skewness-adjusted test statistics to counter the cross-correlation problem. Still, they are not an effective remedy.[44]

Other problems closely related to cross-correlation are autocorrelation and heteroscedasticity. Autocorrelation leads to understated test statistics.[45] A remedy to this problem in connection with the use of the Market Model was developed by Engle (1982). He developed the autoregressive conditionally heteroscedastic model (ARCH) which is a more efficient estimator than ordinary least squares (OLS). Later, the more generalised ARCH (GARCH) was introduced.[46] GARCH processes have been widely discussed among scholars.[47] ARCH/GARCH models account for two issues, namely that the variance of the errors is heteroscedastic and that volatility occurs in clusters, i.e. one can say - slightly abusing the term - that "volatility is autocorrelated".[48] Hence, ARCH models accommodate that volatility consists of a conditional component and an unconditional component. The conditional variance is stationary, i.e. does not change over time, whereas the unconditional variance is constant.[49] The ARCH model has then been advanced by Bollerslev (1986) to GARCH processes which are more flexible in terms of their autoregressive lags.[50]

---

[40] Cf. Lyon et al. (1999), pp. 192-193; Jegadeesh / Karceski (1999), pp. 1-3.
[41] Cf. Mitchell / Stafford (1999), p. 4.
[42] Cf. Khotari / Warner (2004), pp. 31-32.
[43] Cf. Fama (1998), pp. 11-14; Khotari / Warner (2004), p. 33; Cf. Lyon et al. (1999), p. 188.
[44] Cf. Khotari / Warner (2004), p. 38.
[45] Cf. Brown / Warner (1984), p. 25, p. 28.
[46] Cf. Brooks (2002), pp. 437-469; Engle (2001), p. 157; Engle (1982), p. 987.
[47] Cf. Brooks (2002), pp. 444-447; Cf. Brockett et al. (1999), p. 197; Bollerslev (1987), p. 542.
[48] Cf. Brooks (2002), p. 446.
[49] Cf. Engle (1982), pp. 987-988; Bollerslev (1986), p. 307.
[50] Cf. Bollerslev (1986), pp. 307-308; Brooks (2002), pp. 452-455.

Overall, Bollerslev (1987) and Ackert / Racine (1997) find that GARCH (1,1)[51] models fit the time series they examined well.[52] In summary, GARCH appears to be a more sophisticated method than OLS, and thus it is superior in this respect. When it comes to test statistics, Jegadesh et al. (1999) have constructed new test statistics based on BHAR calculations. They praise their methodology as a pancea, especially because they consider it superior to the bootstrap method. However, disadvantages are that it has been developed on the basis of the study conducted by Lyon et al. (1999)[53] and has not been tested widely yet.

From the preceding discussion it is clear that the appropriate model has to be chosen very deliberately. Test statistics in turn depend on the model choice. The next chapter will be more precise on this.

4.2 Methodology Selection

4.2.1 Estimation of Abnormal Returns

The main problem of this study is the comparably small sample. With only five acquirers and nine non-acquirers, the sample has a critical size. This is also the main reason why some methods cannot be considered. Using size decile portfolios and book-to-market decile portfolios is not feasible due to the small sample. The same is true for control firms. Finding a German brewing control firm for Holsten, by far the biggest acquirer in the sample, is impossible. Likewise, forming calendar-time portfolios with small samples makes no sense. Especially when samples are clustered in one industry as they probably would yield unspecified test statistics.[54] This excludes the use of the FFTM or any other similar approach as well. Consequently, one feasible method left over is the Marked Model[55] which is also

---

[51] The (1,1) in parentheses is a standard notation. The first number is the squared residual and indicates how many autoregressive lags appear in the formula. The second number refers to how many lags are included in the moving average component of a variable. Cf. Brooks (2002), p. 452; Engle (2001), p. 160.

[52] Cf. Bollerslev (1987), p. 546; Ackert / Racine (1997), p. 372.

[53] Cf. Jegadeesh / Karceski (1999), p. 1-3, p. 21.

[54] Cf. Lyon et al. (1999), pp. 192-193.

[55] Yet the market adjusted model is also feasible, it is not implemented as it is not widely used in literature and the scope of this paper is limited.

employed by other scholars analysing long-run abnormal returns.[56] A further advantage is that it is a well acknowledged method to measure short event windows. The MDAX was consulted as the benchmark index.[57]

Formula 1

$$R_{it} = \alpha_i + \beta_i R_{mt} + e_{it}$$

whereby α_i and β_i are parameter estimates obtained from the regression of daily returns R_{it} from security i at day t on the MDAX for the respective estimation periods.

Brocket et al. (1999) strongly recommend the use of GARCH(1,1) with classical event study methodologies because in longer horizons the power of classical event studies deteriorates.[58] Thus, GARCH(1,1) is applied to the error term e_{it} :[59]

Formula 2

$$e_{jt} | \Psi_{t-1} \sim N(0, h_t)$$

whereby $N(0,h_t)$ denotes the conditional distribution of e_{it} with a zero mean and the variance h_t. All information available at t-1 is given by ψ_{t-1}. Further, the conditional variance h_t is determined by the past conditional variance and the squared past error:

Formula 3

$$h_t = \alpha_0 + \alpha_1 h_{t-1} + \alpha_2 e_{t-1}^2$$

---

[56] See for example Kothari / Warner (1997), p. 306; Brockett et al. (1999), p. 198; Ising et al. (2004), p. 12; Nahar (2005), p. 23.

[57] This was done by the shirt term Event Studies presented in the course of the project. Consequently, this is done for matters of comparability and because the MDAX is liquid and a well diversified index. It was taken into account to consult the BEX-Germany 15 or Europe Titans 30 which were con structed during the course of the project. Both indices are driven by a few big breweries, which is con sidered as striking disadvantage.

[58] Cf. Brockett et al. (1999), pp. 216-217.

[59] Cf. Brockett et al. (1999), p. 199.

In a first step parameters are estimated during a period of 252 trading days using the maximum likelihood method.[60] It is assumed that there will be no information available on the deal one month prior to the announcement date. Hence, the estimation period is from T= -282 to t= -30. In order to get clean values for the expected return, the estimation period has to be free of any M&A activity. Also, there must not be any M&A event during the event window. In order to weaken the handicap of the small sample size, two non-acquirer portfolios (with the same companies but) with different event dates are set up. These event dates are selected by using a random function (see Table 3).[61]

Table 3: Random-set Distribution of Non-Acquirers

P1	Distribution of Events - Non-Acquirers Portfolio 1												
	Jan.	Feb.	Mar.	Apr.	May	Jun.	Jul.	Aug.	Sep.	Oct.	Nov.	Dec	Total
1990						29						26	2
1991										14			1
1992				4									1
1993										25			1
1994							18					27	2
1995				11									1
1996										4			1
1997													
1998													
Total				2		1	1			3		2	9

P2	Distribution of Events - Non-Acquirers Portfolio 2												
	Jan.	Feb.	Mar.	Apr.	May	Jun.	Jul.	Aug.	Sep.	Oct.	Nov.	Dec	Total
1990												10	1
1991	7						18						2
1992													
1993		12						2	7				3
1994							1						1
1995											24		1
1996	25												1
1997													
1998													
Total	2	1					2	1	1		1	1	9

The event window starts one day after the announcement date and abnormal returns are measured for 12, 24 and 36 months respectively.[62]

[60] Cf. Bollerslev (1986), p. 315.
[61] Cf. Khotari / Warner (1997), p. 305.
[62] See Appendix 4.

After all market models have been estimated, the abnormal return can be calculated:[63]

Formula 4

$$AR_{it} = R_{it} - \left(\hat{\alpha}_i + \hat{\beta}_i R_{mt}\right)$$

Next, CAR and CAAR can be calculated respectively as follows:

Formula 5

$$CAR_{i,[b;B]} = \sum_{t=b}^{B} AR_{it}$$

and

Formula 6

$$CAAR_{[b;B]} = \frac{1}{N} \sum_{i=1}^{N} AR_{i,[b;B]}$$

whereby [b;B] indicates the time period and N the number of firms in the sample.

In a second step the effect of the single acquirer events on non-acquirer performance is examined. The modus operandi is quite similar to the process of the previous step and distinguishes only the event windows. These are set up in short-terms for the monthly periods [-1;1], [-1;3], [-1;6] and [0;2], [0;3], [0;6]. The "-1" periods are used to consider abnormal stock return reaction before the announcement took place and therefore should prevent from test distortions due to insider information.

---

[63] Cf. MacKinlay (1997), p. 20.

4.2.2 Test Statistic

After having computed CARs and CAARs respectively, it has to be determined whether abnormal returns differ statistically significantly from zero. Therefore, the conventional t-test is calculated at first:[64]

Formula 7

$$\frac{\overline{x}}{s}\sqrt{N},$$

whereby $\overline{x}$ denotes the computed CAAR and s denotes the sample standard deviation.

Additionally, the more sophisticated Mikkelson / Partch test is carried out, allowing for a different standard deviation at each calendar day's abnormal return and re-controlling the results obtained from the t-test in order to avoid false inferences. The Mikkelson / Partch standardised cumulative residual is obtained by:[65]

Formula 8

$$SR_{i,[c;C]} = \frac{\sum_{t=c}^{C} AR_{it}}{s_i\sqrt{EP + \frac{EP^2}{T_i} + \frac{\sum_{t=c}^{C} R_{mt} - EP(R_m)^2}{\sum_{t=d_i}^{D_i}(R_{mt} - R_m)^2}}}$$

whereby

AR_{it} = the Abnormal Return at day t of security i;

[c;C] = the examined time window;

EP = the number of days in the event period;

$[d_i;D_i]$ = the estimation period for security i;

T_i = the number of days in the estimation period of security i;

---

[64] Cf. McClave et al. (3001), p. 298.

[65] Cf. Mikkelson / Partch (1988), pp. 121-123; Mikkelson / Partch (1986), pp. 40-41.

s_i = the standard deviation of stock i during the estimation period;
R_m = the average return on the market portfolio during the estimation period

Finally, the Mikkelson / Partch z-statistics will be computed by:

Formula 9

$$\frac{\sum_{i=1}^{N} SR_{i,[c;C]}}{\sqrt{N}}$$

Both tests require the sample to be normally distributed and independent.[66] In addition to these tests, the Wilcoxon Rank Sum Test is consulted to test the hypothesis for probability distributions of acquirers and non-acquirers to be equivalent. If the calculated rank sums are significantly different, then it is implied that the focal samples may stem from different populations.[67] The rank sum test is considered superior to the t-test and the sign test in event studies.[68]

Furthermore, the Boehmer Test will be consulted for shorter and medium terms as it accommodates event induced variance. Also, it is named a hybrid of the standardized-residual and the ordinary cross-sectional method, requiring the error term to be cross-sectional uncorrelated:[69]

Formula 10

$$\frac{\frac{1}{N}\sum_{i=1}^{N} SR_{i,[c;C]}}{\sqrt{\frac{1}{N(N-1)}\sum_{i=1}^{N}\left(SR_{i,[c;C]}-\sum_{i=1}^{N}\frac{SR_{i,[c;C]}}{N}\right)^2}}$$

[66] Cf. Serra (2002), pp. 4-6.
[67] Cf. McClave et. al. (2001), pp. 894-896; Wilcoxon (1945), pp. 80-83.
[68] Cf. Corrado / Zivney (1992), p. 477.
[69] Cf. Boehmer (1991), p. 203; pp. 260-270.

The tests are not well specified if there are cross-sectional correlations within the sample.[70]

5 Empirical Results

5.1 Long-term Results

The findings of the long-term study of the acquirers are exhibited in Table 4. All event windows[71] yield negative CAARs. The pattern suggests that the longer the horizon is the worse the abnormal performance turns out to be. Yet, neither the results of the conventional t-test nor the results of the more sophisticated Mikkelson / Partch Test give indication for the rejection of the null hypothesis.

Table 4: Long-term Performance Acquirers.

n=5	CARs of Acquirers				
Event Window	CAARs	Median	Std. Dev.	t-statistic	Mikkelson / Partch
[0;36]	-40,70%	-30,40%	57,47%	-1,58	-1,07
[0;24]	-27,52%	-14,31%	46,39%	-1,33	-1,01
[0;12]	-15,36%	-7,46%	25,53%	0,91	0,43

Likewise, but as expected, non-acquirers do not show abnormal performance, either.[72] At first sight, it appears odd that Portfolio 1 yields positive abnormal returns whereas Portfolio 2 shows negative CAARs. This difference can be ascribed to the different and randomly chosen event dates. A brief look at the CARs of acquirers and non-acquirers reveals that acquirers' CARs are much more volatile than non-acquirers' CARs during the examination period (Appendix 5). Despite this volatility pattern, there is no evidence that this is an abnormal return pattern that could be ascribed to low speed of adjustment.

Besides, the Wilcoxon Rank Sum Test was carried out to determine whether CARs stem from the same population. In fact, the test results predicate that the CARs are not from different populations (see Appendix 6).

---

70 Cf. Serra (2002), pp. 5-6.
71 Where [0;12] for example denotes the event window starting one day after the announcement day.
72 As explained earlier, the event months were determined randomly.

Overall, the data suggest that there was no long-term abnormal performance for both, acquirers and non-acquirers. Though, these results have to be treated carefully as the sample size is small and thus not representative enough. A multivariate regression was omitted owing to the insignificance of returns on the one hand and to small sample size on the other.

Table 5: Long-term Performance Non-Acquirers

n=9	CARs of Non-Acquirers Portfolio 1				
Event Window	CAARs	Median	Std. Dev.	t-statistic	Mikkelson / Partch
[0;36]	11,10%	8,39%	65,53%	0,51	0,40
[0;24]	6,14%	-6,43%	39,96%	0,46	-0,08
[0;12]	7,77%	-3,10%	25,53%	0,91	0,43
n=9	CARs of Non-Acquirers Portfolio 2				
Event Window	CAARs	Median	Std. Dev.	t-statistic	Mikkelson / Partch
[0;36]	-7,94%	-12,42%	60,79%	-0,39	1,16
[0;24]	-11,03%	-7,21%	47,94%	-0,69	0,92
[0;12]	-5,56%	-1,33%	26,73%	-0,62	0,32

To get a more detailed picture of the behaviour of non-acquirer performance, short windows shall be examined additionally.

5.2 Short-term Results

The inferences of Geiger / Roediger (2005) are that the market seems to honour the consolidation of the German brewery market for bidders proven by their positive abnormal returns.[73] This is underpinned by their findings that cross-boarder M&A is less rewarded.

The question arising is whether non-acquirers show any reaction to the announcement day of acquirers, that is, it is tested if non-acquirers respond to acquirer events. The data exhibits a diffuse picture at first glance.

Table 6 summarises the results from the short-term event window analysis. Nonetheless, most of the significant abnormal returns can be traced back to an outlier.

---

[73] Cf. Geiger / Roedinger (2005).

Table 6: Non-acquirer CAARs at announcement date of acquirers

DOM acquires GIESELER: 30/07/1998					Non-Acquirer CAARs		
Event Window	n	CAARs	Median	Std. Dev.	t-statistic	Mikkelson / Partch	Boehmer
[-1;1]	9	1,05%	0,02	0,04	0,87	0,89	1,27
[-1;3]	9	-2,97%	0,01	0,11	-0,85	-0,30	-0,44
[-1;6]	9	-7,95%	-0,03	0,13	-1,80	-1,37	-1,99 **
[0;2]	9	-0,70%	0,00	0,12	-0,18	0,21	0,22
[0;3]	9	-2,21%	0,00	0,13	-0,50	-0,50	-0,61
[0;6]	9	-7,20%	-0,03	0,16	-1,34	-1,62	-2,00 **

GILDE acquires WUELFEL: 30/09/1991					Non-Acquirer CAARs		
Event Window	n	CAARs	Median	Std. Dev.	t-statistic	Mikkelson / Partch	Boehmer
[-1;1]	9	-2,53%	-0,02	0,05	-1,58	-1,34	-1,63
[-1;3]	9	-1,13%	-0,02	0,05	-0,72	-0,60	-1,03
[-1;6]	9	-7,94%	-0,01	0,61	-0,39	-0,40	-0,56
[0;2]	9	-1,31%	-0,03	0,04	-0,96	-1,26	-2,02 **
[0;3]	9	0,08%	-0,01	0,05	0,04	-0,35	-0,62
[0;6]	9	0,83%	0,01	0,07	0,36	-0,20	-0,31

HOLSTEN acquires NORDGETRANKE: 08/12/1993					Non-Acquirer CAARs		
Event Window	n	CAARs	Median	Std. Dev.	t-statistic	Mikkelson / Partch	Boehmer
[-1;1]	9	1,89%	0,02	0,04	1,48	1,25	1,65 *
[-1;3]	9	6,52%	0,06	0,11	1,84	2,75 ***	1,90 *
[-1;6]	9	10,99%	0,05	0,22	1,50	3,22 ***	1,67 *
[0;2]	9	-0,14%	-0,01	0,05	-0,08	0,24	0,27
[0;3]	9	5,59%	0,06	0,10	1,73	2,82 ***	1,86 *
[0;6]	9	10,06%	0,03	0,21	1,41	3,29 ***	1,59

MAINZER acquires ALLGÄUER: 18/01/1994					Non-Acquirer CAARs		
Event Window	n	CAARs	Median	Std. Dev.	t-statistic	Mikkelson / Partch	Boehmer
[-1;1]	9	1,32%	0,02	0,04	1,07	1,18	1,31
[-1;3]	9	5,56%	0,07	0,09	1,77	2,41 **	1,99 **
[-1;6]	9	11,92%	0,09	0,21	1,73	3,68 ***	1,76 *
[0;2]	9	5,83%	0,04	0,11	1,55	3,66 ***	1,77 *
[0;3]	9	7,16%	0,07	0,12	1,82	3,41 ***	1,97 **
[0;6]	9	11,92%	0,08	0,21	1,73	4,42 ***	1,74 *

SEDLMAYER acquires DINKELACKER: 30/09/1992					Non-Acquirer CAARs		
Event Window	n	CAARs	Median	Std. Dev.	t-statistic	Mikkelson / Partch	Boehmer
[-1;1]	9	-0,03%	0,00	0,03	-0,02	-0,32	-0,43
[-1;3]	9	-0,19%	0,00	0,03	-0,19	-0,05	-0,14
[-1;6]	9	13,28%	0,08	0,24	1,68	3,40 ***	1,68 *
[0;2]	9	1,20%	0,01	0,04	0,91	0,62	0,99
[0;3]	9	-0,20%	0,01	0,03	-0,18	0,18	0,33
[0;6]	9	13,27%	0,06	0,22	1,77	3,93 ***	1,81 *

*, ** and *** denote significance at the 10, 5, and 1 percent level, respectively.

The general pattern to be observed is that the t-test did not detect any abnormal performances of non-acquirers at the announcement date of the respective acquirer. This is different when regarding the Mikkelson / Partch and Boehmer Test statistics. They indicate significance in various event windows. Again, the Wilcoxon Rank Sum Test does not reject the hypothesis that acquirers and non-acquirers stem from different populations (see Appendix 7). When elaborating on these test results, it is obvious that suspicions towards the test results are justified. To begin with the event of Dom, the abnormal return which occurs only during the event windows [-1;6] and [0;6] can be ascribed to a financial distress situation connected with corporate restructuring at Actris-Henninger.[74] Consequently, following the test statistics would lead to wrong inferences, as the negative performance is not driven by the acquisition.

Continuing with the Gilde acquisition, the CAR in the event window [0;2] is significant there according to the Boehmer Test. But as the other tests both are insignificant, this result seems not to be an important abnormal non-acquirer return.

Even stronger abnormal short and mid-term performances of non-acquirers are suggested at the Holsten announcement date. Unfortunately, these test results were mainly caused by Stuttgarter Hofbräu and Moninger. Elaborating on this, it reveals that abnormal returns are the result of the 80% share of Stuttgarter Hofbräu in Moninger since 1993 which means that there is a cross-correlation in the sample.[75] This strategic investment in turn has probably already affected the statistic significance of non-acquirers at the Sedlmayr event windows [-1;6] and [0;6], that is half a year after the take-over announcement of Sedlmayr. The take-over was then accompanied by restructuring activities disturbing again the event of Mainzer: Moninger divested shares in other companies in 1994.[76]

Hence, there are two effects that distort the outcome: Firstly, the investment year of Stuttgarter Hofbräu in Moninger coincided with the event windows of Sedlmeyer and Holsten. Secondly, the restructuring activities of Moninger "spilled over" to its strategic invester Stuttgarter Hofbräu yielding positive abnormal returns.

The inference from this is that Mikkelson / Partch and Boehmer Test statistics seem to be misleading in this sample.[77] Except once, abnormal returns could in

[74] Cf. Ad Hoc News (1998), p. 1.

[75] Cf. Sammleraktien-online.de (2005), p. 1.

[76] Cf. HWPH Historisches Wertpapierhaus AG (2003), p. 1.

[77] When purging the sample of correlating firms, the Mikkelson / Partch as well as the Boehmer Test does not indicate significant abnormal performance any more.

almost every case be explained by coinciding events. Nevertheless, the implication is that it is unlikely that acquirer events have a significant influence on non-acquirer returns. Also, the results imply that the conventional t-test may be the better indicator in very small samples despite correlations across firms. Again, a multivariate regression is omitted as single firm CARs dominate the sample.

6 Summary and Concluding Remarks

The finding of no long-run abnormal acquirer performance is basically not in line with the findings discussed in the literature review. Besides all criticism, sticking to the results would mean that there is no long-term adjustment of acquisitions. The long-term abnormal performance analysis comes to the conclusion that firstly, there is no significant long-term impact of acquisitions and secondly, there is no abnormal performance for non-acquirers in the German brewing industry measured by the same two samples with randomly selected event dates. The question of which group in general performed better cannot be answered satisfactorily, since it depends on the time window investigated. Or in short: In the long-run, acquisitions seem neither to create nor to destroy shareholder value. When it comes to the short-term analysis of event windows surrounding the announcement dates, the findings have to be interpreted even more cautiously. Although the two more sophisticated test statistics, the Mikkelson / Partch Test and the Boehmer Test alike indicated significant abnormal performance, a detailed sample analysis surprisingly showed that a strategic investment connection within the sample had a misleading impact on the results. However, disregarding the disturbances of coinciding events, it is unlikely that the non-acquirers responded to a take-over event by another company. An obvious reason is, that breweries are, as mentioned before, geographically dispersed, meaning that the businesses of regional breweries are not affected by an acquisition far beyond their regional market.

Consequently, the only advice that can be given for managers is that targets should be chosen thoroughly in terms of strategy, synergies and price, of course.

From an investor's point of view, it is important to bear in mind that volatility of abnormal returns was found higher for acquirers in the examined time window. Furthermore, markets are relatively illiquid, thus they are less efficient. Hence, the brewing industry is not necessarily a long-term investment opportunity, particularly not when one considers the declining markets.

Finally, it has to be stressed again that the results obtained from the long-term event study have to be interpreted deliberately. Some major points have to be criticised:

Firstly, the sample was not randomly selected, since it was data from the brewing industry, and secondly, it was not large enough for the Central Limit Theorem to hold. Stocks in the sample suffered from long non-trading periods which implies that markets are rather illiquid and inefficient. Also, long-term event studies often suffer from the bad-model problem, that is, the models are unspecified. This possibility cannot be eliminated. In other words: Another model might have led to other results. A severe problem is also that returns within the sample are correlated, leading to the wrong rejection of the null hypothesis.

Appendix

Appendix 1: Return Distribution of Acquirers

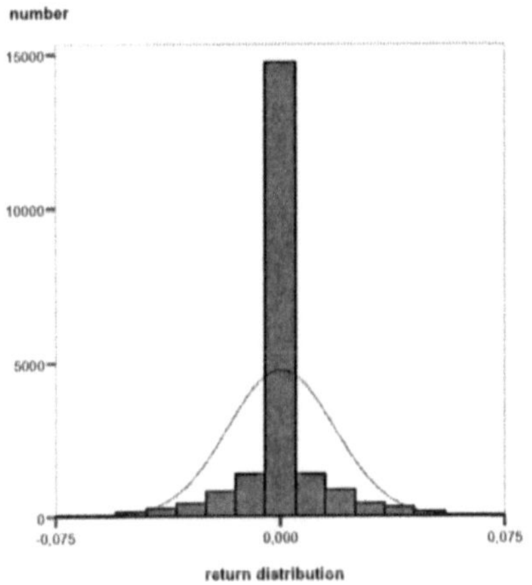

Appendix 2: Return Distribution of Non-Acquirers

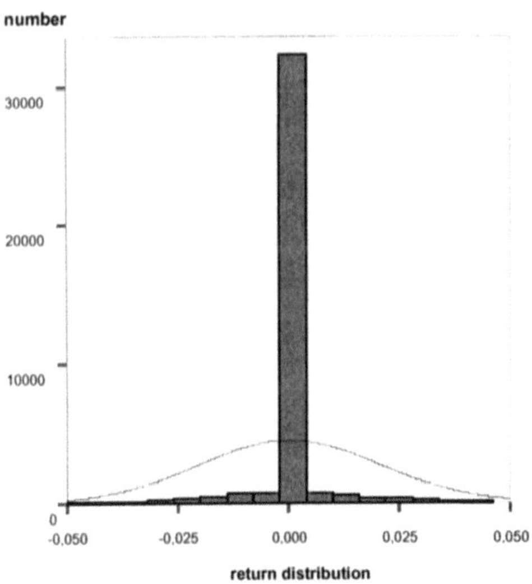

Appendix 3: Data Selection

descr.	targets	acquirers	german	breweries only	2005	2002	2001	1999	1996	1993	1990	#
1	o	*X*	o									***98***
2	o	*X*	*X*									***51***
3		*X*	*X*	*X*	*2*	*4*	*5*	*5*	*7*	*9*	*11*	*11*
4	*X*	*o*	*X*									***175***
5	*X*		*X*									***144***
6	*X*		*X*	*X*								***approx. 100***
7	*X*	*X*	*X*	*X*								***31***
8	*o*		*X*									***153***
9	*o*		*X*	*X*								***approx. 100***
10			*X*	*X*	*4*	*7*	*7*	*9*	*10*	*10*	*11*	*11*

	description/categorization
1	*acquirer*
2	*acquirer and only German*
3	***acquirer only and only German and only breweries***
4	*targets*
5	*targets only*
6	*targets only and only breweries*
7	*as well acquirer as targets*
8	*no acquirer and only German*
9	*no acquirer and only German and only breweries*
10	***no acquirer and no targets and only German and only breweries***

Appendix 4: Event Windows

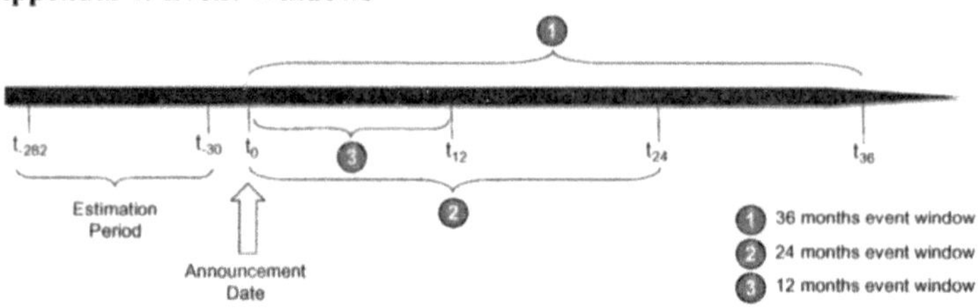

Appendix 5: Average Cumulative Returns

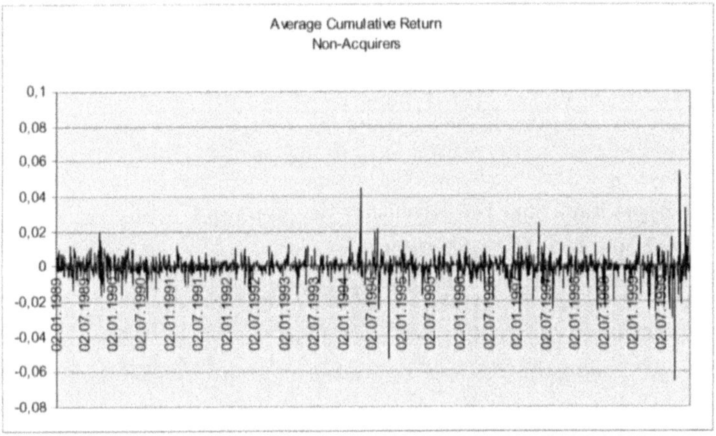

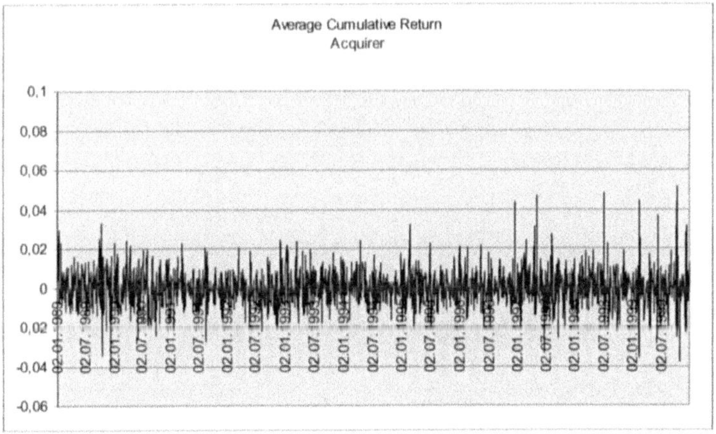

Appendix 6: Wilcoxon Rank Sum Test Results for Acquirers and Non-Acquirers CARs – Long-term.

	Non-Acquirer Portfolio 1			Non-Acquirer Portfolio 2		
	[0;12]	[0;24]	[0;36]	[0;12]	[0;24]	[0;36]
Acquirer Non-Acquirer	-1,133	-0,867	-1,400	-1,400	-0,867	-1,267

Appendix 7: Wilcoxon Rank Sum Test Results for Acquirers and Non-Acquirers CARs – Short-term

	[0;2]	[0;3]	[0;6]	[-1;1]	[-1;3]	[-1;6]
Acquirer Non-Acquirer	-0,501	-1,180	-1,148	-1,472	-1,116	-1,148

References

Ad Hoc News (1998): Henninger neuer Vorstand, <http://www.aktiencheck.de/>, Publication Date: 15/07/1998, Accessed: 06/06/2005.

Agrawal, Anup / Jaffe, Jeffrey F. (2000): The Post-Merger Performance Puzzle, in: Cooper, Cary / Gregory, Alan (Eds.): JAI Series: Advances in Mergers and Acquisitions, Vol. 1, pp. 1-59.

Agrawal, Anup / Jaffe, Jeffrey F. / Mandelker, Gershon N. (1992): The Post-Merger Performance of Acquiring Firms: A Re-examination of an Anomaly, in: The Journal of Finance, Vol. 47, No. 4, pp. 1605-1621.

Andre, Paul / Kooli, Maher / L'her, Jean-Francois (2004): The Long-Run Performance of Mergers and Acquisitions: Evidence from the Canadian Stock Market, in: Financial Management, Vol. 33, No. 4, pp. 27-43.

Asquith, Paul (1982): Merger Bids, Uncertainty, and Stockholder Returns, in: Journal of Financial Economics, Vol. 1, pp. 51-83.

Barber, Brad M. / Lyon, John D. (1997): Detecting Long-Run Abnormal Stock Returns: The Empirical Power and Specification of Test Statistics, in: Journal of Financial Economics, Vol. 43, No. 3, pp. 341-372.

Bhagat, Sanjai / Romano, Roberta (2001): Event Studies and the Law: PART 1: Technique and Corporate Litigation, in: Yale Law School-Center for Studies in Law, Economics and Public Policy, Vol. 4, No.1, pp. 1-33.

Boehmer, Ekkehart / Musumeci, Jim / Poulsen, Anette B. (1991): Event-Study Methodology Under Conditions of Event-Induced Variance, in: Journal of Financial Economics, Vol. 30, No. 2, pp. 253-272.

Bollerslev, Tim (1986): Generalized Autoregressive Conditional Heteroscedasticity, in: Journal of Econometrics, Vol. 31, No. 3, pp. 307-317.

Bollerslev, Tim (1987): A Conditionally Heteroscedastic Time Series Model for Speculative Prices and Rates of Return, in: Review of Economics & Statistics, Vol. 69, No. 3, pp. 542-547.

Brockett, Patrick L. / Chen, Hwei-Mei / Garven, James R. (1999): A New Stochastically Flexible Event Methodology with Application to Proposition 103, in: Insurance: Mathematics & Economics, Vol. 25, No. 2, pp. 197-217.

Brooks, Chris (2002): Introductory Econometrics for Finance, Cambridge.

Brown, Stephen J. / Warner, Jerold B. (1980): Measuring Security Price Performance, in: Journal of Financial Economics, Vol. 8, No. 3, pp. 205-258.

Brown, Stephen J. / Warner, Jerold B. (1985): Using Daily Stock Returns: The Case of Event Studies, in: Journal of Financial Economics, Vol. 14, No. 1, pp. 3-31.

Corrado, Charles J. / Zivney, Terry L. (1992): The Specification and Power of the Sign Test in Event Study Hypothesis Tests using daily Stock Data Returns, in: Journal of Financial and Quantitative Analysis, Vol. 27, No. 3, pp. 465-478.

Credit Suisse First Boston (2003): The German Beer Industry – The Consolidors' Challenge, in: Credit Suisse First Boston Equity Research, Research Paper, Vol. 04/06/2003.

Credit Suisse First Boston (2004): The German Beer Industry – The Consolidation continues, in: Credit Suisse First Boston Equity Research, Research Paper, Vol. 16/02/2004.

Engle, Robert F. (1982): Autoagressive Conditional Heteroscedasticity with Estimates of the Variance of United Kingdom Inflation, in: Econometrica, Vol. 50, No. 4, pp. 987-1008.

Engle, Robert F. (2001): Garch 101: The Use of ARCH/GARCH Models in Applied Econometrics, in: Journal of Economic Perspectives, Vol. 15, No. 4, pp. 157-168.

Faff, Robert (2004): A Simple Test of the Fama and French Model Using Daily Data: Australian Evidence, in: Applied Financial Economics, Vol. 14, No. 2, pp. 83-92.

Fama, Eugene F. (1998): Market Efficiency, Long-Term Returns, and Behavioral Finance, in: Journal of Financial Economics, Vol. 49, No. 3, pp. 283-306.

Fama, Eugene F. / French, Kenneth R. (1993): Common Risk Factors in the Return on Stocks and Bonds, in: Journal of Financial Economics, Vol. 33, No. 1, pp. 3-56.

Fama, Eugene F. / French, Kenneth R. (1996a): Multifactor Explanations of Asset Pricing Anomalies, in: The Journal of Finance, Vol. 53, No. 1, pp. 55-85.

Fama, Eugene F. / French, Kenneth R. (1996b): The CAPM is wanted, dead or alive, in: The Journal of Finance, Vol. LI, No. 5, pp. 1947-1958.

Fama, Eugene F. / French, Kenneth R. (1998): Value versus Growth: The International Evidence, in: The Journal of Finance, Vol. 53, No. 6, pp. 1975-1999.

Ferris, Stephen P. / Park, Kwangwoo (2002): How Differnet is the Long-Run Performance of Mergers in the Telecommunications Industry?, in: Hirschey, Mark / John, Kose / Makhija, Anil (Eds.): Advances in Financial Economics, Vol. 7, No. 1, pp. 1-21.

Franks, Julian R. / Harris, Robert S. / Mayer, Colin (1988): Means of Payment in Takeovers: Results for the United Kingdom and the United States, in: Auerbach, Alan J. (Ed.): Corporate Takeovers: Causes and Consequences, Chicago.

Geiger, Florian / Roediger, Tobias (2005): Announcement Effects M&A of Bidder in Germany, Unpublished Working Paper, Oestrich-Winkel.

Gerbig, Joerg / Zawadsky, Felix (2005): M&A Announcement Effects on Targets in the German Brewery Market, Unpublished Working Paper, Oestrich-Winkel.

HWPH Historisches Wertpapierhaus AG (Ed.) (2003), Auktionskatalog zur 3. Präsenzauktion am 20.09.2003 in Würzburg, <http://www.historisches-wertpapierhaus.de/ auktionen/pa3/pa3_2.html>, Publication Date: 20/09/2003, Accessed: 06/06/2005.

Ising, Jan / Schiereck, Dirk / Simpson Marc W. / Thomas, Thomas W. (2004): Long-Term Market Reactions to Large Price Declines and Increases – The Case of Germany; Witten/Herdecke University working paper, 2nd revised Version (June 2004), Witten, pp. 1-45.

Jegadeesh, Narasimhan / Karceski, Jason (2004): Long-Run Performance Evaluation: Correlation and Heteroskedasticity-Consider Tests, Working Paper Emory University, pp. 1-40.

Kothari, S. P. / Warner, Jerold B. (1997): Measuring Long-Horizon Security Price Performance, in: Journal of Financial Economics, Vol. 43, No. 3 pp. 301-339.

Kothari, S. P. / Warner, Jerold B. (2004): Econometrics of Event Studies, in: Eckbo, Espen (Ed.): Handbook of Corporate Finance: Empirical Corporate Finance, Elsevier.

Lyon, John D. / Barber, Brad M. / Tsai, Chih-Ling (1999): Improved Methods for Tests of Long-Run Abnormal Stock Returns, in: The Journal of Finance, Vol. 54, No. 1, pp. 165-201.

McClave, James T. / Benson, P. George / Sincich, Terry (2001): Statistics for Business and Economics, 8th Edition, Upper Saddle River.

Mikkelson, Wayne H. / Partch, Megan (1986): Valuation Effects of Security Offerings and the Issuance Process, in: Journal of Financial Economics, Vol. 15, pp. 31-60.

Mikkelson, Wayne H. / Partch, Megan (1988): Withdrawn Security Offerings, in: Journal of Financial and Quantitative Analysis, Vol. 23, No. 2, pp. 119-136.

Mitchell, Mark L. / Stafford Erik (1999): Managerial Decisions and Long-Term Stock Price Performance, in: University of Chicago Press: Journal of Business, Vol. 73, No. 3, pp. 1-56.

Nahar, Toby (2005): The Rebound Effect: Long-term Reactions to Large Stock Price Declines and Increases of the AsianTitans50, unpublished Working Paper, Oestrich-Winkel.

Rajand, Mahendra / Forsyth, Michael (2002): Hostile Bidders, Long-Term Performance, and Restructuring Methods: Evidence from the UK, in: American Business Review, Vol. 1, pp. 71-81.

Sammleraktien-Online.de (2005): Moninger Brauerei AG – Brauerei Moninger, Karlsruhe, < http://www.sammleraktien-online.de/html/2/artId/__1112/gid/__deu90deumf90 /article.html >, Accessed: 06/06/2005.

Serra, Paula A. (2002): Event Study Tests – A brief Survey, in: Working Papers da FEP No. 117, pp. 1-15.

Wilcoxon, Frank (1945): Individual Comparisons by Ranking Methods, in: Biometrics Bulletin, Vol. 1, No. 6, pp. 80-83.

E Case Study: The Acquisition of Brau und Brunnen by RB Brauholding

by
Claus Naarmann and Dominikus Priller

1 Introduction

A majority share of the Bau und Brunnen AG (BuB) was acquired on 12th February 2004 by RB Brauholding GmbH, a wholly owned subsidiary of Dr. August Oetker KG. The aim of this acquirement for Dr. August Oetker KG was to integrate BuB AG into a holding with the Radeberger Gruppe AG to form Germany's biggest brewery. It was believed that this company would withstand the growing market difficulties and assure future success of Dr. August Oetker's commitment in the brewing sector. Although the bidder in the transaction was Dr. August Oetker KG through its subsidiary, the RB Brauholding GmbH, the strategic relevance in the deal lies with the Radeberger Gruppe AG. Thus, the description of the bidder will in fact be a portrait of the Radeberger Gruppe AG. The reasons why Radeberger Gruppe AG did not buy BuB directly was mainly due to the facts that the company did not have sufficient funds for the deal and that it found itself in the middle of a difficult conversion process of its trading name.[1] In the present paper, the names RB Brauholding and Radeberger Gruppe will be used as synonyms, since they are both wholly owned subsidiaries of the Dr. August Oetker KG and either financially or strategically involved in the purchasing process.[2]

The acquisition of BuB by Dr. August Oetker KG was the last in a row of acquisitions on the German brewing market. The uniqueness of this deal lies in the fact that this acquisition was accomplished between two German companies without

---

[1] For a better understanding of the ownership structure see Appendix 1.
[2] Cf. Oetker-Gruppe (2004b), pp. 6-11.

any international involvement. Additionally, the deal is of high interest due to the fact that the two companies already had great dimensions before the merger. As the number three and four on the German market, the two companies left most other competitors far behind. In the light of the importance and the uniqueness of this transaction, the deal must be examined in more detail.

The paper at hand tries to deliver all relevant information necessary to fully capture the momentousness of the take-over of BuB by the Radeberger Group. The article covers four main areas: Firstly, the bidder and the target are introduced in detail as they existed before the deal. Secondly, the transaction itself is illustrated by describing the course of the transaction, price and valuation issues and the reaction of the share price. Thirdly, the paper highlights possible rationales for the transaction, like synergies. And fourthly, it will evaluate the transaction in an ex-post analysis. The authors of this paper intend to contribute to a better understanding of the transaction and to give a secluding judgment about the success of the deal.

2 Profiles of the Involved Companies

2.1 The Bidder – RB Brauholding (Radeberger)

The origins of the Radeberger Gruppe AG reach back to the year 1872. In this year, the brewery "Zum Bergkeller", which later developed into the Radeberger Gruppe AG, was founded close to the city of Radeberg. The company "Zum Bergkeller" starts to brew beer applying the pilsner procedure. The company is the first brewery in Germany that strictly uses this method, still giving the company a competitive advantage. After many years of internal growth, Radeberger's activities are completely absorbed in the Binding Gruppe in 1990, which marked the starting point of a new era of external growth. In the following years, several breweries are acquired by the company, resulting in the group as it is known today.
At the time of the take-over, the Radeberger was the third biggest brewery in Germany, with around 7%-8% of the market share.[3] Besides a great variety of different beers, the company also offered several mineral waters on the German beverage

[3] Cf. w/o author (2003).

market. In February 2004, the company was still traded as a public limited company, although the conversion into a private limited company had been decided. The majority shareholder – at that time Dr. August Oetker KG with a stake of 95.8% – had determined on the general shareholder meeting on the 25th September 2003 to squeeze out the minority shareholders. Additionally, Dr. August Oetker KG announced the conversion of the Radeberger into a private limited company. However, due to several law suits, the conversion was not achieved until the 6th August of the subsequent year. The main reason for Dr. August Oetker KG to change the trading name of Radeberger was to avoid the publication obligations all public limited companies have to follow.[4]

The economic results of the Radeberger in the year 2003 were satisfactory in the light of a very difficult market situation. The company realised a sales volume of € 808.6m in 2003 which represented a drop of 10.6% compared to the previous year. This sales figure was achieved mainly through the sales of beer (8.6m hl.) and the sales of mineral water (0.8m hl.). Due to the difficult market situation resulting in a decreasing sales volume, the company executed strong cost cuttings. Main savings were achieved through the reduction of personnel of 12.3%, resulting in a total number of employees of 2,593 at the end of the year 2003. Consequently, despite the dropping sales volume, the company could still increase its EBIT to € 78.6m, an increase of more than 21% compared to the previous year. Nevertheless, these EBIT only led to a net profit of € 43.6m which was equal to a drop of 10.8% with respect to the year 2002. The drop in net profits together with an increased EBIT was caused by augmented tax payments Radeberger had to pay in 2003. The company's tax payments in 2002 were unusually low as the group had realised several non-taxable profits in 2002; consequently the result was an extraordinarily high net profit for the respective year.[5]

Concerning the company's strategy, one has to highlight that Radeberger follows a market leader strategy with a differentiation focus and special emphasis on the German market. Thus, the company aims to be a national and regional market

[4] Radeberger (2004c).
[5] Cf. Radeberger (2004b), p. 2.

leader in the premium segment with its brands. Additionally, it is slowly trying to reach an international market entry, especially with its big brands like Clausthaler. Moreover, the company also follows a consolidation strategy regarding its costs. This strategy was necessary due to the implementation of the deposit on non-returnable packaging, which especially depressed the sales of cans.[6]

The most important brands of the Radeberger have been the Radeberger Pilsener (a pilsner beer), the Clausthaler beer (a non-alcoholic beer), the Schöfferhofer Weizen (a wheat beer) and the brand Selters, the company's only important mineral water. These brands are the company's strategic brands and offered on a national level. In order to round off its brand portfolio, the company has several specialty brands like Corona Extra or Binding Lager and a high number of regional beers, like Henniger or Berliner Kindl. For a detailed overview regarding the company's brands see Chart 1.[7]

Chart 1: Overview and classification of brands, Radeberger Gruppe AG

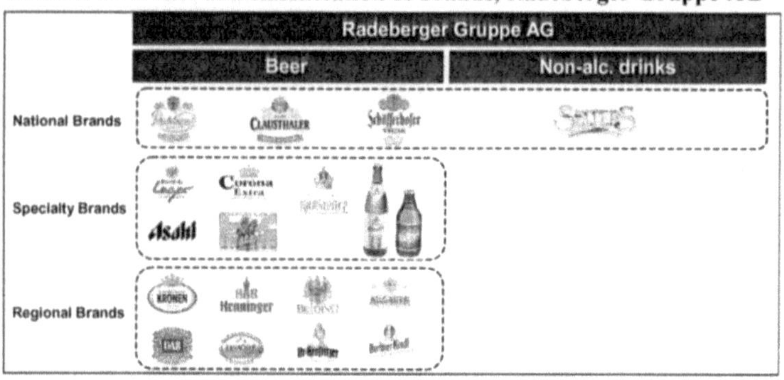

2.2 The Target – Brau und Brunnen AG

Before the take-over by RB Brauholding, Brau und Brunnen AG was the 4th largest beverage group in Germany. Brau und Brunnen's business activities comprise the production and marketing of beer and non-alcoholic drinks and the administration of real estate, which is not part of the core business.

---

[6] Cf. Radeberger (2004b), p. 10 f.
[7] Cf. Radeberger (w/o year).

The origins of Brau und Brunnen reach back to the foundation of the Schultheiss brewery in Berlin (1842) and the Dortmunder Union brewery in 1856. The merger between the two companies in 1972 created the biggest beverage producing company in Germany, Dortmunder Union Schultheiss Brauerei AG. The company had a wide network of investments in other companies, which had to be reduced for reasons of profitability. Since 1956, the Apollinaris Brunnen AG belonged to the Dortmunder Union. After the merger, the non-alcoholic branch grew in importance and further acquisitions strengthened the portfolio (e.g. Sinziger Mineralbrunnen). In 1988, the company was renamed to Brau und Brunnen AG (BuB). After the fall of the Berlin Wall, BuB acquired several breweries in East Germany, among them the Brau und Erfrischungsgetränke AG, breweries in Frankfurt / Oder and Leipzig and in 1994 the St. Pauli brewery, which possessed the national brand Jever.

Due to the costly acquisition history and decreasing demand, BuB had to restructure the company. Michael Hollmann, the new CEO, drove forward the restructuring efforts from the year 2001 onwards. Part of the restructuring programme was the ending of the joint venture with Apollinaris & Schweppes and the sale of the shares. Following the restructuring programme, BuB managed to become profitable again in 2003. BuB then launched an extensive strategic reorganization programme that concentrated on further acquisitions and the extension of the sales network in Germany. BuB acquired the East German Margon Brunnen and Glashäger Brunnen as well as the Rostock brewery. The acquisition of Tucher strengthened the brewery and sales position in the south of Germany. The brand Vita Cola completed the non-alcoholic branch, which was then organized under the name BuB Mineralquellen GmbH. The brewery Iserlohner and the brewery in Frankfurt / Oder were sold. Other brewery facilities (such as the brewery Schlösser) were closed down. Since January 2004, (almost) all brewery activities are organized under the name BuB Brauereien GmbH.[8]

The years 2001 and 2002 were marked by the restructuring of the whole group. As shown in the paragraph above, several breweries were closed or sold when possible. The figures represent these activities. Profit could be raised to € 82m in 2002,

8 Cf. Brau und Brunnen (w/o year).

mainly due to the sale of the Apollinaris shares (about € 150m) and the sale of real estate in Berlin. In 2003, BuB managed to generate a profit of € 7.5m. The growth in turnover (12.1%) can be drawn back to the sales increase in the non-alcoholic branch mainly due to the acquisitions mentioned above.[9]

Just before the announcement of the take-over by RB Brauholding, BuB's market capitalisation amounted to € 335.6m. BuB held almost ten per cent of the share capital. The holding company of the Oetker group, Erste FuB Beteiligungs-GmbH, was shareholder with 0.56% of the shares. These shares had been acquired in the 3-months time period before the announcement date.[10] See Chart 2 for BuB figures and shareholders.

Chart 2: Figures of 2003 and shareholders

Figures (2003)		
Turnover:	647.8m €	(+12.1%)
• Beer:	531.2m €	(-6.6%)
• Non-alc bev.:	114.3m €	(+15.7%)
• Real estate:	2.3m €	(+15.0%)
Sales bev.:	12.0m hl	(+4.3%)
Employees:	3,084	(-6.6%)

Shareholders	
• Free float	27.9%
• Bayrische HypoVereinsbank AG	61.7%
• Erste FuB Beteiligungs-GmbH	0.56%
• Own shares (BuB)	9.80%

BuB's brands can be classified into three groups. Within the beer branch, there is Jever as the only national brand. The specialty brands comprise all Kölsch beers and Schlösser Alt (the brand still belongs to BuB although the brewery was closed-down). The emphasis of BuB's brand portfolio lies in the extensive list of regional brands. These beers are mainly produced in Dortmund (e.g. Dortmunder Union, Brinkhoffs No 1) and in Berlin (Berliner Pilsner, Schultheiss). Among the other brands there is Tucher (Nürnberg), Rostocker and Reudnitzer.

Within the mineral water branch, the most important regional brands are Spreequell (Berlin), Glashäger (Bad Doberan), Margonwasser, Sinziger ("Gerri") and

9 Cf. Brau und Brunnen (2004).

10 Cf. Oetker-Gruppe (2004b), p. 14 f.

Vita Cola. The real estate branch has only limited importance and is expected to be reduced further. See Chart 2 for the brand portfolio of BuB.[11]

Chart 3: Overview and classification of brands, Brau und Brunnen AG

3 The Transaction

3.1 Course of the Transaction

The Bayrische HypoVereinsbank (HVB) initially had a share of about 55% in BuB AG. Due to their own financial problems in the portfolio and a continuing problem crisis at BuB, HVB decided to sell its stake of the company. However, HVB was not able to sell its shares and instead supported the restructuring efforts of Michael Hollmann, the new CEO from the year 2001 onwards. At that time BuB suffered from extreme losses. The share price was below 20 €, which might have been too low for HVB to sell the shares. After the restructuring and reorganization programme, HVB searched for new prospective buyers. Among the most important companies were the Schörghuber group, One Equity Partners (OEP), Radeberger, Holsten, Interbrew and Scottish & Newcastle Breweries. Serious negotiation, however, have only been conducted with OEP. The acquisition by OEP was the favourite alternative that both the HVB and BuB proclaimed to be the optimal solution.

[11] Cf. Brau und Brunnen (2004), p. 2.

Nevertheless, shortly before closing the deal, HVB pulled back and ended the negotiations. The official reason for this was a lack of fairness by OEP as one could read in HVB's press releases from the 1st December 2003. Since the business situation of BuB had improved substantially, BuB announced to continue independently.[12]

At the same time, Carlsberg entered into negotiations with Holsten which, apart from BuB, was the only large brewery available to investors. This fact was to be one critical point in the take-over considerations. All other strategic investors needed to focus on BuB if they desired to invest in a German brewery.

Between the 8th December 2003 and the 30th January 2004, the Oetker group acquired shares in BuB (0.56% of the share capital) through the Dr. Oetker Finanzierungs- und Beteiligungs-GmbH and the Erste FuB Beteiligungs-GmbH (subsidiary of the Oetker Group, see Appendix 1). All shares were then sold to the Dritte Finanzierungs- und Beteiligungs-GmbH, which was renamed to RB Brauholding GmbH (the bidder). On the 12th February 2004, RB Brauholding announced the acquisition of the 61.73% stake from the HVB for € 80 per share. During February, RB Brauholding acquired additional shares on the market and could then count on 75.71% of the share capital. This majority was a necessary condition set out in the sale contract. The company then announced the take-over bid on the 24th March which would expire on the 5th May. Precisely, the take-over bid had the same price as paid to HVB, namely € 80 per share.[13] Apparently, the take-over bid was not sufficiently accepted by the end of the period so that RB Brauholding had to offer a second term from the 11th to 25th May. At the end of the second term, RB Brauholding held 96.68% of the shares.[14]

The whole deal structure was aimed at gaining complete control over BuB without incurring publishing obligations. Firstly, the BuB was bought by a limited liable company, secondly, the Oetker group planned to delist BuB from the stock ex-

[12] Cf. VWD (2003).
[13] Cf. Oetker-Gruppe (2004b), p. 14 f.
[14] Cf. Oetker-Gruppe (2004a).

change. With the majority of over 95% and a profit transfer agreement between the two companies, RB Brauholding could then start the squeeze-out process. The agreement proposed a compensation of € 86.38 per share for the remaining shareholders.[15] At the extraordinary meeting on the 19th November 2004, the shareholders voted in favour of a higher compensation of € 88.51 per share.[16] Initially, many shareholders had hoped for a higher compensation since the squeeze-out of the Radeberger AG shareholders forced Radeberger to increase the compensation substantially. Until the 20th January 2005, RB Brauholding managed to acquire further 16,474 shares (0.37% of the share capital) at the agreed price. Currently, BuB is still in the squeeze-out process.[17]

3.2 Transaction Price and Valuation Issues

RB Brauholding paid € 80 per share for HVB's stake of 61.68%, which means a total of € 221.7m for 2.77m shares. Consequently, the implied value of 100% equity (4,489m shares) is € 359.1m. Assuming 76.84m net debt (from the balance sheet 31/12/2003), the enterprise value is € 435.97m. Taking an EBITDA of € 90.3m, the resulting EV/EBITDA-multiple is 4.8.[18]

The transaction multiple usually contains a strategic premium, i.e. a higher price that the bidder is willing to pay according to the strategic benefits (e.g. synergies) he expects from the deal. The question is whether these strategic considerations were taken into account in the take-over by RB Brauholding. For the finding of the purchase price potential synergies were, however, not explicitly calculated.[19]

[15] Cf. Landmesser (2004b).
[16] Cf. Landmesser (2004a).
[17] Cf. Oetker-Gruppe (2005).
[18] The transaction also included the take-over of pension liabilities of € 225m (Cf. Radeberger Gruppe (2004a): Rede von Herrn Ulrich Kallmeyer [...]) that are not included in this calculation because no information could be retrieved on the exact composition and calculation of the pension liabilities. However, if added to the EV, the resulting EV/EBITDA multiple would be 7.32x.
[19] Cf. Oetker-Gruppe (2004b), p. 24.

Here, it is merely analysed how the calculated multiple actually compares to the deals taken place before this transaction. Chart 4 gives an overview of other transaction multiples in the German market.

Chart 4: EBITDA multiples in previous transactions

Date	Target	Multiple
20/01/2004	Holsten Brauerei AG	7.25/7.40
10/12/2003	Stuttgarter Hofbräu Brau AG	4.18
18/09/2003	Dinkelacker Schwabenbräu AG	6.07
12/02/2003	Hofbrauhaus Wolters AG	17.93
12/02/2003	Gilde Brauerei AG	24.31

Apart from the acquisition of Stuttgarter Hofbräu Brau AG, previous transactions show a significantly higher EBITDA-multiple paid by the bidder. Ignoring the extreme values leads us to an average multiple of around 6 to 7.5.

In the news, Mr. Hollmann stated that the internally set multiple was around 6 to 7 times EBITDA. After the failure of the take-over negotiations with OEP, he assumed an EBITDA of € 113m for the year 2004, resulting in an enterprise value of € 600m to 800m. For the year 2003, potential bidders assumed an EBITDA of € 71m, whereas the internally calculated EBITDA was € 78m. Furthermore, Mr. Hollmann disconfirmed news about the price offered by OEP. "The figure [€ 350m] is not quite right."[20]

What do these pieces of information tell us? Firstly, assuming that OEP offered more or less € 350m, the multiple was about 4.9x which is almost the actual EBITDA-multiple paid by RB Brauholding. Additionally, this multiple is close to the multiple paid for Stuttgarter Hofbräu Brau AG. Secondly, BuB aimed at a multiple of 6 to 7 which is oriented at the price paid for Dinkelacker Schwabenbräu

[20] Cf. VWD (2003b).

AG shortly before (18/09/2003). Thirdly, comparing the actual multiple paid and the internally calculated multiple, one can derive that RB Brauholding obviously did not encounter the synergies or did not share the same positive outlook as BuB. Consequently, the premium paid is only very small (the trading multiple on the 12/02/2004 was 4.57). The low price might also be due to HVB's desire to sell its shares. The buyer's power was therefore stronger, and BuB failed to influence negotiations with high multiple estimates.

If the take-over of pension liabilities is also taken into account, the EV/EBITDA multiple is 7.32. This multiple is more in line with the Holsten acquisition and the internally calculated multiple. Furthermore, this higher multiple includes a premium that would explain Ulrich Kallmeyer's (CEO of Radeberger) statement that the price paid was a strategic one.[21]

3.3 Reaction of the Share Price of Brau und Brunnen AG

The share price of Brau und Brunnen[22] had increased steadily from below 20 € in 2001 to over 90 € in 2003. Two factors are responsible for this development. Firstly, the stock market honored the restructuring efforts of BuB. Secondly, BuB became a potential take-over target. BuB remained constantly in the press with news about ongoing negotiations with possible acquirers. Surprisingly, negotiations with OEP were broken up on the 1st December 2003. The share price fell by over 18% (from € 80.75 to € 65.60) the day after the announcement and further to 58 € a few days later. However, the price recovered due to new take-over rumours. On the day of the announcement of the take-over of HVB's shares (12/02/2003) the price was 74.75 €. The following day the price jumped by 6% to just below € 80, which was the price RB Brauholding paid.

After the announcement dates of the results of the offer acceptance period to all shareholders, the next major price movements were recorded. At the announcement of the squeeze-out offer (€ 86.38) the price rose to just above that level. Other price

[21] Cf. Radeberger (2004a).

[22] The share price of the Radeberger Gruppe AG was not analyzed here because the squeeze-out process was already started and the liquidity of the shares was limited.

movements, e.g. the increase on 12th and 21st July with 330 shares traded, could not be explained with the information available. See Appendix 2 for the graphical illustration of the share price reactions.[23]

4 Strategic Rationale behind the Transaction

Since the transaction itself has been examined in much detail now, the most important question to be answered in a subsequent step is the question concerning the rationale behind such an acquisition. The CEO of the Radeberger Gruppe, Ulrich Kallmeyer, once said that the price paid for BuB was a strategic one, although he rarely highlighted any strategic reasons.[24] Consequently, this paper will now try to identify the most obvious reasons for the transaction at hand. The general and the most important reasons why an M&A-transaction in the brewing industry is carried out are potential synergies, the motivation to optimize the brand portfolio, the hope to attain a greater distribution net, better market coverage and finally the expectation to find hidden reserves. All in all, this refers to increasing competitiveness in the respective market, both through cost advantages and increased sales.

If one takes an overall look at the accomplished company after the 12th February 2004, one expects two ways of achieving synergies. Firstly and almost self-evident is the possibility to consolidate proximate operating sites, in order to reduce costs like labour costs and / or to achieve economies of scale through a combined production. These kinds of synergies could possibly be reached in Berlin and Dortmund. In Berlin the newly formed company can rely on two production facilities after the acquisition, the brewery of BuB (Berliner Schultheiss) and the plant of Radeberger Gruppe (Berliner Kindl). The same situation is found in Dortmund where the corporation acquired the former BuB Brinkhoff's brewery and also possesses an own operating site, the Dortmunder Actien Brewery (DAB). In both cities the plants could be merged to accomplish synergies. Secondly and somewhat less obvious are possible synergies in the financing of the BuB company. The new owner of BuB, the Dr. August Oetker KG, is highly credit worthy and as such has

[23] Share price (Xetra) taken from Yahoo! Finance.
[24] Cf. Radeberger (2004a).

much lower refunding costs than BuB had before. Now, much cheaper credits are achieved. Consequently, it would be very easy to make BuB more profitable, since the company needs fewer funds to pay its debt obligations. Other synergies include procurement costs, IT costs or auditing costs that arise from a bigger buyer power of the larger company. This is another way to jointly reduce costs and could consequently be a possible synergy that convinced the bidder to buy BuB.

Another decisive reason for the acquisition of BuB could be the extensive brand portfolio of the company. The target accounts for some very interesting brands both in the area of beer and in the area of non-alcoholic beverages. Of special interest for the bidder to foster its sales volume are premium brands, since the company follows a differentiation strategy. The premium brand in the portfolio of BuB with respect to beer is Jever. It is located in the national premium segment and can count on a high market reputation. As such, it could be very interesting for the bidder and could be a reason for the purchase. Another interesting aspect in the brand portfolio of BuB is the company's ownership of specialty beers. Here, the target possessed three "Kölsch"-beers (Sion Kölsch, Gilde Kölsch and Kurfürsten Kölsch). "Kölsch"-beers are special beers only brewed in the city of Cologne where this kind of beer is very famous and almost exclusively consumed. The strategic interest in the "Kölsch"-beers could reach from the fact that they are successfully developing beyond the borders of Cologne and that they can count on a very loyal home market. Consequently, the specialty beers of BuB could also be a reason for the company's acquisition.

Concerning its regional brands, the target owned a high number of beer brands and mineral water brands. Of major significance regarding regional beer brands are probably the brand Brinkhoff's in Dortmund, the brand Schultheiss in Berlin, the brand Tucher in Fürth and the brands in Rostock and Leipzig (Rostocker and Reudnitzer). Those brands are strong players in their region and could be of special interest for a brewery that is looking to enter those regional markets. A further interesting feature in the brand portfolio of the target is its high number of regional non-alcoholic beverages. Here the main brands of significance are Sinziger, SpreeQuell in Berlin, Margonwasser in Müglitztal, Glashäger in Bad Doberan and Thüringer Wald-Quell and Vital Cola in Schmalkalden. Those brands could round off a brand portfolio of premium brands that is looking for non-alcoholic beverages in Eastern Germany. Altogether, the brand portfolio could represent a possible reason for Radeberger to buy the target.

A third reason for buying BuB could be the fact that the bidder wants to optimise its distribution net and its market coverage. If one takes a look at the locations of the production facilities BuB owned before the transaction, one sees that most of them are situated on a horizontal strip in the middle of Germany. There are only some that lie apart from that band, Jever in the northwest of Germany, Glashäger and Hanseatische Brauerei Rostock in the northeast of Germany and two facilities in Berlin. For a better understanding of the location net and the market coverage see Appendix 3. If the distribution net and market coverage of the target complements the bidder's network and coverage, this would be a good reason for an acquisition.

The final reason that could have influenced the decision to buy BuB could rest in the expectation to find hidden reserves within the target. Hidden assets that one can find in a brewing corporation like BuB could be real estate. In general, most breweries own, due to their history, a high number of real estate, which is in reality worth much more than the balance sheet shows. Many deals do not fully embrace those value differences between balance sheet and reality in their purchase price due to valuation difficulties and consequently make a deal sometimes a bargain buy. As BuB owns real estate, hidden assets in this respect could have been a reason for its acquisition. The same kind of hidden reserves could be expected in the empties of BuB, like bottles and boxes. The German taxation law allows companies to directly deduct such low-value assets. Therefore, empties, although being of extremely high value, in reality are often not reflected correctly on a company's balance sheet. Due to very high evaluation difficulties with those empties, it is very likely that the true value of those assets is not properly reflected in the acquisition price. If Radeberger expects to find hidden assets in the target's empties it could be a strong reason to buy the company. A third important kind of hidden reserves can be expected in the brands of a target. This is caused by the fact that brands in reality often have a high value that is very difficult to measure. Furthermore, the value of brands as intangible assets does not at all appear on the balance sheet (unlike a brand was acquired instead of built-up), which sometimes makes one even forget their strategic value. As a result the value of brands is often wrongly incorporated in the acquisition price and consequently the price does not correspond to reality. If Radeberger expects to find hidden assets within the brand portfolio, it could be a strong reason to buy BuB.

5 Evaluation of the Transaction

The final and crucial facet when looking at an M&A-transaction is always the evaluation of its success or failure, in an ex-post consideration. The paper has mentioned four dominant rationales one could think of in an M&A-transaction such as the take-over of BuB by Radeberger. The question which of the rationales are supportable and which of them lack plausibility will be answered in this next.

The first aspect the paper mentioned as credible reasons for a take-over were synergies. One way to attain them is to consolidate proximate operating sites. The paper in this respect mentioned two possible locations where such consolidations could take place, the cities of Dortmund and Berlin. Recently, the company officially said that it would close the plant Berliner Kindl in Berlin and the Brinkhoff's facility in Dortmund in the year 2006.[25] The brands should be kept and brewed in the remaining plants, in the Schultheiss brewery and the Dortmunder Actien Brewery. Although, Radeberger did recognise these opportunities to achieve synergies and did mention a couple of times that it will achieve them, up to this point in time no synergies were accomplished. It is important to accomplish synergies as fast as possible after a transaction. This paper arrives at the conclusion that up to this point of time the achievement of synergies must be evaluated negatively. However, as Radebeger has now officially announced to close two facilities till 2006, the negative evaluation for the past and present must be seen at least as neutral for the future. Nevertheless, the merger of the brewery facilities in Dortmund and Berlin will incur high investments of at least € 50m.[26]

[25] Cf. w/o autor (2005).
[26] Cf. Radeberger (2005).

Another possibility to reach synergies in the transaction at hand was found in the likelihood to improve the target's funding situation. In this regard the transaction was absolutely successful. With the help of the highly credit-worthy parent company, the Dr. August Oetker KG, the target's average cost of debt could be reduced by 6% to only 3-4%. Apart from financing costs, also supply, IT and auditing costs could be reduced substantially. Consequently, the achievement of synergies concerning the cost positions must be evaluated positive.

A second aspect mentioned as a plausible take-over reason was the extensive brand portfolio of BuB. A portfolio can have a very high value if it complements the bidder's portfolio. For a good estimation one has to differentiate between national brands, specialty brands and regional brands of the target. Regarding the premium brands, BuB brings in Jever beer. Although this brand has a high value, it does not bring additional value to Radeberger. The reason is that Radeberger Pilsner and Jever Pilsner are players in the same market and do therefore not complement each others but rather clash with each other. Accordingly, the optimisation of the bidder's brand portfolio must be evaluated negatively relating to national brands. However, the evaluation is different when looking at the target's specialty brands. BuB owns three "Kölsch"-beers that are quite interesting. As mentioned earlier, the home market of this type of beer is very loyal and the beer is slowly becoming successful beyond the borders of its home market. Altogether, this beer type is interesting as it is strongly consumed and its forecast for the future quite promising. However, the most common and must successful "Kölsch"-beer in recent times is Gaffel Kölsch, a competitor that is not to be underestimated in this specialty beer segment. Nevertheless, the gain of those specialty beers must be evaluated positively within the deal and as promising for the future.

Finally, the value of the regional brands for the bidder's portfolio must be evaluated. The most important regional brands are Schultheiss in Berlin, Tucher in Fürth and Brinkhoff in Dortmund. Those Brands are strong players in their regional markets and are individually taken again quite interesting. Nevertheless, it is questionable if it was really necessary for Radeberger to foster its brand presence in Berlin and Dortmund, where the bidder already owned strong brands, the Berliner Kindl and the Dortmunder Actien Brewery. Only Tucher in Fürth opens new opportunities for the bidder, although the value of Tucher and its subsidiaries is probably overestimated. Consequently, regarding regional brands, the deal must be evaluated at best neutral. Overall, considering the brand portfolio aspect, the acquisition of BuB must be evaluated neutral or even negative, especially since the national brand Jever is actually competing with Radeberger Pilsner.

Another interesting reason to execute the deal was the possible opportunity to optimise the bidder's distribution net and its market coverage. If one takes a look at all allocations of the newly formed conglomerate (see Appendix 3) it is only Tucher in Fürth, Jever in the North and the "Kölsch"-beers in Cologne that represent a relevant gain with respect to the distribution net and the market coverage. This is not much, but could be evaluated at least as neutral for the deal. However, with an increased number of products the dependency on big retailers grows, too. Furthermore, as the development of the German beer market is not positive at all, the question remains if it would not have been much more interesting to invest internationally in e.g. the strongly developing Eastern European countries like the Czech Republic. Consequently, when evaluating the distribution and market coverage, the deal has to be evaluated negatively.

A final reason for the deal and a strong reason to support such a deal can be identified in hidden reserves. The paper mentioned that possible hidden reserves can be found in the target's real estate, its empties and its brands. However, when one takes a look at the target's real estate portfolio one will find out that most of the company's real estate had already been sold before the deal or remained with the HVB. BuB had followed a strong divestment policy concerning its real estate and had only 22 non-essential real estate assets left at the end of 2003. Consequently, there were only little hidden reserves to be found in the target's real estate portfolio, and thus this aspect has to be evaluated negatively for the transaction. Another area hidden assets could probably be found are the empties of BuB. However, since the CEO of BuB, Michael Hollmann, had executed a sale-and-lease-back transaction to boost liquidity, the empties were no longer in the possession of the target when it was purchased. Accordingly, this aspect must again be assessed negatively. A final area where hidden reserves played a vital role was in the target's brands. As mentioned earlier, Brau and Brunnen did bring in some very interesting brands although most of them did not really fit to the bidder's brand portfolio. Nevertheless, Radeberger does not make profit from them by selling them separately or by giving them a promising, complementary direction for the future. Taking an individual look at the brand Jever, this aspect becomes clearer. The brand by its own has a very high value, as it is a national pilsner beer that is very acerb and characteristic. However, as Radeberger already owns a pilsner beer, the company does not really need Jever. Nevertheless, instead of making profit of it by selling the brand separately to another investor, it seems that Radeberger even destroys the brand's value by possibly demoting the brand into a regional brand. All in all the hidden reserves are not used or do not exist. As a result, this is another aspect evaluated negatively for the transaction.

6 Conclusion

The paper at hand examined the acquisition of BuB by RB Brauholding. The objective was to come up with a critical analysis of the transaction by evaluating the strategic rationale behind the deal. After presenting a profile of BuB and Radeberger, the merely technical details of the transaction itself were described. In a next step, all possible reasons for the acquisition were explained before finally assessing the acquisition in the light of potential synergies, brand portfolio, the distribution network and hidden reserves.

The paper concludes that synergies were clearly overestimated. The close-down of the two breweries is proclaimed, but has not yet been accomplished. Moreover, the merger of the brewery facilities will incur high investments for capacity upgrading. Only synergies in the cost positions can be achieved, e.g. the financing, procurement, IT and auditing costs. With regard to the brand portfolio, the national brands rather compete with than complement each other. The portfolio of regional brands is evaluated as neutral. The distribution was not a reason for the transaction, since it rather made Radeberger more dependent on big retailers. Furthermore, the entry to other international markets would have been more favourable than a concentration on the German market. Also hidden reserves could not be identified.

Ultimately, taking all rationales into account, one has to accept that the acquisition was too expensive. The rationales that would justify the high strategic price can mostly be rejected. The reason for the transaction rather lies in the conclusion that the deal was mainly executed as a reaction to the strong international M&A activities on the German market. Radeberger obviously feared to become a target itself. Behind this conclusion one can also assume that the Oetker group as the actual investor made a strategic decision to strengthen the beer branch rather than to divest it. BuB was the only potential target left on the German market. However, for this strategy the wrong target was selected so that the acquisition must ultimately be evaluated as a mispurchase.

Appendix

Appendix 1: Overview company structure Oetker Group

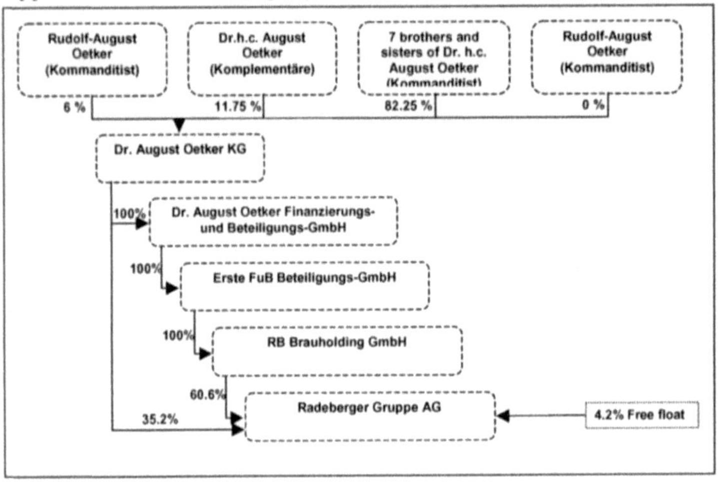

Source: Oetker-Gruppe (2004b), p. 6.

Appendix 2: Share price reaction of Brau und Brunnen AG

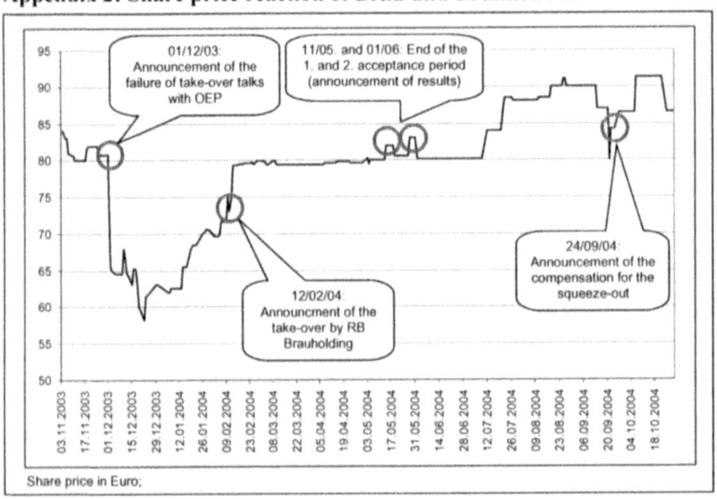

Source: Own illustration, data: Yahoo! Finance.

Appendix 3: Brands and production plants of the Brau und Brunnen AG.

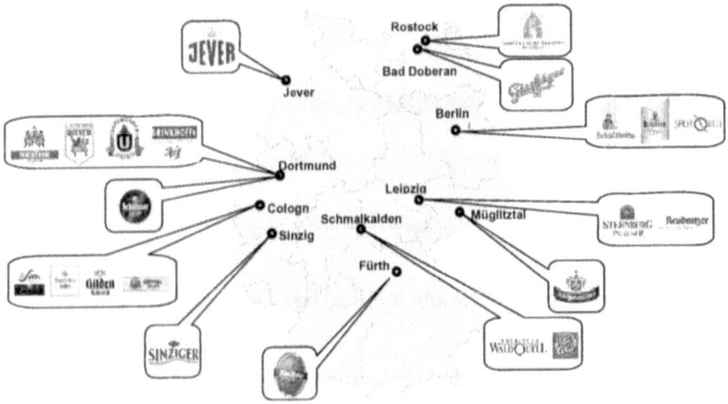

Appendix 4: The combined distribution net and market coverage of Radeberger Gruppe AG and Brau and Brunnen.

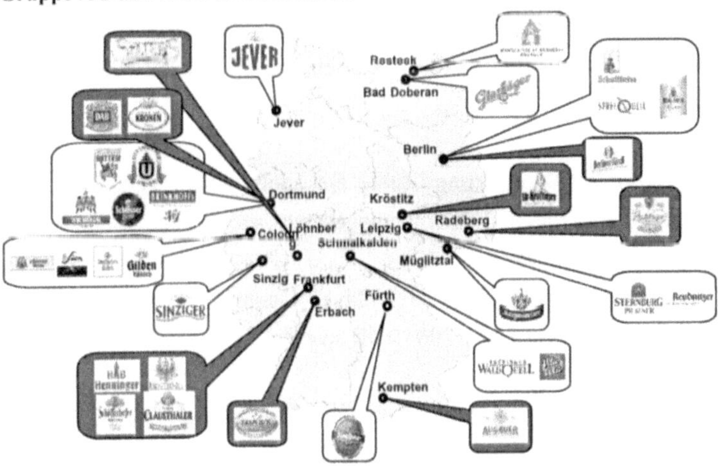

References

Brau und Brunnen (2004): Geschäftsbericht 2003, Brau und Brunnen AG, Dortmund 2004.

Brau und Brunnen (w / o year): Die Geschichte unseres Unternehmens, electronic publication under the URL: http://www.brauundbrunnen.de/index_bub_website.jsp, call up date: 02/05/2005.

Landmesser, D. (2004a): Squeeze-out bei Brau und Brunnen, electronic publication under the URL: http://www.boerse.ard.de/content.jsp?key=document_71311, date: 19/11/2004, call up date: 20/05/2005.

Landmesser, D. (2004b): Squeeze-out bei Brau und Brunnen naht, electronic publication under the URL: http://www.boerse.ard.de/content.jsp?key=document_66713, date: 24/09/2004, call up date: 20/05/2005.

Oetker-Gruppe (2005): RB Brauholding GmbH, Bekanntmachung gemäß § 23 Abs. 2 des Wertpapiererwerbs- und Übernahmegesetzes, electronic publication under the URL: http://www.oetker-gruppe.de/webgate/Oetkergruppe/Gruppe5_2_2.NSF/ContentByKey/DROR-5WYMW4-DE-p, date: 20/01/2005, call up date: 15/04/2005.

Oetker-Gruppe (2004a): RB Brauholding GmbH, Bekanntmachung gemäß § 23 Abs. 2 des Wertpapiererwerbs- und Übernahmegesetzes, electronic publication under the URL: http://www.oetker-gruppe.de/webgate/Oetkergruppe/Gruppe5_2_2.NSF/ContentByKey/DROR-5WYMW4-DE-p, date: 01/06/2004, call up date: 15/04/2005.

Oetker-Gruppe (2004b): Angebotsunterlage – Öffentliches Übernahmeangebot (Barangebot), Pflichtveröffentlichung gemäß § 14 Abs. 3 Wertpapiererwerbs- und –übernahmegesetz, Bielefeld 2004.

Radeberger (2005): Brau und Brunnen und Radeberger Gruppe werden zusammengeführt, electronic publication under the URL: http://www.radeberger-gruppe.de/cms/-startordner/presse/93.html, date: 01/02/2005, call up date: 15/04/2005.

Radeberger (2004a): Rede von Herrn Ulrich Kallmeyer, Generalbevollmächtigter der Dr. August Oetker KG, Mitglied der Oetker Gruppenleitung, Vorstandsvorsitzender der Radeberger Gruppe AG, electronic publication under the URL: http://www.radeberger-gruppe.de/cms/startordner/presse/93.html, date: 13/02/2004, call up date: 25/05/2005.

Radeberger (2004b): Geschäftsbericht 2003, Radeberger Gruppe AG, Frankfurt am Main 2004.

Radeberger (2004c): Radeberger Gruppe AG wird vom Kurszettel genommen, Squeeze out Beschluss im Handelsregister eingetragen, electronic publication under the URL: http://www.radeberger-gruppe.de/cms/start-ordner/presse/104_a5027.html, date: 06/08/2004, call up date: 02/05/2005.

Radeberger (w / o year): Marken, electronic publication under the URL: http://www.radeberger-gruppe.de/cms/startordner/marken/91.html, call up date: 02/05/2005.

VWD (2003a): Brau und Brunnen macht im Alleingang weiter, electronic publication under the URL: http://web.consors.de/CatFront/JspNews.jsp?m_id=561835, date: 02/12/2003, call up date: 15/04/2005.

VWD (2003b): Brau und Brunnen: HVB hält an Engagement fest... (drei), electronic publication under the URL:
http://web.consors.de/CatFront/JspNews.jsp?m_id=561550, date: 02/12/2003, call up date: 15/04/2005.

W / o author (2003): Oetker schluckt Radeberger, electronic publication under the URL: http://www.sueddeutsche.de/wirtschaft/artikel/380/16364/, date: 18/08/2003, call up date: 02/05/2005

W / o author (2005): Traditionsbrauerei in Dortmund schließt, electronic publication under the URL:
http://www.wdr.de/themen/wirtschaft/wirtschaftsbranche/brauereien/brinkhoff/050201.jhtml, date: 01/02/2005, call up date: 02/05/2005.

F The German Brewing Industry in an International Comparison

I Index for listed Breweries in Germany

by
Ulf Dobberke and Florian Voigt

1 Introduction

1.1 Objective of the Study

The German brewing industry has experienced an increasing attention over the last couple of years. Several large and small scale acquisitions could be observed, and breweries from Germany and abroad have intensified their efforts to strengthen their position in a consolidating market environment. In addition to the strategic investors that focus on Germany, more investors have become aware of breweries as an investment opportunity as well. As the majority of German breweries are held privately, the level of market transparency is not very satisfying; however, there are several German breweries are listed at the stock exchange.

By introducing the "Bier Erzeuger Index" (BEX) for Germany, we aim at several targets. First of all, the index is supposed to give an overview of the German brewing industry. Furthermore, the transparency of the market should be increased by the introduction of the BEX-Germany as it should draw more attention to this interesting sector of the German economy. If accepted by the market participants, the BEX-Germany will also serve as a benchmarking tool for brewing companies.

1.2 Course of Analysis

The structure of the paper follows the research objectives. Chapter 2 describes the important basics of indices. Chapter 3 describes the relevant data sample and points out the important key characteristics. Chapter 4 looks into the calculation methodology of the index. In the course of doing so, the two different calculation methodologies are evaluated. Thereafter, the index formula is analysed and illustrated. Furthermore, the chapter provides an analysis, caps and the correction factor. In Chapter 5 we analyse the performance of the index by comparing it to its key driver as well as several established indices. Chapter 6 summarises the findings and draws a conclusion. In addition, an outlook for the future applicability of a German brewing index is profited.

2 Foundations

2.1 Overview of the German Brewing Market

Presently the brewing industry is driven by consolidation,[1] market segmentation and brand building.[2] A strong concentration among leading national brands can be observed in most developed markets at the expense of traditional secondary and regional brands. This is most evident across the US American, British, Spanish, Italian, and German beer markets. Furthermore, a strong link between margin and market share can be identified. Also, large brand portfolios are much more beneficial concerning the developed markets. This involves a powerful negotiation position over wholesalers. Moreover, companies are forced to high marketing investments to ensure their brands to be a priority to the consumers.

Profits and growth are driven by specialty, imports and theme brands. The possession of a leading global brand ensures significant market positions across local markets.[3] For these reasons, M&A activities remain buoyant and optimistic regardless of the very limited number of bidders for each transaction. M&A activities are mainly driven by distribution and segmentation synergies essential for success.[4] Further value is added through best practice of the top industry players. Emerging markets like Eastern Europe open interesting opportunities for higher growth.[5]

---

1 Cf. Credit Swiss First Boston (2003), p. 1.
2 Cf. Deutsche Bank (2004a), p. 3; Deutsche Bank (2004b), p. 6, 174.
3 Cf. Deutsche Bank (2004b), p. 17.
4 Cf. Credit Swiss First Boston (2004b), p. 1.
5 Cf. Credit Swiss First Boston (2004b), p. 4; Deutsche Bank (2004b), p. 17.

Currently the German brewing industry faces two main obstacles. First of all volumes are declining with a negative future trend.[6] Secondly, prices have been on a static level for the past years. Hence, margins are increasingly under big pressure. Therefore, the product mix became a vital factor for any future growth strategy.[7] As far as the mature and emerging markets are concerned, the premium and specialty sectors are growing with a stable outlook. At the global perspective the demand for international brands is increasing. Breweries tend to hold growing excess capacity and prefer off-premise rather than on-premise. However, the purchasing and bargaining power of the major retailers has increased over the past.
In addition to the pressure for consolidation within the German brewing market, global brewing companies continue to acquire German breweries to gain access to the big German beer market.[8] A local brand portfolio is critical for distribution of brands in Germany. Furthermore, it opens the field for synergies.[9] The acquired platforms are utilised to market the imported premium and specialty brands, which further increase profitability. Currently, this strategy seems to be the only way to gain access to the German market as the customers are extremely loyal to "their" brands.[10]

Despite this pressure on the brewing industry, the German market for beer is still the 2nd largest in Europe with consumption per inhabitant of 118 litres.[11] However the year-to-year consumption is continuously decreasing due to the saturation of the market, which is closed to its maximum, the negative demographical development, legal regulations and a change in lifestyle.[12] The German beer market is divided amongst two beer categories: the premium beer and the economy beer. Premium beer is characterised by a high price, high marketing expenses, distribution via restaurants and pubs, and individual packaging. The economy beer is placed at the bottom of the price scale, involves low marketing expenses, wholesalers are cut out and the packaging is standardised.

---

[6] Cf. Credit Swiss First Boston (2004b), p. 5; Deutsche Bank (2004b), p. 13, 174.
[7] Cf. Credit Swiss First Boston (2004b), p. 9.
[8] Cf. Deutsche Bank (2004a), p. 2.
[9] Cf. Credit Swiss First Boston (2004a), p. 3.
[10] Cf. Credit Swiss First Boston (2003), p. 3; Credit Swiss First Boston (2004b), p. 9.
[11] Cf. Credit Swiss First Boston (2004a), p. 3; Deutsche Bank (2004a), p. 6; Deutsche Bank (2004b), p. 14.
[12] Cf. Credit Swiss First Boston (2003), pp. 7, 8; Deutsche Bank (2004a), p. 3.

2.2 Index Basics

Indices are used as statistical measures of changes in an economy or a security market, as it would be extremely difficult and very complex to track every single security by itself.[13] An index indicates changes in the underlying values over a period of time and can be based on regions, sector or any other possible conglomeration of values. In financial markets an index is an imaginary portfolio representing a market, sector or industry or portions of it. An index is communicated in terms of a change from a base value.[14] Financial markets are more interested in the percentage changes rather than the actual numeric changes in value or the value itself. Ideally, a change in the price of an index would represent an exactly proportional change in the stocks included in the index.

With the help of an index investment, opportunities can be identified and evaluated. Furthermore, it can be a useful tool for investors and analysts to identify and track market trends. While an index provides a historical perspective, it can be utilised to serve as a benchmark against a single share, a portfolio or another index. An index also creates attention to the stocks included. This can result in increasing market values or increasing trading volumes.[15]

There are two main criticisms of indices: calculation biases and representative biases. Calculation biases mean the weights of the single stocks with its market capitalisation can lead to large influences of those stocks with a relative big market capitalisation. If the stock of such a big player falls dramatically, the whole market represented by the index goes down. There are also representative biases because the composition of an index changes over time. Therefore, one cannot look at a historical chart of an index and assume that it characterises the trading pattern of the same underlying stocks over a long period of time. Markets, however, are more dynamic than the indices.

[13] Cf. Deutsche Börse Group (2005a), p. 6.
[14] Cf. NYSE (2004), p. 5.
[15] Cf. Dow Jones Indices (2005), p. 4.

For the creation of a German brewing index several reasons can be named. Firstly, the German as well as the European beer sector has been very active in the last five years. An index could help investors and market participants to better analyse the industry as a whole. Secondly, an index helps listed or non-listed breweries to benchmark themselves against the index, i.e. against the industry and their competitors. Especially in a market environment, that becomes more and more unstable, this point is very important for many breweries. Thirdly, a German brewing index could attract more attention to a vital and important business sector in Germany. Finally, indices are oftentimes used as a basis for hedging instruments and other derivative securities.[16] It has to be analysed if a German brewing index can be used for this function.

3 Description of the Data Sample

The membership to the BEX Germany is bound to several requirements.[17] Firstly, the company must be listed at a German stock exchange and a German company, i.e. its headquarters has to be located in Germany. Furthermore, the company has to be active in the brewing industry, and these brewing activities have to be a major business of the company. Therefore, a major part of the annual turnover has to come directly from own brewing activities, indirectly from affiliates, or via a holding structure. Finally, in order to become a member of the index, the free float percentage of the company has to be at least 5 %.

Applying the requirements to the German beer market left us with 18 companies. The companies are or were listed at three different stock exchanges in Germany, namely Frankfurt (8x), Munich (9x) and Stuttgart (1x).[18] For these companies we use historic data over a time period of approximately 42 months. Due to several mergers and acquisitions, the sample has changed during this time frame, which in turn impacted the index composition.

[16] Cf. Deutsche Börse Group (2005a), p. 6; MSCI (2005), p. 1.
[17] These requirements will be discussed in more detail in Chapter 4.3.
[18] For an overview of the data sample refer to Appendix 1.

Market capitalisation is major issue of the data sample. There are a few larger scale companies like Holsten or Brau und Brunnen, but many companies have market capitalisation of well below € 100m. Some are even in the area of € 5m. This huge difference in size between the companies results in an index dominated by a few large companies.

This problem does not really change when taking the free float percentages into account. Here the same spread can be seen. Also, the oftentimes very low free float numbers can be an explanation for the low liquidity.

The lack of liquidity is a problem.[19] Though the market for beer brewing companies is very voluminous, there are only a small number of publicly traded companies. With the exception of Holsten and Brau und Brunnen, the trading volumes are very low. The majority of the listed companies are traded only once or twice a year with volumes below ten shares per deal or even less.

For us another problem while constructing the index has also been caused by the very poor data quality. We used Reuters, DataStream and OnVista as the main sources for the data. While the stock prices seems to be reliable, especially the historic free float data is not. In many cases the free float numbers are not available historically. In other cases they are obviously wrong.[20] Therefore, in order to get relatively reliable results we take the more reliable actual free float numbers for the whole period, assuming that no major changes occurred during this time frame. Only for Holsten and Brau und Brunnen we make adjustments at the time of the respective merger.

4 Index Calculation Methodology

4.1 Performance versus Price Index

For stock indices, two different kinds of indices are used predominantly in practice: performance and price indices. The calculation of a price index is based on

[19] Cf. MSCI (2005), p. 12.

[20] Holsten's free float was stated at 40% even after the acquisition by Carlsberg.

actually observed stock prices. The performance index on the other hand uses adjusted stock prices that assume a reinvestment of distributions to the shareholders.

While all the major European stock indices and several U.S. indices are calculated as performance indices,[21] other important indices like the Dow Jones Industrial Average are calculated as price indices.[22] For the German Brewery Index we stay in line with the European "tradition", i.e. it is calculated as a performance index. The main reason for this choice is the purpose of the index. The German Brewery Index is supposed to reflect the performance of the German brewing industry. A price index only shows the development of share prices, but distributions to the shareholders are a major component of the overall performance.

However, there is one crucial assumption implied in any performance index. As prices are adjusted for distributions, a reinvestment of these distributions into the same company is assumed. As discussed earlier, the shares of listed German breweries tend to be highly illiquid. In many cases shares are only traded occasionally.[23] Therefore, it is not necessarily possible to buy those shares at the ex-dividend date. Still we think the performance index is the right choice as it enables to show a picture of the industry that is not disturbed by different distribution policies, even though this decision might limit the usability of the index as a basis for derivative securities.

4.2 Index Formula

The index formula used for the German Brewery Index is a straight forward Laspeyers formula. As shown in Formula 1, the actual index is basically the sum of the free float-weighted market capitalisation of each security divided by the initial market capitalisation of all securities.[24]

---

[21] DAX, CAC40, FTSE and EuroStoxx are calculated as both, price and performance index. However, usually the performance index is referred to. Cf. Deutsche Börse Group (2005a), p. 9; NYSE (2004), p. 2; MSCI (2005), p. 2.

[22] Cf. Dow Jones Indices (2005), p. 9.

[23] See Appendix 1.

[24] Cf. Dow Jones Indices (2005), p. 23; Deutsche Börse Group (2005b), p. 12; NYSE (2004), p. 13.

Formula 1

$$Index_t = K \times \frac{\sum p_{it} \times ff_{it} \times q_{it}}{\sum p_{i0} \times q_{i0}} \times Basis$$

It can be argued whether a Laspeyers index formula is the best for calculating a stock index or not. A Laspeyers index shows the performance of an investment into a certain basket of securities that is held on to. This is an advantage and a disadvantage at the same time. It ensures the comparability of the index results, but it does not exactly reflect the actual situation of the industry, but only the current situation of an investment into the industry in the past. Still, the comparability seems to be important enough, so that Laspeyers has become the industry standard for index calculations.[25] Therefore, we use it for the brewing index as well.

There are reasons for and against using a free float factor. The major advantage of the regular market capitalisation is that it represents the true economic weight of a company.[26] As an index is supposed to be a picture of the situation in the industry, the market cap weighing could serve as a good proxy for that. However, we prefer the free float-weighted market capitalisation to the regular market capitalisation for several reasons. First of all, investors usually are interested in shares that are actually tradable. Thus, a company, that is large in terms of market capitalisation, can be of relatively low interest to an investor if its free float is too low. The second reason for choosing a free float weighting is that indices are likely to be used as benchmarks for investments. If much capital is invested with a particular market capitalisation weighted index as benchmark, the demand for a security with very low free float could be artificially high, leading to market disturbance even though this is not very likely for the case of a German brewing index. Finally, free float weightings have become the industry standard across Europe. All major European indices reflect the free float in their calculations.[27]

---

[25] Cf. Deutsche Börse Group (2005b), p. 4.

[26] It is obvious that an index can only reflect the performance of an industry reasonably if it is based on the market capitalisation of its members. Even though this is intuitively clear not all of the major indices are calculated accordingly. The Dow Jones Industrial for example is calculated free of any market cap. For some critical thoughts about this as well as the price vs. performance index discussion see Shoven / Sialm (2000).

[27] Cf. Deutsche Börse Group (2005b), p. 5.

4.3 Index Weighting and Free Float

Two different types of caps are employed for the calculation of the German Brewing Index. At first, the weight a company can have in the index is capped. Secondly, a company has to have a minimal free float ratio.[28]

As previously shown in the description of the data sample, listed breweries in Germany vary significantly in terms of size and free float. There are several large companies like Sedlmayr with a market capitalisation of over € 700m as well as small beer producers with about € 4m market capitalisation (Park & Bellheimer). A similar spread can be observed for the free float. As a result there are extreme differences in the free float weighted market capitalisation between the different companies.

The index is supposed to reflect the situation in the industry. Therefore, large companies have to have more influence on the index than smaller ones. However, as the companies are varying in size by a factor of almost 200, the index is likely to replicate the performance of the large players only. Comprising just ten companies, the index is likely to be driven by only one or two companies. In order to limit this influence, and therefore to show the smaller companies' performances as well, the maximum weight one security can have is limited to 15%. This ensures that the industries' situation is somehow reflected by the index, not just that of the number one.[29]

The other cap employed for the German Brewing Index is a free float percentage of at least 5%. It is important to set this lower limit so that only tradable companies are in the index. As soon as a company can squeeze out the minority, shares usually are not traded in a normal manner anymore.[30] Speculations about the compensation then take over as the major driver for the stock price movement. Thus, the

[28] Cf. Deutsche Börse Group (2005a), p. 11; NYSE (2004), p. 5.
[29] Cf. Deutsche Börse Group (2005b), p. 14; MSCI (2005), p. 6.
[30] In Germany a squeeze-out is possible with at least 95% of the shares.

prices do not reflect the company's performance accurately anymore. Therefore, it is preferable to take these companies out of the index.

4.4 Correction Factor

Major events like mergers and acquisitions, but also regular shifts in the industry resulting from different growth rates of the companies make regular adjustments of the index and its composition necessary.[31] Analogous to the DAX and other major European stock indices, we chose quarterly adjustments for the BEX Germany.[32] This ensures that the index always provides an accurate picture of the industry. This rule also allows that the index can be replicated without adjusting it too frequently.[33]

Technically, these adjustments are fairly simple. Calculating the index with its adjusted composition and weightings leads to a different value than before. But this change in the index value is not caused by the development of the individual securities, i.e. the performance of the industry. Therefore, this jump in the index has to be corrected by the correction factor K. K is determined as the ratio of the value of the unadjusted index and the adjusted index for the correction date as shown in formula 2.[34]

Formula 2

$$K_t = \frac{Unadjusted\ \ Index}{Adjusted\ \ Index}$$

This correction factor only accounts for the changes compared to the last index composition. Therefore, at the following adjustment dates, the new correction factor has to be multiplied with the one previously used (Formula 3).

---

[31] Cf. MSCI (2005), p. 17.
[32] Cf. Deutsche Börse Group (2005b), pp. 10, 11.
[33] Cf. NYSE (2004), p. 12.
[34] Cf. Deutsche Börse Group (2005b), p. 23.

Formula 3

$$K_{new} = K_{old} \times K_t$$

Adjusting the index quarterly works well for regular adjustments caused by the company's performance. However, it is obvious that events like take-overs also create the need for index adjustments. As these events can occur any time, i.e. not only at the adjustment dates, extra corrections are necessary. For the BEX-Germany, the final adjustment for these cases is conducted at the following adjustment date. Until then the acquired company is taken out of the index calculation, but no other company will be included as a substitute.

Summing up every aspect, the methodology of the BEX is in line with the other major European indices. The index rules are chosen to guarantee the best picture of the industry possible considering the critical characteristics of the relevant companies. The next chapter will therefore analyse whether the BEX-Germany actually is able to reflect the brewing industry and how this industry is performs compared to the overall market.

5 Performance Analysis

5.1 Holsten as the Key Driver of the BEX

In order to evaluate the quality of the BEX-Germany, it is interesting to analyse the key value drivers of the index. Even without any statistical tools it becomes obvious that until the second quarter of 2004 Holsten had a major impact on the index.

Chart 1: Chart BEX-Germany vs. Holsten

During the pre-acquisition phase of Holsten the stock price was very volatile. In the second half of 2000 Holsten's share price experienced a strong upward movement before it came back down rapidly in early 2001.[35] Looking at the development of the BEX-Germany during that time frame shows almost exactly the same movement just on a smaller scale. Chart 1 shows the development of the BEX-Germany and Holsten with adjusted scales. It is obvious that there is a high degree of correlation between those two.

Actually looking at the number leads to the same result. For the time period from April 2002 to March 2004 the correlation coefficient between Holsten and the BEX-Germany is very high at 0.96. This is a very good indication for Holsten being the key driver of the BEX-Germany. The almost non-existing volatility of the BEX-Germany after Holsten is taken out further strengthens this argument.

[35] Some of the movements of the Holsten stock price are currently subject to enquiries by the BaFin. See also the discussion of the Holsten case by Gast / Johansson (2005).

Chart 2: BEX-Germany vs. BEX-Germany ex Holsten

However, taking Holsten out of the BEX-Germany and analysing the adjusted BEX-Germany, performance gives almost the same result. The correlation between Holsten and the adjusted BEX-Germany is still at very high 0.92.[36] BEX-Germany and BEX-Germany ex Holsten even correlate with 0.99, as can also be seen in Chart 2. Therefore, it is questionable whether Holsten really is the only main driver of the BEX.

Still, the little difference between the data including and excluding Holsten shows that the market – at least during that time frame – behaved very similarly to the Holsten share. This can be interpreted in a positive and a negative way. It is positive that the market participants understand the brewing market as an industry of its own. Therefore, an index for this industry will probably be appreciated and regarded. On the other hand, taking into account the extremely low trading volumes of German brewery shares, it is likely that the movement only reflects the opinion of very few market participants, and therefore cannot be used as a good indicator for the operating performance of the industry.

[36] See Appendix 3 for a chart comparing Holsten and the adjusted BEX-Germany.

Looking at the absolute performance of the BEX-Germany,[37] we are confident that it can be used to further analyse some trends of the German brewing industry. Although at first sight its upward movement does not really fit to the consolidation currently taking place, this upward movement shows that the capital markets do appreciate the outcome of the strategic reorientation taking place in some companies.

5.2 BEX-Germany versus DAX, MDAX and EuroStoxx

Having analysed that the BEX-Germany can be used as an indicator for at least parts of the industry, the next question is how the performance of the listed German breweries looks in a broader context. Therefore, we compared the BEX-Germany to the two major German stock indices DAX and MDAX as well as to the EuroStoxx 50.

Chart 3: BEX-Germany vs. DAX

Chart 3 shows the development of the DAX and the BEX-Germany since mid-2002. In the first half the BEX-Germany, strongly influenced by Holsten's rapid rise, outperforms the DAX significantly. With exception of the dip caused by ru-

---

[37] See Appendix 2.

mours around the Holsten acquisition, it continues this strong development in comparison to the DAX.

When analysing the correlations between DAX and BEX-Germany, they show a moderate correlation of 0.64 for the whole period. This is not really surprising as the DAX represents the 30 largest German companies while even the larger breweries in the BEX-Germany can only be labelled mid-caps.

Therefore, the higher correlation with the MDAX seems to be logical. Here, we observe a correlation coefficient of 0.83, already a strong and positive one. In addition to the stronger correlation between the two indices, the BEX-Germany cannot outperform the MDAX as easily as the DAX. As can be seen on Chart 4, since July 2002 there is an out-performance of about 10%, however, it has mainly been caused by the very strong performance during the first half of this time frame. Therefore, it can be concluded that listed German breweries tend to behave similarly to other German mid-caps.

Therefore, the higher correlation with the MDAX seems to be logical. Here, we observe a correlation coefficient of 0.83, so already a strong positive one. In addition to the stronger correlation between the two indices, the BEX-Germany cannot outperform the MDAX as easily as the DAX. As can be seen on Chart 4, since July 2002 there is an out-performance of about 10%, however it is mainly caused by the very strong performance during the first half of this time frame. Therefore, it can be concluded that listed German breweries tend to behave similar to other German mid-caps.

Chart 4: BEX-Germany vs. MDAX

A final comparison of the BEX-Germany with the European blue-chip index EuroStoxx 50 confirms the results stated above. Here the correlation coefficient is also reasonably moderate with about 0.56. This can not be a surprise, since some DAX companies are included in the EuroStoxx 50. The development of the EuroStoxx 50 is even a little bit weaker than that of the DAX resulting in a slightly higher out-performance by the BEX-Germany as shown in Chart 5.

Chart 5:BEX-Germany vs. EuroStoxx50

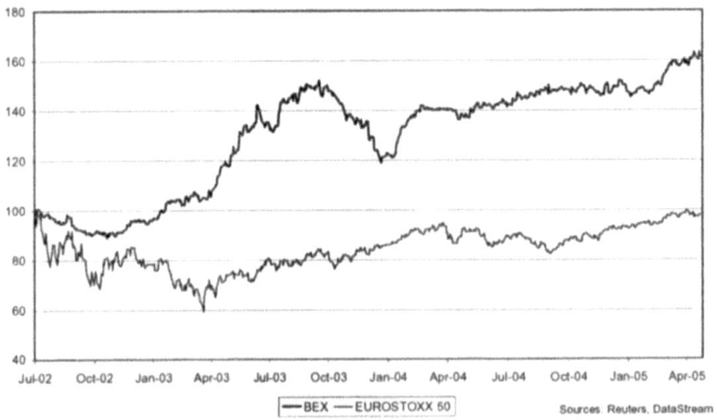

Overall the performance analysis of the BEX-Germany shows that breweries perform in line with other German mid-caps. Relative to large-caps, a significant outperformance and moderate correlation coefficients can be observed for the past three years.

6 Conclusion and Outlook

Summarising the most important facts presented in this paper, we can conclude that the BEX-Germany has a certain potential to be used as an indicator for the German brewing industry. However, the current situation with only very few listed breweries in Germany, that tend to be very illiquid, does not provide the ideal basis for such an index.

For the construction of the BEX-Germany several compromises had to be made. The very small number of listed breweries in Germany resulted in an index comprising a total of 10 companies. Therefore, the danger of one or two companies dominating the index is relatively high. Analysing the final index also confirmed this problem, as prior to the acquisition of Holsten the index almost mirrored Holsten's performance. Furthermore, the free float of most of the companies is fairly low. This fact increases the illiquidity problem of that most companies of the sample already face. But currently it is simply not possible to get around this problem because the universe of listed breweries does not provide enough alternatives yet.

Even though these problems cannot be solved perfectly, the BEX-Germany already shows a performance that can be explained by some trends in the industry. Overall the performance over the past three years was positive. This does not necessarily conflict with the consolidation process taking place in the industry. The BEX-Germany is dominated by the larger listed breweries that obviously can profit relatively to the rest of the industry.

The comparison of the BEX-Germany to the DAX and EuroStoxx also showed a very reasonable result. These indices are moderately positive correlated, implying the brewing industry indeed depends on the overall economic situation. The strong correlation with the German mid-cap index MDAX also perfectly fits the picture. The brewing companies that move the BEX-Germany are mid-size companies, and they also behave similarly to mid-caps from other industries.

Summing up, we come to the conclusion that the BEX-Germany is not a perfect index because it only reflects a part of the German brewing industry. Currently it cannot be used as a basis for derivative securities, as its member's trade is far too illiquid. However, in some parts of the industry trends are recognizable in the BEX-Germany. For breweries it also gives a relatively good picture of where they stand in the competition. With further listed breweries and more active trading in those securities, the BEX-Germany should be able to completely reach its goals.

Appendix

Appendix 1: Data Sample

Name	Exchange	Mcap in EUR	Free Float	Average Volume in EUR
ACTRIS	Frankfurt	115,530,000	1.30%	1,100.00
AKTIEN BRAU.KAUFBEUREN	Munich	12,000,000	14.00%	0.00
ALLGAEUER BRAUHAUS	Munich	23,945,066	9.80%	5.00
BAY.BIERBRAUEREI	Munich	7,490,000	10.00%	0.00
BRAU UND BRUNNEN	Frankfurt	406,266,265	3.32%	661,465.50
BRAUEREI MONINGER	Frankfurt	4,640,000	9.10%	1,020.72
BUERG.BRAUH.INGOLSTADT	Munich	16,800,000	6.22%	0.00
CUSTODIA HOLDINGS	Munich	444,320,000	7.61%	15.00
DOM-BRAUEREI	Frankfurt	7,978,500	23.40%	28.51
EINBECKER BRAUHAUS	Frankfurt	42,787,509	85.34%	5,958.00
HOLSTEN-BRAUEREI	Frankfurt	539,137,500	1.86%	7,706.67
INNSTADT-BRAUEREI	Munich	2,240,000	5.00%	0.00
KULMBACHER BRAUEREI	Munich	79,968,000	11.40%	6,278.00
LANDSHUTER BRAUHAUS	Munich	n.a.	0.00%	64,800.00
PARK & BELLHEIMER	Frankfurt	4,050,000	25.00%	1,988.42
SEDLMAYR	Frankfurt	707,000,000	0.00%	16.75
STUTT.HOFBRAEU	Stuttgart	375,000,000	21.47%	91,598.86
WUERZBURGER HOFBRAEU	Munich	40,100,000	9.30%	0.00

	Mcap in EUR	Free Float	Average Volume in EUR
Low	2,240,000	0.00%	0.00
High	707,000,000	85.34%	661,465.50
Mean	166,426,638	14.36%	45,716.55
Median	40,100,000	9.30%	28.51

Sources: Reuters, DataStream, OnVista

Appendix 2: BEX-Germany

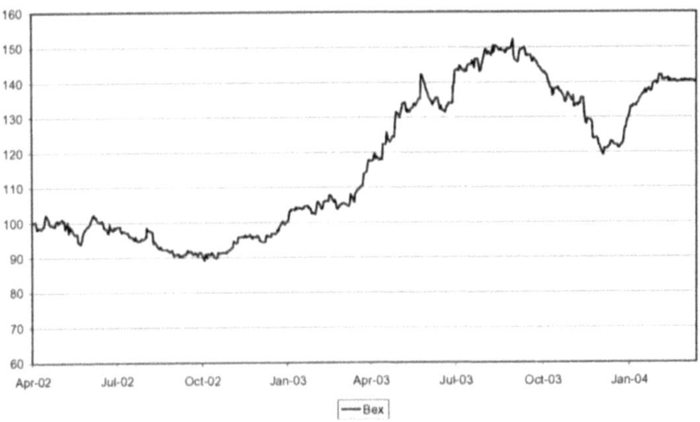

Appendix 3: BEX-Germany ex Holsten vs. Holsten

References

Credit Swiss First Boston (2003): The German beer industry: The consolidators' challenge, in: Theme, June 2003.

Credit Swiss First Boston (2004a): The German beer industry: Consolidation continues, in: Sector Review, February 2004.

Credit Swiss First Boston (2004b): European brewers: Going for growth, in: Sector Review, September 2004.

Deutsche Bank (2004a): Implications of EU accession: Central European Brewing, in: Industry Focus, February 2004.

Deutsche Bank (2004b): Global Brewing: The Global Pitcher 2004 - Volume V, in: Industry Focus, September 2004.

Deutsche Börse Group (2005a): Leitfaden zu den Aktienindizes der Deutschen Börse, January 2005.

Deutsche Börse Group (2005b): Leitfaden zum German Entrepreneurial Index GEX® der Deutschen Börse, January 2005.

Dow Jones Indexes (2005): Guide to the Dow Jones Global IndexesSM, January 2005.

Gast, Jochen / Johansson, Christian (2005): Case Study: The Acquisition of the Holsten Brauerei AG by Carlsberg A/S, Working Paper, Oestrich-Winkel 2005.

MSCI (2005): MSCI Standard Index Series Methodology, May 2005.

NYSE (2004): Methodology Guide for NYSE Indexes, February 2004.

Shoven, John B. / Sialm, Clemens (2000): The Dow Jones Industrial Average: The Impact of Fixing Its Flaws, Stanford, CA.

II Developing a European Brewing Industry Index

by
Nils Steiner and Bastian Biesenbach

1 Introduction

1.1 Objective of the Study

The European brewing industry has been moved by several large scale merger transactions in the recent past.[1] However, the value generating capabilities of these acquisitions have been doubted for various reasons. At about the same time, the European beverage industry has outperformed the general markets by 48%,[2] which has lead to positive quote developments throughout the whole industry. Thus, the underperformance of a single company can not be detected by a simple stock performance analysis, since the general market development is not taken into account. However, through benchmarking the company's track record to the brewing industry's performance, it might be possible to gain insights into the value enhancing or destroying effects of the recent M&A transactions. Thus, this paper has the goal to develop an equity index for the European brewing industry as an industry benchmark. Furthermore, this paper will use the newly calculated index to gain insights into the past merger activities and their impact on the industry.

The analysis will reveal that the European brewing industry has strongly outperformed the European prime standard indices FTSE 100, DAX, and DJ EuroSTOXX. However, the paper will also show, that the main protagonists of the past M&A wave in the brewing industry have performed rather weakly in the past.

---

[1] Cf. Deutsche Bank AG (2003), p. 1.
[2] Cf. Deutsche Bank AG (2002), p. 1.

Thus, the paper's findings seem to be consistent with the expectations of many market analysts.

1.2 Course of Analysis

After the short introduction in this section, the paper will give a brief overview on different types of indices and the European brewery market in Section 2. Based on these findings, the European brewery index (EuroBEX) will be outlined roughly in Section 2.3. The following Section 3 elaborates on the methodology and the sample which is used for the calculation of the index. In Section 4.1 the EuroBEX is presented and tested for its usability. Afterwards in Section 4.2, the index is used to analyse the past merger activities in the brewing industry in order to estimate the value creation potential of the transactions. The study is shortly summarised in Section 5.

2 Indexation for the European Brewing Industry

2.1 Overview on Index Types

Market indices are commonly used in the financial industry to track the performance of a specific portfolio of assets, which are considered to be representative for a market segment or a sector of the financial markets.[3] The most prominent and most regular quoted market indices are the broad-base indices that list the largest companies of an economy, like the Dow Jones Industrial Average (DJIA), the S&P 500, the FTSE 100, and the Nikkei 225. Although all these indices have the same goal to make the markets more transparent and comparable for investors, they all differ in their method of indexation.[4]

Firstly, market indices can be differentiated by the method of calculation. From a statistical point of view there are two ways to estimate a weighted composite market index commonly used in financial markets.[5] The method most often used to calculate a weighted market index is the Laspeyres index, which compares the

[3] Cf. SEC (2000).
[4] Cf. Deutsche Börse AG (2005), p. 6.
[5] Cf. McClave / Benson / Sincich (2001), p. 761.

weighted total of the current prices to the weighted total in the base period. In contrary to this, the Paasche index compares the current, weighted prices to the base period prices, which are weighted by the current weights.[6] The major disadvantage of the Paasche index is that although each period is compared to the base period, it is not possible to compare the index at two other periods since the weights change from period to period. Hence, the Laspeyres is the most preferred index for the estimation of weighed composite market indices.[7]

Secondly, market indices differ by the performance evaluation. This refers mainly to the treatment of dividend payments and similar benefits to the shareholder which have an impact on the price of an asset. Total return or performance indices mathematically reinvest the value of all cash and security payments to the asset holders.[8] Thus, the indices measure the overall performance of the portfolio including the outgoing payments. In contrast to these total return indices, price indices only consider the current price level without any adjustments. Hence, dividend payments and stock splits are not adjusted for and affect the index.[9]

The third dimension by which indices may differ is the method of the portfolio selection. Indices are either a selection index, which means that the index members are selected by a certain rule, an all-share index, or an industry / segment index.[10] All of these three dimensions will be taken into account later on in Section 3 for the derivation of the methodology and the sample selection.

2.2 Reasons for a European Brewery Index

During the past years there has been a strong consolidation in the European brewing industry.[11] These mergers are partially motivated by the ongoing consolidation of the beer markets, like in Germany, and the striving for new markets. Thus, the brewing industry has become an interesting field for investment activities with

---

[6] Cf. ibid pp. 756-759.
[7] Cf. ibid p. 761.
[8] Cf. Harris (2003), p. 445.
[9] Cf. Shoven / Sialm (2000), p. 1.
[10] Cf. Deutsche Börse AG (2005), pp. 6-8.
[11] Cf. Deutsche Bank AG (2003), p. 3.

strong outperforming growth.[12] Therefore, there is an increasing interest for a European brewing industry index in the financial market. In the following, this paper will shortly elaborate on the benefits of such a brewery index in order to be able to analyse and later on evaluate the paper's findings.

The main target of an index is to give information on the portfolio and its performance in the past.[13] Thus, a European brewery index could be used for evaluating investment opportunities by benchmarking individual investments against the overall industry performance. This is especially interesting for the evaluation of the success of past mergers and acquisitions, since the value creation capabilities of some take-overs have been questioned in the past.[14] By a representative European brewing industry index it is possible to test whether merged companies have performed better or worse than the market. Hence, this paper will also test later on how the members of the index perform individually when compared to the aggregated market.

Another important function of indices is that they are an investment guideline for many funds, which try to mimic a specific industry. There by, more attention is drawn to the individual companies and their performance, which should be highly interesting for the companies. Additionally, indices are used increasingly as a basis for financial derivatives like futures, options, and warrants.[15] However, since only few breweries are traded publicly in continental Europe, institutional traders like funds and banks are not too much interested in the industry. Additionally, all major breweries are already covered by analysts, since they are members of various other indices. Hence, this paper will mainly focus on the above discussed benchmarking function of an index, when analyzing the paper's results.

2.3 The European Brewing Industry Index (EuroBEX)

The discussion above has shown that the European brewery index (EuroBEX) has the main objective to compare and benchmark the performance of European beer

[12] Cf. Deutsche Bank AG (2002), p. 1.
[13] Cf. Deutsche Börse AG (2005), p. 6.
[14] Cf. Deutsche Bank AG (2003), p. 1.
[15] Cf. Deutsche Börse AG (2005), p. 6.

producers. Thus, the index will be based on the Laspeyres methodology, since it allows the comparison of index numbers with each other.[16] Furthermore, the index will be constructed as a market capitalisation weighted price index, since this guarantees that the value weighted index corresponds to the changes in the total market value of a company.[17] The selection of the potential members is discussed in detail below. However, the paper will take all continental European publicly listed breweries into account, since the expansion of the European Union in 2004 consequently expanded the EC domestic market. Furthermore, several larger players in the market acquired breweries in eastern European countries; thus, these markets are also considered in the EuroBEX.[18]

3 Methodology and Sample

3.1 Methodology

The methodology for the calculation of a European brewery index used in this paper conforms to the indexation methods applied by most exchanges around the world. However, there are minor differences in the calculation techniques used by the major exchanges, as discussed already above. This paper will therefore follow the practices of the Deutsche Börse AG for the German prime standard index DAX.[19] This methodology was chosen, since it fits the preliminary considerations on the EuroBEX in Section 2.3, where it was demanded that the EuroBEX is a weighted Laspeyres performance index. The applied method uses the market capitalisation of the free-float as index weights, which is considered to be objective: only tradable shares are of interest to investors. In the following the techniques for the EuroBEX used are elaborated on in more detail.

3.1.1 Method of Index member selection

The first question to be considered when constructing an index is the selection of the members. Since the EuroBEX is a European brewing industry index, the mem-

---

[16] Cf. McClave / Benson / Sincich (2001), p. 761.
[17] Cf. Shoven / Sialm (2000), p. 3.
[18] Cf. Deutsche Bank AG (2004), p. 1.
[19] Cf. Deutsche Börse AG (2005).

bers have to generate about 20% of their turnover from brewery activities and have to be publicly listed at a continental European exchange. This relatively broad definition has been chosen, due to the expansion of larger European breweries into Eastern Europe, like the Heineken acquisition of BBAG, which might have implications for the European beer market.[20] Furthermore, the EuroBEX members need to have a free-float of at least 5% in order to ensure sufficient liquidity. Otherwise it would be possible to initiate a squeeze-out if the free-float was below this value in many countries. Thus, it is quite likely, that such a company will not exist in the long run. Hence, companies with a free-float of less than 5% are excluded from the EuroBEX at the adjustment dates. The remaining companies are ranked by their market capitalisation of the free-float the first 30 companies at the adjustment date are included in the EuroBEX for the next three months.

3.1.2 Calculation of the EuroBEX

The EuroBEX covers publicly traded breweries from all over continental Europe; hence, some of the companies in the later introduced sample are not traded in Euro, but in their home currency. In order to be able to compare the stock prices it is necessary to convert the quotes of domestic currencies into a Euro-quote, which is achieved by using daily ECB FX-rates from the Datastream database. Based on the homogenous Euro-quotes, it is then possible to calculate the free-float market capitalisation as shown below in Formula 1.

Formula 1

$$Market\ Capitalization_{Free-Float} = p_t \cdot q_t \cdot ff_t ,$$

where p_t and q_t are the stock price and stocks outstanding at time t and ff_t is the current free-float. In order to prevent the domination of the index by a few corporations with a high market capitalisation caused either by high prices, a large number of shares outstanding or a high free-float, the index weights are capped at a 15% level. This prevents a single company to be able to influence more than one sixth

[20] Cf. Deutsche Bank AG (2004), p. 4-18.

of the EuroBEX. The capping is repeated until all companies have a market capitalisation weight of 15% or lower.

After the adjustment of the weights it is then possible to calculate the EuroBEX. The method is based on the Laspeyres indexation formula; thus, the current value of the index portfolio is compared to the portfolio's value at the base period. Due to the fact that only limited time series data is available for the free-float, the base period is defined as January 1st, 2004. The index number is then calculated to the index basis which is in the case of the EuroBEX 1000 points. Thus, the basic index formula for the EuroBEX is given by Formula 2 as:

Formula 2

$$Euro\ BEX\ Index = \frac{\sum_{i=1}^{n} p_{it} \cdot q_{it} \cdot ff_{it}}{\sum_{i=1}^{n} p_{i0} \cdot q_{i0}} \cdot Basis$$

The formula for the EuroBEX does not include any adjustments for dividends or subscription rights, since the calculations in this paper are done with adjusted prices.[21] Nevertheless, Formula 2 could be easily adjusted to these extraordinary influences by including a factor c_{it}, an adjustment factor to the stock's price. The adjustment factor for individual equities is calculated analogous to the quarterly index adjustment, but on equities level.

3.1.3 Quarterly Index Adjustment

Like the DAX, the EuroBEX is adjusted on a quarterly basis.[22] This means that the composition of the BEX and the index weights are adjusted every three months, in order to update the index to the recent market developments. The period of three months is chosen because the period is not too long and still keeps the calculation effort to a reasonable level. Since a possible modification of the index might result in a change in the EuroBEX, it is necessary to readjust the new index numbers by

[21] This was done, since no reliable dividend and subscription right information was available.
[22] Cf. Deutsche Börse AG (2005), p. 33f.

an adjustment factor which is calculated in a three step process. First of all, the index is estimated with the old weights and members and the old adjustment factor K_t as estimated at the last adjustment date, as shown in Formula 3.

Formula 3

$$Euro\ BEX\ Index = K_T \cdot \frac{\sum_{i=1}^{n} p_{it} \cdot q_{it} \cdot ff_{it}}{\sum_{i=1}^{n} p_{i0} \cdot q_{i0}} \cdot Basis$$

Afterwards the index is calculated with the new weights and index members by using Formula 3 with K_T equaling zero. This so called interim value is then used to calculate the new adjustment factor by multiplying its reciprocal with the old K_T.

Formula 4

$$K_{T+1} = \frac{Index}{Interim\ Value}$$

This method would also be used in the case of an extraordinary adjustment, which could be necessary in the case of a take-over with delisting or bankruptcy. However, since this is not the case for any company in the sample, the paper will not elaborate on this any further.

3.2 Sample

In order to calculate the EuroBEX, a sample of all European publicly traded breweries, which generate about 20% of their turnover from brewery activities, is constructed. The selection is based on data from Datastream, factiva, and the Business & Company Resource Center by Thomson Gale. Companies with a beer related turnover of less than 20% is excluded, since the value of these companies is not expected to correlate with the brewing industry. Due to the fact that most breweries are still privately owned, a sample of only 48 companies was comprised that to a large part are from Germany (18 breweries) and Great Britain (ten companies).

Three breweries are sited in Belgium and Denmark, two are from the Netherlands and Turkey, and the remaining breweries are listed in Russia, Austria, Swiss, Spain, Finland, Hungary, Ireland, Luxembourg, and Poland (one brewery each). Table 1 gives a detailed overview on the sample companies and some descriptive statistics.

Table 1 - Descriptive Statistics for the Euro BEX Sample

					Stock Price in €		Stocks Outstanding		Free Float	
Number	Name	Country	Exchange	Currency	Mean	Std. Dev.	Mean	Std. Dev.	Mean	Std. Dev.
1	Actris	DEU	Frankfurt	EUR	7.75	0.47	14,624	0	37.63%	0.10
2	Aktienbrauerei Kaufbeuren AG	DEU	Munich	EUR	226.71	18.31	50	0	0.00%	0.00
3	Allgaeuer Brauhaus AG	DEU	Munich	EUR	369.98	15.61	87	0	0.00%	0.00
4	Anadolu Efes	TUR	Istanbul	TRL	12.25	2.01	112,877	0	75.12%	0.27
5	BALTIKA BREWERY	RUS	Russian Trading System	USD	11.93	1.53	117,160	0	84.26%	0.36
6	Bay. Bierbrauerei	DEU	Munich	EUR	1004.16	30.31	8	0	0.00%	0.00
7	Belhaven Brewery Group PLC	GBR	London	GBP	657.39	41.23	29,507	119	39.38%	0.10
8	Brau Und Brunnen AG	DEU	Frankfurt	EUR	84.70	7.00	4,489	0	13.81%	0.28
9	Brau Union Hungaria Sorgyarak Rt	HUN	Budapest	HUF	56.64	7.43	674	0	84.26%	0.36
10	Brauerei Moninger AG	DEU	Frankfurt	EUR	2.39	0.37	1,600	0	16.85%	0.07
11	Bryggerigruppen	DNK	Copenhagen	DKK	53.09	5.10	6,542	60	67.14%	0.10
12	Buergerliches Brauhaus Ingolstadt AG	DEU	Munich	EUR	612.20	58.34	30	0	0.00%	0.00
13	C&C Group	IRE	Dublin	EUR	2.00	1.27	321,121	148	0.00%	0.00
14	Carlsberg AS	DNK	Copenhagen	DKK	35.22	2.04	34,076	668	12.48%	0.02
15	Custodia Holding AG	DEU	Frankfurt	EUR	622.86	104.77	601	0	2.70%	0.02
16	Damm SA	ESP	Madrid	EUR	129.00	0.00	0	n/a	0.00%	0.00
17	Diageo PLC	GBR	London	GBP	1068.89	40.21	3,045,180	31,762	63.26%	0.11
18	Dom-Brauerei AG	DEU	Frankfurt	EUR	27.79	6.96	394	0	88.03%	0.28
19	Duvel Moortgat SA	BEL	Brussels	EUR	74.42	1.90	5,341	0	24.34%	0.01
20	Eichhof	CH	Zurich	CHF	672.13	110.90	177	0	45.73%	0.07
21	Einbecker Brauhaus AG	DEU	Frankfurt	EUR	20.98	1.51	2,160	0	0.00%	0.00
22	Fuller Smith & Turner PLC	GBR	London	GBP	1056.30	115.09	12,899	121	62.78%	0.08
23	Greene King PLC	GBR	London	GBP	1987.52	203.70	71,966	178	49.17%	0.10
24	Grupa Zywiec	POL	Warsaw Continuous	PLN	102.18	11.55	11,335	0	95.12%	0.11
25	Harboes Bryggeri	DNK	Copenhagen	DKK	225.05	38.01	536	0	48.76%	0.21
26	Hardys & Hansons PLC	GBR	London	GBP	785.45	88.65	20,000	0	70.27%	0.06
27	Heineken NV	NLD	Amsterdam	EUR	27.43	3.13	464,833	42,860	49.16%	0.01
28	Holsten-Brauerei AG	DEU	Frankfurt	EUR	37.45	2.41	13,750	0	8.37%	0.14
29	InBev SA	BEL	Brussels	EUR	25.90	2.21	499,591	71,664	51.41%	0.22
30	Innstadt-Brauerei	DEU	Munich	EUR	61.62	6.08	72	0	0.00%	0.00
31	Jennings Brothers PLC	GBR	London	GBP	395.94	54.14	10,654	0	35.53%	0.16
32	Koninklijke Grolsch NV	NLD	Amsterdam	EUR	23.46	0.98	16,922	0	86.32%	0.06
33	Kulmbacher Brauerei	DEU	Frankfurt	EUR	22.96	3.73	3,360	0	15.34%	0.09
34	Landshuter	DEU	Munich	EUR	3592.32	74.73	6	0	0.00%	0.00
35	OLVI	FIN	Helsinki	EUR	13.43	1.28	4,023	45	68.52%	0.07
36	Ottakringer Brauerei AG	AUT	Vienna	EUR	60.42	5.59	890	0	29.58%	0.03
37	Park & Bellheimer AG	DEU	Frankfurt	EUR	1.15	0.32	3,300	1,001	31.00%	0.00
38	Quinsa	LUX	Luxembourg	USD	0.68	0.10	647,619	0	19.15%	0.19
39	SAB Miller	GBR	London	GBP	1053.64	141.22	1,020,978	37,546	34.45%	0.14
40	SAKU	EST	Tallinn	EUR	7.03	0.82	8,000	0	88.19%	0.27
41	Scottish & Newcastle PLC	GBR	London	GBP	617.96	38.22	893,621	0	62.90%	0.11
42	Sedlmayr	DEU	Frankfurt	EUR	1971.97	110.50	348	0	86.66%	0.20
43	Societe Commerciale De Brasserie SA	BEL	Brussels	EUR	900.01	110.52	79	0	21.61%	0.02
44	Stuttgarter Hofbrau AG	DEU	Frankfurt	EUR	25.47	1.14	15,000	0	64.40%	0.33
45	Turk Tuborg Bira Ve Malt Sanayii AS	TUR	Istanbul	TRL	3.31	0.64	38,733	12,216	100.00%	0.00
46	Wolverhampton & Dudley Breweries PLC	GBR	London	GBP	1356.00	159.68	73,574	1,618	53.79%	0.10
47	Wuerzburger Hofbraeu AG	DEU	Frankfurt	EUR	396.08	14.98	100	0	84.26%	0.36
48	Young & Co S Brewery PLC	GBR	London	GBP	1832.37	269.68	3,141	0	50.52%	0.20

For each company stock prices, shares outstanding, and free-float data for the period from January 1st, 1991 until April 22nd, 2005 are taken from the Datastream database. However, information about the free-float is only available for the time after April, 18th, 2002. Additionally, the gathered free-float data shows strong inconsistencies with other data sources, especially for the German breweries. Due to this, the free-float data for the Aktienbrauerei Kaufbeuren AG, Allgäuer Brauhaus AG, Bay. Bierbrauerei, Brau und Brunnen AG, Brauerei Moninger AG, Bürgerliches Brauhaus Ingolstadt AG, Dom-Brauerei AG, Holsten-Brauerei AG, Innstadt-Brauerei, Sedlmayer, Stuttgarter Hofbräu AG, Turk Tuborg Bira Ve Malt Sanayii SA, and Würzburger Hofbräu AG has been adjusted according to other sources. In most cases recent changes in the shareholder structure have not yet been adjusted for by Datastream. Although this manipulation of the data might influence its reliability, a few slight amendments are neccessary, since the original data is obviously incorrect. Furthermore, most of the affected companies are rather small; thus, the influence on the index should be of minor importance.

4 Results

The EuroBEX is calculated for the period from January 1st, 2004 to April 22nd, 2005. Thus, the index composition is based on quotes, free-float data, and stocks outstanding dating January 1st, 2004, and afterwards adjusted on a quarterly basis. In order to present a larger track record, the index is counted back to January 1st, 1999 based on the weights calculated for January 1st, 2004. The resulting index chart is displayed below in Chart 1 and the related weights and index members are shown in Table 2.

Chart 1: EuroBEX Performance (01/01/1999 - 04/22/2005)

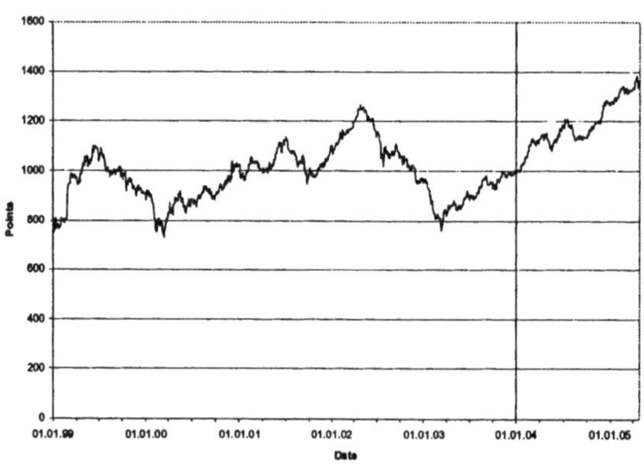

Chart 1 shows that the brewing industry has seen strong growth since 2003, which is highly interesting since several larger M&A transactions took place in 2002 and

2003.[23] Thus, this paper will elaborate on this issue in more detail later on in Section 4.2 after an analysis of the index results itself and their reliability.

Table 2: EuroBEX Index Weights

	Period 1		Period 2		Period 3		Period 4		Period 5
Name	01. Jan 04	Name	01. Apr 04	Name	01. Jul 04	Name	01. Oct 2004	Name	01. Jan 05
DIAGEO	15.00%	DIAGEO	15.00%	DIAGEO	15.00%	DIAGEO	15.00%	DIAGEO	15.00%
SABMILLER	15.00%	SCOTTISH & NEWCASTLE	15.00%	SCOTTISH & NEWCASTLE	15.00%	SCOTTISH & NEWCASTLE	15.00%	SABMILLER	15.00%
SCOTTISH & NEWCASTLE	15.00%	SABMILLER	15.00%	SABMILLER	15.00%	SABMILLER	15.00%	SCOTTISH & NEWCASTLE	15.00%
GREENE KING	15.00%	WOLV & DUDLEY	15.00%	WOLV & DUDLEY	15.00%	GREENE KING	15.00%	WOLV & DUDLEY	15.00%
WOLV & DUDLEY	15.00%	GREENE KING	15.00%	GREENE KING	15.00%	WOLV & DUDLEY	15.00%	GREENE KING	15.00%
HARDYS & HANSONS	4.53%	HARDYS & HANSONS	5.58%	HARDYS & HANSONS	6.12%	HARDYS & HANSONS	5.77%	HARDYS & HANSONS	5.56%
INBEV	4.50%	BELHAVEN GROUP	5.47%	BELHAVEN GROUP	4.96%	FULLER SMITH 'A'	4.66%	FULLER SMITH 'A'	4.41%
BELHAVEN GROUP	4.29%	FULLER SMITH 'A'	3.86%	FULLER SMITH 'A'	4.02%	HEINEKEN	3.64%	INBEV	4.30%
FULLER SMITH 'A'	3.89%	HEINEKEN	3.49%	HEINEKEN	3.44%	INBEV	3.19%	BELHAVEN GROUP	3.47%
HEINEKEN	2.94%	INBEV	1.82%	INBEV	2.04%	BELHAVEN GROUP	2.95%	HEINEKEN	2.93%
YOUNG & CO.BREW.'A'	1.96%	YOUNG & CO.BREW.'A'	1.34%	YOUNG & CO.BREW.'A'	1.30%	YOUNG & CO.BREW.'A'	1.45%	YOUNG & CO.BREW.'A'	1.26%
JENNINGS BROTHERS	1.03%	BALTIKA BREW	0.73%	BALTIKA BREW	0.67%	BALTIKA BREW	0.83%	BALTIKA BREW	0.75%
ANADOLU EFES	0.57%	ANADOLU EFES	0.69%	ANADOLU EFES	0.62%	JENNINGS BROTHERS	0.70%	JENNINGS BROTHERS	0.70%
GRUPA ZYWIEC	0.35%	JENNINGS BROTHERS	0.67%	GRUPA ZYWIEC	0.57%	GRUPA ZYWIEC	0.70%	GRUPA ZYWIEC	0.64%
GROLSCH (KON.)	0.18%	GRUPA ZYWIEC	0.58%	JENNINGS BROTHERS	0.51%	ANADOLU EFES	0.39%	ANADOLU EFES	0.37%
QUINSA	0.13%	GROLSCH (KON.)	0.19%	GROLSCH (KON.)	0.19%	GROLSCH (KON.)	0.19%	GROLSCH (KON.)	0.16%
BRYGGERIGRUPPEN	0.13%	BRYGGERIGRUPPEN	0.14%	BRYGGERIGRUPPEN	0.13%	BRYGGERIGRUPPEN	0.13%	BRYGGERIGRUPPEN	0.10%
BRAU UND BRUNNEN	0.12%	SEDLMAYR	0.11%	SEDLMAYR	0.10%	CARLSBERG 'A'	0.10%	CARLSBERG 'A'	0.08%
SEDLMAYR	0.10%	CARLSBERG 'A'	0.07%	CARLSBERG 'A'	0.06%	STUTT HOFBRAEU	0.05%	STUTT HOFBRAEU	0.04%
HOLSTEN-BRAUEREI	0.07%	STUTT HOFBRAEU	0.04%	STUTT HOFBRAEU	0.05%	EICHHOF 'R'	0.04%	EICHHOF 'R'	0.04%
CARLSBERG 'A'	0.05%	SAKU BREWERY	0.03%	HARBOES BRYGGERI 'B'	0.03%	TURK TUBORG	0.04%	TURK TUBORG	0.03%
STUTT HOFBRAEU	0.04%	QUINSA	0.03%	SAKU BREWERY	0.03%	SAKU BREWERY	0.03%	SAKU BREWERY	0.03%
HARBOES BRYGGERI 'B'	0.02%	HARBOES BRYGGERI 'B'	0.03%	EICHHOF 'R'	0.03%	QUINSA	0.03%	HARBOES BRYGGERI 'B'	0.02%
TURK TUBORG	0.02%	ACTRIS	0.03%	ACTRIS	0.03%	ACTRIS	0.03%	ACTRIS	0.02%
OLVI 'A'	0.02%	TURK TUBORG	0.03%	QUINSA	0.02%	HARBOES BRYGGERI 'B'	0.03%	BRAU UNION HUNGARIA	0.02%
ACTRIS	0.02%	EICHHOF 'R'	0.02%	TURK TUBORG	0.02%	BRAU UNION HUNGARIA	0.02%	OLVI 'A'	0.02%
EICHHOF 'R'	0.01%	OLVI 'A'	0.02%	BRAU UNION HUNGARIA	0.02%	DUVEL MOORTGAT	0.02%	DUVEL MOORTGAT	0.02%
DUVEL MOORTGAT	0.01%	BRAU UNION HUNGARIA	0.02%	OLVI 'A'	0.02%	OLVI 'A'	0.02%	QUINSA	0.02%
KULMBACHER BRAUEREI	0.01%	DUVEL MOORTGAT	0.02%	DUVEL MOORTGAT	0.02%	COMIT DE BRASSERIE	0.01%	OTTAKRINGER BRAUEREI	0.01%
OTTAKRINGER BRAUEREI	0.01%	OTTAKRINGER BRAUEREI	0.01%	OTTAKRINGER BRAUEREI	0.01%	OTTAKRINGER BRAUEREI	0.01%	COMIT DE BRASSERIE	0.01%

4.1 Analysis of the EuroBEX

The EuroBEX consists of strongly differing members. On the one hand, companies like Diageo, SAB Miller, InBev, and Heineken operate world-wide and produce several million hectolitres of beer per year. On the other hand, there are also small regional breweries, like the Kulmbacher Brauerei AG, in the sample. Although the index weights for each company are caped at a level of 15%, there is still a potential danger that the index is dominated by a single company, since 75% of the index's value is caused by five companies, as shown above in Table 2. Hence, the return correlation estimates for each company in the sample with the index calculated in order to detect possible dominant BEX members.

[23] Cf. Deutsche Bank AG (2003), p. 3.

Table 3: Correlation Factors of Index members with the Euro BEX

Number	Name	Country	Correlation Return
1	Actris	DEU	0.0268
2	Aktienbrauerei Kaufbeuren AG	DEU	-0.0046
3	Allgaeuer Brauhaus AG	DEU	-0.0669
4	Anadolu Efes	TUR	0.1524
5	BALTIKA BREWERY	RUS	0.0993
6	Bay. Bierbrauerei	DEU	-0.0658
7	Belhaven Brewery Group PLC	GBR	0.3445
8	Brau Und Brunnen AG	DEU	-0.0762
9	Brau Union Hungaria Sorgyarak Rt	HUN	0.0147
10	Brauerei Moninger AG	DEU	-0.0327
11	Bryggerigruppen	DNK	0.0788
12	Buergerliches Brauhaus Ingolstadt AG	DEU	-0.0079
13	Carlsberg AS	DNK	0.3013
14	Custodia Holding AG	DEU	-0.0965
15	Damm SA	ESP	0.0102
16	Diageo PLC	GBR	0.5958
17	Dom-Brauerei AG	DEU	0.0236
18	Duvel Moortgat SA	BEL	0.0225
19	Eichhof	CH	0.1093
20	Einbecker Brauhaus AG	DEU	0.1033
21	Fuller Smith & Turner PLC	GBR	0.3929
22	Greene King PLC	GBR	0.5566
23	Grupa Zywiec	POL	0.2041
24	Harboes Bryggeri	DNK	0.1202
25	Hardys & Hansons PLC	GBR	0.0696
26	Heineken NV	NLD	0.4400
27	Holsten-Brauerei AG	DEU	0.2819
28	InBev SA	BEL	0.0335
29	Innstadt-Brauerei	DEU	0.2514
30	Jennings Brothers PLC	GBR	-0.0884
31	Koninklijke Grolsch NV	NLD	0.1674
32	Kulmbacher Brauerei	DEU	0.0379
33	Landshuter	DEU	0.0192
34	OLVI	FIN	0.0747
35	Ottakringer Brauerei AG	AUT	0.0207
36	Park & Bellheimer AG	DEU	0.0109
37	Quinsa	LUX	0.0843
38	SAB Miller	GBR	0.6188
39	SAKU	EST	0.1115
40	Scottish & Newcastle PLC	GBR	0.6884
41	Sedlmayr	DEU	0.0857
42	Societe Commerciale De Brasserie SA	BEL	0.0214
43	Stuttgarter Hofbrau AG	DEU	0.0462
44	Turk Tuborg Bira Ve Malt Sanayii AS	TUR	0.2256
45	Wolverhampton & Dudley Breweries PLC	GBR	0.5794
46	Wuerzburger Hofbraeu AG	DEU	-0.0229
47	Young & Co S Brewery PLC	GBR	0.1531

Table 3 shows that most of the larger, international breweries like SAB Miller or Scottish & Newcastle PLC correlate highly with the BEX, while the local, German Breweries only show little evidence of a connection to the EuroBEX. This shows that the index is strongly influenced by the larger international companies, which is caused by the market capitalisation weighting of the index. Nevertheless, since the European brewing industry consists of a few larger companies dominating the numerous local beer producers, the index seems to represent the European market.

Thus, it is possible to use the EuroBEX to benchmark the performance of the European brewing industry against the performance of the general markets in the following in order to investigate the success of European breweries and their M&A activities.

4.2 Analysis of the BEX in an M&A Context

The European brewing industry has been affected by several large scale M&A transactions in recent years, which have been doubted to be value enhancing.[24] In the following sections, this paper will analyse the performance of the European brewing industry by means of the earlier constructed EuroBEX index in order to gather some evidence of the success of the M&A activities.

In a first step, the performance of the EuroBEX is plotted against the several major European indices. The analysis reveals that the EuroBEX significantly outperforms all major European market indices, as shown in Figure 2. This indicates that the industry has been successful over the past 18 months and that the mergers have not harmed the industry's profitability. However, the EuroBEX is outperformed by the Datastream index for European (Non-EC) beverage producers; thus, the good performance of the EuroBEX in comparison to the prime standard indices might be caused alone by the non-EC companies. Hence, the performance of the sample companies will be compared to the EuroBEX itself, in order to identify the value-enhancing and value-destroying members of the industry.

Chart 2: Cumulated Return of EuroBEX and European prime standard indices

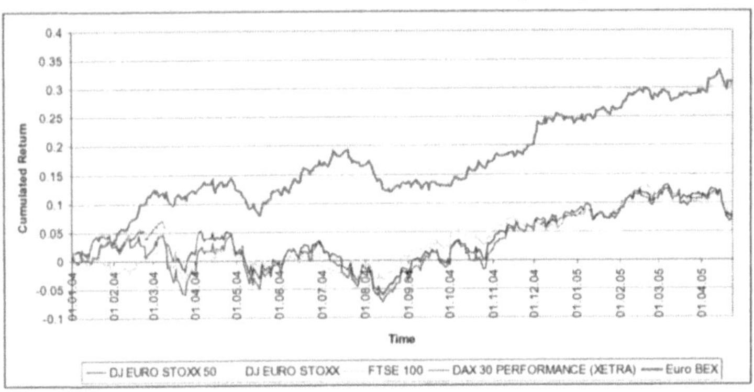

In order to measure the performance of the individual sample members, the cumulated return in the period from January 1st, 2004 until April 22nd, 2005 of each

[24] Cf. Deutsche Bank AG (2004), p. 4.

company is compared to the EuroBEX. The results of this analysis are shown in Table 4 which reveals some indications for the evaluation of the recent "merger wave" in the brewing industry. The major acquirers in the past transactions, Scottish & Newcastle (- 2%), Heineken (- 43%), Carlsberg (- 16.5%), and InBev (- 5%) have not performed as well as the industry, represented by the EuroBEX. This indicates that the concerns about the value destruction through past M&A transactions in the brewing industry might be legitimate. Especially the weak performances of Carlsberg and Heineken are striking, since the underperformance is so severe. The latter even generated a negative return over the whole period, which shows that the company has destroyed value in the past 18 months, compared to the market. Only SAB Miller, as the last of the big European breweries, is able to outperform the EuroBEX by 8.5%, which shows that the merger of South African Breweries and Miller has to be analysed from a different perspective, since the synergies in this merger might have been of a different nature.

Furthermore, the benchmark analysis reveals that most of the east European breweries outperformed the EuroBEX significantly, which could be caused by the strong growth opportunities in these markets.[25] The strong performance of Park & Bellheimer can be explained by a partial take-over through the Actris AG in 2004 and the announcement of insolvency in 2003, which therefore caused high returns during the turnaround. The good performance of some of the British breweries might have been caused by their strong vertical integration activities, which could have resulted in higher than average profits.

---

[25] Cf. Deutsche Bank AG (2004), p. 7.

Table 4: Performance Benchmark Analysis on Company level

Name	Cum. Return	Diff. To BEX
PARK & BELLHEIMER	1.77	1.45
JENNINGS BROTHERS	0.68	0.37
YOUNG & CO.BREW.'A'	0.63	0.32
SAKU BREWERY	0.58	0.27
EICHHOF 'R'	0.57	0.26
LANDSHUTER BRAUHAUS	0.56	0.25
HARBOES BRYGGERI 'B'	0.56	0.24
ANADOLU EFES	0.53	0.21
BALTIKA BREW.	0.47	0.16
GREENE KING	0.45	0.14
KULMBACHER BRAUEREI	0.45	0.13
BRAUEREI MONINGER	0.44	0.13
HARDYS & HANSONS	0.44	0.13
HOLSTEN-BRAUEREI	0.43	0.12
COMIT.DE BRASSERIE	0.42	0.10
QUINSA	0.41	0.10
WOLV.& DUDLEY	0.40	0.09
SABMILLER	0.40	0.09
BRAU UNION HUNGARIA	0.39	0.08
FULLER SMITH 'A'	0.39	0.08
BRAU UND BRUNNEN	0.35	0.04
DUVEL MOORTGAT	0.33	0.02
ACTRIS	0.32	0.01
Euro BEX	**0.31**	**0.00**
SCOTTISH & NEWCASTLE	0.29	-0.02
GRUPA ZYWIEC	0.29	-0.02
INBEV	0.26	-0.05
BELHAVEN GROUP	0.26	-0.05
AKTIEN BRAU.KAUFBEUREN	0.25	-0.06
BRYGGERIGRUPPEN	0.25	-0.07
BAY.BIERBRAUEREI	0.20	-0.11
OTTAKRINGER BRAUEREI	0.18	-0.13
OLVI 'A'	0.17	-0.14
SEDLMAYR	0.16	-0.15
CARLSBERG 'A'	0.15	-0.16
STUTT.HOFBRAEU	0.12	-0.19
ALLGAEUER BRAUHAUS	0.09	-0.22
DIAGEO	0.09	-0.22
GROLSCH (KON.)	0.04	-0.27
DAMM	0.00	-0.31
WUERZBURGER HOFBRAEU	0.00	-0.31
EINBECKER BRAUHAUS	-0.06	-0.37
INNSTADT-BRAUEREI	-0.11	-0.43
HEINEKEN	-0.12	-0.43
BUERG.BRAUH.INGOLSTADT	-0.21	-0.52
TURK TUBORG	-0.24	-0.55
CUSTODIA HOLDINGS	-0.32	-0.63
DOM-BRAUEREI	-0.43	-0.74

5 Conclusion

This paper has developed a market capitalisation weighted performance index for the European brewing industry consisting of the 30 largest breweries in continental Europe. The index is constructed for the period from January 1st, 2004 to April 22nd, 2005. During this period the brewing industry shows a strong growth, which outperforms the prime standard indices Dow Jones EuroStoxxs, FTSE 100, and DAX. This illustrates that the industry has been growing strongly in the past, which might be influenced on the one hand by the ongoing consolidation through

M&A transaction as well as the good growth perspectives in Eastern Europe. However, the EuroBEX is outperformed by the DJ Europe (Non-EC) beverage index, which emphasizes the possibility of a strong growth effect, especially in Russia. A benchmarking analysis on the performance of all individual stocks in the industry sample has revealed that the major acquirers, like Heineken, Carlsberg, and InBev, have rather underperformed during the analyzed time interval. Most Eastern European breweries have performed better than the index at the same time, which leads the paper to the conclusion, that most of the strong performance has to be attributed to the growth opportunities in Eastern Europe. Furthermore, it seems that the concerns about a value destroying effect from the increased M&A activities in the European brewing industry holds true.

References

Deutsche Börse AG (2005): Leitfaden zu den Aktienindizes der Deutschen Börs, Version 5.6, January 2005.

Deutsche Bank AG (2002): European Beverages - Calling time?, in: DB Global Equity Research, May 8th, 2002.

Deutsche Bank AG (2003): European Brewing - Dangerous Liasons, in: DB Global Equity Research, June 5th, 2003.

Deutsche Bank AG (2004): Central European Brewing - Implications of EU accession, in: DB Global Equity Research, February 12th, 2004.

Mcclave, James T. / Benson, P. George / Sincich, Terry (2001): Statistics for Business and Economics, 8th edition, Upper Saddle River 2001.

Shoven, John B. / Sialm, Clemens (2000): The Dow Jones Industrial Average: The Impact of Fixing Its Flaws, Workingpaper Stanford University, February 28th, 2000.

U.S. Securities And Exchange Commission (SEC) (2000): Market Indices, http://www.sec.gov/answers/indices.htm, November 9th, 2000, downloaded: June 4th, 2005.

III Performance Index UK versus Germany

by

Jens Tegelaers

1 Introduction

The European brewery market has experienced strong consolidation during the last few years. Many breweries and brands have been target of M&A activities in this branch. However, there is little information on the overall market development. Particular measurement of brewer's share performance is rare. But is the brewing industry an attractive investment for share holders? And how do different countries perform compared to other or the whole European markets?

The objective of this paper is to compare the performance of listed brewers in Germany and the UK. Since the comparison is about stock prices of listed companies, the study uses performance indices. German and European performance indices are already covered by papers also published in this book[1]. The index calculated now is the Breweries of United Kingdoms index, BUK 10.

Starting with a general overview of the two countries UK and Germany, the comparability of the economic and demographic environment will be examined. Assumptions and methodology of the index set up in the second part then lead to the final comparison of the different performances. At the end problems and constraints are looked at before concluding.

---

[1] Cf. Dobberke / Voigt (2005); Steiner / Biesenbach (2005).

2 General Overview

The two countries UK and Germany are not equal, but most of their economic and demographic data is nearly proportional. While Great Britain has 60m people living on 240,000 km² Germany has 83m inhabitants and 360,000 km² of surface. The UK has a slightly higher GDP per capita.

Table 1: General information Germany / UK

	UK	Germany
Inhabitants	59,329,000	82,541,000
Surface	242,910 km²	357,027 km²
GDP / capita (2002)	28,320 $	25,270 $
Beer brands	2,000	3,200
Breweries	475	1200
People employed in brewing industry	20,000	35,000
Ranking beer market Europe (sales)	#3	#1
Ranking world beer market (sales)	#7	#3

Source: weltalmanach.de, xs4all.nl , wer-zu-wem.de

The UK counts approximately 2,000 beer brands[2] brewed in 475 breweries[3] and Germany around 3,500 brands and 1,200 breweries. UK beer is sold in about 140,000 pubs (2001)[4] and there are roughly 20,000 people employed in the brewing industry. In Germany 35,000 earn their living in the brewing industry.

With 104m hl, beer production in Germany nearly doubles UK production (54m hls). Overall consumption is a bit lower than production because beer is also exported, but the proportions are quite similar. Germany imports only 3% of the consumed beer, the UK 15%. But this changes when it comes to per capita consumption: Germans drink 120 l per head and year, British people only 100 l. Beer accounts for 47% of household expenditure on alcoholic beverages in the UK.[5]

[2] Cf. SIBA (2004) p. 6.
[3] Cf. xs4all.nl (2005).
[4] Cf. Liquor Licensing England and Wales, July 1997 - June 1998, cited on: xs4all.nl (2005).
[5] Cf. SIBA (2004).

Chart 1 and Chart 2 show production and consumption for the time from 1999 until 2003. 2005 and 2008 figures are Deutsche Bank's estimates.[6]

Chart 1: Beer production UK / Germany

Source: Deutsche Bank (2005).

Chart 2: Per capita beer consumption

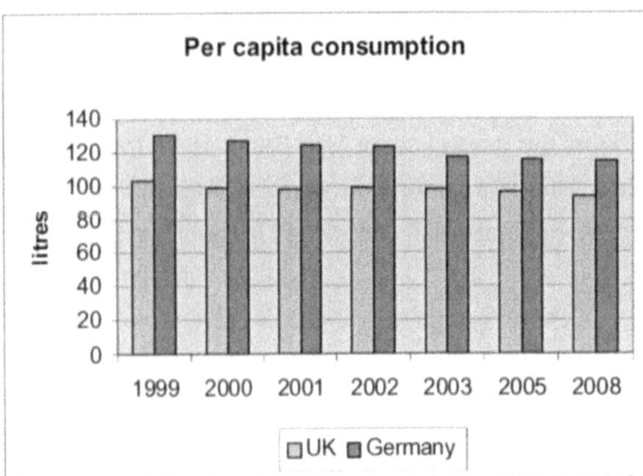

Source: Deutsche Bank (2005).

Taking production and sales figures, the UK is ranked the third largest beer market in Europe and number 7 in the world. Germany is number one in Europe and num-

---

[6] Cf. Deutsche Bank (2004).

ber three in the world. Only the USA and China are ranked higher. In per capita consumption the Czech Republic is ranked number one, Germany follows as number two.[7]

The German beer consumption declines by approximately 3% per year after a peak of 118m hl in 1994. The market has been especially affected by the new deposit rules for cans and non-returnable bottles introduced in 2003. Even though it was the hottest summer of the last decade, overall consumption declined and beer was affected dramatically. The market volume of beer declined by about 10%.[8]

However, the UK's beer market grew by 1% from 2002 to 2003. This was mainly induced by a 7% raise in off-trade. Consumption has been declining since 2003.[9]

3 Market Structure

Besides global players in both domestic markets there is a significant number of small brewers. UK counts currently with over 400 micro brewers with individual capacity of less than 5,000 hl, and it is argued that some are not captured by official statistics due to their size and 93% on-trade sales.[10] In Germany small and micro brewers account for 42% of the market share (see Chart 3), in the UK only for 17% (Chart 4). Nevertheless, this is a significant share in both markets. How the markets are divided among the big and small companies is shown in the following paragraphs.

3.1 German Brewers

The German market shows a nearly equal distribution of market share among eight to ten big players which together account for two thirds of the total. Chart 3 shows the market share for 2003. Today Brau & Brunnen belongs to Radeberger, so their market share of 7% and 8% respectively can be added together and represents

[7] Cf. Xs4all.nl (2005).
[8] Cf. Deutsch Bank (2004).
[9] Cf. Deutsche Bank (2004).
[10] Cf. SIBA (2004).

Radeberger market share. The "others", which account for the last third, consist of small and micro breweries, mostly local or regional.

Chart 3: German beer brewer's market share 2003

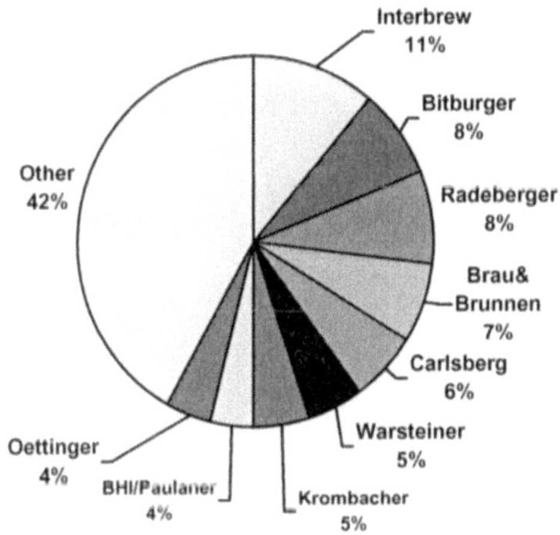

Source: Deutsche Bank (2005).

3.2 UK Brewers

The UK beer market is more consolidated than the German. Therefore, the UK brewing industry shows a different structure compared to the German industry. In the most recent market share distribution only two companies account for nearly half of the total market share. Scottish & Newcastle and Bass both have a 24% stake. Coors, Interbrew and Carlsberg-Tetley bring in their weight with 18%, 16% and 12% respectively. Chart 4 shows the market share distribution.

Chart 4: UK brewers' market share 2003

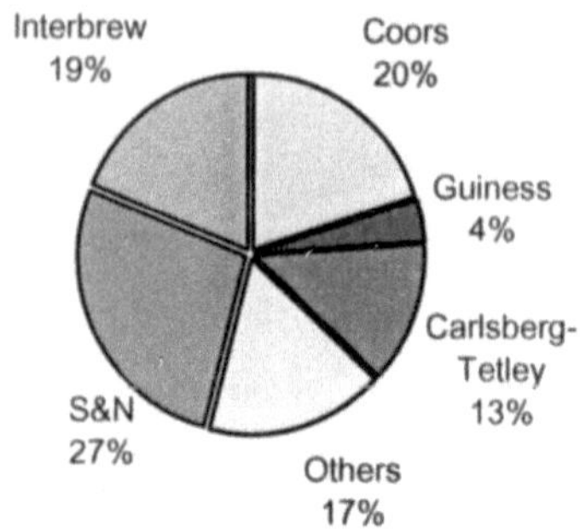

Source: Deutsche Bank.

Taking into account that the market volume is about 50% of Germany's volume it is logical that there are less competitors. Both countries count with a high percentage of small and micro breweries, although in Germany they play an even bigger role. Nevertheless, they are two of the leading European beer markets and although a bit different in structure and size, they are comparable. And in addition to all that numbers and statistics Germany and the UK both count with an incredible variety of beer brands and types. Hop and malt are part of their cultures.

4 Setting up the Index

The index to be set up is a performance index that should reflect the performance of listed brewers in the UK. The potential index members are shown in Table 2. Due to the small sample it was decided to choose the ten biggest players as index members out of the portfolio of twelve. The index portfolio shall be adjusted quarterly.

4.1 Sample

Potential BUK members are the companies shown in Table 2. They are all listed at the London Stock Exchange.

Table 2: Potential index members and key figures (as of 19.04.2005)

Name	Share Price £	# of Shares Outstanding	Market Cap.	DS Mnemonic	DS Code	SEDOL
Belhaven Brewery Group PLC	517	29784	15.398.328	BHG	876181	90539
Diageo PLC	770	2979452	2.294.178.040	DGE	900251	237400
Fuller Smith & Turner PLC	890	13075	11.636.750	FLLRA	917579	355186
Greene King PLC	1277	71790	91.675.830	GRNK	900250	387242
Hardys & Hansons PLC	700	20000	14.000.000	HDYS	906032	410278
Heavitree Brewery PLC	455	2026	921.830	HVT	926003	418250
Jennings Brothers PLC	411	10654	4.378.794	JENB	952536	472665
Scottish & Newcastle PLC	478	893621	427.150.838	SCTN	900261	783969
South African Breweries PLC	815,5	1101816	898.530.948	SAB	695504	483548
Tom Hoskins PLC	0,75	26751	20.063	TMH	870924	439132
Wolverhampton & Dudley Breweries PLC	1083	76371	82.709.793	WOLV	900274	3122945
Young & Co S Brewery PLC	1687,5	3141	5.300.438	YNGBA	910018	988203

Obviously there are large players in the group, with *Diageo* in the pole position. Diagoe has by far the biggest number of shares outstanding, the second highest share price and a free float of 50-70% on average it plays the major role, followed by Scottish & Newcastle. Due to these inequalities the weights were capped to 15%, i.e. no member can be weighted with more than 15% in the index. The 15% mark is chosen because in this relatively small sample it is a reasonable trade off between letting the big players keep some of their weight and letting the index reflect the whole sample.

4.2 Index Method

Since portfolio performance has to be measured, Laspeyres' price index is used for calculations. It suits the purpose because it uses the same quantity scheme for different periods and therefore allows statements of price performance.[11] "p" in the formula stands for a share price while "q" represents the number of shares. The numerator of this Laspeyres-formula is adjusted for the free float of the individual stocks.

[11] Cf. Hartung (2002), p. 63.

Formula 1: Laspeyres' price index formula[12] with freefloat adjustment

$$P_{0,t} = \frac{\sum_{i=1}^{n} p_{ti} q_{0i} \times freefloat\%}{\sum_{i=1}^{n} p_{0i} q_{0i}}$$

4.3 Examination Period and Data

The BUK is calculated for the last three years starting in April 2002 until April 2005. This guarantees most actual figures. The three year time frame seems good for a relatively fast changing market.

Most of the data was kindly provided by Dobberke / Voigt (2005) and Steiner / Biesenbach (2005). There are Datastream[13] figures adjusted with some OnVista[14] data regarding the free float. FX rates used are from Datastream.

4.4 Weightening and Capping

The weight adjustments are calculated in iterative steps. A soon as a company exceeds the 15% cap it is cut down to that 15%. This leads to a missing percentage, since the excess is missing in the sum with which the index is calculated. Therefore the exceeding percentage is equally distributed to the other companies in the index that are still under the 15% mark. This step is repeated until there was no excess percentage to be distributed any more.

Table 3 shows the unadjusted average weights during the examination period and the average weights after capping. Diageo, Scottish & Newcastle and SABMiller still dominate the index, but it now reflects the sample's performance far better. Without capping, Diageo would have represented more than 77% of the index on average during the last three years.

[12] Cf. Hartung (2002), p.63.
[13] Cf. datastream.com (2005).
[14] Cf. onvista.de (2005).

Table 3: Average weights with and without capping during examination period

Company	Ø weighting w\ capping	Ø weighting after capping
BELHAVEN GROUP	0,343%	7,650%
DIAGEO	77,239%	15,000%
FULLER SMITH 'A'	0,261%	7,568%
GREENE KING	1,386%	8,694%
HARDYS & HANSONS	0,430%	7,737%
JENNINGS BROTHERS	0,138%	7,446%
SCOTTISH & NEWCASTLE	9,443%	15,000%
SABMILLER	9,403%	14,933%
WOLV.& DUDLEY	1,215%	8,522%
YOUNG & CO.BREW.'A'	0,142%	7,449%

5 Results and Observations

The BUK 10 is mostly dependent on the brewery market and therefore M&A driven, not beer market driven. However, it roughly reflects the overall beer market development. This is a feature which the BEX-Germany does not count with; the German brewery index performance is totally dominated by Holsten's share price and its reaction to M&A activities.[15] Of course it can be argued that the UK market is not as heavily influenced by M&A events during the examination period as the German market is.

[15] Cf. Dobberke / Voigt (2005); Steiner / Biesenbach (2005).

Chart 5: BEX-Germany, EuroBEX and BUK 10, April 2002 – April 2005

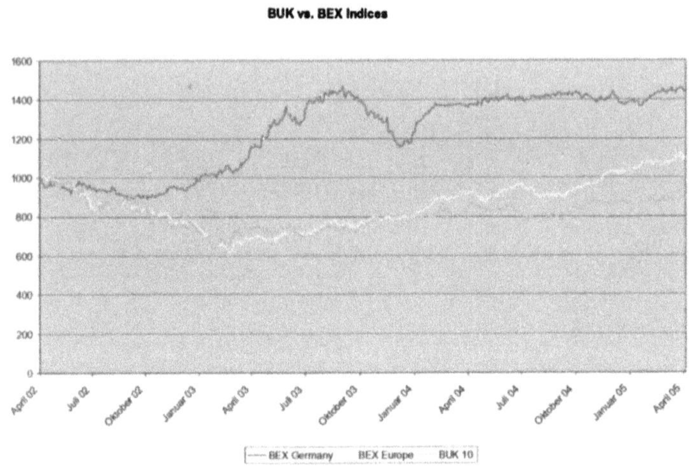

Some words concerning the sample: due to the small sample size there is no change in index members during the whole examination period. Furthermore, Scottish & Newcastle and Diageo are capped all the time. (See Table 5 for capping impact on average weights)

5.1 Currency Adjustment

The original BUK 10 currency, of course, is the British Pound (£). Nevertheless, it would be interesting to see how BUK 10 performes from a European investor's perspective. If we adjust the index for FX rates, we get a slightly different result due to a strong euro. Chart 4 shows FX rate development. The currency adjusted BUK 10 reflects a European investor's view from outside the UK. The impact is illustrated in Chart 7. Due to a relatively weak euro in the beginning and its strengthening later on, a foreign €-investor would have lost even more on the investment.

Chart 6: FX rates, British Pounds (£) paid for 1€ during examination period

Source: Datastream.

Chart 7: € FX rate impact on BUK 10 performance from European investor's perspective

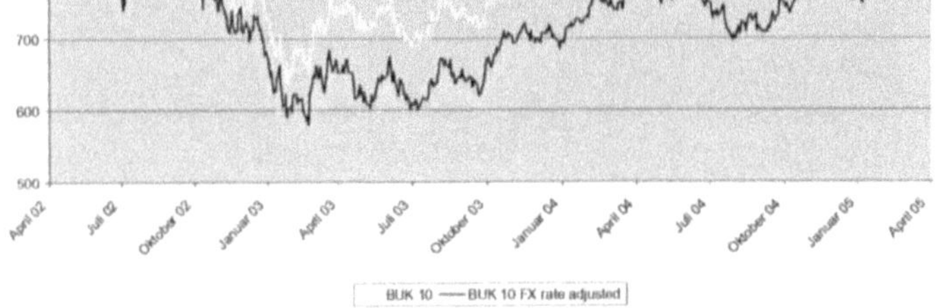

5.2 Risk and Return

An investment in a BUK 10 portfolio would have led to poor results compared to possible returns in Germany and Europe. While a UK national investor would have lost approximately 9% on his investment, a foreign euro investor would have lost on portfolio value and currency, which would have amounted to an 18% loss.

However, UK brewing industry investment is relatively save with a standard deviation of 7,59%. A European brewery shares portfolio is more volatile with a standard deviation of 12%. Germany has a lead here with 17%. But the German index shows a positive performance of 44,35% during the last three years. The overall results are stated in Table 6.

Table 4: Overall performances during examination period

	BUK 10 (£)	BUK 10 (€)	German Gnomes 15	Europe Titans 30
Variance	5759,38	7537,25	28874,37	14412,67
Standard Deviation	7,59%	8,68%	16,98%	12,00%
Median	809,27	742,47	1.127,27	860,45
Average	810,94	741,26	1.040,31	860,80
Index Value end / beginning	90,81%	81,96%	144,35%	110,17%
Overall Performance	-9,19%	-18,04%	44,35%	10,17%

Even compared to other British stock market indices the brewing industry would have been a poor investment. Although the market declined in general, a FTSE 100 portfolio would have lost only -7,3% instead of -9,1% during the same period.[16] But as Chart 6 shows, FTSE100 would have been a more risky investment.

[16] Cf. www.handelsblatt.com (2005).

Chart 8: FTSE100 during the last 3 years

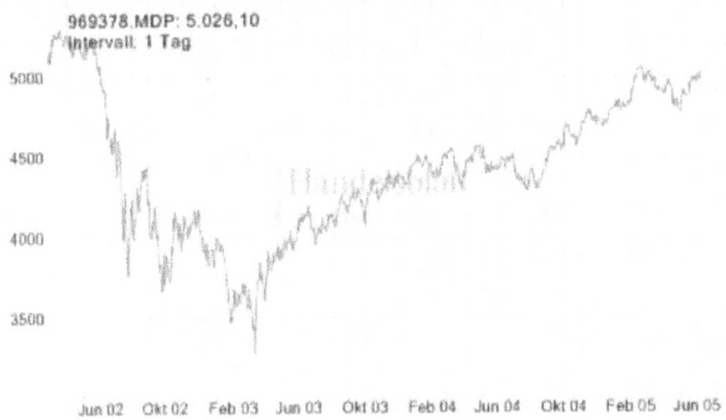

Source: handelsblatt.com.

5.3 Problems and Constraints

A general problem in analysing shares in this industry is the diversification of the companies. Diageo's main business for example is high percentage alcoholic beverages and the fast food franchise business Burger King, not brewing. Unfortunately there are no figures available to adjust this bias. There is a similar problem with Scottish & Newcastle. Although it has a completely separated brewing division called Scottish Courage, it does not allow separating since this division is not listed. Hence, the two heavy weights do not reflect pure beer business. Other companies are affected, too.

So generally speaking, there is no exact and direct measure for "beer performance" in terms of a stock price based analysis. However, at this point of time, there is no way to separate the beer business completely from other activities. However, this fact is accepted. Calculating a volume-based index instead of an share-price-based index would have implied a shift from a performance index to a market share model and would therefore have led away from the original goal.

BEX-Germany is definitely driven by Holsten Brewery and the corresponding M&A activities impact on the share price. The BUK 10, after capping and re-weighting, is also influenced by the three big players Diageo, Scottish & Newcastle and SABMiller, but still reflects UK beer market performance. This might be due to coincidence and only apply for the period of examination, but generally it can be said that with declining market consolidation and therefore less M&A activity, the index gains reasonability in terms of reflection of overall market conditions as well as demographic and macro economic factors.

5.4 Additional Remarks

The BUK 10 is similar to a branch index that can be used in the Financial Times' online chart analysis tool. While looking at any listed UK brewer stock prices, it is possible to underlay a branch index for comparison. Unfortunately, it is impossible to separate this from the stock price chart, and there was no information available about how that index is set up or calculated. Information requests are not answered until the date of publishing. Chart 7 shows the Fuller Smith Turner stock price chart and trading volume during the period of examination as an example. The dark line in the lower part is the branch index. It shows a nearly similar performance as the BUK 10 does.

Chart 9: Fuller Smith Turner stock price and trading volume with branch index

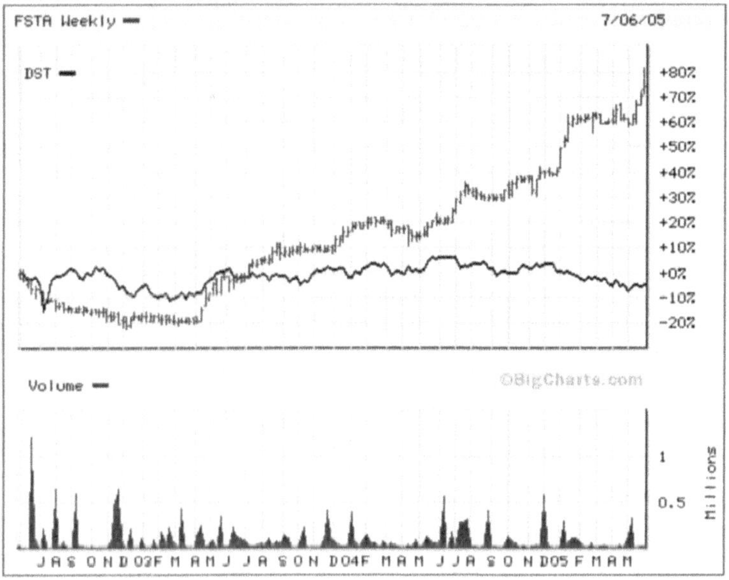

Source: Financial Times.

6 Conclusion

To conclude it can be said that the UK brewery market has performed worse than its German or European counterparts. However, compared to the overall performance of British shares, the FTSE 100 for example, the return of a portfolio of brewery shares was nearly equal during the examination period, but offered a significantly lower risk due to far lower volatility.

Despite some decline in the recent past breweries and the beer market are interesting markets. Since both markets still not have finished their consolidation phase, there will be more movement in the future. It will be interesting to see how BUK and BEX-Germany will develop.

However, results have to be used with care and are only useful when taking into account the overall picture, market development and M&A activities. The indices do not necessarily reflect the breweries' core business of selling beer.

References

datastream.com, http://www.datastream.com, last accessed 05.06.2005.

Deutsche Bank Equity Research (2005), Global Brewing – The global Pitcher Vol. V, London.

Dobberke, Ulf / Voigt, Florian (2005): Index for listed Breweries in Germany, Working Paper, Oestrich Winkel 2005.

Handelsblatt.com, http://www.handelsblatt.com, last accessed 04.06.2005.

Hartung, Joachim (1999), Statistik, Lehr- und Handbuch der angewandten Statistik, München.

SIBA, Society of Independent Brewers (2004), Small Brewing Industry Report 2004, available at http://www.siba.co.uk/ , last accessed: 04.06.2005.

Steiner, Nils / Biesenbach, Bastian (2005): Developing the European Brewing Industry Index for Benchmarking M&A Transactions in Continental EU, Working Paper, Oestrich-Winkel 2005.

onvista.de, http://www.onvista.de, last accessed 04.06.2005.

Xs4all.nl , http://www.xs4all.nl/~patto1ro/ukstatsn.htm, last accessed: 04.06.2005.

IV A Consolidated View on Central and Eastern European Beer Markets Including Russia and China

by

Philip Janßen and Carsten Düber

1 Introduction

1.1 Objective of the Study

The global beer industry is the one of the largest beverage industries in the world. Its sales increased by 2.3% in 2003 and totalled 1,484m hl (million hectolitres) and its consumer value is expected to be about 250-300b. Over the years, there has been an observable shift from a conglomerate of national markets to a truly global industry in which the leading national brands have been gradually acquired by the leading international brewers.[1]

After the fall of the Iron Curtain and the related liberalisation of industry politics, all international brewers except Anheuser Bush, started significant acquisitions in Eastern Europe and Russia to generate growth opportunities. Therefore, the industry structure in most of these countries largely resembles that of Western Europe concerning ownership and consolidation levels. But it is expected that national brands will still remain important due to a different consumer market in those countries. Margins and price points are also still quite high in some countries, but they are expected to decrease as a result of an increase in competition.[2]

The main impulse for growth derived from the increased consumption in the emerging markets of Eastern Europe, Russia and some parts of South America, but

[1] Cf. Euromonitor (Ed.) (2005), p. 1; Rabobank (Ed.) (2004), p. 5.

[2] Cf. Rabobank (Ed.) (2004), p. 5.

especially of China which recently overtook the US as the world's largest beer market. In established beer markets, the volume growth has been low due to market saturation. Additionally, due to shifts in lifestyle trends, health consciousness has increased and induced consumers to drink less alcoholic beverages. Furthermore, fashion trends in the beverages industry and stricter legislation also constrain consumption.[3]

International operating breweries are aware of these developments and their impacts on the beer market and seek possibilities to invest in emerging beer markets or to discover alternatives to cut costs and to improve profitability. In the process of investment decisions, international brewers make these decisions on the basis of economic developments and their individual product portfolio. In this context, the paper analyses the recent markets trends, isolates the most interesting markets for West European brewers and contributes to the understanding of market dynamics.

1.2 Course of Analysis

In the first section of the paper, the choice of the topic is explained by emphasising the importance of Central and Eastern European markets including Russia and China, in particular for West European brewers. After having analysed the specific macro- and microeconomic attributes of mature and emerging markets, principles about the brewing industry's consolidation tendencies are presented in the context of the contemporary brewing industry's development. In the course of this description, buyers' and sellers' motivations for consolidation transactions are revealed to get an understanding of industry dynamics.

In connection to the strong consolidation tendency in the brewing business, in a next step, the market environment in Eastern European markets including Russia and China will be analysed. Starting with the description of recent consumption trends, over the analysis of beer markets' prices and market life cycles, a framework for the beer market development will be created that allows for strategic considerations for West European brewers. Plausible strategic alternatives are going to be recalled in order to reflect their applicableness to the given market

[3] Cf. Technology Centre AS CR (Ed.) (2005), p. 10; Euromonitor (Ed.) (2005), p. 1.

environment. After having pointed out the interconnection between market maturity and strategic options, the most promising countries will be looked at in detail to provide a background for individual assessments. Finally, the conclusion will summarise the recent situation in the brewing industry and give thought-provoking impulses to West European brewers.

2 Comparative Analysis of Global Beer Markets

2.1 Mature Versus Emerging Markets

On the background of markets' maturity and saturation in combination with intensified competition in the developed markets of North America, Western Europe, Japan and Australia, volume sales declined or at best remained stable.[4] This is partly due to the shift in consumption habits, from beer to wine consumption and several more trendy beverages.[5] Another reason is the recent development in demographics because a reduction of the male age-group between 15 and 29 in Western Europe has caused reduced sales of beer.[6] Only South Europe experienced a slight increase in beer consumption which is not expected to be sustainable because of fierce competition of other beverage industries. [7]

In Latin America, volume sales increased only by 0.4% in 2003 with fast growth in Colombia and Argentina, but heavy slumps in Venezuela. It is projected that about one-third of the growth of beer sales in the next decade will arise from Central and South America.[8] The merger between Interbrew and Ambev of March 2004 has demonstrated how important brewers assess this market. With nearly 35% of the population in Brazil under the age of 18, and the overall beer per capita under 50 litres, Brazil could become a key market with potential, but competition from domestic and regional suppliers is expected to be enormous. Additionally, due to economic crisis, crawling performance in Mexico and Brazil and fragile disposable

[4] Cf. Appendix 1: World Beer Consumption in the main regions world-wide 1997-2002.
[5] Especially in UK, Germany and the Netherlands. Cf. Den Butter / Delifotis / Koning (1997), pp. 2-10; Uk Trade And Investment (Ed.) (2005), p. 16.
[6] Cf. Lutz (2003), pp. 1-8.
[7] Cf. Gual / Colom (1997), pp. 21-24.
[8] Based on figures from Brazil, Mexico, Venezuela and Argentina. Cf. Rabobank (Ed.) (2004), p. 14.

income, Latin America is not in a favourable condition to invest in.[9] Apart from economic reasons, it is simply geographical distance that complicates an investment in these countries for West European brewers.

The South African market, after having reached maturity, stagnated with its sales. Elsewhere, e.g. in the Egyptian and Moroccan markets, the beer market boomed relatively well, but on an absolute scale this is less interesting because sales increased mostly due to tourist consumption, since Islamic traditions generally forbid alcohol.[10]

Consequently, in the period of 1997-2003, growth mainly came from Eastern Europe including Russia and China.[11] The net result shows continuing growth in the industry with a world-wide production increase of 2.1%, despite of the difficult international political and economic situation in the past years.[12]

2.2 Macroeconomic Analysis

2.2.1 Drivers of Growth

An ongoing volume growth is likely to be seen in those markets on average, because of the upward potential in terms of per capita consumption.[13] An analysis of the key value drivers in the beer industry proves that the GDP growth and demographics are directly correlated with an increase in the per capita consumption of beer and the level of prices.[14]

Analysing the Eastern European markets including China, other factors seem to apply better there than to the developed markets. In this context, regulations on beer consumption have become tighter in Europe with restrictions being imposed on consumption in markets like Spain, Ireland, France and presumably in the UK.[15]

---

[9] Cf. Euromonitor (Ed.) (2005), p. 1.
[10] Cf. Euromonitor (Ed.) (2005), p. 1.
[11] Cf. TGI (Ed.) (2005), p. 4; Rabobank (Ed.) (2005), p. 1.
[12] Cf. Council Of New Zealand (Ed.) (2002), p. 2; Rabobank (Ed.) (2004), p. 9.
[13] Cf. Appendix 2, 3, 4 and 5: GDP and Per Capita Growth Western versus Eastern Europe.
[14] Cf. Bentzen / Smith (2004), p. 12.
[15] Cf. Bleakley / Bowley / Matthews (2004), p. 5.

Smoking bans in Ireland, Norway, Sweden and parts of the US have also slightly reduced the consumption of beer in bars and restaurants.

On the basis of a study of the EIU (Economist Intelligence Unit), the risk associated with the different beer markets world-wide, as measured by political and economic policy, economic structure and liquidity risks, has decreased for the emerging beer markets of Central and Eastern Europe, Asia and Africa, whereas it has remained broadly the same for the US and Western Europe. Furthermore, there is a clear positive correlation between country risk and volume growth rates.[16]

Recapitulating, with an improvement of economic conditions, the emergence of political stability, high GDP growth rates and low per capita consumption of beer, Eastern Europe, Russia and China are considered to be the main drivers of growth in global beer sales in the near future.

2.2.2 Focal Point Emerging Markets

According to PLATO LOGIC, Eastern Europe registered an annual growth of almost 10% on average for the last five years, with total consumption close to 20 billion litres.[17] On average, Eastern Europeans drink only 46 l of beer per capita, although there are significant regional differences. Compared with the West European average beer consumption per capita, which accounts for 77 litres, the potential of development for the market is considerable. Much of the growth of the Eastern European region can be attributed to the Russian market which was provided with extraordinary high foreign investments.[18] But international competition in Eastern Europe and China also increased, forcing domestic breweries to upgrade their facilities. For the future, PLATO LOGIC expects that the growth will be primarily led by Russia and the Ukraine.[19] With a per capita consumption in Russia

[16] Cf. Bleakley / Bowley / Matthews (2004), p. 6; Appendix 6: Declining Risk from Emerging Markets.
[17] Cf. Rexam (Ed.) (2005), p. 1.
[18] Cf. Yudaeva / Kozlov / Melentieva et al. (2001), pp. 36-38;
Rogacheva / Mikerova (2003), pp. 5, 8, 13, 52-53.
[19] Cf. Deutsche Bank (Ed.) (2004), p. 166.

of 52 litres and in the Ukraine of 32 litres there is a lot of upward potential, generating a huge market.[20]

After a growth of 6%, China has finally overtaken the US to become the world's largest beer market; it will reach 26b litres in 2005.[21] With a low per capita consumption at around 19 litres, its underdeveloped beer market, increasing disposable incomes, rising standards of living and greater levels of foreign investments, China seems to add significant further volume over the next 5-10 years, consolidating its status as the world's largest beer market. [22]

In addition to the rise in disposable incomes and a low per capita consumption, the growth of the beer market in Eastern Europe is further driven by external investments from international brewers seeking for growing markets in an increasingly competitive market place. [23]

As a result, this study focuses on Eastern Europe including Russia and China, since they represent the world's most interesting beer markets with an annual growth of about 4% on average to 2010.[24]

2.3 Microeconomic Analysis

The profitability of emerging markets compared to developed markets is vital for investors. Higher volume growth in Eastern Europe, Russia and China apparently compensates for the higher risk levels in these countries. But profitability largely contributes to the investment decision.

Since purchasing power in these countries is lower than in Western Europe or the US, the absolute profitability per unit sold is anticipated to be lower as well. However, in many emerging markets, beer operations generate higher margins than in

[20] Cf. Deutsche Bank (Ed.) (2004), pp. 200, 212.
[21] Cf. Asahi (Ed.) (2005), pp. 29-30.
[22] Cf. Anheuser Busch (Ed.) (2004), pp. 17-19; Deutsche Bank (Ed.) (2004), p. 166.
[23] Cf. Rexam (Ed.) (2005), p. 1.
[24] Cf. Appendix 7: The World Beer Market Volume to 2010; A.T. Kearney (Ed.) (2005), p. 6.

their developed market counterparts.[25] This is mainly due to the consolidated nature of those beer markets.[26] Whereas anti-trust regulations and historic competitive rivalry have left many mature markets relatively fragmented with intense competition that limits the upside potential for margins, Central and Eastern European markets including Russia and China are more consolidated markets concerning domestic breweries, allowing targeted acquisitions of a significant market share.[27]

As a conclusion of this enquiry, emerging markets are more profitable than developed markets. Margins in these countries are on average significantly higher. In the light of attractive market dynamics and the possibility to increase relative market positions by consolidation efforts, Eastern European countries attract investors' attentions.[28] Additionally, restructuring opportunities for breweries in emerging markets are expected to offer comparable upside potential in cost savings, on average up to 15% of their current market value.[29]

In terms of cash conversion cycles, brewers need to invest before growth in order to build up local production facilities to supply the market efficiently at the right time. Since high capacity utilisation directly results from increasing demand that requires machinery installations ex ante, brewers always reap their investments temporally delayed. Especially if the brewer's business is balanced between emerging and developed markets, good growth prospects; a high cash conversion should be on hand, because brewers can invest reaped income from their home market in emerging markets. On the basis of relatively high capex rates (more than 55%) in the start-up phase of emerging markets, the situation will eventually stabilize (at around 7% on average) and improve, depending on market maturity.

Additionally, it has to be pointed out that the cost of building a brewery is very low in Russia or China compared to Western European countries.[30] On average, the cost of the construction of a brewery per hl of yearly production capacity amount to US

[25] Cf. Appendix 8: Emerging Market Delivering High Margins to InBew and SABMiller.
[26] Cf. Appendix 9: Profitability Increases with Market Consolidation.
[27] Cf. Appendix 10: Consolidation Phases.
[28] Cf. Bleakley / Bowley / Matthews (2004), p. 11.
[29] Cf. Bleakley / Bowley / Matthews (2004), pp. 11-13; Appendix 11: NPV of Savings.
[30] Cf. Sabmiller (Ed.) (2004), p. 4.

$ 25 in Russia and US $ 27 in China compared to US $ 85 in the Netherlands.[31] In connection with the superior profitability in emerging markets, it has to be accentuated that these higher margins combined with lower cost of incremental capacity cause the emerging market brewers to be able to cover capex cost more easily.[32] Consequently, markets are more dynamic in terms of tactical or strategic investments.

3 Consolidation in the Global Beer Market

3.1 Long-Term Benefits for the Buyers

It is a general rule of the beer industry that higher levels of market concentration lead to higher levels of profitability.[33] Consolidation induced profitability improvements arise in several different areas:

Integration benefits from reducing head office administration costs,
Pricing power benefits due to concentration levels of demand and supply,
Cost of production benefits due to economies of scale (capacity utilisation),
Distribution benefits through the abolishment of intermediary trade depending on whether the relevant market has sufficient critical mass or through the consolidation of former separate distribution networks. [34]

But since improvements of production efficiency go along with the consolidation of the brewing industry, it is not traceable which part of industry lay-offs is directly attributable to the consolidation effects caused by economies of scale and synergy effects and which part results from efficiency gains in the beer production itself. In fact, the whole European brewing industry has been able to reduce its overall workforce by around 20,000 employees in the last ten years.[35] Moreover, due to

---

[31] Cf. Bleakley / Bowley / Matthews (2004), p. 13.
[32] Cf. Bleakley / Bowley / Matthews (2004), pp. 11-13. Appendix 12: Cash Conversion Cycle.
[33] Cf. Appendix 13: Average Cost Structure of a Brewing Company.
[34] Cf. Thommen / Achleitner (2001), p. 916.
[35] Cf. Bowley / Shackleton / Bleakley / Matthews (2003), p. 27; Appendix 14: Declining Employee numbers driving Productivity Improvements.

consolidation, volume and mix gains from cross-selling of brands can be achieved.[36]

3.2 Contemporary Development

Nevertheless, the global beer industry is still very fragmented compared to other drink industries, taken into account that the global three global brewers only control around 30% of market share whereas it is 85% in the soft drink industry.[37] Especially the recent years, however, have shown a distinct shift towards consolidation in the beer industry world-wide. Because many brewers from domestic markets reach their saturation of consumption, it has become necessary to look for opportunities to expand their business.[38]

The dominant global breweries have set up their own territories.[39] They can gain market share by buying or ruining local breweries and by increasing beer consumption in undersold markets. These global players have tried to prevent a fierce competition against each other.[40] In national markets, however, breweries are highly consolidated with market shares over 60% of the top three.[41] Mergers and acquisitions were especially numerous in the German market, which is currently still very fragmented and an exception of this rule.[42] The business environment in the beer industry in Germany facilitates the production of speciality beers which could offer strong growth potential in international markets if sufficient financial capabilities and effective marketing are provided.[43]

The international brewers like Interbrew, Heineken and SABMiller play an important role in the international consolidation process and are changing the world's top ten list of brewers continuously while the traditional beer markets with family owned breweries have become a battlefield. Concerning required capital for con-

---

[36] Cf. Bowley / Shackleton / Bleakley / Matthews (2003), p. 22.
[37] Cf. Matraves (1999), p. 23-25 in connection with A.T. Kearney (Ed.) (2005), pp. 15-17.
[38] Cf. Mannsperger (2000), pp. 30-31.
[39] Consider Appendix 15: Number one and two Positions of Int. Brewers in Eastern Europe.
[40] Cf. Oligopoly Watch (Ed.) (2003), pp. 1-3.
[41] Cf. Appendix 16: Local Consolidation.
[42] Cf. Rost (2002), p. 2.
[43] Cf. Euromonitor (Ed.) (2005), p. 2.

solidation, in particular companies like SABMiller that are able to resort to financial resources which do not belong to their core business, have enough unused liquidity to realize acquisitions continuously.[44]

A number of key deals also have taken place in China, for example the struggle between Anheuser-Busch and SABMiller for Harbin, with SABMiller gaining the upper hand. Prepared with some acquisitions already performed, international companies try to scoop up remaining local companies, which have optimum margin potential, as well as to ensure that they gain strategic geographical advantage.[45]

3.3 Long-Term Benefits for the Sellers

When it comes to the question of the take-over of privately held breweries, the rationale of the seller needs to be accounted for. As in every case, there are numerous reasons for why a sale could make sense.

Especially in the Chinese and Russian market two important reasons seem to be most plausible. The first reason is a consequence of the opening of these markets to the western world. From that time on many aspects of market economy were introduced to the Chinese market. However, the smaller Chinese companies could well be troubled by the thought of having to adopt these aspects and might rather sell their companies. Especially right now, as the bidders are competing fiercely about every brewery for sale in China, the prices paid are quite high.[46] The same is true of the Russian beer market where the free market economy has to be slowed down in order to find its way into the management teams. Big global brewers are familiar with the market economy, and thus might be able to profit from their predominance. Another trigger for international consolidation, especially in China, is the planned privatisation of state-owned companies.[47] A number of breweries are still

[44] Cf. Rabobank (2003), pp. 18, 23.
[45] Cf. Euromonitor (Ed.) (2005), p. 2.
[46] A good example fort he fierce competition is the battle about Harbin Breweries 2004. For a more detailed analysis of this bidding Cf. Moffet / Ramaswamy (2005).
[47] This seems not to be true in Russia, where the tendency seems to shift back to more state control over companies like in the case of Yukos.

held by the state, and thus might be easy and suited targets for those internationally operating breweries that try to increase their market share in China.

More generally, in some countries of Eastern Europe, and in particular in Russia and China, many breweries are remarkably old in terms of technology, which weakens their market position on the background of increased global competition. As those mostly private breweries are usually quite small, they lack financial resources to stem the required heavy investments in new machinery which could secure their ability to compete on a sustainable basis. Therefore, a global brewer equipped with sufficient financial resources is a potential source of providing financial sources for these breweries. This leads to numerous co-operations where the big companies buy a stake in these breweries (e.g. Anheuser-Busch's investment in Tsingtao, in China, where Anheuser-Busch will gradually increase its share to 27% in 2007).[48] Another reason in the same context is the lack of adequate infrastructure in the Eastern countries. This problem means that a smaller brewery is not able to expand its target market without buying other breweries or building new production sights. Since these transactions require financial leverage, financial capabilities are again the impeding factor.

Finally, it is the overall antiquated picture of domestic Eastern brewers that points up the exigency of efficiency enhancements, which can only be achieved through initial investments and the transmission of professional expertise. This, in turn, suggests acquisitions by West European brewers.

4 Market Environment and Related Strategies

4.1 Consumption Trends

Before reviewing the beer markets' potential and action alternatives, the main influencing factors in the beer consumption have to be taken into consideration for further analysis.

[48] Cf. Moffet / Ramaswamy (2005), p. 10.

Firstly, the substitution of beer by other drinks has to be taken into account. Mineral water, juice and wine have been taking advantage of their image as being healthier. People from 15 to 29 years of age tend to prefer mixed drinks such as Barcadi Breezer and energy drinks like Red Bull. The ready-to-drink beverages (RTDs) gained around 2% of the market share of beer in 2001 in Europe, 3-4% in the US and around 15% in Australia. But the popularity of these drinks has already passed its peak in some countries.[49]

Secondly, the demand for premium beers as a substitution of generic beer products has increased, and this is directly linked to the disposable income. These speciality and premium segments are expected to grow by around 5% at the expense of mainstream beer brands.[50] The consumption of premium beers increases especially in the on-trade, whereas, in general, at-home (off-trade) consumption of generic beers increases in most markets of Western Europe. Therewith the bargaining power of beverage retailers has increased as the food retail sector is also highly consolidated.[51]

Due to the rivalry for shelf space in the retail stores and reduced prices, increasing competition among the breweries in different markets has amplified itself. This phenomenon has formed another dimension of market entry barrier.[52]

Furthermore, legislation and politics usually can have an enormous impact on the beer industry. Examples are on-trade restrictions, monopoly legislation, alcohol abuse legislation and legislation against the misuse of market power.

4.2 Analysis of Beer Prices

After having reviewed possible market trends in Eastern Europe, it is adequate to analyse present beer prices in these markets in order to derive conclusions about current brand segments and future potentials. To make the gathered data comparable, prices are calculated in euros per 0.5 litre, excluding VAT and excise duties.

[49] Cf. Heineken (Ed.) (2005), p. 44.
[50] Cf. INBEV (2002), p. 41.
[51] Cf. Rabobank (Ed.) (2004), pp. 9 -10.
[52] Cf. Rabobank (Ed.) (2004), p. 10.

Consequently, the costs purely reflect the sales price of beer, consisting of costs of production and selling as well as the trade margin. In order to refer to prices of mature markets for comparison, the Netherlands is taken as a representative country.

Chart 1: Beer Prices in Selected Countries

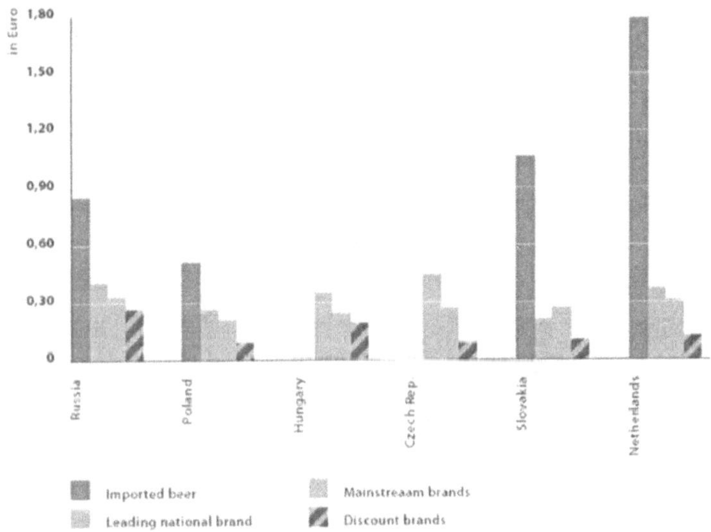

Source: Rabobank (Ed.) (2004), p. 24.

As illustrated in the graphs, the respective leading national brand's beer prices are not on the same level. Slovakia and Poland are cheap whereas Russia and the Czech Republic are relatively expensive. Since the prices reflect the category of beer as well as the costs to create and support the brand (included in selling cost), it is especially important to review the prices of discount brands as they should incur no cost for marketing, hardly any overheads and almost no margin. With these assumptions taken into account, these prices should be able to assist as an estimate for the production cost of 0.5 litre of beer. Remarkably, the price for the cheapest discount beer brands are all about the same even compared to the Dutch discount prices. Only Russia and Hungary deviate enormously. For Hungary, further analysis determines the distribution costs as the decisive factor for this mark-up, because the cheapest beer available is a German import. In Russia, an inefficient retail structure and higher purchasing costs of imported malt and hop are the main reason for the price difference.[53] As these costs are apparently very high, some ground in these markets could probably be gained by efficiently distributing beer in this cheap price segment. Additionally, a reduction of the price of discount beer in Russia and Hungary could even induce a higher consumption of discount beer as an increased price differentiation between discount and mainstream beers might drive price sensitive customers to switch from mainstream to discount beers.

Reviewing beer price differences of the countries' leading national brands and their cheapest discount brands, it is striking to see the resulting premium mark-ups (the price difference between discount to leading or mainstream beers) vary tremendously. Considering that the discount prices will probably decrease in Russia and Hungary in future, a clearer positioning of premium brands will be the consequence. As price differentiation is not the only attribute for a premium brand, brand building has to be accompanied with heavy marketing efforts to stimulate brand recognition.[54] Based on the GDP development and forecast for Russia and Hungary, it is expected that consumers' disposable income at hand will increase in the next years. As a result, the demand for premium beers will rise. So either the discount beer prices will decrease or the prices of mainstream and leading brands have to increase in order to create the necessary price discrimination.

Summarizing the results of this section, Hungary and Russia are both very promising markets for West European brewers to establish both cheap and premium beer brands.

4.3 Market Life Cycles

Generally, the growth possibilities of beer markets can be illustrated by means of the life cycle diagram which describes the dynamic beer markets using a phase approach.

---

[53] Cf. USDA (Ed.) (2000), p. 1.
[54] Cf. World-Health Organisation (Ed.) (2001), pp. 8, 13.

Using this life cycle diagram, it can be illustrated that Asia is still in the starting phase, whereas China, Russia and Eastern Europe are examples of growth markets with a relatively low per capita consumption and a high upward potential. The North American market does not show any growth, just as Japan and Australia do not. These markets are saturated, and growth can be realized mainly by more expensive premium brands, imports and speciality beers. In the US, some innovative products like low-calorie beers have been introduced successfully over the last years. In Japan also, brewers are successfully attracting new customers to consume new types of beer. These innovations result in a "second life phase" which is illustrated by the slightly rising graph.

Chart 2: Mature Markets versus Emerging Markets

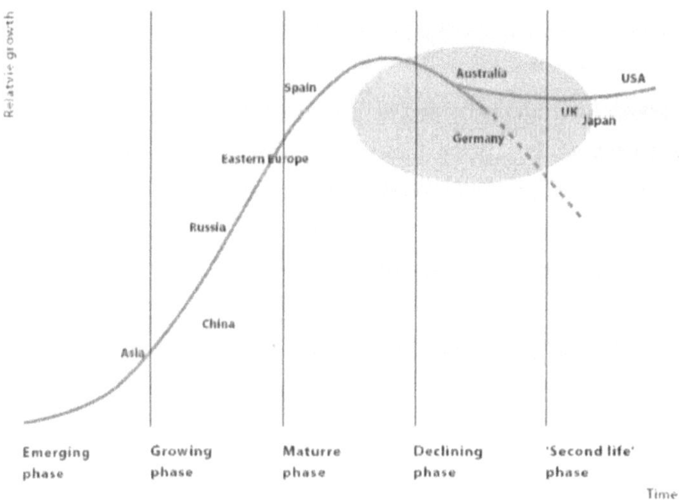

Source: Rabobank (Ed.) (2004), p. 13.

The Eastern European beer market including Russia and China is still in a growing phase, although the prospects for the individual markets can differ considerably. The Czech Republic and, to a lesser extend, Slovakia are traditional beer markets. Thus, no further rise in per capita consumption is expected. Only the premium beer, due to improvements of economic conditions and increasing disposable income, has potential for growth. The Baltic States and Poland have also become mature markets with growth opportunities in the premium segment only.

4.4 Developments in Eastern Europe Including Russia and China

Contradicting these developments, Russia, the Ukraine, Hungary and Romania were immature beer markets where the consumption of wine or spirits has traditionally been very high. As beer is perceived as being healthier than spirits, beer consumption has continuously substituted spirits in consumer preferences.[55] International brewers like SABMiller, Interbrew, Scottish & Newcastle, Carlsberg and Heineken have all become active in this region after the fall of the Iron Curtain in order to compensate for the lack of growth prospects in their traditional markets, which had become increasingly mature or even declined.

Eastern Europe is both geographically and demographically a very interesting and convenient market offering legislation that may further adapt to EU standards, strong GDP growth, a trend towards Western habits and an easy cross-border trade.[56] Only the economic and political risks in Russia and the Ukraine could have a negative impact on the beer consumption there.

Chart 3 shows the different beer markets according to the estimated change in per capita GDP and the estimated change in per capita beer consumption. The size of each bubble reveals the expected market size in 2008.

[55] Cf. Rexam (Ed.) (2004), p. 15.
[56] Cf. Rabobank (Ed.) (2004), p. 15.

Chart 3: Growth per capita Beer Consumption against per capita GDP Growth

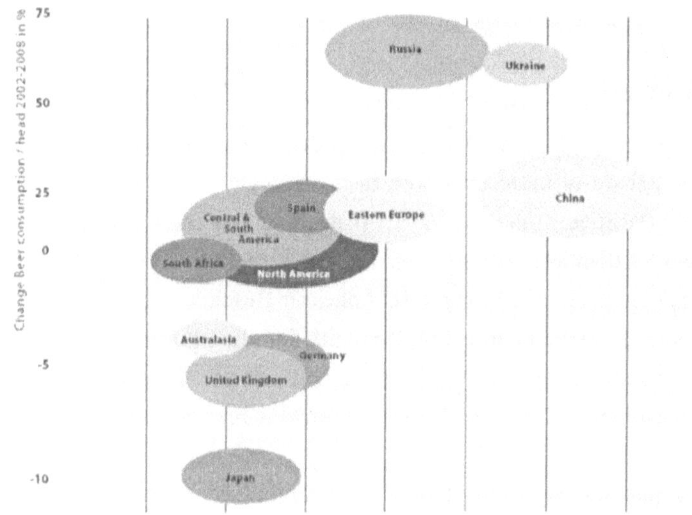

Source: Rabobank (Ed.) (2004), p. 16; Canadean and EIU figures 2004.

Long-term demand trends for beer mainly depend on three different factors: demographics, GDP and absolute consumption.

As pointed out in Section 4.1, it is in particular the age group of 15 to 29 year-olds that is important to the beer industry. In almost all Eastern European countries, the number of people in this particular age group is expected to decline dramatically between 2010 and 2015. Only Turkey and Albania are the two exceptions with an expected growth of 5-10% until 2015. After all, this trend is a major concern for all brewers.[57]

In terms of the GDP and the beer consumption for the individual markets from 2002 to 2008 demand will have reached its peak with 160 litres in the Czech Republic and a 100 litres in Slovakia. Especially in Russia and the Ukraine, potential for further growth is obvious. At a level of 80 to 90 litres per capita consumption,

[57] Cf. Appendix 17: Population Distribution Development for 15-29 age group.

most markets will reach their peak when beer consumption starts to shift from volume to premium beer.[58]

4.5 Main Brewers

Beer markets in Eastern Europe are highly consolidated. The largest beer companies have a market share of more than 60% in many countries. Since the 1990s, four international breweries - Interbrew, BBH (Carlsberg and Scottish & Newcastle), Heineken and SABMiller – have moved into the Eastern European beer market, capturing strategic positions. In contrast, Anheuser Busch has decided to concentrate on its home US market and is only committed to the Chinese beer market. EFES, a Turkish midsize brewer with a large market share in Turkey and establishments in Russia and the Ukraine, is the fastest growing brewer in this region.[59]

Thinking about acquisition possibilities, only a few targets seem to be left. Chart 4 illustrates which markets would still be interesting for global players as potential consolidation targets, and which global breweries act in which markets:

Chart 4: Market Share of International Brewers in Eastern Europe, Russia and China

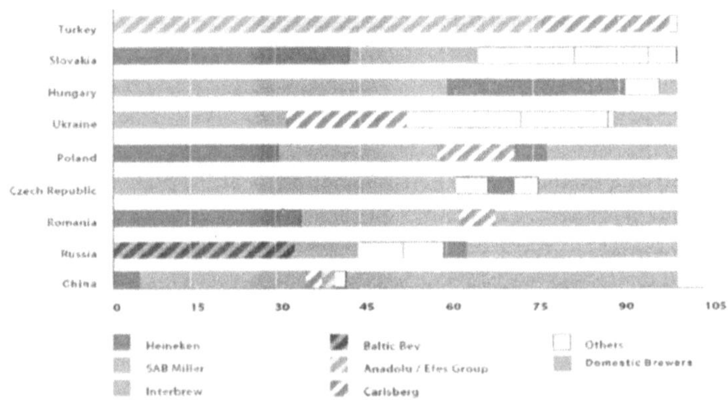

Source: Rabobank (Ed.) (2004), p. 13 with own adjustments.

[58] Cf. also Appendix 18: Beer consumption in Relation to GDP 2002 to 2008.
[59] Cf. EFES (Ed.) (2004), p. 1.

4.6 Strategic Considerations

4.6.1 Plausible Alternatives

First of all the brewers have to decide for one of the three main options in terms of markets to compete. Afterwards the decision on one of three basic strategies has to be made.

Cost leadership

Cost leadership is a strategy in which the brewer mainly focuses on reducing the sales price of the beer, generating customer value with cheap prices delivery. All value chain processes are performed at minimal cost. As economies of scale drive down costs, growth is a way to success and operational excellence the key to it.[60]

Brand strategy

With this option companies focus on their marketing of premium beer brands. The focal point is to take influence on consumer preferences. Marketing, branding and distribution are mandatory core competencies. The aim is market leadership. Therefore, the critical mass is decisive as well, but not as important as in the cost leadership strategy.[61]

Niche strategy

This strategy focuses on the establishment of speciality beers with superior images and qualities for which a group of customers is willing to pay higher prices. It usually focuses on smaller market segments which makes the size of the brewery less relevant.[62]

4.6.2 The Influence of Scale and Market Fragmentation

Apart from the different competitive battlefields, the common denominator is the scale of beer companies. Scale is necessary in both saturated and emerging markets. In saturated markets the large beer companies equipped with sustainable mar-

---

[60] Cf. Besanko / Dravone / Shanley (2000), pp. 412-413.
[61] Cf. Besanko / Dravone / Shanley (2000), pp. 413-414.
[62] Cf. Besanko / Dravone / Shanley (2000), pp. 429-430.

ket power are most successful in promoting their brands. In emerging markets, large financial reserves are of great importance. Companies equipped with sufficient financial background are able to acquire local brands that give them access to the markets. Taking the global beer industry structure into account, further consolidation in the beer markets can be expected.

Referring to Chart 4 again, there are only a few targets left. In accordance to the determined value drivers of the global beer industry, there are two major implications:
The international brewers will now shift from acquisitions to more organic growth in order to increase their market share. This induces significant investments in brand marketing and value chain optimisation to resist competition and to realize high margins. Since the beer market seems to be divided into two parts, new market entrants experience high market entry barriers. As a consequence, Russia and China are the markets where important further consolidation can be expected.

4.6.3 Choices Depending on Market Maturity

Taking the most recent trends of the world beer market into account and considering the market analysis of Chart 4, there are different strategies to apply for different markets.[63] Competition in mature markets involves a fierce competition for market share and margins. Cost leadership has practically no potential for growth in those markets as they are highly consolidated and driven by economies of scale. The marketing of premium brands is the decisive key factor in the fight for market share in those markets where large consolidated retailers offer the customer a wide choice of beers and other beverages.

In the emerging markets "[…] gaining the market access is the name of the game […]"[64] because usually local low price brands dominate these markets. But international brewers leveraging economies of scale through consolidation advantages have reasonable chances to enter and succeed in these markets. Additionally, since the economic expectations promise an increase in per capita beer consumption and

[63] Cf. Appendix 15: Number one and two Positions of Int. Brewers in Eastern Europe.
[64] Cf. Rabobank (Ed.) (2004), p. 12.

an increase in disposable income, premium beer brands could be able to substitute the cheap local beer and increase their market share. However, it is still questionable whether these premium and in particular niche strategies will be won by foreign owned international premium brands or local ones.

Experts are confident that the emerging markets will remain different from the Western beer markets with regard to cultural identities, consumer preferences and lifestyle issues. As these markets will not have the same character, it could be possible that international premium brands might remain a niche, failing in competition against the strong local premium brands.[65]

According to FLETCHER, consultant at FIRST KEY, who researched a consultancy specialised on the brewing industry, companies should leverage their technical and marketing competencies and simultaneously adjust to local market conditions.[66]

5 Portraying Outperformers

Eastern Europe is going through a process of transformation. The following chapter portrays the three most interesting countries in the scope of this paper's topic.

5.1 Ukraine

History

The Ukrainian beer market saw a steady growth throughout the second half of the 1990s. Starting at a low point in consumption of only 5 litres per capita in 1996, the market showed a good recovery with about 25 litres per capita in the early 1990s (Chart 6). This turnaround was made possible by three developments. Firstly, the Ukrainian population experienced an income growth (Chart 7). Secondly, the brewers were able to improve beer quality significantly, and another factor was the improved efficiency in production and distribution.[67]

---

[65] Cf. Euromonitor (Ed.) (2005), p. 1.
[66] Cf. Appendix 19: Interview with Mr. Tony Fletcher, First Key Consulting.
[67] Cf. Rabobank (Ed.) (2004), p. 51.

Current Development

Currently the market is dominated by the three big companies InBev, Obolon and BBH. The market shares of these three add up to 74% of the total market with Inbev being the clear leader controlling 34% alone. Obolon is the biggest independent brewery and has a market share of 20%. In addition to the other three big breweries, Saramt (again privately held) has a considerable market share of 17%. This goes to show that the big four companies own 91% of the market.[68]

The beer industry continues to strongly benefit from economic growth and favourable changes in the personal tax environment. However, despite the economic growth the Ukraine remains a poor country resulting in relatively low per capita consumption of beer (Chart 5).[69]

Outlook

The above mentioned drivers of the rising beer consumption of the last years should have some further impact on the beer market. Especially the expected continuing improvement of beer quality and distribution channels should yield in higher returns for the big four breweries in the Ukrainian market. The current distribution of the market share makes it appear quite likely that Heineken and SAB-Miller could try to enter the market by acquiring one of the two big independent breweries.[70]

[68] Cf. Deutsche Bank (Ed.) (2004), p. 212.
[69] Cf. Deutsche Bank (Ed.) (2004), p. 212.
[70] Cf. Deutsche Bank (Ed.) (2004), p. 212.

Chart 5: Total and per capita beer consumption - Ukraine

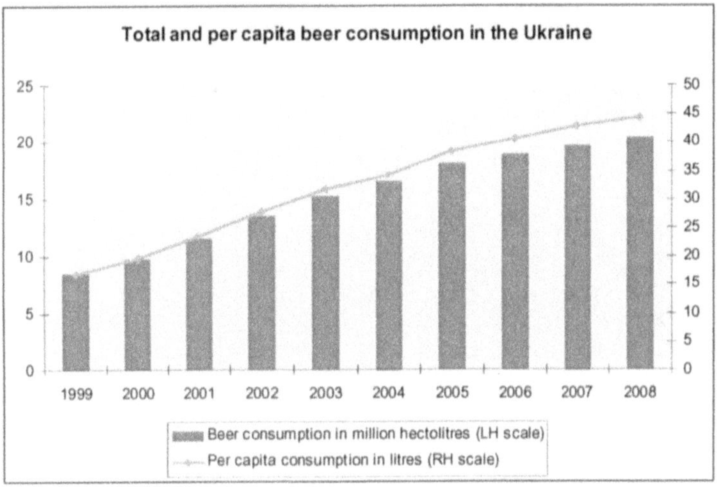

Source: Deutsche Bank (Ed.) (2004), p. 212.

Chart 6: Per capita Growth versus GDP growth – Ukraine

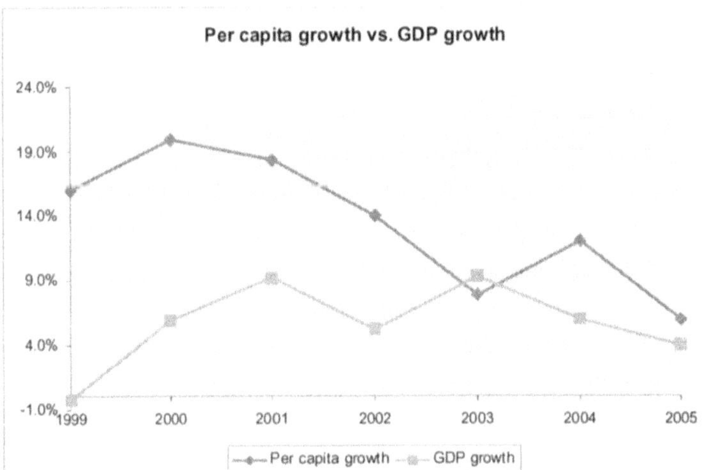

Chart 7: Cumulated per capita growth versus cumulated GDP growth - Ukraine

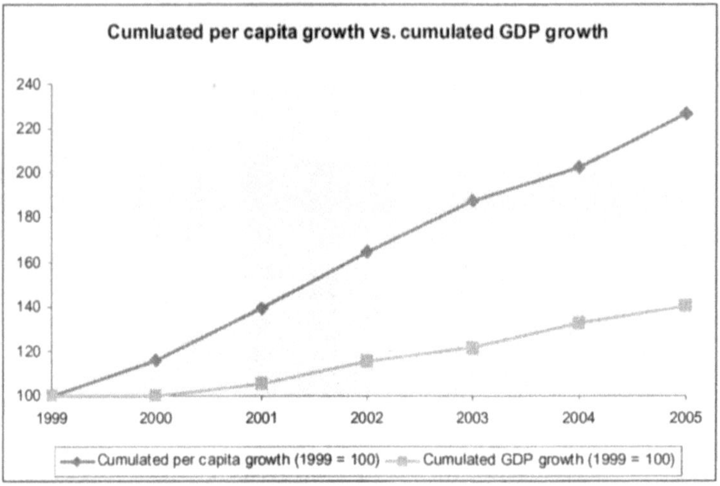

5.2 Russia

History

After the beer consumption has risen dramatically in the last five years, the Russian government has introduced new laws restricting the advertisement of beer in the country (Chart 8). Despite the fact that these regulations go even further than EU regulations, analysts say that the growth of the sector should continue for the next 20 years. As vodka consumption in Russia has traditionally been widespread in high volumes, a general perception developed assuming beer a healthier alternative. Together with advertisements associated with social, sporting or individual success, this has partly accounted for the shift from spirits to beer. As the vodka lobby was distressed about this dramatic change, the Duma had to constrain this shift. Beer advertisements were banned from health magazines, environment or education, and every billboard poster must be at least 100 metres away from educational institutions, hospitals and cultural centres or sports clubs. Furthermore, every advertisement has to contain a government warning about the effects of alcohol on health and the warning must take up no less than 10 percent of the advertising space.[71]

[71] Cf. Beveragedaily (Ed.) (2004), p. 21.

Current Development

The current driving forces of growth in the Russian beer market remain the strong economic growth and the increased availability of high quality beer (Chart 10).[72] Although there is still some room left for switch-overs from vodka to beer, this factor of growth should lose influence as soon as the above mentioned political measures show their impact. Although the three market leaders BBH, SUN Interbrew and Krasny Vostok account for 52% of the market share, the market is still quite fragmented with a few acquisition opportunities still at hand.

In 2003 over 300 local and international players acted on the Russian market implying further consolidation potential which should be especially interesting for Heineken, as its market share only adds up to roughly 4%.[73]

Outlook

Compared to Germany or the UK, both average about 100 litres per capita, the beer consumption in Russia is still quite low with 51 litres (Chart 8). Assuming it would be possible to raise the per capita consumption to a Western level, a huge additional market potential of about 70 mhl could be generated.[74] Even with less optimistic assumptions, the Russian market still has a future of high growth ahead with an estimated total consumption of roughly 90 mhl, equalling a per capita consumption of 62 litres.[75]

This outlook makes Russian breweries a likely target for acquisitions, especially in the light of the fact that the two big breweries Krasny Vostok and Ochakovo are still privately held and thus make a good acquisition target. In particular Heineken and SABMiller should be interested in these companies as they still have a market share of only 4% and 3% respectively.[76] However, not only those two Russian companies could help build a higher market share. Also other smaller companies can be the target of acquisitions. For example, on the May 6th, 2005, Heineken agreed to buy the Russian brewery Patra for an undisclosed sum, increasing Heine-

---

[72] Cf. Deutsche Bank (Ed.) (2004), p. 200.

[73] Cf. Rabobank (Ed.) (2004), p. 48.

[74] Cf. Food & Drink (Ed.) (2004), p. 1.

[75] Cf. Deutsche Bank (Ed.) (2004), p. 200; Rabobank (Ed.) (2004), p. 47 even has a more optimistic outlook for Russia estimating a per capita consumption of beer of 82 litres for the year 2008.

[76] Cf. Deutsche Bank (Ed.) (2004), p. 200.

kens market share by about 3%.[77] As pointed out before, rapid economic growth and an improving standard of living in these countries enable consumers to increase their spending on quality beers.

Chart 8: Total and per capita Beer consumption - Russia

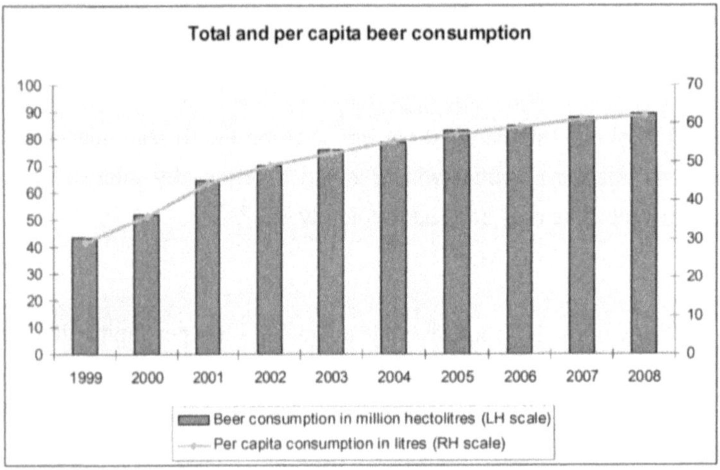

Source: Cf. Deutsche Bank (Ed.) (2004), p. 200; Datamonitor (2004b), p. 14.

[77] Cf. Heineken (Ed.) (2005b), p. 16.

Chart 9: Per capita Growth versus GDP Growth - Russia

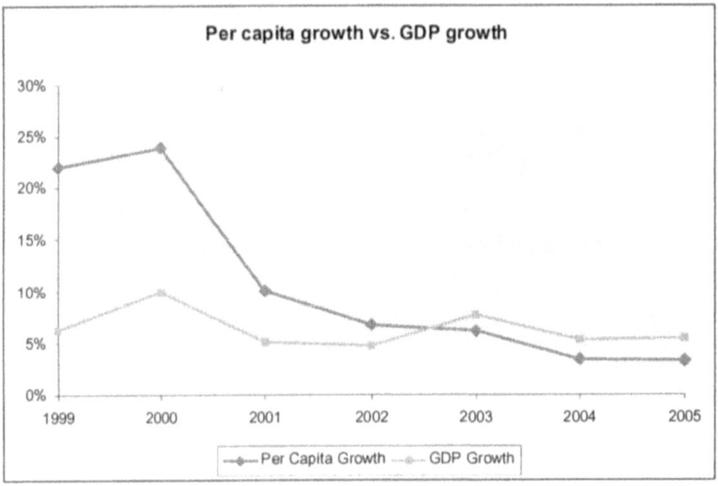

Chart 10: Cumulated Per Capita Growth versus Cumulated GDP Growth - Russia

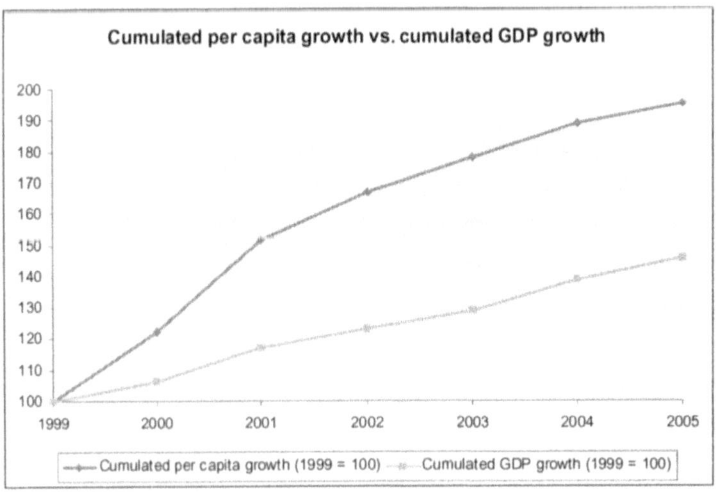

5.3 The People's Republic of China

History

Since the People's Republic of China ("China") opened its borders for world trade in the beginning of the 1990s, many foreign brewers have entered this market of more than one billion potential consumers. It took some years for the brewers to realise that the Chinese market was far from being homogenous. Generally, it could be seen as a combination of regional markets where low-cost and low-priced regional or partly even local beers were preferred to the more premium type beers for foreign brewers like San Miguel, Heineken, SABMiller and Anheuser-Busch. The consolidation process really started in 1996 when over 700 breweries were active in China. Another indicator for the high fragmentation at that time is the information given by the official statistical office which announced that the 10 biggest breweries accounted for a market share of 17.7% in 1997.[78]

Current Development

Until 2002 the consolidation process resulted in 300 acquisitions, reducing the number of independent breweries to 400. After this wave of consolidation the top four breweries Tsingtao, Yanjing, SABMiller and InBev had a market share of 43%. Despite this consolidation process, which reduced the number of breweries significantly, 57% of the market share is still distributed in the hands of many smaller breweries. [79]

Outlook

China is still the leading country for the beer industry's growth on a worldwide scale (Chart 9). The consolidation process is bound to move on, giving foreign investors the chance to gain their shares of this market. Anheuser-Busch has already started for this direction by entering an agreement with Tsingtao that will grant Anheuser-Busch a 27% share Tsingtao by 2007.[80]

However, a problem foreign and regional players face as a downside of the Chinese market is the strong brand loyalty in the rural areas. Each region is dominated by its own brand, and thus it will be difficult for other regional competitors to enter. The future will probably see a fast changing Chinese market environment for

[78] Cf. Deutsche Bank (Ed.) (2004), p. 166.
[79] Cf. Deutsche Bank (Ed.) (2004), p. 166.
[80] Cf. Moffet / Ramaswamy (2005), p. 10.

the beer industry with market shares changing often with every acquisition of one of the larger players.[81]

Chart 11: Total and per capita beer consumption - China

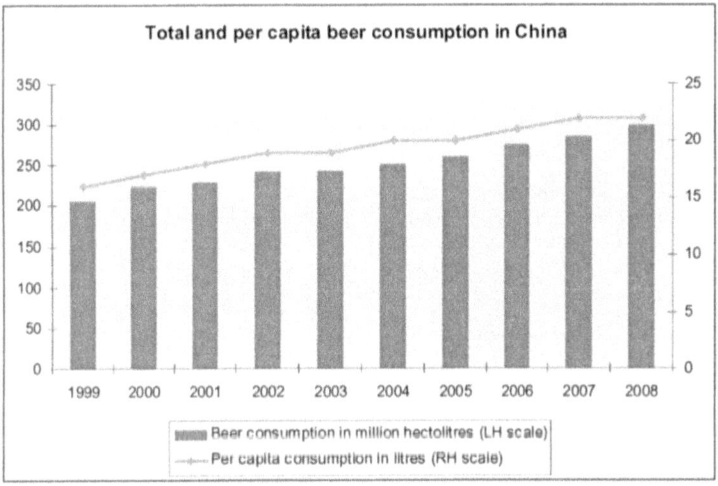

Source: Deutsche Bank (Ed.) (2004), p. 166.

[81] Cf. Deutsche Bank (Ed.) (2004), p. 166.

Chart 12: Per capita growth versus GDP growth - China

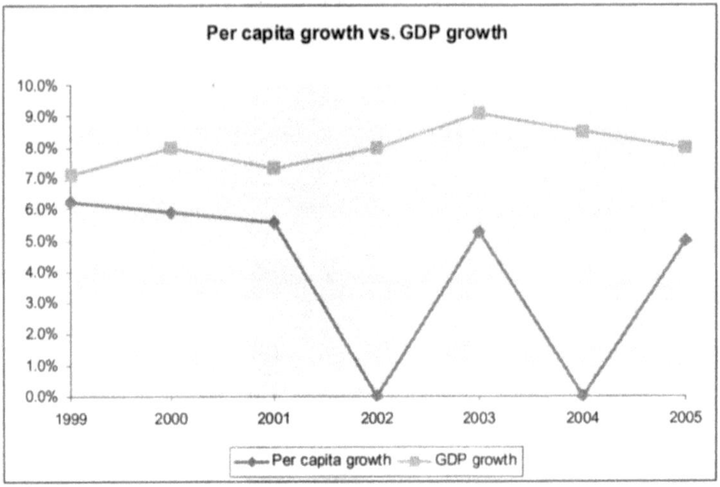

Chart 13: Cumulated per capita growth versus cumulated GDP growth

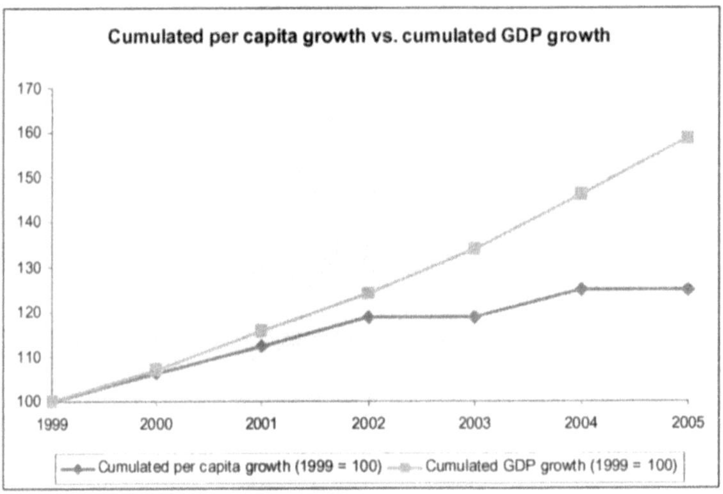

6 Conclusion

The expected economic growth in Eastern Europe between 2004 and 2008 will result in an increase in beer consumption in Hungary and Russia. In many other countries, the saturation point of about 90 litres of beer per capita will be reached by 2005 whereas it is not foreseeable for Hungary, Russia and China yet. At this point, an increase in countries' GDPs will not result in a rise of the volume of consumed beer; it will rather induce a shift to premiums brands. This tendency should have a positive impact on the sales of the big European brewers.

Currently, there is an enormous potential for growth in Eastern Europe, but with only few independent targets left for acquisition. Consequently, overall growth will be rather organic and the resulting increased competition will go hand in hand with investments into brands and restructuring in order to resist competition and to generate the required margins. As scale is the common denominator, mostly large companies equipped with sustainable market power and financial leverage are able to acquire local brands in the respective target markets.

Recapitulating, European brewers have to consider two major factors for acquisitions in their target markets: they have to concentrate financial reserves and in due time must consider the situation. As a result, European brewers face a dilemma. On the one hand, they could wait, accumulate their financial resources to be able to stem larger acquisition targets, and possibly accept a reduction of acquisition opportunities as well as a probable increase of targets' prices due to greater acquisition demand in the industry. On the other hand they can also contemporarily acquire smaller target companies, but have to accept higher financing risks and put considerably more effort into consolidation and integration.

As was shown in this paper, each beer market has its unique characteristics and growth opportunities. Modern beer brands seem to attract the attention of many younger consumers who shun the traditional spirits drunk by older generations, especially in Russia and the Ukraine. This development is an opportunity as well as a threat to the big breweries. The threat is directly related to the future demographics in these countries, where the proportion of the population between 15 and 29 year-olds is expected to decrease considerably by 2008. Since this is an important age group for beer consumption, this reduction will have a negative impact on it. The opportunity on the other hand is founded on the possibility to create sustainable brand recognitions for the new foreign beer brands.

Recapitulating all prospects for development, Western European brewers would be well advised with acting tactically through targeted immediate acquisitions to secure relevant geographical footprints in accordance to their individual company profiles. Simultaneously, Western European brewers should think strategically with regard to their long-term business goals when it comes to effective penetration alternatives for these markets and the planning of other acquisitions.

Appendix

Appendix 1 World Beer Consumption in the Main Regions World-Wide 1997-2002

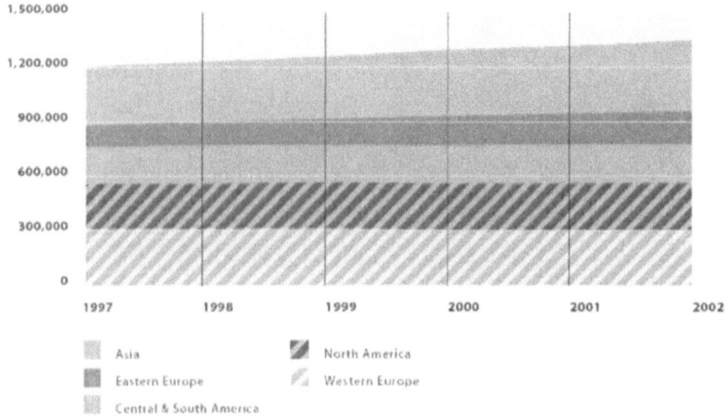

Source: Canadean (2004); Rabobank (Ed.) (2004), p. 10.

Appendix 2: GDP-Growth Western versus Eastern Europe (Median)

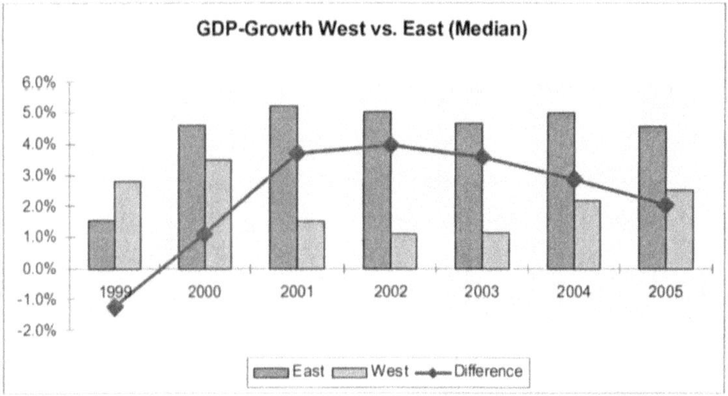

Source: Deutsche Bank (2004), pp. 166-212.

Appendix 3: GDP-Growth Western versus Eastern Europe (Median)

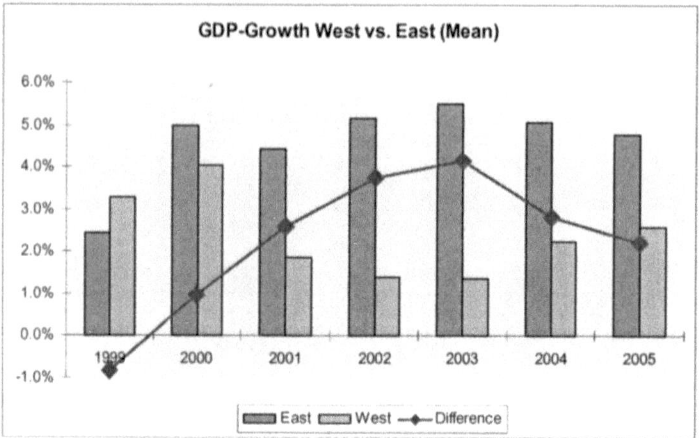

Source: Deutsche Bank (2004), p. 166-212.

Appendix 4: Mean of per capita growth

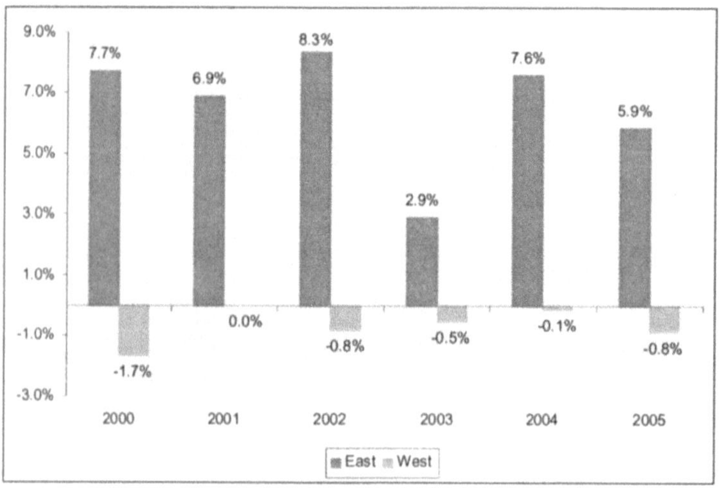

Source: Deutsche Bank (2004), p. 166-212; Euromonitor; Canadean.

Appendix 5: Median of per capita growth

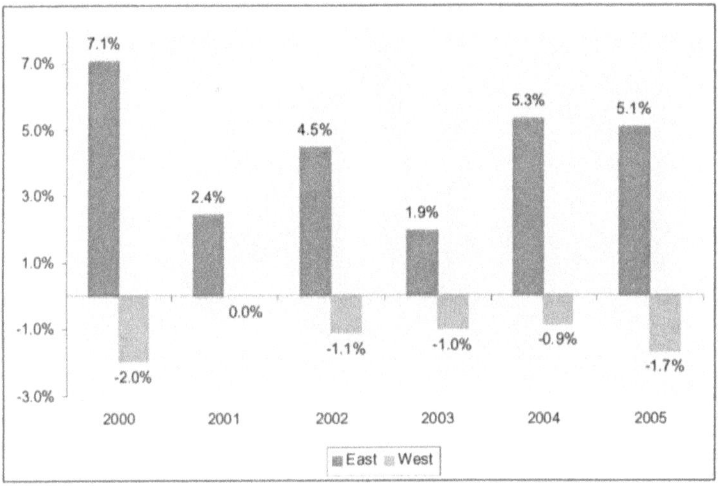

Source: Deutsche Bank (2004), p. 166-212; Euromonitor; Canadean.

Appendix 6: Declining Risk from Emerging Markets

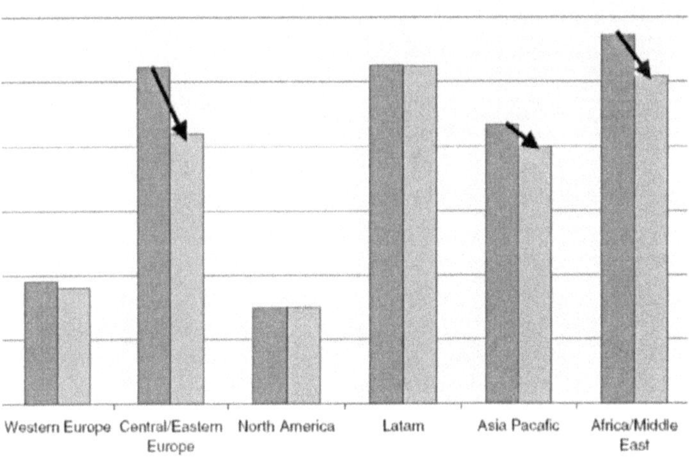

Source: Bleakley / Bowley / Matthews (2004), p. 6.

Appendix 7: The World Beer Market Volume to 2010

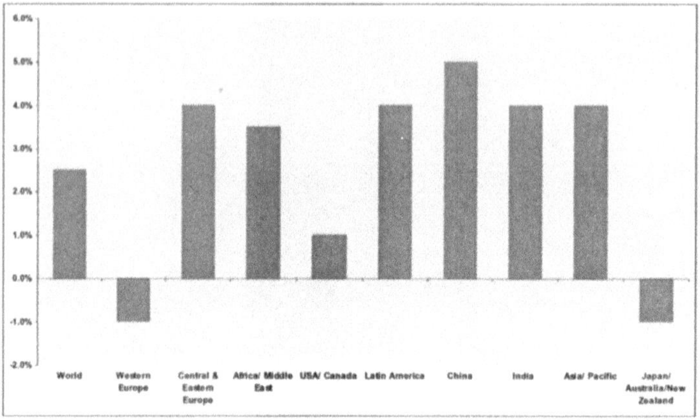

Source: A.T. Kearney (Ed.) (2005), p. 6.

Appendix 8: Emerging Market Delivering High Margins to InBew and SABMiller

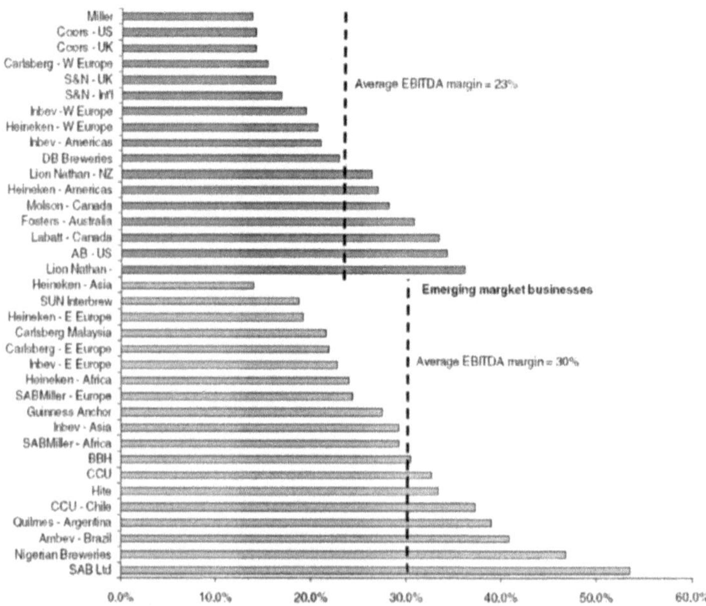

Source: Bleakley / Bowley / Matthews (2004), p. 9.

Appendix 9: Profitability Increases with Market Consolidation

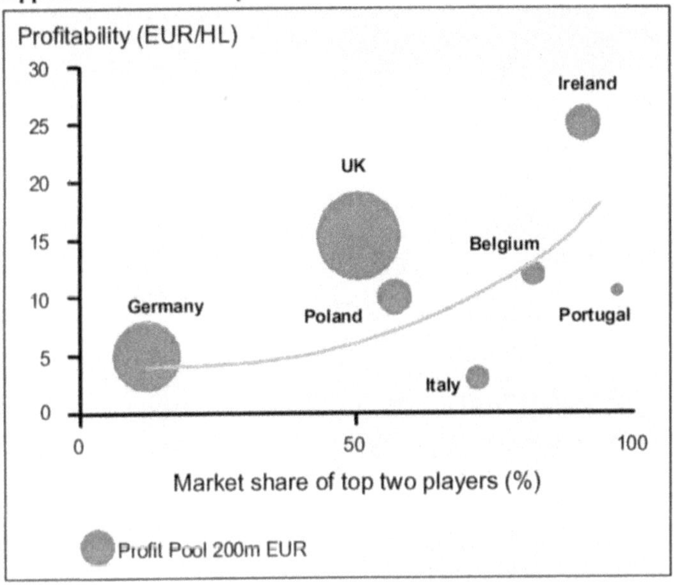

Source: A.T. Kearney (Ed.) (2005), p. 8; Plato Logic; ABN Amro.

Appendix 10: Consolidation Phases

	Opening Phase	Scale Phase	Focus Phase	Balance/ Alliance Phase
Market share of the 3 leaders	• 30-15% • Decreasing	• 15-45% • Increasing	• 45-75% • Increasing	• 75-90% • Stable
Market structure	• National	• Most players national • Leaders play internationally	• Major players international • Only national niches	• Mainly international
M&A activity	• Merger success: 59%	• Significant M&A activity • Merger success: 58%	• Decreasing merger success: 50%	• Low merger succes: 30%
Profitability	• High, but decreasing	• Under pressure • Triggers shake-outs	• Increasing	• High • Close parity among major competitors
Strategy implications	• Grow and take the leadership	• Reduce costs through greater economies of scale • Take charge and „win the battle"	• Strengthen core competencies • Clean up portfolio	• The remaining companies collaborate through alliances where applicable

Source: A.T. Kearney (2005), p. 16.

Appendix 11: NPV of Savings

Target cost savings € m	2006	NPV	Mkt value	NPV % of Mkt value
S&N	45	563	5,716	10%
Carlsberg	27	336	2,934	11%
Heineken	100	1,250	12,434	10%
Inbev	230	2,875	14,974	19%

Source: Bleakley / Bowley / Matthews (2004), p. 15.

Appendix 12: Cash Conversion Cycle

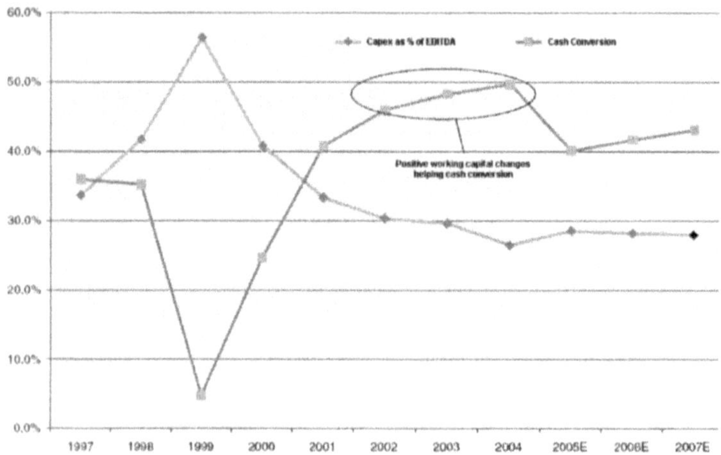

Source: Bleakley / Bowley / Matthews (2004), p. 13.

Appendix 13: Average Cost Structure of a Brewing Company

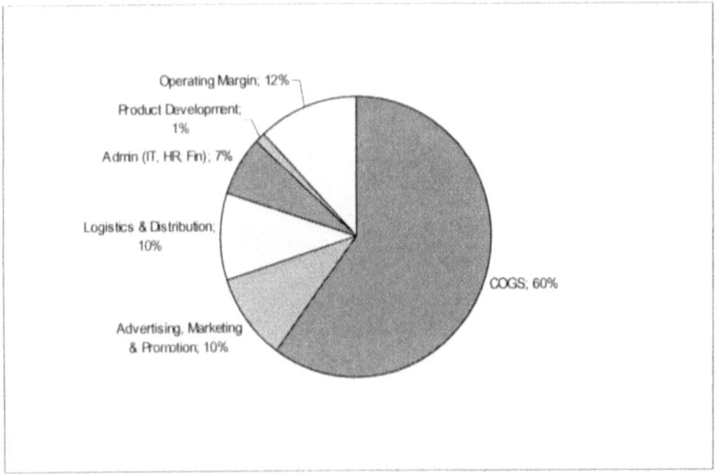

Source: A.T. Kearney (Ed.) (2005), p. 2.

Appendix 14: Declining Employee Numbers Driving Productivity Improvements

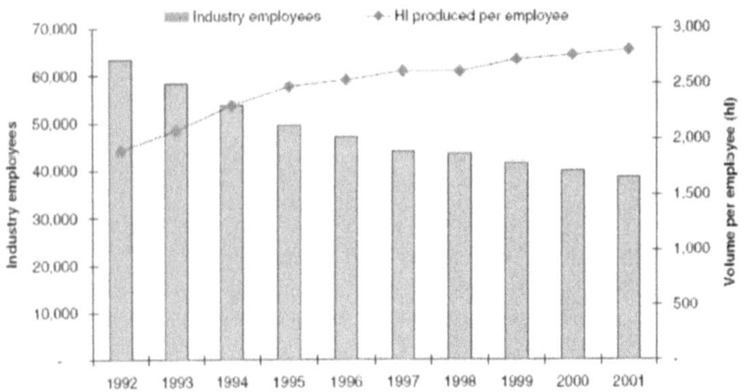

Source: Bowley / Shackleton / Bleakley et al. (2003), p. 27.

Appendix 15: Number one and two Positions of Int. Brewers in Eastern Europe

	Czech Rep.	Slovakia	Hungary	Poland	Romania	Russia	Ukraine	Estonia	Latvia	Lithuania	Turkey
Interbrew	2	2	2			2	1				
BBH*						1		1	1	1	
Heineken		1		1	1						
SABMiller	1		1	2	2						
Efes											1
Carlsberg											2

Source: Rabobank (Ed.) (2004), p. 23.

Appendix 16: Local Consolidation

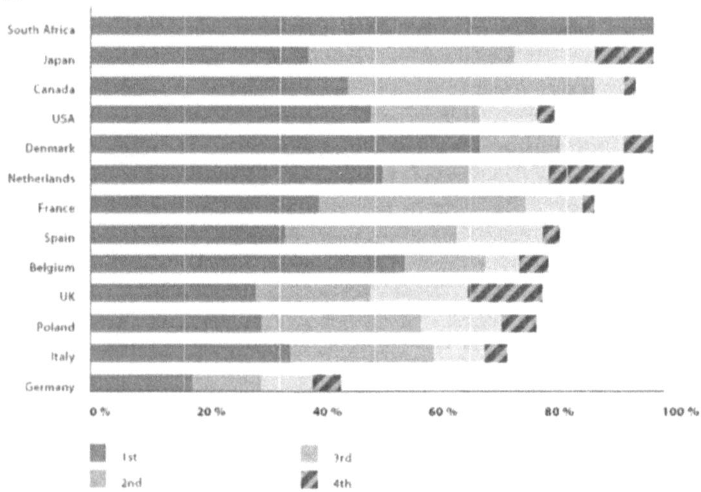

Source: Rabobank (Ed.) (2004), p. 12.

Appendix 17: Population Distribution Development for the 15-29 Age Group

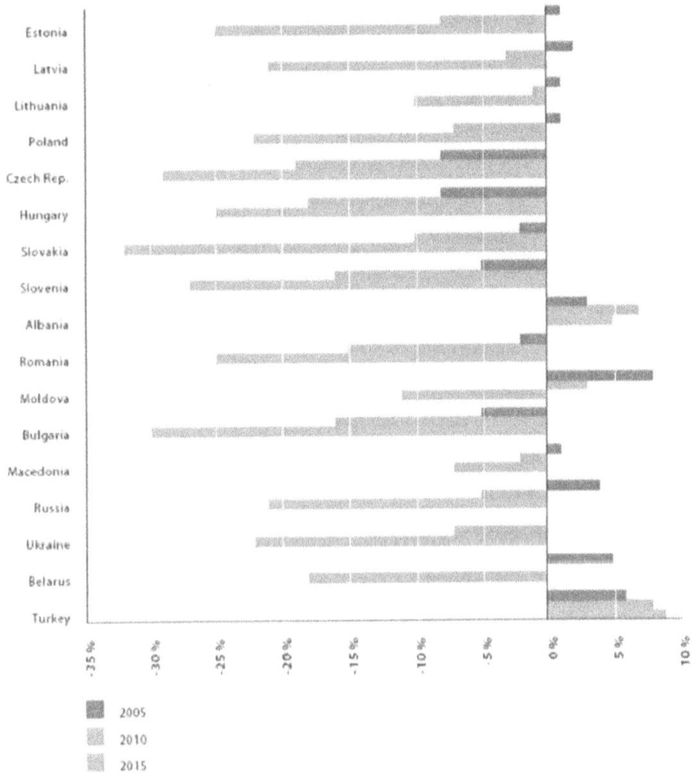

Source: Rabobank (Ed.) (2004), p. 20, based on figures from the United Nations (2004).

Appendix 18: Beer Consumption in Relation to GDP 2002 to 2008

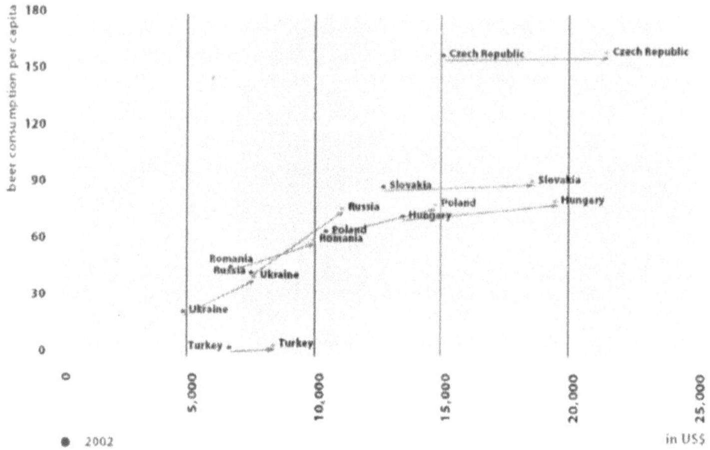

Source: Rabobank (Ed.) (2004), p. 21; Canadean and EIU figures 2004.

Appendix 19

Interview with Tony Fletcher

Business Development Manager, Eastern Central Europe

at First Key – Consultants to the Brewing and Malting Industry

First Key Eastern & Central Europe

V Lesicku 93/8

150 00 Prague

Czech Republic

http://www.firstkey.com

Question:

The South American market compared to the Central & Eastern European one – which of both is generally more favourable to invest in from the perspective of a European brewer?

Answer:
It is not really an either/or. In general the most attractive markets for European Brewers are
1) Large beer markets preferably with further growth potential:
2) Developing economies (spending power increasing)
3) Fragmented competition
4) Cultural/Religious 'tolerance' to alcohol
5) Younger and growing population.
6) Propensity to switch from spirits and wine.

In general, developed markets have little or no scope for volume growth and with their aging populations will tend to switch towards spirits and wine. Assets are more expensive and markets less fragmented.

Of the top ten beer markets, the following are possibly the most favourable:

China/ Brazil/ Russia/ Mexico/ Poland

Question:
Did the integration in the European Union bring along any fundamental changes concerning the consolidation tendencies in the brewing industry?

Answer:
No because consolidation was already well underway driven by globalization and market forces.

Question:
How do you evaluate the market positioning of the breweries in the new EU countries. Do they suffer from the competition that emerges from Western European breweries (crowding out)? Or are there rather new positive possibilities emerging?

Answer:
Many breweries in the new EU countries are already owned by multinationals, especially InBev, Heineken, SAB Miller, Carlsberg and Heineken. In general, a

freer movement of goods across borders will favour the new countries such as the Czech Republic. Western retail prices are three times higher than domestic ones.

Question:
What are the possible threats and uncertainties, a Western European brewer has to take into account when investing in Central & Eastern Europe, Russia or China? (e.g. the strength of local beer brands, different consumption habits, etc.)

Answer:
There are all the usual political/socio/economic uncertainties. More specifically for Brewers local preferences and tastes must be taken into account. Beer is not like coca cola. The largest selling beer brand in the world accounts for only about 3% of the world markets. Many brewers entered China in the 1990s and made huge losses by failing to understand culture and consumer preferences. Another threat is posed by inability or failure to control the distribution chain.

Question:
Which Central & Eastern European countries/markets including China and Russia do you expect to be the most promising for acquisitions and for organic growth?

Answer:
Probably China in that consumption levels are currently much lower at about 17 litres per head/year. Russia has already experienced outstanding growth from less than 20 litres in the mid 90's to current levels of about 60. Some further growth is likely but at much slower rate. Ukraine lags Russia on per capita consumption but should grow strongly in the next few years. Central Europe already has high consumption levels (Czech Republic has highest in the world). Apart from a few pockets such as former Yugoslavia potential for organic growth is limited. The big Brewers are aiming for revenue as opposed to volume growth in developed markets (in 2003 they increased value by 10% against volume by 3%)

Question:
How many consolidations do you expect to see in the coming years in Central & Eastern European markets including Russia and China?

Answer:
Consolidation in world markets is likely to continue. At present the global top 10 own about 45% of total market. Interbrew recently merged with AmBev (Brazil) to become the biggest beer company. Molson has merged with Coors and SAB with Miller Further mergers between larger companies are likely.
Consolidation is well under way in Central and Eastern Europe. In Russia and Ukraine the four largest players in each control 80 to 85% of assets. The major players (InBev, Heineken, Carlsberg (JV with S&N) are all making and looking for further acquisitions
Multinationals such as AB, InBev, SAB Miller, Heineken, and Carlsberg are acquiring in China so further consolidation is inevitable.

Question:
On the background of favourable market conditions in Central & Eastern Europe, Russia and China, for which reasons do domestic breweries sell their businesses to bigger internationally operating brewers?

Answer:
Because of either necessity or profit. Smaller operations cannot compete with the investment needed to upgrade, distribution muscle, purchasing power, marketing spend etc.
Investors with local knowledge (banks, entrepreneurs) can buy up assets, add value and eventually sell to multinationals at good profit.

Question:
Where should a European brewer invest in the moment and at which scale?

Answer:
Obviously Eastern Europe, South America and China remain favourite but competition and increasing price of assets mean these will be tough markets to dominate. For a long shot as yet undeveloped markets in former Soviet Union (Belarus, Kazakhstan) and India should be looked at.

Question:

What should international operating breweries do to be successful in emerging markets? Should they leverage their technical and marketing competencies and simultaneously adjust to the local market conditions?

Answer:

Yes but with big emphasis on taking 100% control of running the business at the same time as understanding and fulfilling local market requirements.

References

Asahi (Ed.) (2005): Annual Report 2004, 2005.

Anheuser Busch (Ed.) (2004): Annual Report 2003, 2004.

A.T. Kearney (Ed.) (2005): International Beer Industry Case, 2005.

BBC (Ed.) (2005): Heineken to buy Russian beer firm, URL: http://news.bbc.co.uk/2/hi/business/4520401.stm, released on the 6th of May 2005, accessed on the 26th of May 2005, 2005.

BBH (Ed.) (2005): Carlsberg Annual Report 2004, 2005.

Bentzen, Jan / Smith, Valdemar (2004): Are the fluctuations in the consumption of alcohol pro- or countercyclical? - Empirical evidence from the Scandinavian countries using long-run time series data, Research Paper of the Department of Economics, The Aarhus School of Business in Denmark, May 2004.

Besanko, David / Dravone, David / Shanley, Mark (2000): Economics of Strategy, Second Edition, New York, 2000.

Beveragedaily (Ed.) (2004): Russia tightens beer regulations, 11.08.2004, URL: http://beveragedaily.com/news/ng.asp?id=54092&n=wh34&c=%23emailcode, released on the 20th of May 2004, accessed on the 27th of May 2005, 2004.

Bleakley, Michael / Bowley, Andy / Matthews, Jennifer (2004): European Brewers – Going for growth, Credit Suisse First Boston (Ed.) Sector Review on Beer & Alcoholic Beverages, 06. September 2004.

Bowley, Andy / Shackleton, Ian / Bleakley et al. (2003): The German beer industry - The Consolidators' challenge, Credit Suisse First Boston (Ed.), 04th of June 2003.
Brock, John F. (2005): InBev Announces – Organic EBITDA Growth of 8,0%, InBev Results 2004, Presentation to Investors & Analysts, 2005.

Ceeretail.com (Ed.) (2005a): Retail: Hungary: German imports cause difficulties for beer producers, in: Emerging Europe Economy 2005, 05.04.2005, 2005.

Ceeretail.com (Ed.) (2005b): Retail: Hungary: Cheap canned bear disappearing, in: Emerging Europe Economy 2005, 19.04.2005, 2005.

Ceeretail.com (Ed.) (2005c): Retail: Hungary: Plzensky Prazdroj sells more beer in 2004, in: Emerging Europe Economy 2005, 05.04.2005, 2005.

Ceeretail.com (Ed.) (2005d): Retail: Czech Republic: Downmarket beer enrages Czech brewers, in: Emerging Europe Economy 2005, 19.04.2005, 2005.

Council Of New Zealand (Ed.) (2002): Beer, Wine & Spirits – Facts & Figures, autumn 2002.

Den Butter, F. A. C. / Delifotis, A. / Koning, R.H. (1997): Serie research memoranda – Preference shifts in costumer demand for beer and wine, a study in conjunction with the applied labour economics research team (alert), Unversity of Amsterdam, September 1997.

Deutsche Bank (Ed.) (2004): Global Brewing, The Global Pitcher 2004 – Volume V, Deutsche Bank Global Equity Research – Industry Focus, September 2004.

Euromonitor (Ed.) (2005): The global beer market: a world of two halves, URL: http://www.euromonitor.com/article.asp?id=4764, released on the 25th of February 2005, accessed on the 26th of May 2005, 2005.

EFES (Ed.) (2004): Message from the CEO, in: EFES Annual Report 2003, 2004.

EFES (Ed.) (2005): Annual Report 2004, 2005.

Food & Drink (Ed.) (2004): Russia cracks down on domestic beer advertising, URL: http://www.foodanddrinkeurope.com/news/printNewsBis.asp?id=54078, released on the 10th of August 2004, accessed on the 26th of May 2005, 2004.

Gual, A. / Colom, J. (1997): Why has alcohol consumption declined in countries of southern Europe?, in: Addiction, vol. 92, no. Supplement 1 to Issue 3, pp. 21-32(12), 1997.HEINEKEN (Ed.) (2005a): Annual Report 2004, 2005.

Heineken (Ed.) (2005): Annual Report 2004, 2005.

Heineken (Ed.) (2005b): Heineken acquires Patra brewery in Russia, URL: http://www.heinekeninternational.com/images/2005-05-06%20Heineken%20acquires%20Patra%20brewery%20in%20Russia_tcm4-13066.pdf, 2005, released on the 6th of May 2005, accessed on the 28th of May 2005, 2005.

Inbev (Ed.) (2002): Annual Report 2001, 2002.

Oligopoly Watch (Ed.) (2003): Oligopoly brief: SABMiller, in: Monthly Report July 2003, 2003.

Kahn, Meyer (2003): The chairman's statement, in: SABMiller Annual Report 2002, p. 4-5, 2003.

Lutz, Wolfgang (2003): Addressing the Challenges of Europe's new demography, in: Population Network Newsletter – POPNET Europe, No. 35, p.1-8, summer 2003.

Mannsperger, Patrick (2000): Structure and dynamics of the European brewing industry, a presentation of Roland Berger Strategy Consultants in Rimini February 2000.

Matraves, Catherine (1999): Market Integration and Market Structure in the European Soft Drinks Industry: Always Coca-Cola?, Working Paper at the Lowry Mays College and Graduate School of Business and Texas A&M University USA, Discussion Paper FS IV 99-12, 1999.

Moffet, Michael H. / Ramaswamy, Kannan (2005): Anheuser Busch and Harbin Brewery Group of China, Casestudy of Thunderbird - The Garvin School of International Management, 2005.

Rabobank (Ed.) (2003): The Dutch beer market in an international perspective: Dynamics of a mature market, F&A Research and Advisory Review, 2003.

Rabobank (Ed.) (2004): The Eastern European Beer Market – Its place and prospects, F&A Research and Advisory Review, May 2004.

Rabobank (Ed.) (2005): The global malt industry – A changing industry structure, driven by emerging beer markets, F&A Research and Advisory Review, March 2005.

Rexam (Ed.) (2004): busy lives – Consumer Packaging Report 2004.

Rexam (Ed.) (2005): Development Markets Drive Global Beer, URL: http://www.rexam.com/index.asp?pageid=735, released on the 1th of January 2005, accessed on the 26th of May 2005, 2005.

Rogacheva, Elena / Mikerova, Julia (2003): European FDI in Russia: Corporate strategy and the effectiveness of Government promotion and facilitation, September 2003.

Rost, Andreas (2002): Address to the 120th Annual General Meeting of Holsten-Brauerei AG on the 26 June in Hamburg, 2002.

SABMILLER (Ed.) (2000): Notes to the financial statements, in: SAB Annual Report 1999, p. 25-39, 2000.

SABMILLER (Ed.) (2004): Chief Executive's Review, in: Interim Report 2004, 2004.

Technology Centre AS CR (Ed.) (2005): BACKGROUND REPORT on the state and prospects of development, and the implementation of innovations in small and medium enterprises in the agricultural industry, with the focus on food-processing industry, Prague, 2005.

TGI (Ed.) (2005): Beer Drinking in Asia-Pacific and Around the World, in: TGI trans-global comparisons, URL: http://www.tgisurveys.com/quiz/China%20TGI.pdf, released on the 4th of April 2005, accessed on the 29th of May 2005, 2005.

Thommen, Jean-Paul / Achleitner, Ann-Kristin (2001): Allgemeine Betriebswirtschaftslehre – Umfassende Einführung aus managementorientierter Sicht, 3. Aufl., Wiesbaden, 2001.

SABMILLER (Ed.) (2005): Annual Report 2004, 2005.

USDA (United States Department of Agriculture) (2000): Making Malt for Moskow, in: FASonline, URL: http://www.fas.usda.gov/info/agexporter/2000/May/russians.htm, released on the 2nd of September 2000, accessed on the 29th of May 2005, 2000.

UK Trade And Investment (Ed.) (2005): Food and Drink Opportunities in the UK – A World Market with World-wide Tastes, 2005.

World Health Organisation (Ed.) (2001): Global Status Report on Alcohol, Internal Research Document, 2001.

Yudaeva, Ksenia / Kozlov, Konstantin / Melentieva, Natalya et al. (2001): Does Foreign Ownership Matter? – Russian Experience, GET project paper, Working Paper # WP/2001/027, 2001.

MIX
Papier aus verantwortungsvollen Quellen
Paper from responsible sources
FSC® C105338

Printed by Libri Plureos GmbH
in Hamburg, Germany